Partnership Taxation

Partnership Taxation

An Application Approach

SECOND EDITION

Joni Larson

PROFESSOR OF LAW,
THOMAS COOLEY LAW SCHOOL

CAROLINA ACADEMIC PRESS
Durham, North Carolina

Library of Congress Cataloging-in-Publication Data

Larson, Joni.
  Partnership taxation : an application approach / Joni Larson. -- Second Edition.
    pages cm
  Includes bibliographical references and index.
  ISBN 978-1-61163-272-9 (alk. paper)
  1. Partnership--Taxation--United States. I. Title.

  KF6452.L37 2013
  343.7305'2662--dc23

                    2013009768

Carolina Academic Press
700 Kent Street
Durham, NC 27701
Telephone (919) 489-7486
Fax (919) 493-5668
www.cap-press.com

Contents

Partnership Taxation

I.

Introduction

Chapter 1

Introduction

Partnership taxation often is considered one of the most difficult areas of tax. However, given the growing number of limited liability companies (which generally are taxed as partnerships for tax purposes), it is extremely beneficial to have a working knowledge of this area. In addition, partnership tax provides a flexibility found nowhere else in the Code, affording the attorney or accountant an unparalled opportunity to engage in tax planning on behalf of his client.

In approaching partnership tax, it is helpful to understand a few basic concepts. First, a partnership is a "flow-through" entity. It does not pay any tax. Rather, the taxable items flow through the partnership and are reported by the partners. Second, in designing the flow-through system, Congress was not always consistent in its treatment of the status of the partnership. Sometimes it is respected as an entity, separate and distinct from its partners. At other times, the entity is ignored and instead the arrangement is treated as an aggregation of the partners. And, finally, at other times, a hybrid approach is used.

The chapters that follow organize the partnership tax concepts and provisions into cohesive groups. However, one of the things that makes partnership tax so difficult is that the provisions are often interrelated and intertwined. In some respects, it is only after the entire area has been studied that the overall system will make sense. As a result, trying to fit the pieces together along the way can feel a bit like putting together a puzzle without having seen the picture. But, once the pieces are in place, the overall picture does make sense. And then, planning can begin.

II.

Formation of a Partnership

Overview Problem

Stacey, Bill, and Olivia, close friends, decided to form a general partnership to operate a coffee shop. They discussed what they each could contribute. After having discussed the issue for an hour, they developed a plan.

Stacey would contribute an inventory of gourmet coffee beans that she had purchased for $1,000 and that was currently valued at $500. Bill would contribute an industrial strength espresso machine that he had purchased for $5,000 and that was currently valued at $7,000. He had used the machine in a similar business and had held it for two years. Olivia would contribute $5,000 cash.

They intended to be equal partners.

After the partnership was formed, they would look for an appropriate location from which to operate the coffee shop. The partnership would either purchase the building or lease space, depending on what options they could find.

They have asked you to advise them regarding the formation of the partnership.

Formation of a Partnership

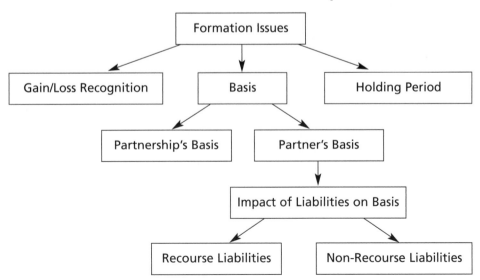

7

Chapter 2

Deferral of Gain or Loss

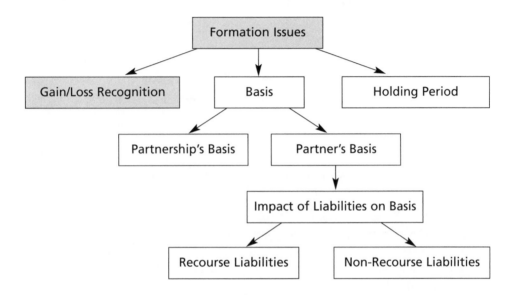

Read:

Code Sections 721(a), (b); 1245(b)(3); 1250(d)(3).
Treas. Reg. §§ 1.721-1(a), -1(b)(1); 1.453-9(c)(2); 1.1245-4(c)(1), -4(c)(2).

A. Background

1. Federal Law

Gross income includes income from all sources derived.[1] One of the items enumerated in Section 61(a) is gain derived from dealings in property.[2] The amount of gain is the excess of the amount realized over the adjusted basis.[3] Unless otherwise provided, the gain realized must be recognized, *i.e.*, reported on the taxpayer's income tax return.[4]

---

1. Code Sec. 61.
2. Code Sec. 61(a)(3).
3. Code Sec. 1001(a).
4. Code Sec. 1001(c).

The amount of loss from a disposition of property is the excess of the adjusted basis over the amount realized. The taxpayer can recognize the loss, *i.e.,* report the loss on his tax return, if it was incurred while engaged in a business or in a transaction entered into for profit.[5]

Example: Allison owns land with a basis of $100 and a fair market value of $500. Blake owns equipment with a basis of $700 and fair market value of $500. Allison sells the land for $500 and Blake sells the equipment for $500. Upon disposition of the land, Allison would realize gain as follows:

Amount realized = $500
Adjusted basis =   100
Gain realized = $400

As provided by Sections 61(a)(3) and 1001(c), Allison must recognize the $400 gain.

Upon disposition of the equipment, Blake would realize a loss as follows:

Amount realized = $500
Adjusted basis =   700
Loss realized =   <$200>

If Blake held the equipment in his business or through a transaction entered into for profit, he can recognize the $200 loss.

The Code has several non-recognition provisions based on the concept of "continuity of interest." In general, to the extent the taxpayer has retained an investment in property that is essentially the same type as the originally held property, any gain or loss on the transaction may be deferred. For example, the taxpayer generally is not required to recognize gain or loss in the following types of transactions:

- Gains or losses from like-kind exchanges;[6]
- Gains from some involuntary conversions;[7] or
- Gains or losses from transfers between spouses or former spouses.[8]

The gain or loss realized in such transactions is deferred until the taxpayer sufficiently disposes of his investment in the property so that there is no longer a continuity of interest.

2. State Law

State law establishes which entities can be created in the state. State law also sets forth the rights, obligations, and responsibilities of the entity owners to each other, to the entity, between the entity and a third party, and between the owners and a third party. In general, states provide, at a minimum, for partnerships, limited liability companies, and corporations.

---

5. Code Sec. 165(a), (c)(1), (c)(2).
6. Code Sec. 1031.
7. Code Sec. 1033.
8. Code Sec. 1041.

Under the Revised Uniform Partnership Act a partnership exists when two or more people carry on as co-owners a business for profit.[9] The partners share the profits of the business and, in addition to the partnership, are individually liable for its debts.[10] While a partnership can arise by operation of law, regardless of whether a certificate has been obtained, all states provide for creation of a partnership by filing with the state.

B. Discussion of Rules

1. Requirements for Tax-Free Transaction

A partnership is a legal entity, separate from the taxpayer-partner. Thus, a transfer of property by a partner to a partnership is a disposition of property. Gain must be recognized, unless authority provides otherwise, and loss can be recognized if provided for under Section 165.

When a taxpayer disposes of property by transferring it to a partnership in exchange for a partnership interest, he continues to have an indirect ownership interest in the property. Stated differently, he has a continuity of his investment. Accordingly, Congress chose not to require taxpayers to recognize gain or loss from the transfer of property to a partnership in which the taxpayer is a partner. Rather, any gain or loss is deferred. Similarly, from the perspective of the partnership, no gain or loss is recognized.

> **Practice Tip:** Services are not considered property for purposes of the non-recognition provision.

To come within the non-recognition provision (Section 721), property must be transferred to the partnership in exchange for an interest in the partnership. This rule applies regardless of whether the partnership is being created or a contribution is being made to a partnership already in existence. In addition, unlike with corporations, there is no requirement that the partner have a certain amount of control over the partnership in order to come within the non-recognition provision.

> **Practice Tip:** If the Internal Revenue Service questions the value of the property contributed to the partnership, the taxpayer-partner has the burden of establishing the value. Thus, the partner should maintain records establishing the value of property contributed.

---

9. RUPA §§ 101(b); 202.
10. RUPA §§ 401(b); 306.

2. Special Rules

Contribution of an installment note. If a taxpayer sells property to an unrelated party and at least one payment for the property is to be received in a year after the year of disposition, the gain[11] from the disposition can be reported using the installment method. Rather than the gain being reported all in the year of sale, a portion of the gain is reported each time an installment payment is received.[12]

If an installment note is disposed of, the disposition is treated as a disposition of property.[13] Gain or loss is recognized based on the difference between the amount realized and the remaining adjusted basis. However, if an installment note is transferred to a partnership in exchange for a partnership interest, the non-recognition provision controls and no gain or loss is recognized.

Recapture. In general, if a taxpayer disposes of tangible or intangible personal depreciable property and realizes a gain, he must characterize the gain as ordinary to the extent of depreciation previously claimed. This gain commonly is referred to as "recapture" gain.[14]

If a taxpayer disposes of depreciable real property, he generally must characterize the gain as ordinary to the extent of depreciation taken in excess of that allowed under the straightline method.[15] Because the straightline method is the only method available for property placed in service after 1986, the recapture provision applicable to real property generally does not re-characterize any of the gain.

If the transfer qualifies as a tax-free contribution to a partnership under Section 721, for both depreciable personal property and depreciable real property, no gain is recognized and no depreciation recapture is required.

Noncompensatory options. A taxpayer may contribute property to the partnership in exchange for an option to acquire a partnership interest. The transfer of property in exchange for the option does not come within Section 721. The taxpayer recognizes gain or loss on the transfer and the partnership takes a cost basis in the property.[16] When the taxpayer transfers property to the partnership to exercise the option, the transfer is covered by Section 721. While the taxpayer holds a noncompensatory option, he is not treated as a partner for purposes of allocating partnership income. However, if the option gives the taxpayer rights substantially similar to those of a partner, then he is treated as a partner for purposes of allocating partnership income.[17]

---

11. The gain must qualify to be reported using the installment method. In general, gain from inventory and Section 1245 recapture is not eligible to be reported using the installment method. Code Sec. 453(b)(2), (i).
12. See Code Sec. 453.
13. See Code Sec. 453B.
14. See Code Sec. 1245.
15. See Code Sec. 1250.
16. Treas. Reg. § 1.721-2(a), (b).
17. Treas. Reg. § 1.761-3(a).

3. Failing Tax-Free Status

Sale or rental to partnership. Rather than make a contribution, a partner may sell the property to the partnership or lease or rent the property to the partnership. If the transaction is structured as a sale or lease, the property has not been contributed to the partnership. The partner must include any rental or lease payment in his gross income and the partnership, to the extent allowed, may claim a deduction for the payments. The substance of the transaction, rather than the form, will be determinative of whether the transaction is a contribution, sale, or rental of property.[18]

Section 721(b) — diversification of appreciated securities. If partners owning various securities were allowed to transfer them to a partnership without recognizing gain, they could use the non-recognition provisions to diversify their appreciated securities on a tax-free basis. The Code does not permit such tax-free diversification.[19] Rather, if the partnership would be treated as an investment company if incorporated, the partner must recognize any gain in the securities contributed to the partnership.

The transfer of property will be considered a transfer to a partnership treated as an investment company if the transfer results, directly or indirectly, in diversification of the partner's interests and the transfer is made to a partnership, more than 80 percent of the value of whose assets are held for investment and are:

- readily marketable stocks or securities;
- interests in regulated investment companies; or
- real estate investment trusts.

In making this determination, the following items are treated as stocks and securities:

- Money;
- Stocks and other equity interests in a corporation, evidence of indebtedness, options, forward or futures contracts, notional principal contracts, and derivatives;
- Foreign currency;
- Any interest in a real estate investment trust, a common trust fund, a regulated investment company, a publicly traded partnership, or other equity interest; and
- Any interest in precious metals, unless such metal is used or held in the active conduct of a business after contribution.

A transfer ordinarily results in the diversification of the partner's interest if two or more partners transfer non-identical assets to a partnership. A transfer of stock and securities is not treated as resulting in a diversification of the partners' interests if each partner transfers a diversified portfolio of stocks and securities. For purposes of determining whether there has been diversification, if any transaction involves one or more transfers of non-identical assets that, taken in the aggregate, constitute an insignificant portion of the total value of assets transferred, such transfers are disregarded in determining whether diversification has occurred.

---

18. For a complete discussion of the tax treatment of a partner not acting in the capacity of a partner, see Chapter 29.

19. Code Sec. 721(b).

If the transfer is part of a plan to achieve diversification without recognition of gain, the original transfer will be treated as resulting in diversification. For example, a plan that contemplates a subsequent transfer, however delayed, of the partnership assets to a partnership treated as an investment company in a transaction purporting to qualify for non-recognition treatment will be treated as resulting in diversification.

If the partnership is treated as an investment company, gain is recognized on all transfers, not just on transfers of securities. In addition, if a loss is realized upon contribution of property, it cannot be recognized.

C. Application of Rules

Example 1. Allison and Blake formed Circle Partnership. They agreed that they each would contribute $500 of assets in exchange for 50 percent of the partnership interests, each 50-percent partnership interest being worth $500. Specifically, Allison contributed land with a basis of $100 and a fair market value of $500, and Blake contributed equipment with a basis of $700 and fair market value of $500.

Upon disposition of the land (contribution to the partnership), Allison realized gain as follows:

Amount realized =	$500
Adjusted basis =	100
Gain realized =	$400

Unless otherwise provided, under Sections 61(a)(3) and 1001(c), the gain realized must be recognized. Section 721(a) provides that any gain realized on the disposition of property to a partnership is not recognized. Thus, Allison will not recognize the $400 of gain upon her contribution of property to the Circle Partnership.

Upon disposition of the equipment, Blake realized a loss as follows:

Amount realized =	$500
Adjusted basis =	700
Loss realized =	<$200>

Usually, Blake will recognize the loss if the property were held in his business or for profit. However, Section 721(a) provides that any loss realized on the disposition of property to a partnership is not recognized. Thus, Blake cannot recognize the $200 of loss upon his contribution of property to the Circle Partnership.

The Circle Partnership does not recognize any gain or loss upon receipt of the land or equipment.

Example 2. Alex contributed a machine used in his business with a fair market value of $110,000 to a partnership in exchange for a 50-percent partnership interest. He originally purchased the machine two years earlier for $100,000 and had claimed $52,000 in depreciation.

If Alex had disposed of the machine in a taxable transaction for $110,000, rather than contributed it to the partnership, he would have been required to recognize $62,000 of gain:

Amount realized =	$110,000
Adjusted basis ($100,000 − $52,000) =	48,000
Gain realized =	$62,000

Of the $62,000 of gain, $52,000 would be recapture gain, characterized as ordinary income under Section 1245. The remaining gain would continue to be characterized as hotchpot (Section 1231) gain. However, because Alex transferred the equipment to the partnership, the transfer qualifies as a tax-free exchange; he recognizes no gain, and no portion of the gain must be reported as ordinary income pursuant to the Section 1245 recapture provision.

Example 3. David and 50 other people formed a partnership. David transferred $10,000 worth of ABCo stock to the partnership in exchange for a 50-percent interest in the partnership. Each of the other partners transferred $200 worth of marketable securities, other than ABCo stock, in exchange for a one-percent interest. Diversification is present. All partners must recognize gain on the transfer; no loss may be recognized.

D. Problems

1. Able, Beth, and Claire formed an equal general partnership. They contributed the following assets:

Able:

Asset	Adjusted Basis	Fair Market Value
Equipment (all § 1245 gain)	$500	$2,000
Goodwill	-0-	4,500
Accounts receivable	-0-	500

Beth:

Asset	Adjusted Basis	Fair Market Value
Land	$10,000	$6,000
Installment note (from the sale of land)	500	1,000

Claire:

Asset	Adjusted Basis	Fair Market Value
Cash	$7,000	$7,000

Able used the equipment in his business for three years prior to contribution. The goodwill was generated over three years. Beth held the land for investment and had purchased it five years prior to contribution. The installment note is from the sale of land Beth held for investment purposes. She held the land for four years prior to selling it.

(a) Able:

    (1) What is the amount of gain or loss realized by Able upon his contribution of the equipment, goodwill, and accounts receivable to the partnership?

      (2) What is the amount of gain or loss recognized by Able on each asset? Why? What is your authority?

(b) Beth:

      (1) What is the amount of gain or loss realized by Beth upon her contribution of the land and installment note to the partnership?

      (2) What is the amount of gain or loss recognized by Beth on each asset? Why? What is your authority?

(c) Claire:

      (1) What is the amount of gain or loss realized by Claire upon her contribution of cash to the partnership?

      (2) What is the amount of gain or loss recognized by Claire? Why?

---

2. Drita, Ethel, and Frank formed a limited liability company in which they were equal members. They contributed the following assets:

Drita:

Asset	Adjusted Basis	Fair Market Value
Cash	$5,000	$5,000

Ethel:

Asset	Adjusted Basis	Fair Market Value
Accounts receivable	$-0-	$4,000
Installment note (from the sale of inventory)	700	1,000

Frank:

Asset	Adjusted Basis	Fair Market Value
Land	$9,000	$5,000

Frank held the land for investment and had purchased it six years prior to contribution.

(a) How is a limited liability company treated for tax purposes? Hint: See Treas. Reg. § 301.7701-3(a), (b)(1).

(b) Drita:

      (1) What is the amount of gain or loss realized by Drita upon her contribution of cash to the limited liability company?

      (2) What is the amount of gain or loss recognized by Drita? Why?

(c) Ethel:

      (1) What is the amount of gain or loss realized by Ethel upon her contribution of the accounts receivable and installment note to the limited liability company?

      (2) What is the amount of gain or loss recognized by Ethel on each asset? Why? What is your authority?

(d) Frank:

      (1) What is the amount of gain or loss realized by Frank upon his contribution of the land to the limited liability company?

(2) What is the amount of gain or loss recognized by Frank on the land? Why? What is your authority?

3. Application:

(a) How would you explain to the soon-to-be partners what the tax consequences of forming a partnership are?

(b) As part of forming the partnership, what documentation would you advise your clients acquire and maintain? Why?

(c) How would you document the transfer of cash or property by a partner to the partnership?

E. Advanced Problems — Looking Forward

Without conducting any research, consider the following questions:

1. For tax purposes, can a partner ever interact with a partnership not in his capacity as a partner? If so, how should the transaction be treated for tax purposes?

2. If no gain or loss is recognized on the contribution of property by a partner to a partnership, but rather deferred, how might the deferral be accomplished?

3. If a contribution of property to a partnership reflects a continuity of the partner's interest in the property, what impact, if any, should that have on the partner's holding period in his partnership interest?

4. If a partnership interest is given in exchange for services:

a. How should the transaction be treated by the partner who performed the services?

b. Is the partnership entitled to an expense deduction for the salary payment as an ordinary and necessary expense (under Section 162)? If yes, which partners should get the benefit of the deduction? Specifically, should the service-provider (who will become a partner) be entitled to benefit from the deduction?

Chapter 3

Basis and Holding Period

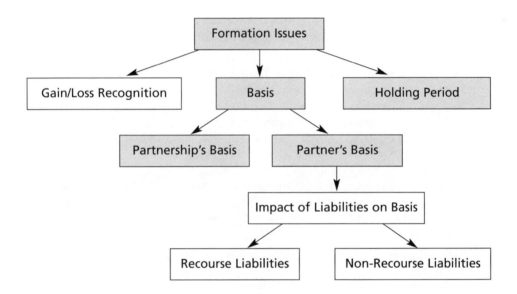

Read:

Code Sections 722; 723; 1223(1), (2); 7701(a)(43), (a)(44).
Treas. Reg. §§ 1.722-1 (omit examples); 1.723-1; 1.1223-3(a), -3(b)(1), -3(e),
-3(f) Ex. 1(i).

A. Background

1. Basis

A partnership can be viewed as an aggregate of the partners or as a separate entity. The Uniform Partnership Act follows the approach that a partnership is an aggregate of the partners. As such, all property contributed to or acquired by the partnership is partnership property.[1] However, each partner is a co-owner of partnership property with the other partners, holding it as tenants-in-partnership.[2]

---

1. UPA § 8(1).
2. UPA § 25(1).

The Revised Uniform Partnership Act follows the approach that a partnership is a separate entity.[3] Property acquired by the partnership, either through contribution or direct acquisition, is considered property of the partnership and not of the partners individually.[4]

2. Holding Period

The taxpayer's holding period of an asset is relevant when considering those Code sections that are dependent on how long the asset has been held. For example, an asset is a hotchpot (Section 1231) asset if it is land or depreciable property used in a business that the taxpayer has held for more than one year. In general, a net hotchpot gain becomes a long-term capital gain and a net hotchpot loss becomes an ordinary loss.

Determination of Which Assets Are Hotchpot (Section 1231) Assets: Section 1231 addresses quasi-capital assets. But for the application of Section 1231, any gain or loss recognized on Section 1231 assets would be characterized as ordinary gain or loss. Through application of Section 1231, it is possible for a net gain to be characterized as a long-term capital gain, while a net loss continues to be treated as an ordinary loss.

In general, hotchpot (Section 1231) assets include the following:[5]
- Depreciable property used in the taxpayer's business and held for more than one year; and
- Real property used in the taxpayer's business and held for more than one year.

Hotchpot (Section 1231) assets do not include the following:
- Capital assets;
- Inventory;
- Real property held primarily for sale to customers in the ordinary course of the taxpayer's business; or
- Certain copyrights.

For capital assets, the characterization as long-term or short-term gain determines whether a preferential tax rate will be applied to the gain recognized on disposition. An asset is held long term if it has been held for more than one year. An asset is held short term if it has been held for one year or less.

Determination of Which Assets Are Capital Assets: In general, capital assets include all property except:[6]
- Inventory;
- Real property held primarily for sale to customers in the course of the taxpayer's business;

---

3. RUPA § 201(a).
4. RUPA § 203.
5. See Code Sec. 1231(b).
6. See Code Sec. 1221(a).

- Depreciable property used in the taxpayer's business;
- Real property used in the taxpayer's business;
- Certain copyrights;
- Accounts receivable acquired in the ordinary course of the taxpayer's business; and
- Supplies used in the taxpayer's business.

Summary of Tax Results

	Ordinary	**Capital**
Gain	Taxed at regular rates.[7]	• Net long-term gain—taxed at preferential rates.[8] • Net short-term gain—taxed at regular rates.
Loss	In general, if otherwise allowable, no limitation on the amount of loss that can be claimed.	• To the extent it exceeds capital gains, the amount allowed is limited to $3,000.[9] • Any excess loss can be carried forward, retaining its character as long-term or short-term capital loss.[10]

B. Discussion of Rules

1. Basis

The partner's basis. For purposes of determining the partner's basis in his continuing interest (the partnership), the Code follows the entity approach. Thus, rather than owning an interest in the underlying assets of the partnership, the partner owns an interest in the partnership (which, in turn, owns all the assets contributed).

The contribution of property to a partnership generally is not a taxable event. However, the ability of a partner to transfer property to a partnership free of any tax consequences does not completely relieve the partner from the tax liability associated with appreciation in the asset. Nor does it eliminate any loss. Rather, it postpones the recognition event, generally until the time the partnership disposes of the asset or the partner disposes of his partnership interest.

The gain or loss inherent in the property is preserved in the partner's basis in the partnership interest. This concept is similar to the treatment of the basis of property received in a like-kind exchange, replacement property acquired after an involuntary con-

---

7. There is one exception—dividends. Dividends, while ordinary income, are taxed at preferential rates. See Code Sec. 1(h)(11).

8. See Code Sec. 1(h).

9. See Code Sec. 1211(b).

10. See Code Sec. 1212(b).

version, and property transferred from a spouse or former spouse. Any gain or loss that has been deferred is reflected in the basis of the new property.

The partner's basis in his partnership interest is the amount of money and the adjusted basis of contributed property at the time of the contribution, increased by the amount (if any) of gain recognized under Section 721(b).[11] The partner's basis in his partnership interest is referred to as his "outside basis."

Formula: When there are no liabilities involved, to determine the partner's basis in the partnership interest acquired by a contribution to a partnership, complete the following steps:

Step 1: Determine the adjusted basis of the asset(s) contributed to the partnership.

Step 2: Determine the amount of cash contributed to the partnership.

Step 3: Determine the amount of gain under Section 721(b), if any.

Step 4: Add the amounts determined under the first three steps.

The total is the partner's outside basis in the partnership interest.

If a partner contributes his promissory note to the partnership, it is not treated as cash. Rather, it is considered a contractual obligation to the partnership, and the partner has basis from the note only to the extent he makes payments on the note.

If a cash basis taxpayer contributes accounts receivable to the partnership, the basis in the accounts receivable is zero. The zero basis reflects the fact that the accounts receivable have not been reported in income.

Practice Tip: If the Internal Revenue Service questions the basis of the property contributed to the partnership, the taxpayer-partner generally has the burden of proof. Thus, the partner should maintain records establishing the basis of property contributed.

Practice Tip: If a partner acquires a partnership interest through a purchase, he will have a basis equal to cost, as provided for under Section 1012. [Code Sec. 742. See discussion in Chapter 22.]

The partnership. The partnership is continuing the ownership interest in the assets contributed by its partners. Because the gain or loss inherent in that property has not yet been recognized, it must be preserved in the basis of the asset. In essence, the partnership steps into the shoes of the contributing partner.

The basis of assets contributed to a partnership is the basis in the hands of the contributing partner, increased by the amount (if any) of gain recognized under Section

---

11. Code Sec. 722.

721(b) by the contributing partner at the time of the contribution.[12] The partnership's transferred basis in the assets is referred to as the "inside basis."

> **Practice Tip:** The concept of the partnership's inside basis is similar to that of appreciated property received as a gift. The donee takes the donor's basis in the property. Upon disposition of the property, the donee has to recognize not only the appreciation that occurred while he held the property, but also the appreciation that occurred while the donor held the property.

The partner's basis as assumed by the partnership is used for all purposes. Such purposes include determining gain or loss upon disposition of the asset, calculating depreciation, and determining availability of credits. For depreciable property, in addition to the partner's basis being transferred to the partnership, the partnership succeeds to the cost recovery method used by the partner.[13]

Note that, by treating the partnership as an entity separate from the partners, one asset can be viewed from two different perspectives. First, the basis of all the assets contributed will be reflected cumulatively in the partner's basis in his partnership interest. Second, the partnership will have a basis in each individual asset that has been contributed to the partnership.

> **Example:** As part of the purchase of a business, Tanya paid $15,000 for goodwill. Under Section 197, goodwill is amortizable over 15 years. Thus, Tanya will recover the cost of the goodwill over 15 years. After using the goodwill in her business for one entire year (and claiming $1,000 of amortization), Tanya contributed the goodwill to a partnership. Upon contribution, the partnership steps into Tanya's shoes for purposes of determining the amount of amortization allowed. To the extent of the $14,000 carryover basis ($15,000 cost less $1,000 of amortization), the partnership will continue to amortize the goodwill over the remaining 14 years.

2. Holding Period

The partner. In general, a partnership interest is a capital asset. Because the partnership interest represents a continuation of the partner's interest in the contributed assets, the length of time the individual held contributed capital assets should tack onto the length of time the partner has held the partnership interest. Thus, by including the

---

12. Code Sec. 723. If the property being contributed to the partnership was not being used in a trade or business or investment activity, the basis in the hands of the partnership is the lesser of its adjusted basis or fair market value.

13. Code Sec. 168(i)(7).

time the underlying capital assets were held, if the partner held the partnership interest for more than one year, the gain would be eligible for long-term capital gain preferential treatment. Accordingly, if the property contributed by the partner to the partnership is a capital asset or hotchpot (Section 1231) asset, the partner's holding period in the asset is tacked onto the holding period of his partnership interest. If the partner contributes cash or ordinary income assets, the holding period of the partnership interest begins on the day following the date of contribution.[14] If a partner contributes assets whose holding period tacks and those that do not, the holding period will be allocated between the two.[15] For purposes of this determination, Section 1245 recapture gain is not treated as a capital or Section 1231 asset.

Formula: The percentage of the partnership interest that has a holding period that tacks is:

Fair market value of capital and Section 1231 assets
Fair market value of entire partnership interest

The percentage of the partnership interest that has a holding period that does not tack is:

Fair market value of ordinary income assets and cash
Fair market value of entire partnership interest

The partnership. Consistent with the concept of continuing the partner's interest in the property and preserving the tax ramifications inherent in the property until disposition of the asset by the partnership, the partnership can tack the partner's holding period in the asset onto the partnership's holding period.[16] However, there is no distinction between the various types of assets; the holding period for all assets tacks. Because each asset continues to be a separate and distinct asset, the character of the gain or loss and holding period can be determined at the partnership level.

Example: Pat contributed inventory he had held for two years to a partnership in exchange for a partnership interest. The partnership can tack on Pat's holding period; it is considered as holding the asset for two years.
If the inventory is sold over the next three months, the character will continue to be ordinary. Note, however, that because the income is ordinary, the length of time the partnership is considered as having held the property is irrelevant.

---

14. Rev. Rul. 99-5, 99-1 C.B. 434; Rev. Rul. 66-7, 1966-1 C.B. 188.
15. Treas. Reg. § 1.1223-3(a)(2).
16. Code Sec. 1223(2).

C. Application of Rules

Example 1. Partner's basis in partnership. Allison contributed land to a partnership. Her basis in the land was $100 and its fair market value was $500. Upon contribution to the partnership, she exchanged her ownership in the land for ownership in the partnership which then owned the land. She exchanged her $100 basis in the land for a $100 basis in the partnership interest.

Example 2. Partner's basis in partnership. Blake contributed equipment to a partnership. His basis in the equipment was $700 and its fair market value was $500. Upon contribution to the partnership, he exchanged his ownership in the equipment for ownership in the partnership which then owned the equipment. He exchanged his $700 basis in the equipment for a $700 basis in the partnership interest.

Example 3. Partner's basis in partnership. Callie and Denver formed an equal general partnership. Callie contributed $500 cash and land with a basis of $100 and a fair market value of $300. Denver contributed $600 cash and equipment with a basis of $700 and fair market value of $200.

To determine Callie's outside basis in the partnership:

Step 1: Basis in land	$100
Step 2: Cash contributed	500
Step 3: Section 721(b) gain	0
Step 4: Total –> outside basis	$600

To determine Denver's outside basis in the partnership:

Step 1: Basis in equipment	$700
Step 2: Cash contributed	600
Step 3: Section 721(b) gain	0
Step 4: Total –> outside basis	$1,300

Example 4. Partnership's basis. Allison contributed land to a partnership. Her basis in the land was $100 and its fair market value was $500. Upon contribution to the partnership, the partnership's basis in the land is $100.

Example 5. Partnership's basis. Blake contributed equipment to a partnership. His basis in the equipment was $700 and its fair market value was $500. Upon contribution to the partnership, the partnership's basis in the equipment is $700.

Example 6. Partnership's basis. Callie and Denver formed an equal general partnership. Callie contributed $500 cash and land with a basis of $100 and a fair market value of $300. Denver contributed $600 cash and equipment with a basis of $700 and fair market value of $200.

The partnership steps into the shoes of the partner and has an inside basis in the assets as follows:

Asset	Basis
Land	$100
Equipment	700

The partnership also has $1,100 of cash.

Example 7. Partner's holding period. Charlie and Deidre formed an equal general partnership. Charlie contributed $300 cash and land he held for investment for four years with a basis of $100 and a fair market value of $300. Deidre contributed $400 cash and equipment used in her business that she held for two years with a basis of $700 and fair market value of $200.

The portion of Charlie's holding period that will tack is:

$$\frac{\text{(fmv of land)}}{\text{(fmv of entire partnership interest)}} \quad \frac{300}{600} = \frac{1}{2}$$

The portion of Charlie's holding period that does not tack is:

$$\frac{\text{(fmv of ordinary assets + cash)}}{\text{(fmv of entire partnership interest)}} \quad \frac{300}{600} = \frac{1}{2}$$

Thus, Charlie is treated as having held ½ of his partnership interest for four years. The holding period for the remaining ½ of his partnership interest begins on the day following contribution.

The portion of Deidre's holding period that will tack is:

$$\frac{\text{(fmv of equipment)}}{\text{(fmv of entire partnership interest)}} \quad \frac{200}{600} = \frac{1}{3}$$

The portion of Deidre's holding period that does not tack is:

$$\frac{\text{(fmv of ordinary assets + cash)}}{\text{(fmv of entire partnership interest)}} \quad \frac{400}{600} = \frac{2}{3}$$

Thus, Deidre is treated as having held 1/3 of her partnership interest for two years. The holding period for the remaining 2/3 of her partnership interest begins on the day following contribution.

Example 8. Partner's holding period (Section 1245 property). Evelyn contributed equipment to a partnership in exchange for a partnership interest. She had held the equipment for two years. It had a basis of $100 and fair market value of $400. All the potential gain is Section 1245 recapture gain.

The Section 1245 recapture gain is not treated as a capital or Section 1231 asset. Thus, $100 of the asset is a Section 1231 asset whose holding period tacks and $300 of the asset is an ordinary income asset whose holding period does not tack.

The portion of Evelyn's holding period that will tack is:

$$\frac{\text{(non-recapture portion of the equipment)}}{\text{(fmv of entire partnership interest)}} \quad \frac{100}{400} = \frac{1}{4}$$

The portion of Evelyn's holding period that does not tack is:

$$\frac{\text{(recapture (ordinary income) portion of the equipment)}}{\text{(fmv of entire partnership interest)}} \quad \frac{300}{400} = \frac{3}{4}$$

Thus, Evelyn is treated as having held 1/4 of her partnership interest for two years. The holding period for the remaining 3/4 of her partnership interest begins on the day following contribution.

Example 9. Partnership's holding period. Charlie and Deidre formed an equal general partnership. Charlie contributed $300 cash and land he held for four years with a basis of $100 and a fair market value of $300. Deidre contributed $400 cash and equipment she held for two years with a basis of $700 and fair market value of $200.

The partnership can tack Charlie's holding period in the land onto its holding period in the land and, thus, is treated as having held it for four years. The partnership can tack Deidre's holding period in the equipment onto its holding period and, thus, is treated as having held it for two years.

D. Cases and Materials

Oden v. Commissioner
T.C. Memo 1981-184, aff'd without opinion,
679 F.2d 885 (4th Cir. 1982)

[Author's note: The taxpayers contributed $16,250 cash and a promissory note in the amount of $18,750 to the Ohio Products partnership in exchange for a partnership interest. The issue before the court was whether the taxpayer-partners were entitled to a deduction for losses from the partnership. Because the taxpayer-partners could only deduct a loss up to the amount of their outside basis, resolution of the issue turned on the determination of the taxpayer-partners' basis in the partnership during that year.]

* * *

Section 722 provides in pertinent part that the basis of an interest in a partnership acquired by a contribution of property, including money, to the partnership shall be the amount of such money and the adjusted basis of such property to the contributing partner at the time of the contribution. A partner's distributive share of partnership loss (including capital loss) shall be allowed only to the extent of the adjusted basis of such partner's interest in the partnership at the end of the partnership year in which the loss occurred. Section 704(d). Petitioner's cash contribution to the Ohio Producers partnership was $16,250. Additionally, he argues that he tendered a note for $18,750 at the time of the creation of the partnership. Petitioner claims that under section 742 he is entitled to a $35,000 basis in his partnership interest.

Petitioner's application of section 742 to the instant case is in error. That section provides that a transferee's initial basis in his partnership interest is determined under the rules generally applicable to acquisitions of other types of property. See section 1.742.-1, Income Tax Regs. Accordingly, if a partnership interest is purchased or acquired in a taxable exchange, the transferee's basis is his cost under section 1012. Where, however, the partnership interest is acquired by a contribution of property to the partnership, the contributor's basis in the acquired interest is determined by reference to the adjusted basis of the property so contributed. Section 722. See section 1.722-1, Income Tax Regs.

Petitioner urges that we determine that his basis in the Ohio Producers partnership includes the face amount ($18,750) of a note allegedly executed and delivered by him to the partnership. Petitioner has not shown that any payments were made on the note during 1971.

Petitioner advances an elaborate argument which points to the alleged transfer of his own note to the partnership. He emphasizes that the note created a bona fide indebtedness to the partnership, while he minimizes the importance of the question of whether the note was recourse or nonrecourse. While we agree that it is irrelevant in the present context whether the note was either recourse or nonrecourse, we believe that such irrelevancy stems from the fact that petitioner's basis in his partnership interest is to be determined under section 722. Since petitioner incurred no cost in making the note, its basis to him was zero. Petitioner has not shown that any payments on the note were made in 1971. Thus, pursuant to the mandate of section 722, petitioner is not entitled to increase his partnership basis by the face amount of the allegedly transferred note. Cf. Alderman v. Commissioner, 55 T.C. 662 (1971) (shareholder's personal note had a zero basis for purposes of applying section 357(c)); Rev. Rul. 68-629, 1968-2 C.B. 154 (to the same effect). See Rev. Rul. 80-235, 1980-35 I.R.B. 7, 8. Accordingly, petitioner is not entitled to deduct any partnership loss in excess of his cash contribution of $16,250. Section 704(d).

Other arguments aired by the parties are rendered moot by our holding above and thus we do not address them.

Decision will be entered for the respondent.

E. Problems

1. Able, Beth, and Claire formed an equal general partnership. They contributed the following assets:

Able:

Asset	Adjusted Basis	Fair Market Value
Equipment (all § 1245 gain)	$500	$2,000
Goodwill	-0-	4,500
Accounts receivable	-0-	500

Beth:

Asset	Adjusted Basis	Fair Market Value
Land	$10,000	$6,000
Installment note (from the sale of land)	500	1,000

Claire:

Asset	Adjusted Basis	Fair Market Value
Cash	$7,000	$7,000

Able used the equipment in his business for three years prior to contribution. The goodwill was generated over three years. Beth held the land for investment and had purchased it five years prior to contribution. The installment note is from the sale of land Beth held for investment purposes. She held the land for four years prior to selling it.

(a) Able:
 (1) What is his basis in his partnership interest?
 (2) What is his holding period for his partnership interest?

(b) Beth:
 (1) What is her basis in her partnership interest?
 (2) What is her holding period for her partnership interest?

(c) Claire:
 (1) What is her basis in her partnership interest?
 (2) What is her holding period for her partnership interest?

(d) The partnership:
 (1) What is the partnership's basis in each asset?
 (2) What is the partnership's holding period for each asset?
 (3) How will the partnership calculate depreciation on the equipment?

---

2. Drita, Ethel, and Frank formed a limited liability company in which they were equal members. They contributed the following assets:

Drita:

Asset	Adjusted Basis	Fair Market Value
Cash	$5,000	$5,000

Ethel:

Asset	Adjusted Basis	Fair Market Value
Accounts receivable	$-0-	$4,000
Installment note	700	1,000
(from the sale of inventory)		

Frank:

Asset	Adjusted Basis	Fair Market Value
Land	$9,000	$5,000

Frank held the land for investment and had purchased it six years prior to contribution.

(a) Drita:
 (1) What is her basis in her member interest?
 (2) What is her holding period for her member interest?

(b) Ethel:
 (1) What is her basis in her member interest?
 (2) What is her holding period for her member interest?

(c) Frank:
 (1) What is his basis in his member interest?
 (2) What is his holding period for his member interest?

(d) The limited liability company:

(1) What is the limited liability company's basis in each asset?

(2) What is the limited liability company's holding period for each asset?

3. Application:

(a) How would you explain to the soon-to-be partners what the tax consequences of a transfer of property to a partnership are?

(b) Specifically with respect to the transfer of property to a partnership, what documentation would you advise your clients obtain and maintain? Why?

F. Advanced Problems — Looking Forward

Without conducting any research, consider the following questions:

1. Characterization Issue:

    a.   What would be the character of gain if a taxpayer sold inventory at a profit?

    b.   What would be the character of gain if a taxpayer sold a partnership interest?

    c.   What should be the character of gain if a partner transfers inventory to a partnership, then sells the partnership interest?

2. Deferral Issue:

    a.   A partner contributed appreciated property to the partnership.

        (1) Who should be responsible for the tax due on the appreciation that occurred prior to contribution? How might that be accomplished?

        (2) Who should be responsible for the tax due on appreciation that occurs after the property was contributed to the partnership? How might that be accomplished?

    b.   A partner contributed depreciated property to the partnership.

        (1) Who should be able to recognize the loss due to the depreciation that occurred prior to contribution? How might that be accomplished?

        (2) Who should be able to recognize the loss that occurs after the property was contributed to the partnership? How might that be accomplished?

Chapter 4

The Balance Sheet

Read:
Treas. Reg. § 1.704-1(b)(2)(iv)(a), -1(b)(2)(iv)(b), -1(b)(2)(iv)(d)(1), -1(b)(2)(iv)(d)(2), -1(b)(2)(iv)(h).

A. Background

For tax purposes, the partnership is treated as separate from the partners. By treating the partnership as an entity separate from the partners, one asset can be viewed from two different perspectives. First, the basis of all the contributed assets will be reflected in the partner's basis in his partnership interest. Second, the partnership will have a basis in each individual asset that has been contributed to the partnership.

B. Discussion of Rules

A partnership balance sheet is a document that can be used to keep track of the relationship of the partnership to the partners and the partners to each other, both from a tax perspective and an economic perspective.

The left half of the balance sheet reflects the assets from the partnership's perspective. Generally, assets are listed starting with the most liquid and moving towards the most illiquid.

For each asset, both the adjusted basis (inside basis) and the fair market value are reflected. The adjusted basis is the partnership's basis (inside basis) in each asset. Generally, the fair market value will be the value of the asset upon contribution (book value), reduced to reflect any depreciation taken by the partnership. In general, for purposes of the balance sheet, except to reflect depreciation, the fair market value, or book value, does not change, even if it does change in the marketplace.[1]

The right half of the balance sheet reflects partnership liabilities and ownership from the perspective of the partners. Liabilities include not only obligations to third parties,

---

1. There are some events that trigger a revaluation of the partnership assets.

but also obligations to partners who have loaned funds to the partnership, acting other than in their capacity as a partner.

For each partner, both the adjusted basis of the partner in his partnership interest (outside basis) and his economic investment are reflected. A partner's basis was discussed in Chapter 3. A partner's economic investment is his "capital account" or the "book value" of his partnership interest.

The method of computing a partner's capital account is set forth in the regulations. The partner's initial capital account is computed by adding the amount of money and the net fair market value of property contributed to the partnership. "Net fair market value" is the fair market value of the property, less any liabilities the property is taken subject to. The regulations provide detailed rules for how the capital accounts are adjusted during the life of the partnership.

Example: Quinn and Russ formed an equal general partnership. Quinn contributed $5,000 cash and Russ contributed Whiteacre, which had a basis of $4,000, a fair market value of $7,000, and was subject to a $2,000 debt.

In general, to be equal partners, Quinn and Russ must contribute the same amount of equity to the partnership. Quinn contributed $5,000. Russ contributed land valued at $7,000. However, because the partnership took the land subject to the debt of $2,000, the equity the partnership will have in Whiteacre is $5,000 (fair market value of $7,000, less $2,000 debt). Thus, each partner has an equity interest, and capital account, of $5,000.

In general, except to reflect depreciation claimed by the partnership and allocated among the partners, the partner's capital account is not adjusted to reflect changes in the value of the contributed assets.[2]

Finally, a partner's capital account reflects the amount each partner would receive if the partnership were liquidated, all assets were sold for their fair market value, all debts were paid, and the net proceeds distributed among the partners. It also reflects the ownership interest of each partner as compared to the other partners. Noteworthy, the method of computing a partner's capital account does not follow Generally Accepted Accounting Principles (GAAP).

Formulas:

Assets = Liabilities + Equity

Assets – Liabilities = Equity

---

2. There are some events that trigger a restatement of capital accounts.

C. Application of Rules

Example. Finney and Garth formed an equal general partnership. Finney contributed $2,000 cash and land with a basis of $4,000 and a fair market value of $8,000. Garth contributed $5,000 cash and equipment with a basis of $2,000 and a fair market value of $5,000. Upon formation, the balance sheet would appear as follows:

Asset	Adj. Basis	FMV	Liabilities:		0
Cash	$7,000	$7,000		Basis	Cap. Acct.
Equipment	2,000	5,000	Finney	$6,000	$10,000
Land	4,000	8,000	Garth	7,000	10,000
Total:	$13,000	$20,000		$13,000	$20,000

The fact that the partners are equal partners is reflected in the capital accounts—they each own an equal economic interest in the partnership. Or, seen from another perspective, if the partnership sold all its assets (ignoring selling costs), the $20,000 received would be distributed according to Finney and Garth's capital accounts, or $10,000 each.

Note that the total of the partnership's inside bases is equal to the total of all partners' outside bases and that the total fair market value of the partnership assets is equal to the total of all liabilities plus the partners' capital accounts.

D. Problems

1. Able, Beth, and Claire formed an equal general partnership. They contributed the following assets:

Able:

Asset	Adjusted Basis	Fair Market Value
Equipment (all § 1245 gain)	$500	$2,000
Goodwill	-0-	4,500
Accounts receivable	-0-	500

Beth:

Asset	Adjusted Basis	Fair Market Value
Land	$10,000	$6,000
Installment note (from the sale of land)	500	1,000

Claire:

Asset	Adjusted Basis	Fair Market Value
Cash	$7,000	$7,000

Able used the equipment in his business for three years prior to contribution. The goodwill was generated over three years. Beth held the land for investment and had purchased it five years prior to contribution. The installment note is from the sale of land Beth held for investment purposes. She held the land for four years prior to selling it.

Prepare a balance sheet for the partnership.

2. Drita, Ethel, and Frank formed a limited liability company in which they were equal members. They contributed the following assets:

Drita:

Asset	Adjusted Basis	Fair Market Value
Cash	$5,000	$5,000

Ethel:

Asset	Adjusted Basis	Fair Market Value
Accounts receivable	$-0-	$4,000
Installment note (from the sale of inventory)	700	1,000

Frank:

Asset	Adjusted Basis	Fair Market Value
Land	$9,000	$5,000

Frank held the land for investment and had purchased it six years prior to contribution.

Prepare a balance sheet for the limited liability company.

---

3. Application:

Two people want to form an equal partnership. Mary will contribute $10,000 cash. Nora will contribute Blackacre, with a basis of $7,000, fair market value of $10,000, and subject to a $1,000 liablity. Since both are contributing items with a total value of $10,000, how would you explain to them that they would not be equal partners?

E. Advanced Problems — Looking Forward

Without conducting any research, consider the following questions:

1. If property held by the partnership depreciated, what affect (if any) would the depreciation have on the balance sheet?

2. If property held by the partnership appreciates, what affect (if any) would the appreciation have on the balance sheet?

3. If your client were interested in purchasing an interest in a partnership, what information could be obtained by reviewing the partnership balance sheet? What else would the client (and you) want to know?

Chapter 5

Receipt of Partnership Interest for Services

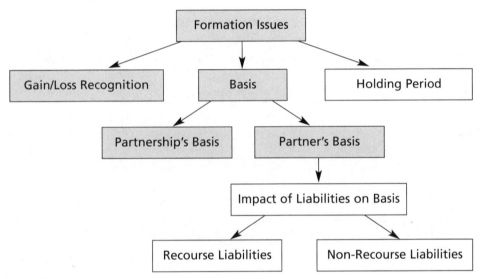

Read:

Code Sections 722; 723.
Treas. Reg. §§ 1.721-1(b)(1); 1.722-1 (omit examples); 723-1.

A. Background

When a taxpayer disposes of property by transferring it to a partnership in exchange for a partnership interest, he continues to have an indirect ownership interest in the property. Stated differently, he has a continuity of his investment. Accordingly, Congress chose not to require taxpayers to recognize gain or loss from the transfer of property to a partnership in which the taxpayer is a partner. Rather, any gain or loss is deferred. Similarly, from the perspective of the partnership, no gain or loss is recognized.

To come within the non-recognition provision (Section 721), property must be transferred to the partnership in exchange for an interest in the partnership. This rule applies regardless of whether the partnership is being created or a contribution is being made to a partnership already in existence. In addition, unlike with corporations, there is no requirement that the partner have a certain amount of control over the partnership in order to come within the non-recognition provision.

Practice Tip: Services are not considered property for purposes of the non-recognition provision.

B. Discussion of Rules

A partner can receive a capital interest or profits interest in the partnership. A capital interest is an interest that would give the partner a share of the proceeds if the partnership's assets were sold at fair market value and then the proceeds were distributed in a complete liquidation of the partnership. A profits interest is only the right to participate in the earnings and profits of the partnership.

Capital interest. When a partner receives a capital interest in a partnership in exchange for services provided (or to be provided) to the partnership, the non-recognition provision does not apply to the entire transaction. Rather, the tax consequences are based on the two component parts of the transaction. First, the partner receives compensation in exchange for his services. The amount of the compensation received will be the value of the capital account; this amount must be included in his gross income. Second, the partner contributes the amount received as compensation for services to the partnership in exchange for the partnership interest. The contribution is tax-free.

In *McDougal v. Commissioner*,[1] the McDougals' horse trainer, Gilbert McClanahan, encouraged them to buy Iron Card, a two-year-old race horse that suffered from a protein allergy. The McDougals purchased Iron Card for $10,000 and entered into an agreement with McClanahan. If McClanahan trained and attended to Iron Card, he would receive a one-half interest in the horse after the McDougals recovered their costs and acquisition expenses. McClanahan successfully treated Iron Card's protein allergy and the horse had great success as a race horse. When the McDougals had recovered their costs and expenses from the race winnings, they transferred a one-half interest in the horse to McClanahan.

The Tax Court found that when the one-half ownership interest in Iron Card was transferred by the McDougals to McClanahan, a partnership was formed; the McDougals contributed the horse and McClanahan contributed past services. However, the court analyzed the transaction in three steps.

First, the McDougals transferred a one-half interest in Iron Card to McClanahan. Because the McDougals had disposed of property, they had to recognize gain to the extent the amount realized (value of the services performed by McClanahan) exceeded their adjusted basis. Second, McClanahan received a one-half interest in Iron Card as com-

---

1. 62 T.C. 720 (1974).

pensation for his prior services. This amount of compensation paid to him had to be included in his gross income. He had a basis in his one-half of Iron Card equal to the amount of compensation income he reported. Finally, the McDougals and McClanahan each contributed their respective one-half interests in Iron Card to the partnership. This transfer was tax-free.[2]

Note that, when the partnership transfers a capital interest to an incoming partner in exchange for services, the current partners are transferring a portion of their indirect interest in the partnership assets to the service-provider partner. Accordingly, the partnership can be viewed as disposing of property to the incoming partner as compensation for his services. The partnership may be required to recognize gain or loss on the disposition of those assets.

Profits interest. When a partner receives a profits interest in a partnership in exchange for services provided to the partnership, generally the partner does not have any income to report. This result is due to the fact that the profits interest does not have any current value or is too difficult to value because it is speculative. However, there are situations where the taxpayer was in fact able to sell his partnership interest, belying any argument that the profits interest was valueless or was too difficult to value.

In *Hale v. Commissioner*,[3] in exchange for future services, the taxpayer received a right to the partnership's future profits. Before receiving any income from the partnership, the taxpayer sold 90 percent of its interest. The issue before the court was the character of the income received. The taxpayer argued that it disposed of a capital asset, a partnership interest, and, therefore, that the gain should be capital.

The Tax Court found that what the taxpayer disposed of was not a partnership interest, but the right to receive future income. Because the taxpayer received the present value of what would otherwise have been ordinary income (compensation for services paid at some point in the future), it had received ordinary income in exchange for its profits interest.

In *Diamond v. Commissioner*,[4] the taxpayer received a profits interest in exchange for services. After the taxpayer had rendered his services but before the partnership showed any profit, the taxpayer sold his partnership interest for $40,000. As in *Hale*, the taxpayer argued that the character of the gain should be capital due to the disposition of a partnership interest. The Seventh Circuit followed the holding of the Tax Court and concluded that the value of the partnership interest was $40,000 and that the interest was received as compensation for services.

Both *Hale* and *Diamond* support the proposition that if you dispose of a right to receive compensation for services, the amount received in the exchange must be included in income as ordinary income. However, neither the value of the profits interest nor the year the accession to wealth occurred was at issue in either case.

In *Campbell v. Commissioner*,[5] the court addressed the issue of whether receipt of a profits interest could result in ordinary income upon receipt and before sale. In this

---

2. See Code Sec. 721(a).
3. T.C. Memo. 1965-274.
4. 492 F.2d 286 (7th Cir. 1974) *aff'g* 56 T.C. 530 (1971).
5. 943 F.2d 815 (8th Cir. 1991), *affg in part and revg in part* T.C. Memo. 1990-162.

case, the taxpayer did not sell the profits interest. The Tax Court used a present value methodology to value the profits interest and find that the taxpayer had gross income. On appeal, the Eighth Circuit reversed the Tax Court on the valuation issue, finding the interest too speculative for the value to be determined.

To provide some certainty in this area, the Service issued Revenue Procedure 93-27. The Service stated that receipt of a profits interest in a partnership is not required to be included in income unless:

- The profits interest relates to a "substantially certain and predictable stream of income from partnership assets;"
- Within two years of receipt, the partner disposes of the profits interest; or
- The profits interest is a limited partnership interest in a publicly traded partnership.

Practice Tip: The partnership agreement should clearly state whether a partner is receiving a capital interest or a profits interest.

Further guidance from the Service provides that the determination of whether an interest given to a service provider is a tax-free receipt of a profits interest is made at the time of the grant, irrespective of whether the interest has vested. However, the service provider and partnership must treat the service provider as owning a partnership interest from the date of the grant.[6]

Practice Tip: The service-provider and the partnership should clearly identify whether the service-provider is providing services in exchange for a partnership interest or as a third party (not as a partner).

Vesting issues. If the interest is not substantially vested when acquired, arguably, the timing of when it should be included in income is governed by Section 83. Section 83 provides that if a taxpayer is paid for services with property, the taxpayer must include the value of the property in gross income unless the property is subject to a substantial risk of forfeiture. In such situations, the taxpayer can either elect to include the fair market value of the property valued, without the restriction, in gross income in the year the property is received. Or the taxpayer can include the fair market value of the property in income in the year the property is no longer subject to the substantial risk of forfeiture. If the taxpayer elects to include the property in the year of receipt, but the right never vests, the taxpayer cannot subsequently take a deduction for the previously included amount.

---

6. *See* Rev. Rul. 2001-43, 2001-2 C.B. 191. The ruling also provides some guidance with respect to the applicability of Section 83.

The Service has issued proposed regulations[7] and a proposed Revenue Procedure[8] addressing the receipt of a partnership interest in exchange for services. They treat both a capital and a profits interest as property for purposes of Section 83. They provide a safe harbor provision for valuing the transferred interest. In addition, they permit the partnership to make the transfer tax free.

C. Cases and Materials

Mark IV Pictures, Inc. v. Commissioner
T.C. Memo. 1990-571, aff'd 969 F.2d 669 (8th Cir. 1992)

[Author's note: The taxpayers developed or otherwise obtained rights to the original story ideas and prepared the scripts for each motion picture before any limited partnerships were formed. The general partners assigned their film rights to their respective limited partnerships. The value of each original story idea and script was never expressed or determined by the general partners in a specific dollar amount. The general partners reported their assignment of film rights to the partnerships as non-taxable contributions of property in exchange for general partnership interests. The Commissioner determined that the general partnership interests received by the general partners were capital interests representing additional compensation for services rendered to the partnerships.]

* * *

OPINION

I. What did the general partners contribute?

The threshold issue we must decide is whether the general partners contributed property, services, or some combination of both in exchange for general partnership interests in certain limited partnerships.

Section 721(a) provides that no gain or loss is recognized to a partnership, or to any of its partners in the case of a contribution of property to the partnership in exchange for an interest in the partnership. The nonrecognition treatment provided by section 721(a) does not apply to the contribution of services. Diamond v. Commissioner, 56 T.C. 530, 544–545 (1971), affd. 492 F.2d 286 (7th Cir. 1974); sec. 1.721-1(b)(1), Income Tax Regs.

Petitioners argue that the general partners assigned film rights and goodwill to their respective limited partnerships in exchange for general partnership interests. Respondent argues that no goodwill was transferred to the partnerships, and that the general partners received their partnership interests in exchange for services performed for the limited partnerships and not in exchange for the contribution of film rights.

The nonrecognition treatment provided by section 721 only applies to the extent that property is contributed in exchange for a partnership interest. United States v.

---

7. Treas. Reg. § 1.83-3(e); REG-105346-03, 70 Fed. Reg. 29675 (May 24, 2005).
8. Notice 2005-43, 2005-1 C.B. 1221.

Stafford, 727 F.2d 1043, 1055 (11th Cir. 1984); sec. 1.721-1(b)(1), Income Tax Regs. The determination of whether a taxpayer contributed property, services, or some combination of both in exchange for a partnership interest is a question of fact. United States v. Stafford, supra at 1054; United States v. Frazell, 335 F.2d 487, 490–491 (5th Cir. 1964). See James v. Commissioner, 53 T.C. 63, 69 (1969). A taxpayer bears the burden of proving that property was actually contributed to a partnership and the value of such property at the time of contribution. United States v. Stafford, supra at 1054–1055; United States v. Frazell, supra. See Rule 142(a).

* * *

Accordingly, we uphold respondent's determination that the general partnership interests were received entirely in exchange for services.

II. Were the general partnership interests capital or mere profits interests?

We must next decide whether the general partnership interests were capital interests or mere profits interests.

Although section 704(e) does not directly apply to this case, the regulations issued thereunder provide helpful definitions of capital and profits interests:

> [A] capital interest in a partnership means an interest in the assets of the partnership, which is distributable to the owner of the capital interest upon his withdrawal or upon liquidation of the partnership. The mere right to participate in the earnings and profits of a partnership is not a capital interest in the partnership.

Sec. 1.704-2(e)(1)(v), Income Tax Regs. The pertinent regulation issued under section 721 provides:

> Normally, under local law, each partner is entitled to be repaid his contributions of money or other property to the partnership (at the value placed upon such property by the partnership at the time of contribution) whether made at formation of the partnership or subsequent thereto. To the extent that any of the partners gives up any part of his right to be repaid his contributions (as distinguished from a share in partnership profits) in favor of another partner as compensation for services (or in satisfaction of an obligation), section 721 does not apply. The value of an interest in such partnership capital so transferred to a partner as compensation for services constitutes income to the partner under section 61. * * *

Sec. 1.721-1(b)(1), Income Tax Regs. The approach suggested by these two regulations has been summarized as follows:

> a capital interest is defined as any interest which would entitle the holder to receive a share of partnership assets upon a hypothetical winding up and liquidation of the partnership immediately following acquisition of the interest, while a profits interest is any interest which would not entitle the holder to receive assets on an immediate liquidation, but does give the holder the right to share in future partnership profits or earnings.

W. McKee, W. Nelson & R. Whitmire, Federal Taxation of Partnerships and Partners, supra at par. 5.05[1], p. 5-22. See St John v. United States, 84-1 USTC par. 9158, 53 AFTR2d 84-718 (C.D. Ill. 1983).

Petitioners argue that because the partnerships were required under their Articles and Iowa law to repay the limited partners their capital contributions before making any payments to the general partners upon liquidation, they did not receive capital interests in the limited partnerships. Respondent, on the other hand, contends that the limited partners gave up part of their right to be repaid their contributions in favor of the general partners, that the capital interests were compensation for services, and that the amount of compensation equals the fair market values of the interest in capital transferred at the time the transfers were made for services.

Paragraph 2.4 of the Articles states that the general partners "shall be entitled to receive Fifty Percent (50%) of the liquidation proceeds of the Partnership in the event of liquidation." Paragraph 9.2 of the Articles requires the liquidation proceeds to be distributed in accordance with the order provided in section 545.42 of the Iowa Code Ann. (West 1950) and, thereafter, between the partners in proportion to the shares of partnership income. Section 545.42 of the Iowa Code provides that the limited partners must be repaid their capital contributions before the general partners.

Deciding whether a partner's interest in a partnership is a capital interest, rather than a mere profits interest, turns on whether that partner has the "right to receive" a share of the partnership's assets upon a hypothetical winding up and liquidation immediately following acquisition of the interest, rather than the mere right to share in future partnership earnings or profits. Here, a fair reading of paragraphs 2.4 and 9.2 of the Articles indicates that the general partners had the right to receive a specified share of the partnerships' liquidation proceeds (assets). Thus, even if no partnership proceeds remained to be distributed to the general partners after distributing the liquidating proceeds in accordance with section 545.42, they nevertheless had the right to receive a share of the partnerships' assets.

Based on the foregoing, we conclude that the general partners received a capital interest in their respective limited partnerships. See sec 1.721-1(b)(1), Income Tax Regs.

III. Do the capital interests have determinable market values?

The final issue for decision is whether the capital interests have determinable market values.

When a taxpayer contributes services in exchange for a partnership interest, the taxpayer may be required to include the fair market value of the interest in gross income upon receipt. Diamond v. Commissioner, 56 T.C. 530, 545 (1971), affd. 492 F.2d 286 (7th Cir. 1974); Campbell v. Commissioner, T.C. Memo. 1990-162; Section 1.721-1(b)(1), Income Tax Regs., provides that the amount of income included under section 61 "is the fair market value of the interest in capital so transferred * * * at the time the transfer is made for past services."

Petitioners contend that the capital interests do not have any determinable market value. Alternatively, they argue that if the section 1.721-1(b)(1), Income Tax Regs., method applies, respondent erred in computing the total value of the capital interests. Petitioners also contend that section 83 precludes inclusion of the value of the interests in their income for the years in issue because there existed a substantial risk of forfeiture.

Respondent contends that the value of petitioners' respective capital interests is determinable under section 1.721-1(b)(1), Income Tax Regs. Accordingly, respondent calculates the value of petitioners' capital interests by adding together (1) the total capital contributions made by the limited partners, and (2) the value of the film rights transferred by petitioners, and multiplying that amount by each general partner's ownership percentage. Respondent does not assign any value to the film rights and therefore, arrives at the following values:

[chart omitted]

We agree with respondent that the value of the capital interests is determinable, that section 1.721-1(b)(1), Income Tax Regs., applies, and that section 83 does not serve to preclude income recognition for the years in issue. However, we agree with petitioners that respondent erred in calculating the value of petitioners' capital interests.

Section 83

Under section 83 if property is received "in connection with the performance of services," the person performing the services receives ordinary income in an amount equal to the excess of the fair market value of the interest over the amount, if any, paid for the property, at the earlier of the first time the property becomes (1) freely transferable, or (2) not subject to a substantial risk of forfeiture. Although petitioners were to perform substantial services in the future, the transfer of their capital interest was not conditioned upon their future performance of services. At the time the partnerships were formed, the capital interests vested in petitioners. See sec. 83(c)(1), secs. 1.83-3(b), (c)(1), Income Tax Regs.

Accordingly, we conclude that petitioners' general partner interests were freely transferable and not subject to substantial risk of forfeiture.

Value of capital interests

Petitioners received their capital interests in the partnerships in the year the partnerships were formed. However, not all the limited partnership units were sold in the year of formation. Accordingly, after reviewing all the evidence we find that the limited partnership units were sold as follows:

[chart omitted]

Thus, petitioners' service income for each of their taxable year(s) in issue must be calculated by considering the year the limited partnership interests were actually sold. Moreover, consideration must be given to the contributions the general partners made in acquiring their limited partnership interest.

Based on the foregoing we conclude that petitioners had the following service income for the years in issue:

[chart omitted]

To reflect the foregoing and concessions,

Decisions will be entered under Rule 155.

Rev. Proc. 93-27, 1993-2 C.B. 343

SECTION 1. PURPOSE

This revenue procedure provides guidance on the treatment of the receipt of a partnership profits interest for services provided to or for the benefit of the partnership.

SEC. 2. DEFINITIONS

The following definitions apply for purposes of this revenue procedure.

.01 A capital interest is an interest that would give the holder a share of the proceeds if the partnership's assets were sold at fair market value and then the proceeds were distributed in a complete liquidation of the partnership. This determination generally is made at the time of receipt of the partnership interest.

.02 A profits interest is a partnership interest other than a capital interest.

SEC. 3. BACKGROUND

Under section 1.721-1(b)(1) of the Income Tax Regulations, the receipt of a partnership capital interest for services provided to or for the benefit of the partnership is taxable as compensation. On the other hand, the issue of whether the receipt of a partnership profits interest for services is taxable has been the subject of litigation. Most recently, in *Campbell v. Commissioner*, 943 F.2d 815 (8th Cir. 1991), the Eighth Circuit in dictum suggested that the taxpayer's receipt of a partnership profits interest received for services was not taxable, but decided the case on valuation. Other courts have determined that in certain circumstances the receipt of a partnership profits interest for services is a taxable event under section 83 of the Internal Revenue Code *See, e.g., Campbell v. Commissioner*, T.C.M. 1990-236, *rev'd*, 943 F.2d 815 (8th Cir. 1991); *St. John v. United States*, No. 82-1134 (C.D. Ill. Nov. 16, 1983). The courts have also found that typically the profits interest received has speculative or no determinable value at the time of receipt. *See Campbell*, 943 F.2d at 823; *St. John*. In Diamond v. Commissioner, 56 T.C. 530 (1971), *aff'd*, 492 F.2d 286 (7th Cir. 1974), however, the court assumed that the interest received by the taxpayer was a partnership profits interest and found the value of the interest was readily determinable. In that case, the interest was sold soon after receipt.

SEC. 4. APPLICATION

.01 Other than as provided below, if a person receives a profits interest for the provision of services to or for the benefit of a partnership in a partner capacity or in anticipation of being a partner, the Internal Revenue Service will not treat the receipt of such an interest as a taxable event for the partner or the partnership.

.02 This revenue procedure does not apply:

(1) If the profits interest relates to a substantially certain and predictable stream of income from partnership assets, such as income from high-quality debt securities or a high-quality net lease;

(2) If within two years of receipt, the partner disposes of the profits interest; or

(3) If the profits interest is a limited partnership interest in a "publicly traded partnership" within the meaning of section 7704(b) of the internal Revenue Code.

D. Problems

1. The Rectangle Partnership operates a rental real estate business. Ms. Orange is given the opportunity to receive a capital interest in the partnership in exchange for managing three of the rental properties owned by the partnership. If Ms. Orange accepts, what are the tax consequences to Ms. Orange and the Rectangle Partnership?

2. The Square Partnership is a law firm. Mr. Green is given the opportunity to receive a one-quarter non-forfeitable profits interest in the partnership in exchange for future services. He would not be required to contribute any property to the partnership. If Mr. Green accepts, is the profits interest taxable?

---

3. The Triangle Partnership operates a deli. Mr. Blue is given the opportunity to receive a one-third non-forfeitable profits interest in the partnership in exchange for managing the deli. Mr. Blue accepts, but one year later sells his partnership interest. What are the tax consequences to Mr. Blue?

---

4. The Circle Partnership owns a hotel. The hotel is leased to a national chain that operates the hotel on a net basis. The lessee pays all interest, taxes, insurance, and mortgage related to the hotel. Mr. Yellow is given the opportunity to receive a one-fifth non-forfeitable profits interest in the partnership. Mr. Yellow would not be required to contribute any property to the partnership. However, he would be expected to render services to the partnership in the future. If Mr. Yellow accepts, is the profits interest taxable?

---

5. Application:

(a) Could you explain the difference between a capital interest and a profits interest to the partners?

(b) What documentation would you use to identify whether a partner is receiving a capital interest or a profits interest?

(c) If a partner wanted to contribute his services to the partnership in exchange for a partnership interest, how would you explain the tax consequences to the partner?

Overview Problem—Putting It All Together

Stacey, Bill, and Olivia, close friends, decided to form a general partnership to operate a coffee shop. They discussed what they each could contribute. After having discussed the issue for an hour, they developed a plan.

Stacey would contribute an inventory of gourmet coffee beans that she had purchased for $1,000 and was currently valued at $500. Bill would contribute an industrial strength espresso machine that he had purchased for $5,000 and was currently valued at $7,000. He had used the machine in a similar business and had held it for 2 years. Olivia would contribute $5,000 cash.

They intended to be equal partners.

After the partnership was formed, they would look for an appropriate location from which to operate the coffee shop. The partnership would either purchase the building or lease space, depending on what options they could find.

They have asked you to advise them regarding the formation of the partnership.

1. Contributions to the partnership:
   (a) What documentation would you prepare for the three friends to establish that the inventory, espresso machine, and cash had been transferred to the partnership and had become partnership property?
   (b) Why is it important to establish that the property has (or has not) become partnership property?
   (c) From a tax perspective, what other documentation do you believe would be important to obtain at the time of contribution?
   (d) What problems would you anticipate if one of the friends wanted to contribute his or her services to the partnership, rather than cash or an asset?

2. Ownership issues:
   (a) What problem do you see with the three wanting to be equal partners?
   (b) What solutions would you offer to this problem?
   (c) How would you explain this issue to the friends?

3. If the three intended to go forward and not be equal partners:
   (a) Will each partner receive a capital interest or a profits interest? How do you know?
   (b) What percentage interest in the partnership would each partner own?
   (c) What would each partner's basis in the partnership be?
   (d) What would each partner's holding period in the partnership interest be?
   (e) What would the partnership's basis in each asset be?
   (f) What would the partnership's holding period in each asset be?

4. Operations issues:
   (a) Have the partners contributed the assets necessary for the partnership to operate a coffee shop?
   (b) If the partnership does not have the assets needed to operate a coffee shop, how will the partnership acquire such assets?
5. Construct a balance sheet for the partnership at the time of formation.
6. Draft language for a partnership agreement establishing:
   (a) That the partners intend to be equal partners.
   (b) That each partner has received a capital interest in the partnership.

Practitioner's Checklist

- ☐ State law that will apply to the partnership: _____.
- ☐ List of all assets each partner will be contributing to the partnership.

For each asset contributed, obtained the following documentation or information (to the extent applicable):

- ☐ If the asset is depreciable:
  - ☐ partner's purchase price (for determining 1245 gain recapture)
  - ☐ asset class life
  - ☐ number of years asset has been in service
  - ☐ whether bonus depreciation was elected
- ☐ Adjusted basis on the date of transfer
- ☐ Fair market value of the property on the date of transfer
- ☐ Partner's holding period of each asset contributed
- ☐ Character of each asset in hands of the partner.

- ☐ Confirmed partners' expected ownership interest is consistent with relative fair market values of contributed assets and understanding of all partners.
- ☐ Transfer documents completed for each asset transferred to the partnership.
- ☐ Confirmed no partner will be contributing services in exchange for partnership interest (and, if a partner is, explain tax consequences).
- ☐ Partners understand what additional assets the partnership will need to operate the business and how they will be obtained.
- ☐ Each partner's outside basis and holding period for the partnership interest calculated.
- ☐ Original balance sheet prepared.

Items to include in the partnership or operating agreement:

- ☐ Statement of what each partner is contributing.
- ☐ Statement of ownership interests (i.e., equal partnership? Something else?).
- ☐ How decisions will be made (i.e., one partner given authority, majority vote, etc.).
- ☐ Efforts each partner is expected to give to the partnership business.
- ☐ Whether the partner is receiving a capital or profits interest.

III.

Effect of Liabilities—Introduction

Overview Problem

Stacey, Bill, and Olivia, close friends, formed a partnership to operate a coffee shop. Stacey contributed an inventory of gourmet coffee beans that she had purchased for $1,000 and was valued at $500. She also contributed $6,500 cash. Bill contributed an industrial strength espresso machine that he had purchased for $5,000 and was currently valued at $7,000. Olivia contributed $7,000 cash.

After the partnership was formed, they found an appropriate location from which to operate the coffee shop. The property owner was willing to either lease the space or sell them the building.

The partners held a partnership meeting and discussed whether they should purchase the building. They were in agreement that they wanted to purchase the building. However, because the partnership did not have the funds, it would have to obtain a loan. If it could, the partnership would obtain a non-recourse loan to finance the purchase. If it could not obtain a non-recourse loan, the partnership would obtain a recourse loan. Finally, if the partnership was unable to obtain financing, whether non-recourse or recourse, Olivia would obtain a loan, purchase the building, then contribute the building subject to the loan to the partnership.

They have come to you for advice about the impact the loan will have, if any, on the partners in the partnership.

Effect of Liabilities

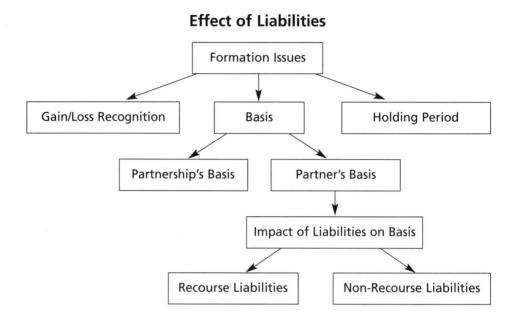

Chapter 6

Recourse Liabilities

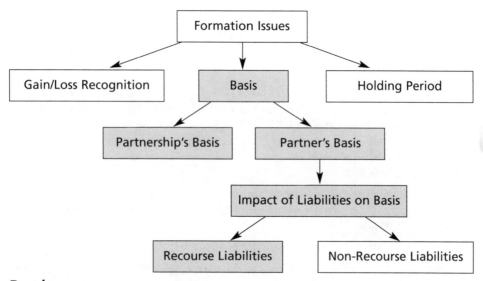

Read:

Code Section 752(a)-(c).
Treas. Reg. §§ 1.704-1(b)(2)(iv)(a), -1(b)(2)(iv)(b), -1(b)(2)(iv)(c), -1(b)(2)(iv)(d)(1),
-1(b)(2)(iv)(d)(2); 1.752-1(a)(1), -1(a)(2), -1(a)(4)(i), -1(b)-(f), -1(g) Ex. 1; 1.752-2(a),
-2(b), -2(f) Ex. 1, 4, -2(h)(1)-(4), -2(j)(1)-(3).

A. Background

So far, no consideration has been given to the impact of liabilities to the partners or the partnership. However, without a doubt, liabilities regularly play a role in a partnership. The property the partner contributes to the partnership may be subject to a liability that the partnership assumes or the partnership itself may acquire debt.

Debt. In general, a recourse liability is one for which the borrower is personally liable. A non-recourse liability is one for which the borrower is not personally liable. Most often, a non-recourse loan is secured by the property purchased with the borrowed funds.

UPA and RUPA. Under the Uniform Partnership Act (UPA), all partners generally are jointly liable for the debts of the partnership.[1] Under the Revised Uniform Partnership Act (RUPA), the partners are jointly and severally liable.[2] Under either the UPA or RUPA, a partner who joins an existing partnership is not personally liable for pre-existing debts.[3] Finally, under the Uniform Limited Partnership Act, a limited partner generally is not personally liable for an obligation of the limited partnership solely by reason of being a limited partner.[4]

Role of debt in amount realized. If, as part of the disposition of property, a third party agrees to pay a liability of the taxpayer, the amount of the debt relief is included in the amount realized.[5] In essence, because the buyer is assuming the debt, it is as if the buyer transferred cash to the taxpayer and the taxpayer used the cash to pay off the debt.

Role of debt in basis. If the taxpayer purchases an asset, his basis in the asset is the cost of the asset. Financing all or a part of the purchase price of the asset does not alter the basis; basis is still equal to the cost of the property. The source of the money used to purchase the asset is irrelevant.[6]

Example: Yolanda decided to sell her land to Zorrido. The land was worth $500 and was subject to a $200 liability. To purchase the land, Zorrido paid Yolanda $300 in cash and assumed the $200 liability. Yolanda's amount realized was the total amount she received from Zorrido, or $500 ($300 cash and $200 debt relief).

Zorrido's cost, or basis in the property, was the amount he paid for the land, or $500. The $500 purchase price consisted of $300 in cash and $200 of assumption of debt.

Debt and the partnership. Similarly, when a partner contributes property subject to a liability to a partnership, the amount of the debt relief (the debt assumed by the partnership) is part of the partner's amount realized (*i.e.,* what the partner is receiving in exchange for the property being contributed to the partnership).[7] In essence, because the partnership is assuming the debt, it is as if the partnership transferred cash to the partner and the partner used the cash to pay off the debt. As such, the assumption of the debt is treated as a distribution of cash from the partnership to the partner.

If the partnership acquires debt in conjunction with the purchase of property, the partnership's basis in the property is the cost of the property. The source of the money used to purchase the asset is irrelevant.

Whether a partnership assumes a debt on property transferred to the partnership by a partner or incurs the debt directly, the partnership is liable for repayment. In ad-

---

1. UPA § 15.
2. RUPA § 306(a).
3. UPA § 17, RUPA § 306(b).
4. ULPA § 303.
5. Tufts v. Commissioner, 461 U.S. 300 (1983); Crane v. Commissioner, 331 U.S. 1 (1947); Old Colony Trust Co. v. Commissioner, 279 U.S. 716 (1929).
6. *Crane, supra.*
7. See Code Sec. 752(c).

dition, under the UPA or RUPA, each partner is secondarily liable for the payment of the debt.

B. Discussion of Rules

1. Definition of Liability

The regulations provide a specific definition of what constitutes a liability. An obligation is a liability to the extent that incurring the obligation—[8]

- Creates or increases the basis of the obligor's assets;
- Gives rise to an immediate deduction to the obligor; or
- Gives rise to an expense that is not deductible and not properly chargeable to capital.

If a cash basis taxpayer contributes accounts payable to a partnership, the accounts payable are not treated as a liability for purposes of Section 752.[9]

2. Capital Accounts and Obligation of Partners to Partnership to Make Capital Contributions

Recall that capital accounts reflect a partner's economic interest in the partnership. The account is increased by cash and the net value of property contributed to the partnership. As will be discussed in greater detail in Chapter 11, the account is increased by gain or income allocated to the partner. Similarly, as will be discussed in greater detail in Chapter 11 and 23, the account is decreased by partnership expenses and losses allocated to the partner and the amount cash and the net value of property distributed to the partner from the partnership.[10]

Because capital accounts reflect a partner's economic interest in the partnership, they reflect the amount a partner generally expects to receive from the partnership upon liquidation. Accordingly, the partnership agreement and, in some situations, state law will impose on the partner an obligation to restore a negative capital account balance.

Example: Oscar, Bert, and Ernie each contributed $50 to a partnership. Assume that the partnership's income and gains for the past year have exactly equaled its expenses and losses so that there has been no change to any partner's financial situation.

At the end of the first year, the partnership still has $150 and each partner's capital account is $50. Assume the partnership liquidates. It will distribute the amount of each partner's capital account, or $50, to each of Oscar, Bert, and Ernie.

---

8. Treas. Reg. § 1.752-1(a)(4)(i).
9. Rev. Rul. 88-77, 1988-2 C.B. 129.
10. Treas. Reg. § 1.704-1(b)(2)(iv)(b).

Alternatively, during the first year, Oscar withdrew $100 from the partnership. At the end of the year, the partnership has $50 ($150 less the $100 withdrawn by Oscar). Oscar's capital account is reduced to a negative $50 ($50 original balance, less $100 he withdrew). Bert and Ernie's capital accounts are still $50 each. If the partnership liquidates, the partnership's remaining $50 is insufficient to pay Bert and Ernie the amount in their capital accounts.

If the partnership agreement requires partners to restore negative capital account balances, Oscar will be required to restore his $50 negative account balance. When he has done so, his capital account will be zero (<$50> increased by the $50 contribution) and the partnership will have $100. The partnership, now having $100, can liquidate, distributing $50 to Bert and $50 to Ernie. Oscar will receive nothing, as indicated by his capital account of zero.

Practice Note: Because it can not only create an obligation to make a payment to the partnership but also impact a partner's outside basis, the partnership agreement should clearly state whether a partner is obligated to restore a negative capital account balance.

---

3. Decrease in Individual Liabilities

When property subject to a liability is contributed by a partner to the partnership, the partnership is treated as having assumed the liability to the extent the liability does not exceed the fair market value of the property at the time of contribution.[11] Thus, the partner's individual liability has decreased. Any decrease in a partner's liabilities by reason of the partnership's assumption of the liabilities is treated as a distribution of money by the partnership to that partner. While distributions from a partnership to a partner have not yet been considered, in general, a distribution of cash from a partnership to a partner will result in a decrease in the partner's basis by the amount distributed.[12]

4. Increase in Partnership's Liabilities

When the partnership acquires debt, the debt generally becomes the responsibility of the general partners. To the extent a partner has increased his share of responsibility for a partnership liability, he is treated as having advanced to the partnership his

---

11. Code Sec. 752(c); Treas. Reg. § 1.752-1(e). A liability is treated as having been assumed if the assuming person is personally obligated to pay the liability. A partner assumes a partnership liability if the creditor knows of the assumption and can directly enforce the partner's obligation and no other partner would bear the economic risk of loss for the liability immediately after the assumption. Treas. Reg. § 1.752-1(d).

12. Code Sec. 752(b).

portion of the funds needed to repay the debt. Because a partner's outside basis reflects all contributions, the partner's outside basis is increased by the amount of the liability for which the partner would be responsible.[13]

Practice Note: The extent to which a limited partner is liable to make additional contributions to the partnership, or is in any way personally liable for a partnership debt, may affect his outside basis. Thus, the partnership agreement or other relevant documentation should clearly state the extent to which a limited partner is liable for a debt of the partnership or has an obligation to contribute to the partnership in the future.

---

5. Net Change in Liabilities

If, in a single transaction, there is an increase in the partner's share of the partnership's liabilities and a decrease in the partner's individual liabilities, only the net amount will affect the partner's basis. If there is a net increase, the net amount is considered a contribution of money by the partner to the partnership. If there is a net decrease, the net amount is considered a distribution of money from the partnership to the partner.[14]

Example: Yolanda became a 50-percent general partner in the XY Partnership by contributing land with a basis of $500, fair market value of $500, and subject to a $200 liability. The partnership assumed the liability.

Yolanda's individual liabilities decreased by $200 (the amount of debt assumed by the partnership). Assume that her share of liabilities as a partner in the partnership increased by one-half of the new partnership debt, or $100. Thus, the net change in her liabilities is a decrease of $100. Her basis in the partnership is $400, determined as follows:

Adjusted basis in land:	$500
Cash contribution:	0
Net change in liabilities:	<100>
Basis:	$400

Rules:
- A partner's outside basis is decreased by any decrease in his share of partnership liabilities or decrease in his individual liabilities due to the partnership's assumption of the liability.

---

13. Code Sec. 752(a).
14. Treas. Reg. § 1.752-1(f).

- A partner's outside basis is increased by any increase in his share of partnership liabilities.
- If, in a single transaction, there is an increase in the partner's share of the partnership's liabilities and a decrease in the partner's individual liabilities (or vice versa), only the net amount will affect the partner's basis.

6. Determination of Partner's Share of Recourse Liability

A partner's basis depends, in part, on the partner's share of partnership liabilities. In turn, the extent to which a partner is liable with respect to a partnership liability depends on whether the liability is a recourse or non-recourse liability and on related facts, such as whether a partner has guaranteed the debt or is entitled to be reimbursed for amounts paid with respect to the debt.

A partnership liability is a recourse liability to the extent that any partner bears the economic risk of loss for that liability or would be obligated to contribute to the partnership to satisfy the liability.[15] To ascertain whether a partner bears the economic risk of loss, the regulations create a doomsday scenario and then consider which partners would have to contribute to the partnership to satisfy the liability. Note that whether a partner is required to contribute to the partnership to satisfy a liability is based on economic, or book, value, not on tax values. Specifically, a partner bears the economic risk of loss if:[16]

- The partnership constructively liquidated;
- As a result of the liquidation, the partner would be obligated to make a payment because the liability became due and payable; and
- The partner would not be entitled to reimbursement from another partner.

When the partnership constructively liquidates, several events are deemed to occur:

- All of the partnership's liabilities become payable in full.
- All of the partnership's assets (including cash) become worthless. The only exception is separately-held property that secures a partnership liability. Such property is transferred to the creditor to fully or partially satisfy the debt.
- Considering fair market, or book, values, the partnership sells all of its assets in a taxable transaction. Any property that secures a non-recourse debt is sold for the amount of the debt. Because all other property has become worthless, it is sold for nothing.
- All resulting items of book gain or loss are allocated among the partners and their capital accounts are adjusted accordingly.[17]

---

15. Treas. Reg. § 1.752-2(a).
16. Treas. Reg. § 1.752-2(b)(1).
17. In general, all allocations will be based on each partner's respective ownership interest in the partnership. See Code Sec. 704(a). This issue is discussed in Chapter 11.

• The partnership liquidates.

Whether a partner has an obligation to make a contribution to the partnership is based on all the facts and circumstances.[18] All obligations are taken into consideration, such as guarantees. In addition, obligations imposed by the partnership agreement or state law are taken into consideration, including the obligation to restore negative capital account balances.[19] Similarly, if the partner is entitled to be reimbursed or indemnified by another partner, in determining the amount of that partner's required contribution, the amount of reimbursement or indemnification is taken into consideration.[20] There is a presumption that any partner required to reimburse another partner does so, even if the partner does not have the funds to make the payment (unless there is a plan to circumvent or avoid the payment).[21] However, if an obligation is subject to a contingency that makes it unlikely it would ever be paid, the obligation is disregarded.[22]

> **Practice Tip:** The extent to which a partner bears the economic risk of loss for a partnership liability cannot be determined by considering the partner's basis in the partnership. Furthermore, note that the extent to which a partner bears the economic risk of loss is not determined by simply allocating to each partner a portion of a recourse liability based on his ownership interest in the partnership.

Steps in Constructive Liquidation: To determine the partner's economic risk of loss, the regulations create a doomsday scenario based on the following steps:

Step 1: All of the partnership liabilities become due and payable.

Step 2: Any separate property pledged by a partner to secure a partnership liability is transferred to the creditor in full or partial satisfaction of the liability.

Step 3: Any asset subject to a non-recourse debt is sold for the amount of the debt.

Step 4: All remaining partnership assets (including cash) become worthless.

---

18. Treas. Reg. § 1.752-2(b)(3). In determining the extent to which a partner bears the risk of loss, obligations of related parties are also taken into consideration. A related person includes a person related to a partner as defined in Section 267(b) or 707(b)(1), except that 80 percent is substituted for 50 percent; brother and sisters are excluded; and Section 267(e)(1) and 267(f)(1)(A) are disregarded. Treas. Reg. § 1.752-4(b)(1).

If the obligation to make a payment is not required to be satisfied within a reasonable time after the liability becomes due, or the obligation to make a contribution to the partnership is not required to be satisfied before the later of the end of the year in which the partnership interest is liquidated or 90 days after the liquidation, then the liability is only taken into account to the extent of its value. Treas. Reg. § 1.752-2(g)(1).

19. Treas. Reg. § 1.752-2(b)(3).

20. Treas. Reg. § 1.752-2(b)(5).

21. Treas. Reg. § 1.752-2(b)(6). Special rules apply if the partner is a disregarded entity. See Treas. Reg. § 1.752-2(k).

22. Treas. Reg. § 1.752-2(b)(4).

Step 5: Considering fair market, or book, value, the partnership sells the remaining assets in a taxable transaction for nothing.

Step 6: Any resulting gain or loss is allocated among the partners based on
how they have agreed to share profits and losses. Their capital accounts are adjusted accordingly.

Step 7: The partnership liquidates.

Taking into account all relevant agreements or laws, as a result of the liquidation,
is a partner obligated to make a payment to the partnership so that the partnership can discharge a liability that has become due and payable?

Formula: To determine the partner's basis in the partnership interest where
the partnership has recourse liabilities, complete the following steps:

Step 1: Determine the adjusted basis of the asset(s) contributed to the
partnership.

Step 2: Determine the amount of cash contributed to the partnership.

Step 3: Determine the net change in liabilities.*

Step 4: Determine the amount of gain under Section 721(b), if any.

Step 5: Combine (subtracting when necessary) the amounts determined
under the first four steps.

The total is the partner's outside basis in the partnership.

* Amount of partnership debt assumed—amount of individual debt relief

---

7. Effect on Balance Sheet

Each partner's outside basis will reflect the amount of recourse liability for which
he is responsible.

Capital accounts reflect only a partner's economic investment in the partnership.
Stated another way, it reflects the amount a partner would expect to receive if the partnership where liquidated. Because all creditors would be paid before any net proceeds
were distributed to a partner, a partner's capital account does not include any liabilities. Thus, the total of all capital accounts must equal the value of all the partnership
assets less all partnership liabilities.

Note that the impact of recourse liabilities on a partner's basis will be addressed in
greater detail in Chapter 19.

C. Application of Rules

Example 1. Recourse debt incurred by partnership. Mindy and Nelson formed an equal
general partnership. They both contributed $500 cash. The partnership agreement pro-
vided that, upon liquidation, all partners must restore a negative capital account. The

partnership purchased a building for $10,000. It paid $1,000 in cash and obtained a $9,000 recourse loan for the remaining purchase price.

Mindy and Nelson's basis depends, in part, on their share of partnership liabilities. The partnership's $9,000 liability is a recourse liability to the extent that any partner bears the economic risk of loss for that liability or would be obligated to contribute to the partnership to satisfy the liability. To ascertain whether Mindy or Nelson bears the economic risk of loss, the partnership must go though the constructive liquidation of the doomsday scenario.

First, the partnership is constructively liquidated. As part of the liquidation, the $9,000 obligation becomes due. All assets become worthless. Considering fair market, or book, value, the partnership sells the building for nothing. The tax consequences from the sale are as follows:

Amount realized:	$0
Book basis:	10,000
Loss:	<$10,000>

The $10,000 loss is allocated equally between Mindy and Nelson, or <$5,000> each. The impact to Mindy and Nelson's capital accounts would be as follows:

	Mindy	Nelson
Capital account on formation	$500	$500
Loss from sale of building:	<5,000>	<5,000>
Balance:	<$4,500>	<$4,500>

The partnership liquidates. The partnership agreement requires the partners to restore a negative capital account to the partnership upon liquidation. Thus, both Mindy and Nelson have an obligation to contribute $4,500 to the partnership. The total of the contributions, $9,000, will be used to satisfy the $9,000 debt.

The liability is a recourse liability because one or more partners bear the economic risk of loss. Specifically, Mindy and Nelson each bears an economic risk of loss of $4,500. Their basis would be determined as follows:

	Mindy	Nelson
Cash:	$500	$500
Increase in liabilities:	4,500	4,500
Basis:	$5,000	$5,000

After the partnership purchases the building, the balance sheet would appear as follows:

Asset	Adj Basis	FMV	Liabilities:			$9,000
Building	$10,000	$10,000			Basis	Cap. Acct.
			Mindy		$5,000	$500
			Nelson		5,000	500
Total:	$10,000	$10,000			$10,000	$10,000

Example 2. Recourse debt incurred by partnership. Tex and Ursula formed a general partnership. They both contributed $500 cash. The partnership agreement provided that profits and losses would be divided 40 percent to Tex and 60 percent to Ursula

and that, upon liquidation, all partners must restore a negative capital account. The partnership purchased a building for $10,000. It paid $1,000 in cash and obtained a $9,000 recourse loan for the remaining purchase price.

Tex and Ursula's basis depends, in part, on their share of partnership liabilities. The partnership's $9,000 liability is a recourse liability to the extent that any partner bears the economic risk of loss for that liability or would be obligated to contribute to the partnership to satisfy the liability. To ascertain whether Ted or Ursula bears the economic risk of loss, the partnership must go though the constructive liquidation of the doomsday scenario.

First, the partnership is constructively liquidated. As part of the liquidation, the $9,000 obligation becomes due. All assets become worthless. Considering fair market, or book, value, the partnership sells the building for nothing. The tax consequences from the sale are as follows:

Amount realized:	$0
Book basis:	10,000
Loss:	<$10,000>

The $10,000 loss is allocated 40 percent to Tex and 60 percent to Ursula, or $4,000 to Tex and $6,000 to Ursula. The impact to Tex and Ursula's capital accounts would be as follows:

	Tex	Ursula
Capital account on formation	$500	$500
Loss from sale of building:	<4,000>	<6,000>
Balance:	<$3,500>	<$5,500>

The partnership liquidates. The partnership agreement requires the partners to restore a negative capital account. Thus, Tex has an obligation to contribute $3,500 and Ursula has an obligation to contribute $5,500. The total of the contributions, $9,000, will be used to satisfy the $9,000 debt.

The liability is a recourse liability because one or more partners bear the economic risk of loss. Specifically, Tex bears an economic risk of loss of $3,500 and Ursula bears an economic risk of loss of $5,500. Their basis would be determined as follows:

	Tex	Ursula
Cash:	$500	$500
Increase in liabilities:	3,500	5,500
Basis:	$4,000	$6,000

After purchase of the building, the balance sheet would appear as follows:

Asset	Adj Basis	FMV	Liabilities:		$9,000
Building	$10,000	$10,000		Basis	Cap. Acct.
			Tex	$4,000	$500
			Ursula	6,000	500
Total:	$10,000	$10,000		$10,000	$10,000

Example 3. Recourse debt incurred by partnership, debt guaranteed. Willie and Xander formed a general partnership. Willie and Xander each contributed $5,000.

The partnership agreement provided that profits and losses would be divided 20 percent to Willie and 80 percent to Xander and that, upon liquidation, all partners must restore a negative capital account. The partnership purchased a building for $25,000. It paid $10,000 in cash and obtained a $15,000 recourse loan for the remaining purchase price. Willie guaranteed the debt.

Willie and Xander's basis depends, in part, on their share of partnership liabilities. The partnership's $15,000 liability is a recourse liability to the extent that any partner bears the economic risk of loss for that liability or would be obligated to contribute to the partnership to satisfy the liability. To ascertain whether Willie or Xander bears the economic risk of loss, the partnership must go though the constructive liquidation of the doomsday scenario.

First, the partnership is constructively liquidated. As part of the liquidation, the $15,000 obligation becomes due. All assets become worthless. Considering fair market, or book, value, the partnership sells the building for nothing. The tax consequences from the sale are as follows:

Amount realized:	$0
Book basis:	25,000
Loss:	<$25,000>

The $25,000 loss is allocated 20 percent to Willie and 80 percent to Xander, or $5,000 to Willie and $20,000 to Xander. The impact to Willie and Xander's capital accounts would be as follows:

	Willie	Xander
Capital account on formation	$5,000	$5,000
Loss from sale of building:	<5,000>	<20,000>
Balance:	$0	<$15,000>

The partnership liquidates. The partnership agreement requires the partners to restore a negative capital account. Thus, Xander has an obligation to contribute $15,000 to the partnership and the $15,000 would then be used to satisfy the $15,000 debt. Willie would not be called upon to pay the debt pursuant to his guaranty.

The liability is a recourse liability because one or more partners bear the economic risk of loss. Specifically, Xander bears the economic risk of loss for the $15,000 liability. Willie and Xander's basis would be determined as follows:

	Willie	Xander
Cash:	$5,000	$5,000
Increase in liabilities:	0	15,000
Basis:	$5,000	$20,000

After purchase of the building, the balance sheet would appear as follows:

Asset	Adj. Basis	FMV	Liabilities:			$15,000
Building	$25,000	$25,000			Basis	Cap. Acct.
			Willie		$5,000	$5,000
			Xander		20,000	5,000
Total:	$25,000	$25,000			$25,000	$25,000

Example 4. Individual debt assumed by partnership. Omar and Pasha formed an equal general partnership. Omar contributed $500 cash and Pasha contributed a building with a basis of $9,500, with a fair market value of $9,500, and subject to a $9,000 recourse liability. The partnership agreement provided that, upon liquidation, all partners must restore a negative capital account.

Omar and Pasha's basis depends, in part, on their share of partnership liabilities. The partnership's $9,000 liability is a recourse liability to the extent that any partner bears the economic risk of loss for that liability or would be obligated to contribute to the partnership to satisfy the liability. To ascertain whether Omar or Pasha bears the economic risk of loss, the partnership must go though the constructive liquidation of the doomsday scenario.

First, the partnership is constructively liquidated. As part of the liquidation, the $9,000 obligation becomes due. All assets become worthless. Considering fair market, or book, value, the partnership sells the building for nothing. The tax consequences from the sale are as follows:

Amount realized:	$0
Book basis:	9,500
Loss:	<$9,500>

The $9,500 loss is allocated equally between Omar and Pasha, or <$4,750> each. In addition, the $500 cash becomes worthless, resulting in a $500 loss that would be allocated $250 to each partner. The impact to Omar and Pasha's capital accounts would be as follows:

	Omar	Pasha
Capital account on formation	$500	$500
Loss from cash:	<250>	<250>
Loss from sale of building:	<4,750>	<4,750>
Balance:	<$4,500>	<$4,500>

The partnership liquidates. The partnership agreement requires the partners to restore a negative capital account. Thus, both Omar and Pasha would have an obligation to contribute $4,500 to the partnership. The total of the contributions, $9,000, could then be used to satisfy the $9,000 debt.

The liability is a recourse liability because one or more partners bear the economic risk of loss. Specifically, Omar and Pasha each bears an economic risk of loss of $4,500 and their basis would be determined as follows.

	Omar	Pasha
Cash:	$500	$0
Property:	0	9,500
Net change in liabilities:	4,500	<4,500>*
Basis:	$5,000	$5,000

* $4,500 of partnership debt assumed, less $9,000 of individual debt relief.

After purchase of the building, the balance sheet would appear as follows:

Asset	Adj. Basis	FMV	Liabilities:			$9,000
Cash	$500	$500			Basis	Cap. Acct.
Building	9,500	9,500	Omar		$5,000	$500
			Pasha		5,000	500
Total:	$10,000	$10,000			$10,000	$10,000

D. Cases and Materials

Logan v. Commissioner
51 T.C. 482 (1968)

Respondent determined a deficiency of $2,146.19 in petitioners' income tax for the taxable year 1961. The only issue is the proper treatment of money received in 1961 from the sale in 1960 of a partnership interest owned by petitioner Frank A. Logan.

FINDINGS OF FACT

Some of the facts are stipulated and are found accordingly.

Petitioners are husband and wife and were legal residents of Anchorage, Ky., at the time of the filing of the petition herein. They filed a joint Federal income tax return for the taxable year 1961 with the district director of internal revenue, Louisville, Ky. Since petitioner Margaret S. Logan is before this Court only because she filed a joint return with her husband, subsequent references to petitioner should be taken to mean Frank A. Logan.

Prior to March 1959, petitioner practiced law as a sole proprietor in Louisville. On March 1, 1959, he and Thomas S. Dawson (Dawson) formed a law partnership under the name of Logan & Dawson, agreeing to share profits and losses equally. Petitioner contributed assets to the partnership with an adjusted basis of $9,654.36. Dawson contributed no assets to the partnership. The partnership assumed a $7,500 personal note owed by petitioner but assumed no liability of Dawson's.

When the partnership was formed, petitioner had legal work in progress, some on a contingent fee basis, all of which had a zero basis. Petitioner contributed this work to the partnership, so that when the fees of some $60,000 were received therefor they became partnership income, rather than petitioner's personal income.

* * *

The second issue relates to the adjusted basis of partnership interest. The root of the disagreement lies in the treatment of the liabilities of the partnership. We agree with respondent's treatment.

When the partnership was formed, petitioner contributed property with a basis of $9,654.36. The partnership assumed one of his personal liabilities in the amount of $7,500. Theoretically, this assumption by the partnership is treated as a distribution of money to petitioner, with a consequent decrease in the basis of his partnership interest. Secs. 705(a) (2) and 752(b). On the other hand, petitioner was simultaneously entitled to increase his basis by one-half of this amount. Sec. 1.722-1, ex. (1), Income Tax Regs. His basis in the partnership was therefore $5,904.36 ($9,654.36 less $7,500 plus $3,750).

* * *

Petitioner seeks to increase his basis in two ways. First, he argues that some amount representing work in progress which he brought into the firm at its inception, and for which some $60,000 in fees was ultimately received, should be included. We disagree. Since petitioner's basis in those unbilled fees was zero, his contribution adds nothing to the basis of his partnership interest. Secs. 721 and 722.

* * *

E. Problems

1. Kyle, Linda, Mona, and Ned formed an equal general partnership and each contributed $25,000. The partnership agreement provided that, upon liquidation, all partners must restore a negative capital account. The partnership purchased a building for $1,000,000, using the $100,000 of cash and obtaining a $900,000 recourse loan.

(a) What is each partner's outside basis? Prepare a balance sheet to reflect the situation of the partners and the partnership.

(b) Alternatively, assume that Linda guaranteed the debt. What is each partner's outside basis? Prepare a balance sheet to reflect the situation of the partners and the partnership.

(c) Alternatively, assume that Mona pledged $100,000 of stock, basis of $80,000, as partial security for the liability and all income, gain, or loss on the stock is allocated to Mona. What is each partner's outside basis?

---

2. Ollie, Paul, and Quincy formed an equal general partnership. The partnership agreement provided that, upon liquidation, all partners must restore a negative capital account. Ollie and Paul each contributed $30,000 cash. Quincy contributed land with a basis of $60,000 that he had held for investment purposes for more than one year. The land had a fair market value of $60,000 and was subject to a $30,000 recourse liability, which the partnership assumed.

What is each partner's outside basis? Prepare a balance sheet to reflect the situation of the partners and the partnership.

---

3. Randy, Sandy, and Ted formed an equal general partnership. Randy and Sandy each contributed $25,000 cash. Ted, a cash method taxpayer, contributed accounts receivable with a fair market value of $35,000. In addition, the partnership assumed $10,000 of Ted's accounts payable. What is Ted's outside basis? How much is his capital account?

4. Application:

(a) With respect to a recourse liability:
   (1) What documentation would you ask to review in determining the impact of a liability?
   (2) How would you explain to the partners what the consequences are of a recourse liability?
   (3) How would you explain to the partners the effect of a liability on the partner's basis?

(b) With respect to a negative capital account:
   (1) How would you explain to the partners what the consequences of having a negative capital account are?
   (2) Will the partners have an obligation to restore a negative capital account? Who gets to make the decision?
   (3) If the partners agree to an obligation to restore a negative capital account, what language would you include in the partnership agreement?

(c) With respect to partnership liabilities:
   (1) Are all partners liable for every recourse liability? How would you know? What documentation would you want to see?
   (2) If a partner is not liable for obligations that arose prior to joining the partnership, what impact will that fact have?

(d) Considering only the jurisdiction in which you practice (or intend to practice), to what extent are limited partners liable for partnership obligations?

F. Advanced Problems — Looking Forward

Without conducting any research, consider the following questions:

1. The partner's outside basis includes his share of the partnership's recourse debt, even though he has not made any payments towards that debt. Can you think of situations in individual income tax where the taxpayer's basis includes amounts that have not yet been paid? Does it provide any opportunities for abuse? Might it provide an opportunity for abuse in the partnership arena?

2. If the partnership went through the constructive liquidation of the doomsday scenario, who would be responsible for making a contribution to the partnership to pay a non-recourse debt? What does this say about whether non-recourse liabilities can be allocated based on which partner bears the economic risk of loss for that liability or would be obligated to contribute to the partnership to satisfy that liability?

3. In the doomsday scenario, any property that secures a non-recourse debt is sold for the amount of the debt. Because all other property has become worthless, it is sold for nothing. Why might the regulations provide that property that secures a non-recourse debt be sold for the amount of the debt?

4. If there is a net change in the partner's liability and the change is a net decrease in liability, the partner's basis is reduced by the net amount. What if the amount of the net decrease exceeds the partner's outside basis? Can the partner have a negative basis? How might the partnership rules address this potential problem?

Chapter 7

Non-Recourse Liabilities

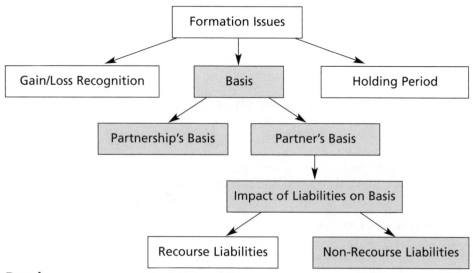

Read:

Code Section 752(a)-(c).
Treas. Reg. §§ 1.752-1(a)(2); 1.752-3(a)(3).

A. Overview of Rules

In general, a recourse liability is one for which the borrower is personally liable. A non-recourse liability is one for which the borrower is not personally liable. Most often, a non-recourse loan is secured by the property purchased with the borrowed funds.

Pursuant to the regulations, a partnership liability is a non-recourse liability to the extent that no partner bears the economic risk of loss for that liability.[1] Accordingly, the constructive liquidation of the doomsday scenario can be used to determine which liabilities are recourse liabilities. Any remaining liabilities will be non-recourse liabilities.

Noteworthy, because no partner will bear the economic risk of loss for a non-recourse liability, such risk cannot be used to allocate the liability among the partners. How-

---

1. Treas. Reg. § 1.752-1(a)(2).

ever, because a partnership generally finances the repayment of a non-recourse debt out of profits, it makes sense to allocate non-recourse debt based on how the partners share profits. As we learn more about the intricacies of partnership tax, we will see that other principles come into play to require that some or all of the non-recourse liability be allocated based on something other than how the partners share profits.[2]

Practice Note: If non-recourse liabilities are allocated, in part, based on the partner's share of partnership profits, the partnership agreement should clearly state how the partners will share profits.

Note that the impact of non-recourse liabilities on a partner's basis will be addressed in greater detail in Chapter 20.

B. Application of Rules

Example. Non-recourse debt incurred by partnership. Garrison and Hal formed an equal general partnership. They both contributed $500 cash. The partnership purchased a building for $10,000. It paid $1,000 in cash and obtained a $9,000 non-recourse loan, secured by the building, for the remaining purchase price.

Because the debt is a non-recourse debt, neither Garrison nor Hal bears the economic risk of loss. The constructive liquidation of the doomsday scenario confirms this fact. The partnership's $9,000 liability is a recourse liability to the extent that any partner bears the economic risk of loss for the liability or would be obligated to contribute to the partnership to satisfy the liability. To ascertain whether Garrison or Hal bears the economic risk of loss, the partnership must go though the constructive liquidation of the doomsday scenario.

First, the partnership is constructively liquidated. As part of the liquidation, the $9,000 obligation becomes due. Any asset subject to a non-recourse debt is sold for the amount of the debt. Accordingly, the building is sold for $9,000. The economic, or book, consequences from the sale are as follows:

Amount realized:	$9,000
Book basis:	10,000
Loss:	<$1,000>

The $1,000 loss is allocated equally between Garrison and Hal, or $500 each. The impact to Garrison and Hal's capital accounts would be as follows:

	Garrison	Hal
Capital account on formation:	$500	$500
Loss from sale of building:	<500>	<500>
Balance:	-0-	-0-

---

2. Treas. Reg. § 1.752-3(a)(1), (2).

The partnership liquidates. Because neither partner has an obligation to contribute to the partnership, neither bears the risk of loss with respect to the liability; the liability is a non-recourse liability. Accordingly, the liability will be allocated based on how the partners share profits, or $4,500 each. Their basis would be as follows.

	Garrison	Hal
Cash:	$500	$500
Increase in liabilities:	4,500	4,500
Basis:	$5,000	$5,000

After purchase of the building, the balance sheet would appear as follows:

Asset	Adj. Basis	FMV	Liabilities:		$9,000
Building	$10,000	$10,000		Basis	Cap. Acct.
			Garrison	$5,000	$500
			Hal	5,000	500
Total:	$10,000	$10,000		$10,000	$10,000

C. Cases and Materials

Elrod v. Commissioner
87 T.C. 1046 (1986)

* * *

The amendment [to an optional sales contract between petitioner as seller and Hahn as purchaser] also provided for petitioner to convey fee title to the 100-acre shopping center site to EWH Woodbridge Associates (EWH), the limited partnership to be formed by petitioner and Hahn. A written limited partnership agreement was executed concurrently with the closings on both the 100-acre and 29-acre parcels. Title to the 29-acre parcel was conveyed by petitioner directly to Hahn. The specific provisions of the EWH limited partnership agreement are discussed in detail in the special allocation of partnership losses section below.

On August 24, 1977, petitioner, as grantor, executed a deed to "grant, bargain, sell and convey, with General Warranty" the 100-acre parcel to EWH and represented that EWH was "to have quiet possession" of the land. EWH issued a promissory note to petitioner for the $2.5 million balance of the purchase price of the 100-acre parcel. The note was payable in full in 3 years from the earlier of its date of execution or upon the date of construction of the shopping center. Although the note purported to be a non-interest-bearing instrument, it provided for monthly payments of "option extension" fees calculated at an annual rate of 6 percent of the outstanding note balance. The note also contained the following provisions:

* * *

On August 19, 1977, a certificate of limited partnership and limited partnership agreement were executed with respect to the formation of EWH as a Virginia limited partnership, in accordance with the provisions of the Virginia Uniform Limited Partnership Act. The partnership was formed with Hahn as its general partner, holding a 95-percent partnership interest, and petitioner as its limited partner, holding a 5-percent partnership interest. The stated purpose of the partnership was to "acquire and develop certain real property in Prince William County, Virginia," consisting of 100 acres of land "as a regional shopping center."

* * *

a. *Petitioner's Basis in the Partnership*

Petitioner's distributive share of partnership loss is deductible to the extent of his basis in the partnership Sec. 704(d). Therefore, before we discuss whether the special allocation of partnership loss may be respected, we first must determine petitioner's basis in the partnership, based upon the adjusted basis of property deemed contributed by petitioner to the partnership. Sec. 722.

Petitioner and Hahn have agreed that the purchase price of the 100-acre parcel constitutes only 95 percent of its fair market value. The remaining 5-percent value, $175,000, was deemed to be a contribution of capital by petitioner to the partnership and was so reflected in petitioner's partnership capital account. As of the formation of EWH, petitioner's adjusted basis in this 5-percent interest in the land equaled $7,500.

Petitioner's basis in the partnership also must be increased by his share in certain partnership liabilities. Sec. 752. In 1977, EWH executed a promissory note in the amount of $1.8 million to the Virginia National Bank for the development of the shopping center site. At trial, petitioner conceded that, because Hahn was personally liable for the satisfaction of this note, as a limited partner petitioner is not entitled to any increase in his partnership basis with respect to this partnership debt. Sec. 752; sec. 1.752-1(e), Income Tax Regs.

EWH also executed a promissory note in the amount of $2.5 million to petitioner with respect to the purchase of the 100-acre parcel. We note that petitioner contends that he also is not entitled to any increase in his partnership basis with respect to this note, on the belief that the note does not constitute a fixed and unconditional obligation of EWH. We disagree, based upon the reasons set forth in the option versus sale section, and restate that this note constitutes a valid debt issued pursuant to the completed sale of petitioner's land. Therefore, as a limited partner, petitioner is entitled to share in this nonrecourse liability in the same proportion as he shares in partnership profits, that is, 5 percent. Sec. 752; sec. 1.752-1(e), Income Tax Regs.

We conclude that, as of 1977, petitioner's total basis in the partnership equaled $132,500, that is, $7,500 for the land deemed contributed plus $125,000 (5% × $2,500,000) for the nonrecourse partnership debt, as respondent has determined in the notice of deficiency. Secs. 722, 752(a); sec. 1.722-1, Income Tax Regs. Petitioner did not make any additional capital or cash contributions to the partnership and he does not present any other arguments to increase his partnership basis for any of the taxable years in issue. Therefore, under section 704(d), the total amount of partnership losses deductible by petitioner for all of the taxable years in issue cannot exceed $132,500.

* * *

D. Problems

1. Ann, Bob, Cathy, and Dennis formed an equal partnership and each contributed $25,000. The partnership purchased a building for $1,000,000, using the $100,000 of cash and obtaining a $900,000 non-recourse loan.

(a) Assume the partnership is a general partnership. What is each partner's outside basis? Prepare a balance sheet to reflect the situation of the partners and the partnership.

(b) Alternatively, assume the partnership is a limited partnership. Ann is the sole general partner and Bob, Cathy, and Dennis are limited partners. What is each partner's outside basis? Prepare a balance sheet to reflect the situation of the partners and the partnership.

---

2. Application:

(a) With respect to a non-recourse liability:
   (1) What documentation would you ask to review in determining whether a liability is a non-recourse liability?
   (2) How would you explain to the partners what the consequences are of a non-recourse liability?
   (3) How would you explain to the partners the effect of a liability on the partner's basis?

(b) With respect to how a non-recourse liability will be allocated among the partners:
   (1) How would you explain to the partners what the consequences of allocating a non-recourse liability are?
   (2) How will the partners allocate a non-recourse liability? Who gets to make the decision?
   (3) What language would you include in the partnership agreement to reflect the partners' agreement?

E. Advanced Problems — Looking Forward

Without conducting any research, consider the following questions:

1. Recall the rule from *Commissioner v. Tufts*, 461 U.S. 300 (1983), that provides non-recourse liabilities are included in the amount realized even if they exceed the fair market value of the property. Might this case have any relevance in how non-recourse debt should be allocated among the partners?

2. No partner bears the economic burden with respect to the repayment of a non-recourse debt. However, is it possible to make a connection between economic benefit derived from the property, for example from depreciation deductions claimed, and allocation of the debt?

3. If a partner contributed property to the partnership, subject to a non-recourse debt, who should be responsible for any gain that accrued prior to contribution of the property to the partnership? Is it possible to make a connection between this pre-contribution gain and allocation of the debt?

Overview Problem—Putting It All Together

Stacey, Bill, and Olivia, close friends, formed a partnership to operate a coffee shop. Stacey contributed an inventory of gourmet coffee beans that she had purchased for $1,000 and was valued at $500. She also contributed $6,500 cash. Bill contributed an industrial strength espresso machine that he had purchased for $5,000 and was currently valued at $7,000. Olivia contributed $7,000 cash.

After the partnership was formed, they found an appropriate location from which to operate the coffee shop. The property owner was willing to either lease the space or sell them the building.

The partners held a partnership meeting and discussed whether they should purchase the building. They were in agreement that they wanted to purchase the building. However, because the partnership did not have the funds, it would have to obtain a loan. If it could, the partnership would obtain a non-recourse loan to finance the purchase. If it could not obtain a non-recourse loan, the partnership would obtain a recourse loan. Finally, if the partnership was unable to obtain financing, whether non-recourse or recourse, Olivia would obtain a loan, purchase the building, then contribute the building subject to the loan to the partnership.

They have come to you for advice about the impact the loan will have, if any, on the partners in the partnership.

1. Importance of the Kind of Debt:

    (a) How would the documentation reflect that the debt is a liability of the partnership as opposed to a partner? How will you know if a partner has guaranteed a debt? Or is entitled to indemnification?

    (b) Does it matter to the partnership, from an economic perspective, whether the debt is recourse or nonrecourse?

    (c) Does it matter to the partners if the debt is obtained by Olivia, then assumed by the partnership?

2. Acquisition of Debt:

    (a) Assume that the partnership purchases a building for $300,000, financed entirely with a recourse loan. What impact would the debt have on the partnership and partners? Create a balance sheet for the partnership after it acquires the building.

    (b) Alternatively, assume the partnership obtains a nonrecourse loan in the amount of $300,000. What impact would the debt have on the partnership and partners? Create a balance sheet for the partnership.

    (c) Alternatively, assume Olivia purchases the building for $300,000 financed entirely with a recourse loan, then transfers the property, subject to the liability, to the partnership. What impact would the debt have on the partnership and partners?

Practitioner's Checklist

General Partners:

- ☐ Confirm (general) partners have agreed to restore a negative capital account and have included appropriate language in the partnership agreement.
- ☐ Confirm (general) partners are liable for all recourse debts.

New Partners:

- ☐ If a new partner is joining an existing partnership, identify all debts for which the new partner will not be liable.

Limited Partners:

- ☐ To what extent are limited partners liable for partnership debt?
- ☐ To what extent (if at all) does a limited partner have an obligation to contribute to the partnership or restore a negative capital account? _____.

All Partners:

- ☐ Partners will share non-recourse debt based on the following percentages: _____.

Partnership Assumption of Partner Debt:

- ☐ Review loan documents for each loan assumed by the partnership and confirm:
  - ☐ For each loan, confirm it could be transferred to partnership without triggering a "due on sale" clause.
  - ☐ Confirm whether the debt is recourse or non-recourse.
- ☐ If debt is assumed by the partnership, determined the net change in liability to the contributing partner.

Items to include in the partnership or operating agreement:

- ☐ Obligation of the partner to restore a negative capital account balance.
- ☐ The extent to which (if any) a limited partner is liable for a partnership obligation.
- ☐ The extent to which (if any) a limited partner has an obligation to restore a negative capital account balance.
- ☐ How partners will allocate non-recourse debt.

IV.

Partnership Operations

Overview Problem

Stacey, Bill, and Olivia formed a general partnership to operate the coffee shop. Stacey, Bill, and Olivia own 20 percent, 50 percent, 30 percent, respectively. This past year it performed fairly well. The following is a summary of the partnership's income, expenses, and depreciation:

Income from sales:		$150,000
Expenses:		
Coffee:	$30,000	
Cups:	10,000	
Sugar:	1,000	
Milk:	3,000	
Salaries:	40,000	
Interest:	4,000	
Depreciation:	12,000	
	100,000	100,000
Profit:		$50,000

In addition, the partnership sold a piece of land for $50,000. The land had been contributed by Bill to the partnership when its fair market value was $40,000. He had originally purchased the land for $20,000.

Stacey has a substantial amount of income from investments that she owns individually. Bill has a modest amount of income he made from working at the coffee shop. Olivia has a net loss that will be carried forward from the previous year.

While things had been going well for the partnership, the partners decided it was time to be more proactive in planning the management and operation of the shop and in planning for tax consequences. The partners set a time for a partnership meeting to discuss the taxable year of the partnership, how the partnership items will be allocated, when (and how) the items will be subject to tax, who will be responsible for running the day-to-day operations of the coffee shop, and any other item a partner thinks is important. You have been invited to the meeting to advise them.

Partnership Operations

```
                    ┌─────────────────────────────┐
                    │ Operation of the Partnership │
                    └─────────────────────────────┘

┌──────────────┐   ┌──────────────────┐   ┌──────────────────┐
│ Taxable Year │   │  Computation of  │   │   Allocation of  │
└──────────────┘   │  Taxable Income  │   │ Partnership Items │
                   └──────────────────┘   └──────────────────┘

                   ┌──────────────────┐
                   │  Start-Up Costs  │
                   └──────────────────┘

┌──────────────────┐        ┌──────────────────┐
│ Varying Interests │        │  Special Issues  │
└──────────────────┘        └──────────────────┘

       ┌──────────────────────┐   ┌──────────────┐   ┌──────────────┐
       │ Limitation on Losses │   │ Allocations  │   │  Contributed  │
       └──────────────────────┘   └──────────────┘   │   Property    │
                                                      └──────────────┘

   ┌──────────────────────────┐     ┌──────────────┐   ┌──────┐
   │   At Risk and Passive    │     │ Depreciation │   │ Sale │
   │ Activity Loss Limitations │     └──────────────┘   └──────┘
   └──────────────────────────┘

        ┌────────────────────┐   ┌────────────────────────┐
        │ Recourse Deductions │   │ Non-Recourse Deductions │
        └────────────────────┘   └────────────────────────┘
```

Chapter 8

Partnership Taxable Year

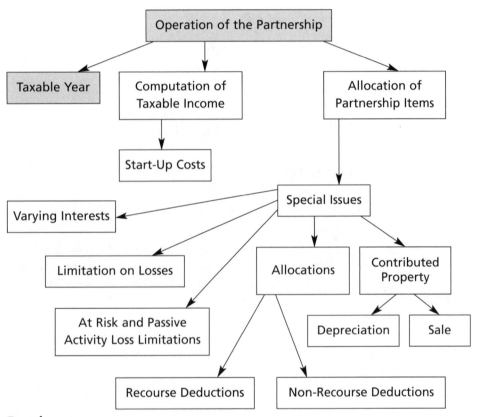

Read:

Code Sections 706(a), (b); 6031(a); 6031(b); 6072(a).
Treas. Reg. § 1.706-1(a)(1), -1(b)(1), -1(b)(2), -1(b)(3)(i).

A. Background

An individual is required to file an annual income tax return reporting his income, gain, deductions, losses, credits, etc. The filing date depends on whether the individual is a calendar year or fiscal year taxpayer. If a calendar year taxpayer (without consideration of any available extensions), the return must be filed on or before April 15th.

In general, a taxpayer wants to defer income to later years and accelerate deductions to the current filing year. However, the taxpayer's accounting method will dictate when items must be reported on his return. In most cases, the taxpayer will be either a cash basis or an accrual basis taxpayer. If the taxpayer is a cash basis taxpayer, he must report amounts actually received, constructively received, or that are cash equivalents. With respect to deductions, he may deduct items that have actually been paid and for which a deduction is allowed.[1] A loss may be reported only if allowed under the Code.

If the individual is an accrual basis taxpayer, income must be reported at the earlier of actual receipt of the income or meeting the all events test (the right to the income is fixed and the amount can be determined with reasonable accuracy). A deduction may be claimed if he can meet the all events test — the fact of the liability is established, the amount can be determined with reasonable accuracy, and economic performance has occurred.[2]

B. Discussion of Rules

1. Partnership Return

A partnership is treated as a separate entity (*i.e.*, separate from the partners) for some purposes and as an aggregation of partners for other purposes.

Partnership return. For purposes of computing the partnership's taxable income, the partnership is treated as a separate entity.[3] The partnership is required to prepare and file an information income tax return reflecting income, gains, deductions, losses and credits.[4] The information return is a Form 1065, U.S. Return of Partnership Income. If the partnership is a calendar year taxpayer, it must file its return on or before April 15 (without consideration of any available extensions). If a fiscal year taxpayer, the partnership must file its return on or before the 15th day of the fourth month after the close of its taxable year.

Partnership accounting method. The partnership's accounting method will dictate when items must be reported on the partnership tax return. In general, it may select any method of accounting, as long as it clearly reflects the partnership's income, even if that method differs from its partners' method of accounting.[5] However, there are some limitations.

If the partnership is a "tax shelter," it may not use the cash method of accounting.[6] A partnership is a "tax shelter" if—

---

1. See Code Secs. 446; 451; 461.
2. See Code Secs. 446; 451; 461.
3. Code Sec. 703(a).
4. Code Secs. 6031; 6072(a).
5. Code Secs. 446(c); 703(b).
6. Code Secs. 448(a), (d)(3); 461(i)(3).

- Interests in the partnership have been offered for sale in an offering required to be registered with any federal or state securities agency;
- More than 35 percent of the partnership's losses during the tax year are allocable to limited partners or limited entrepreneurs who do not actively participate in management of the partnership; or
- A significant purpose of the partnership is the avoidance or evasion of federal income tax.

If a C corporation is a partner in the partnership, the partnership may not use the cash method of accounting.[7] The prohibition on use of the cash method does not apply if:[8]

- The C corporation is a qualified personal service corporation;[9]
- The business is farming; or
- Average annual gross receipts do not exceed $5,000,000 for the three-year period preceding the taxable year.

Flow through of partnership items. The partnership does not pay any tax.[10] Rather, for such purposes, the partnership is treated as an aggregate of its partners and the partners are responsible for reporting partnership income, gain, deduction, and loss on their individual income tax returns.[11] A partner includes his share of partnership items on his tax return for the taxable year in which the partnership's taxable year ends.[12]

Given that both the partnership and the partners file on a yearly basis, a partner may attempt to utilize the disparity between the time a partnership files an information return and the time partnership items are included on the partner's individual return to defer income.

Examples:

Kyle, a calendar year taxpayer, is a partner in a partnership with a taxable year that begins October 1, 2006, and ends September 30, 2007. Kyle will report his share of partnership items on his 2007 individual return. Kyle is able to defer reporting the partnership items for three months.

Lavanda, a calendar year taxpayer, is a partner in a partnership with a taxable year that begins February 1, 2006, and ends January 31, 2007. Lavanda will report her share of partnership items on her 2007 individual return. Lavanda is able to defer reporting the partnership items for 11 months.

To prohibit this deferral, the Code limits the taxable year that may be used by the partnership.

---

7. Code Sec. 448(a), (b)(2).
8. Code Secs. 447; 448(a), (b)(1), (b)(2), (c).
9. A corporation is a "qualified personal service corporation" if substantially all its activities involve the performance of services in the fields of health, law, engineering, architecture, accounting, actuarial service, performing arts, or consulting and substantially all its stock is owned by employees, retired employees, or their estates. Code Sec. 448(d)(2).
10. Code Sec. 701.
11. Id.
12. Treas. Reg. § 1.706-1(a)(1).

2. Taxable Year

To prohibit taxpayer-partners from deferring the reporting of partnership items, the Code sets forth three mechanical rules that identify the partnership's taxable year. There are three exceptions to the mechanical rules.

Mechanical rules. The mechanical rules are applied in order. The first rule that is satisfied will determine the taxable year of the partnership.

First, if the owners of more than 50 percent of the partnership profits and/or capital interests have the same taxable year, that taxable year is the partnership's taxable year.[13] If a partnership is required to change its taxable year under this rule, it is not required to change to another tax year for either of the two tax years following the year of change.[14]

Second, if all the principal partners have the same taxable year, that taxable year is the partnership's taxable year.[15] A partner is considered a principal partner if he owns a five percent or more interest in the partnership profits or capital.[16]

Third, the partnership taxable year is the year that would result in the least aggregate amount of deferral of income to the partners.[17] For this test, the aggregate deferral with respect to each partner's taxable year must be determined. For each such year, first determine the number of months of deferral for each partner. The months of deferral is the number of months from the end of the partnership's taxable year forward to the end of the partner's taxable year. Then, multiply the number of months of deferral for each partner by the partner's interest in partnership profits for that year. Finally, add together all the products to determine the aggregate deferral with respect to that taxable year. The partner's taxable year that produces the lowest sum when compared to the other partners' taxable years is the taxable year that results in the least aggregate deferral of income.

If the calculation results in more than one taxable year qualifying as the taxable year with the least aggregate deferral, the partnership may select any one of those taxable years as its taxable year. But, if one of the qualifying taxable years is the partnership's existing taxable year, the partnership must maintain its existing taxable year.[18]

Exceptions to mechanical rules. There are three exceptions to the statute's mechanical rules.

First, a partnership can use a taxable year not provided for in the mechanical rules if it can establish a business purpose.[19] While both tax and non-tax factors must be considered, generally those that relate to taxpayer convenience are not sufficient to establish a business purpose. Non-tax factors include:[20]

---

13. Code Sec. 706(b)(1)(B)(i), (b)(4).
14. Code Sec. 706(b)(4)(B).
15. Code Sec. 706(b)(1)(B)(ii).
16. Code Sec. 706(b)(3).
17. Code Sec. 706(b)(1)(B)(iii); Treas. Reg. §1.706-1(b)(2)(i)(C).
18. Treas. Reg. §1.706-1(b)(3)(i).
19. Code Sec. 706(b)(1)©.
20. Rev. Rul. 87-57, 1987-2 C.B. 117.

- The use of a particular year for regulatory or financial accounting purposes;
- The seasonal hiring patterns of a business;
- The use of a particular year for administrative purposes, such as retirements, promotions, or salary increases; and
- The fact that a business involves the use of price lists, a model year, or other items that change annually.

Second, a partnership can use a taxable year not provided for in the mechanical rules if it can establish a business purpose and obtain approval from the Service under Section 442.[21] A business purpose can be established by showing there is a "natural business year" under the gross receipts test.[22] A natural business year exists if 25 percent or more of the partnership's gross receipts for the selected year are earned in the last two months. This test must be satisfied in each of the preceding three 12-month periods that correspond to the requested fiscal year.

Under the third exception, a partnership may elect a taxable year that results in up to three months of deferral. However, because the rules for determining a partnership's taxable year are designed to prevent partners from deferring the reporting of income (and payment of tax) to later years, the deferral is allowed only if the partnership is willing to pay the tax on the deferred income.[23] Because of the required tax payment, there is no tax benefit to deferring the income. Accordingly, the partnership must have some other reason for selecting a taxable year other than the one provided for in the statute or regulations.

21. Treas. Reg. § 1.706-1(b)(2)(ii).
22. Rev. Proc. 2002-38, 2002-1 C.B. 1037.
23. Code Secs. 444; 7519; Treas. Reg. § 1.706-1(b)(2)(ii).

Taxable Year of the Partnership

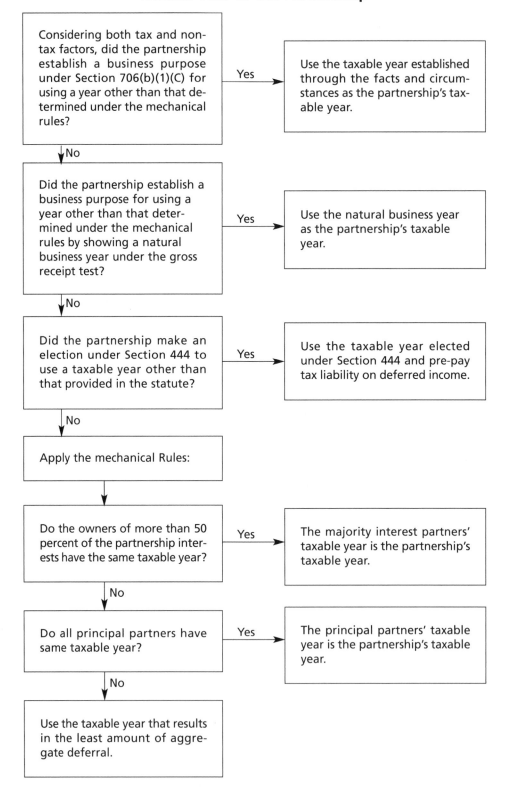

C. Application of Rules

Example 1. Majority-interest taxable year. Leslie, Maynard, and Nathan are partners in the LMN Partnership. Their ownership interest and individual taxable years are as follows:

Partner	Ownership	Taxable Year
Leslie	30%	July 31
Maynard	30%	July 31
Nathan	40%	Dec. 31

The partnership makes no elections.

Together, Leslie and Maynard own more than 50 percent of the LMN Partnership and they have the same taxable year. Thus, the partnership's taxable year is the year ending July 31.

Example 2. Taxable year of all principal partners. Tallie is a 10-pecent owner of the partnership. The remaining 90 percent interest is held by 90 partners, each of whom owns one percent. Tallie's taxable year ends June 30. Of the one-percent partners, 30 have a taxable year that ends on July 30, 30 have a taxable year that ends on August 31, and 30 have a taxable year that ends on December 31. The partnership makes no elections.

No combination of partners who own more than 50 percent of the partnership have the same taxable year. Thus, there is no majority-interest taxable year. As the owner of a 10-percent interest, Tallie is the only principal partner. Thus, the partnership's taxable year is the year ending June 30.

Example 3. Taxable year resulting in the least aggregate deferral. Annie and Betty are equal owners of the AB Partnership. Annie reports her income on a calendar year and Betty reports her income on a taxable year ending November 30. The partnership makes no elections.

No combination of partners who own more than 50 percent of the partnership have the same taxable year. There is no majority interest taxable year. Annie and Betty are both principal partners. However, because they do not have the same taxable year, there is no principal partner taxable year. Thus, the partnership must use whichever of Annie's or Betty's taxable year would result in the least aggregate deferral. That determination is made as follows:

Amount of deferral if the partnership used Annie's calendar year:

Partner	Ownership	Taxable Year	Deferral to 12/31	Interest x Deferral
Annie	50%	Dec. 31	0	0
Betty	50%	Nov. 30	11	5.5
Aggregate deferral				5.5

Amount of deferral if the partnership used Betty's taxable year ending November 30:

Partner	Ownership	Taxable Year	Deferral to 11/30	Interest x Deferral
Annie	50%	Dec. 31	1	0.5
Betty	50%	Nov. 30	0	0
Aggregate deferral				0.5

The partnership is required to have a taxable year ending November 30 because it results in the least aggregate deferral of income.

D. Cases and Materials

Rev. Rul. 87-57, 1987-2 C.B. 117

ISSUE

In the situations described below, has a partnership, an S Corporation, or a personal service corporation established, to the satisfaction of the Secretary, a business purpose for adopting, retaining, or changing its tax year?

FACTS

In each of these situations, the taxpayer is a partnership, an S corporation, or a personal service corporation. In addition, in each instance the owners of the taxpayer have tax years that differ from the tax year requested by the taxpayer. The requested tax year is not a "grandfathered fiscal year" within the meaning of section 5.01(2) of Rev. Proc. 87-32, page 396, this Bulletin.

Situation 1. The taxpayer desires to use a January 31 tax year. The taxpayer's reason for the requested tax year is that that year corresponds to the natural business year for the taxpayer's type of business as suggested by the Natural Business Year Committee of the American Institute of Certified Public Accountants (AICPA) in an official release published in 100 Journal of Accountancy 59 (December 1955). In addition, the taxpayer is using a January 31 fiscal year for financial reporting purposes.

Situation 2. The taxpayer desires to use a September 30 tax year. The taxpayer's reasons for the requested tax year are that the taxpayer's accountant is extremely busy during the first six months of the year and that, if the taxpayer were to have a September 30 tax year, the taxpayer would receive a reduced charge for the accountant's services.

Situation 3. The taxpayer desires to retain its November 30 tax year. The taxpayer's reasons for the requested tax year are that the taxpayer has used a November 30 tax year since the inception of its business 15 years ago and that, if the taxpayer is required to change its tax year, it would lose its recordkeeping consistency and thus would suffer a financial hardship in changing the records to another year.

Situation 4. The taxpayer desires to use a tax year ending September 30. The taxpayer's reason for the requested tax year is that the taxpayer desires to issue timely tax information (for example, Schedules K-1, Form 1065 Partner's Share of Income, Credits, Deductions, Etc.) to its owners to facilitate the filing of timely returns by its owners.

Situation 5. The taxpayer desires to use a November 30 tax year. The taxpayer can establish a natural business year ending on January 31 under section 4.01(1) of Rev. Proc. 87-32. If the taxpayer had not satisfied the natural business year test for January 31, it would have met the natural business year test for November 30.

Situation 6. The taxpayer desires to use a June 30 tax year. The taxpayer's reason for the requested tax year is that it coincides with the taxpayer's natural business year. For this taxpayer, June 30 is not a "natural business year," within the meaning of section 4.01(1) of Rev. Proc. 87-32. This failure to satisfy section 4.01(1) of Rev. Proc. 87-32 is caused by unusual gross receipts figures for several months during the 47-month period (36-month period for requested tax year plus additional 11-month period for comparing requested tax year with other potential tax years) covered by the test. The figures for those months were unusual because a labor strike closed the taxpayer's business during a period that included its normal peak season. The taxpayer has data for the most recent five years demonstrating that the requested tax year would have satisfied the definition of a natural business year within the meaning of section 4.01(1) of Rev. Proc. 87-32, if the strike had not occurred.

Situation 7. The taxpayer desires to use a May 31 tax year. The taxpayer's reason for the requested tax year is that due to weather conditions the business is operational only during the period of September 1 through May 31. For the 10 years it has been in business, the taxpayer has had insignificant gross receipts for the period June 1 through August 31. The facility used by the taxpayer is not used for any other purpose during the three months of insignificant gross receipts. This taxpayer does not have a "natural business year," within the meaning of section 4.01(1) of Rev. Proc. 87-32.

Situation 8. The taxpayer desires to continue to use a March 31 tax year. The taxpayer changed its method of accounting to the accrual method for the tax year ended March 31, 1987. The taxpayer's reason for the requested tax year is that it coincides with the taxpayer's natural business year. For this taxpayer, March 31 is not a "natural business year," within the meaning of section 4.01(1) of Rev. Proc. 87-32. The 25-percent test in section 4.01(1) of Rev. Proc. 87-32 requires the taxpayer to compute the gross receipts on the basis of the method of accounting used to file its return for each year of the test. Therefore, the taxpayer must compute gross receipts on the cash method of accounting for tax years prior to the tax year ended March 31, 1987. The taxpayer has audited financial statements that were prepared on the basis of an accrual method that is acceptable for tax purposes. The taxpayer's gross receipts based on the accrual method would satisfy the 25-percent test for a tax year ending March 31.

LAW AND ANALYSIS

* * *

With respect to the establishment of a business purpose for the use of a tax year, the Conference Report states that the Secretary may prescribe tests to be used to establish the existence of a business purpose if, in the discretion of the Secretary, such tests are desirable and expedient towards the efficient administration of the tax laws. Rev. Proc. 87-32 sets forth a mechanical natural business year test and an ownership tax year test that, if either is satisfied, establish, to the satisfaction of the Secretary, a business purpose (as described in sections 441(i), 706(b)(1)(C), and 1378(b)(2) for a taxpayer to retain, and in limited situations, adopt or change to a tax year.

A taxpayer that cannot satisfy any of the tests set forth in Rev. Proc. 87-32 must establish a business purpose based on consideration of all the facts and circumstances, including the tax consequences. The tax consequences to be considered include: (1) deferring a substantial portion of a taxpayer's income or shifting a substantial portion of a taxpayer's deductions from one year to another to reduce substantially a taxpayer's tax liability; (2) causing a similar deferral or shift in the case of any other person, such as a partner, a beneficiary, or a shareholder in an S corporation; and (3) creating a short period in which there is a substantial net operating loss.

The Conference Report lists various nontax factors that will ordinarily not be sufficient to establish that the business purpose requirement for a particular tax year has been met. These factors are: (1) the use of a particular year for regulatory or financial accounting purposes; (2) the hiring patterns of a particular business—for example, the fact that a firm typically hires staff during certain times of the year; (3) the use of a particular year for administrative purposes, such as the admission or retirement of partners or shareholders, promotion of staff, and compensation or retirement arrangements with staff, partners, or shareholders; and (4) the fact that a particular business involves the use of price lists, a model year, or other items that change on an annual basis.

Both tax factors and nontax factors must be considered for purposes of determining whether a taxpayer has established a business purpose for the requested tax year. In this context, the Conference Report demonstrates the significant weight that must be assigned to tax factors. The four nontax factors that the report identifies as ordinarily insufficient all involve issues of convenience for the taxpayer. Accordingly, if a requested tax year creates deferral or distortion, the taxpayer's nontax factors must demonstrate compelling reasons for the requested tax year.

The taxpayer in each of the eight situations must establish, to the satisfaction of the Secretary, a business purpose for the use of the requested tax year. Each taxpayer has nontax, business reasons for the use of the requested tax year. However, because the requested tax year is different from the tax year of the taxpayer's owners, the taxpayer's use of the requested tax year would inherently create deferral or distortion. Under these circumstances, the taxpayer can establish, to the satisfaction of the Secretary, a business purpose for the requested tax year only if the nontax reasons for the use of that year are compelling.

The taxpayer's reason for the requested tax year in *Situation 1* is that the requested tax year is the natural business year suggested by the Natural Business Year Committee of the AICPA and the taxpayer uses the requested tax year for financial statement purposes. As stated in the Conference Report, the use of a particular year for financial accounting purposes is not sufficient to establish that the business purpose requirement for that year has been met. In addition, the natural business year suggested by the AICPA is not based upon the taxpayer's own facts and circumstances.

In *Situations 2–4*, the taxpayers' reasons for the requested tax years are to take advantage of an accountant's reduced rate (*Situation 2*), to have recordkeeping consistency (*Situation 3*), and to issue timely tax information forms to partners (*Situation 4*). The reasons given in these three situations are ones of convenience to the taxpayers. Although the reasons are not among those specifically enumerated in the Conference Report, they are very similar to the convenience reasons listed there as being insufficient to establish that the business purpose requirement for a requested tax year has been met.

The taxpayer's reason in *Situation 5* is that the requested November 30 tax year would be a natural business year but for the fact that the January 31 year produces a higher percentage under the 25-percent test of Rev. Proc. 87-32. Because a November 30 fiscal year satisfies the 25-percent test and results in less deferral to the shareholders than January 31, the Commissioner, in his discretion, considers it desirable and expedient for the efficient administration of the tax laws for this taxpayer to use November 30 as its tax year. Accordingly, the taxpayer has established a business purpose for using the requested tax year. See 2 H.R. Rep. No. 99-841 at II-319.

The taxpayer's reasons in *Situation 6* are that the requested tax year coincides with the taxpayer's natural business year and that, if the strike had not occurred, the requested year would have been a natural business year according to the test set forth in Rev. Proc. 87-32. The taxpayer's failure to establish a natural business year under the 25-percent test is due to unusual circumstances that occurred during the test period and that were beyond the taxpayer's control. The historical data support the taxpayer's contention that, in the absence of these unusual circumstances, the requested year would have qualified as the taxpayer's natural business year. Thus, the Commissioner is satisfied that the taxpayer has established a business purpose for the requested tax year.

The taxpayer's reason in *Situation 7* is that the requested May 31 tax year coincides with the time the taxpayer has closed down operations for the past 10 years. That closing is not within the taxpayer's control. Accordingly, the taxpayer has established a business purpose for using the requested tax year.

The taxpayer's reason in *Situation 8* is that the requested March 31 tax year coincides with the taxpayer's natural business year and that, if the taxpayer had used the accrual method of accounting, the requested year would have been a natural business year according to the test set forth in Rev. Proc. 87-32. The taxpayer has changed its method of accounting to the accrual method. Therefore, it is reasonable for the Commissioner, to allow the taxpayer to use a March 31 tax year if the accrual method, which will be used for all future tax years, would establish a natural business year ending on March 31.

HOLDING

Each taxpayer in *Situations 1–4* has failed to establish, to the satisfaction of the Secretary, a business purpose for the use of its requested tax year. Each taxpayer in *Situations 5–8* has established, to the satisfaction of the Secretary, a business purpose for the use of its requested tax year.

E. Problems

1. Peter, Quinn, and Roy are 40-percent, 30-percent, and 30-percent partners, respectively, in the PQR partnership. Peter's taxable year ends June 30. Quinn's taxable year

ends June 30. Roy's taxable year ends September 30. The partnership has made no elections. What taxable year must the PQR Partnership use?

---

2. Alpha owns a 20-percent interest in the Beta Partnership. Twenty other individuals each own a 4-percent interest in the partnership. Alpha's taxable year ends September 30 and the twenty other partners all have taxable years that end December 31. The partnership has made no elections. What taxable year must the Beta Partnership use?

---

3. The Green Partnership has 21 partners. The ownership interest of each partner and the taxable year ending is as follows:

No. of partners	Percentage Ownership	Tax Year Ending
2	20 percent each	July 31
11	4 percent each	December 31
8	2 percent each	September 30

The partnership has made no elections. What taxable year must the Green Partnership use?

---

4. Sam and Tess, equal partners, form the ST Partnership. Sam's taxable year ends June 30. Tess's taxable year ends July 31. The partnership has made no elections. What taxable year must the ST Partnership use?

---

5. Marsha, Jan, and Cindy are 40-percent, 30-percent, and 30-percent partners, respectively, in the Brady Partnership. Marsha, Jan, and Cindy's taxable years end December 31. The partnership would like to adopt a taxable year that ends October 31 so that it has sufficient time to complete its tax return before the returns of its partners are due. May the partnership adopt a taxable year that ends October 31? How? Must it make a payment under Section 7519?

---

6. Greg, Peter, and Bobby are 40-percent, 30-percent, and 30-percent partners, respectively, in the United Partnership. Greg, Peter, and Bobby's taxable years end December 31. The partnership owns and operates a ski resort. For the past six years, 30 percent of its business occurs in December and 10 percent in January. Currently, the partnership's taxable year ends December 31. The partnership would like to adopt a taxable year that ends January 31. May the partnership adopt a taxable year that ends January 31? How? Must it make a payment under Section 7519?

F. Advanced Problems — Looking Forward

Without conducting any research, consider the following questions:

1. If the partner receives a payment from the partnership, but it is not in his capacity as a partner, in which year should he report the income?

2. If the partner is guaranteed to receive a payment from the partnership, in his capacity as a partner but the payment is not dependent on whether or not the partnership has profits for the year, in which year should he report the income?

3. Since the return filed by the partnership is only an information return, who is responsible for making any applicable elections, the partnership or the partners?

4. If the partnership does not pay any tax, and the partners are responsible for reporting all items of income, gain, deduction, and loss on their individual income tax returns, how does the partnership divide up the partnership items among the partners?

5. Since the partners are responsible for reporting all items of income, gain, deduction, and loss on their individual income tax returns, how does the partner determine the character of those items?

6. Should there be a limit on the amount of deductions or losses a partner could claim? If so, what should that limit be?

Chapter 9

Computation of Taxable Income

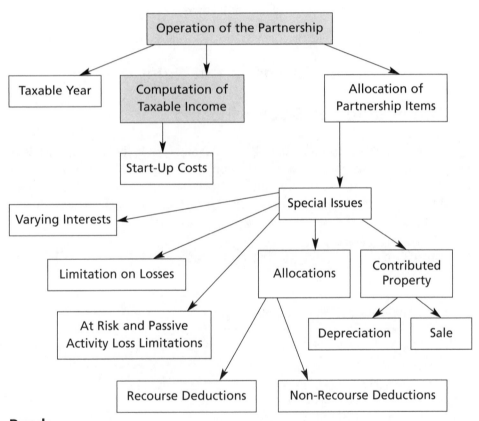

Read:

Code Sections 701; 702; 703.
Treas. Reg. §§ 1.701-1; 1.702-1(b); 1.703-1(a), -1(b)(1).

A. Background

On his individual income tax return, the taxpayer must report all gross income for the taxable year. Next, he reduces his gross income by all allowable deductions. He may be allowed certain "above-the-line" deductions and can claim either itemized deductions or the standard deduction. Finally, he deducts all allowable exemptions to determine net taxable income.

He calculates the tax due on his net taxable income. Ordinary income and gain are taxed at ordinary rates. Similarly, net short-term capital gain is taxed at ordinary rates. However, long-term capital gain is taxed at preferential, or reduced, rates.

Finally, the total tax liability is reduced by any relevant credits, leaving the amount of the taxpayer's current tax liability, which he is personally responsible for paying.

In determining the amount of his tax liability, the individual may have to make a number of decisions, such as the method of accounting, whether to elect out of the modified accelerated cost recovery system, whether to elect bonus depreciation, or whether to report gain using the installment method.

B. Discussion of Rules

1. Computation of Taxable Income

In general, the partnership's taxable income is computed in the same manner as an individual's taxable income.[1] First, the partnership must report all gross income for the taxable year. Next, it reduces its gross income by all allowable deductions. It is allowed the same deductions as an individual, except it is not allowed a deduction for the following items:

- Personal exemptions;
- Taxes paid to foreign countries or U.S. possessions;
- Charitable contributions;
- Net operating losses;
- Certain itemized deductions including:
  - Expenses incurred in the production of income;
  - Medical and dental expenses;
  - Alimony paid;
  - Moving expenses;
  - Qualified retirement contributions;
  - Interest paid on education loans;
  - Qualified tuition and related expenses; and
  - Amounts paid to a health savings account.

To the extent a partnership has the above expenses (except the personal exemption and certain of the itemized deductions), they are separately stated and may be deductible by the partners.

---

1. Code Sec. 703(a).

Form 1065:

Form 1065

U.S. Return of Partnership Income

OMB No. 1545-0099

Department of the Treasury
Internal Revenue Service

For calendar year 2012, or tax year beginning _____ , 2012, ending _____ , 20 _____ .
▶ Information about Form 1065 and its separate instructions is at *www.irs.gov/form1065*.

2012

A Principal business activity	Name of partnership		D Employer identification number
B Principal product or service	**Print or type.**	Number, street, and room or suite no. If a P.O. box, see the instructions.	E Date business started
C Business code number		City or town, state, and ZIP code	F Total assets (see the instructions) $

G Check applicable boxes: **(1)** ☐ Initial return **(2)** ☐ Final return **(3)** ☐ Name change **(4)** ☐ Address change **(5)** ☐ Amended return
(6) ☐ Technical termination - also check (1) or (2)

H Check accounting method: **(1)** ☐ Cash **(2)** ☐ Accrual **(3)** ☐ Other (specify) ▶ _____

I Number of Schedules K-1. Attach one for each person who was a partner at any time during the tax year ▶ _____

J Check if Schedules C and M-3 are attached . . . . ☐

Caution. *Include **only** trade or business income and expenses on lines 1a through 22 below. See the instructions for more information.*

Income

1a	Gross receipts or sales	1a	
b	Returns and allowances	1b	
c	Balance. Subtract line 1b from line 1a	1c	
2	Cost of goods sold (attach Form 1125-A)	2	
3	Gross profit. Subtract line 2 from line 1c	3	
4	Ordinary income (loss) from other partnerships, estates, and trusts (attach statement) . .	4	
5	Net farm profit (loss) (attach Schedule F (Form 1040))	5	
6	Net gain (loss) from Form 4797, Part II, line 17 (attach Form 4797)	6	
7	Other income (loss) (attach statement)	7	
8	**Total income (loss).** Combine lines 3 through 7	8	

Deductions (see the instructions for limitations)

9	Salaries and wages (other than to partners) (less employment credits)	9	
10	Guaranteed payments to partners	10	
11	Repairs and maintenance	11	
12	Bad debts	12	
13	Rent	13	
14	Taxes and licenses	14	
15	Interest	15	
16a	Depreciation (if required, attach Form 4562)	16a	
b	Less depreciation reported on Form 1125-A and elsewhere on return	16b	16c
17	Depletion **(Do not deduct oil and gas depletion.)**	17	
18	Retirement plans, etc.	18	
19	Employee benefit programs	19	
20	Other deductions (attach statement)	20	
21	**Total deductions.** Add the amounts shown in the far right column for lines 9 through 20 .	21	
22	**Ordinary business income (loss).** Subtract line 21 from line 8	22	

Sign Here

Under penalties of perjury, I declare that I have examined this return, including accompanying schedules and statements, and to the best of my knowledge and belief, it is true, correct, and complete. Declaration of preparer (other than general partner or limited liability company member manager) is based on all information of which preparer has any knowledge.

▶ _____ ▶ _____
Signature of general partner or limited liability company member manager   Date

May the IRS discuss this return with the preparer shown below (see instructions)? ☐ **Yes** ☐ **No**

Paid Preparer Use Only

Print/Type preparer's name	Preparer's signature	Date	Check ☐ if self-employed	PTIN
Firm's name ▶			Firm's EIN ▶	
Firm's address ▶			Phone no.	

For Paperwork Reduction Act Notice, see separate instructions.   Cat. No. 11390Z   Form **1065** (2012)

Form 1065 (2012)   Page **2**

Schedule B   Other Information

			Yes	No
1	What type of entity is filing this return? Check the applicable box:			
a	☐ Domestic general partnership **b** ☐ Domestic limited partnership			
c	☐ Domestic limited liability company **d** ☐ Domestic limited liability partnership			
e	☐ Foreign partnership **f** ☐ Other ▶ _____			
2	At any time during the tax year, was any partner in the partnership a disregarded entity, a partnership (including an entity treated as a partnership), a trust, an S corporation, an estate (other than an estate of a deceased partner), or a nominee or similar person?			
3	At the end of the tax year:			
a	Did any foreign or domestic corporation, partnership (including any entity treated as a partnership), trust, or tax-exempt organization, or any foreign government own, directly or indirectly, an interest of 50% or more in the profit, loss, or capital of the partnership? For rules of constructive ownership, see instructions. If "Yes," attach Schedule B-1, Information on Partners Owning 50% or More of the Partnership			
b	Did any individual or estate own, directly or indirectly, an interest of 50% or more in the profit, loss, or capital of the partnership? For rules of constructive ownership, see instructions. If "Yes," attach Schedule B-1, Information on Partners Owning 50% or More of the Partnership			
4	At the end of the tax year, did the partnership:			
a	Own directly 20% or more, or own, directly or indirectly, 50% or more of the total voting power of all classes of stock entitled to vote of any foreign or domestic corporation? For rules of constructive ownership, see instructions. If "Yes," complete (i) through (iv) below			

(i) Name of Corporation	**(ii)** Employer Identification Number (if any)	**(iii)** Country of Incorporation	**(iv)** Percentage Owned in Voting Stock

b Own directly an interest of 20% or more, or own, directly or indirectly, an interest of 50% or more in the profit, loss, or capital in any foreign or domestic partnership (including an entity treated as a partnership) or in the beneficial interest of a trust? For rules of constructive ownership, see instructions. If "Yes," complete (i) through (v) below . .

(i) Name of Entity	**(ii)** Employer Identification Number (if any)	**(iii)** Type of Entity	**(iv)** Country of Organization	**(v)** Maximum Percentage Owned in Profit, Loss, or Capital

			Yes	No
5	Did the partnership file Form 8893, Election of Partnership Level Tax Treatment, or an election statement under section 6231(a)(1)(B)(ii) for partnership-level tax treatment, that is in effect for this tax year? See Form 8893 for more details			
6	Does the partnership satisfy **all four** of the following conditions?			
a	The partnership's total receipts for the tax year were less than $250,000.			
b	The partnership's total assets at the end of the tax year were less than $1 million.			
c	Schedules K-1 are filed with the return and furnished to the partners on or before the due date (including extensions) for the partnership return.			
d	The partnership is not filing and is not required to file Schedule M-3 . . . . If "Yes," the partnership is not required to complete Schedules L, M-1, and M-2; Item F on page 1 of Form 1065; or Item L on Schedule K-1.			
7	Is this partnership a publicly traded partnership as defined in section 469(k)(2)?			
8	During the tax year, did the partnership have any debt that was cancelled, was forgiven, or had the terms modified so as to reduce the principal amount of the debt?			
9	Has this partnership filed, or is it required to file, Form 8918, Material Advisor Disclosure Statement, to provide information on any reportable transaction?			
10	At any time during calendar year 2012, did the partnership have an interest in or a signature or other authority over a financial account in a foreign country (such as a bank account, securities account, or other financial account)? See the instructions for exceptions and filing requirements for Form TD F 90-22.1, Report of Foreign Bank and Financial Accounts. If "Yes," enter the name of the foreign country. ▶			

Form **1065** (2012)

Schedule B	Other Information *(continued)*		

		Yes	No
11	At any time during the tax year, did the partnership receive a distribution from, or was it the grantor of, or transferor to, a foreign trust? If "Yes," the partnership may have to file Form 3520, Annual Return To Report Transactions With Foreign Trusts and Receipt of Certain Foreign Gifts. See instructions		
12a	Is the partnership making, or had it previously made (and not revoked), a section 754 election? . . . . . . See instructions for details regarding a section 754 election.		
b	Did the partnership make for this tax year an optional basis adjustment under section 743(b) or 734(b)? If "Yes," attach a statement showing the computation and allocation of the basis adjustment. See instructions		
c	Is the partnership required to adjust the basis of partnership assets under section 743(b) or 734(b) because of a substantial built-in loss (as defined under section 743(d)) or substantial basis reduction (as defined under section 734(d))? If "Yes," attach a statement showing the computation and allocation of the basis adjustment. See instructions.		
13	Check this box if, during the current or prior tax year, the partnership distributed any property received in a like-kind exchange or contributed such property to another entity (other than disregarded entities wholly-owned by the partnership throughout the tax year) . . . . ▶ ☐		
14	At any time during the tax year, did the partnership distribute to any partner a tenancy-in-common or other undivided interest in partnership property?		
15	If the partnership is required to file Form 8858, Information Return of U.S. Persons With Respect To Foreign Disregarded Entities, enter the number of Forms 8858 attached. See instructions ▶		
16	Does the partnership have any foreign partners? If "Yes," enter the number of Forms 8805, Foreign Partner's Information Statement of Section 1446 Withholding Tax, filed for this partnership. ▶		
17	Enter the number of Forms 8865, Return of U.S. Persons With Respect to Certain Foreign Partnerships, attached to this return. ▶		
18a	Did you make any payments in 2012 that would require you to file Form(s) 1099? See instructions		
b	If "Yes," did you or will you file required Form(s) 1099?		
19	Enter the number of Form(s) 5471, Information Return of U.S. Persons With Respect To Certain Foreign Corporations, attached to this return. ▶		
20	Enter the number of partners that are foreign governments under section 892. ▶		

Designation of Tax Matters Partner (see instructions)

Enter below the general partner or member-manager designated as the tax matters partner (TMP) for the tax year of this return:

Name of designated TMP ▶		Identifying number of TMP ▶	
If the TMP is an entity, name of TMP representative ▶		Phone number of TMP ▶	
Address of designated TMP ▶			

Form 1065 (2012)   Page **4**

Schedule K		Partners' Distributive Share Items			Total amount
Income (Loss)	1	Ordinary business income (loss) (page 1, line 22)		1	
	2	Net rental real estate income (loss) (attach Form 8825)		2	
	3a	Other gross rental income (loss)	3a		
	b	Expenses from other rental activities (attach statement)	3b		
	c	Other net rental income (loss). Subtract line 3b from line 3a		3c	
	4	Guaranteed payments		4	
	5	Interest income		5	
	6	Dividends: **a** Ordinary dividends		6a	
		b Qualified dividends	6b		
	7	Royalties		7	
	8	Net short-term capital gain (loss) (attach Schedule D (Form 1065))		8	
	9a	Net long-term capital gain (loss) (attach Schedule D (Form 1065))		9a	
	b	Collectibles (28%) gain (loss)	9b		
	c	Unrecaptured section 1250 gain (attach statement) . .	9c		
	10	Net section 1231 gain (loss) (attach Form 4797)		10	
	11	Other income (loss) (see instructions) Type ▶		11	
Deductions	12	Section 179 deduction (attach Form 4562)		12	
	13a	Contributions		13a	
	b	Investment interest expense		13b	
	c	Section 59(e)(2) expenditures: **(1)** Type ▶ _____ **(2)** Amount ▶		13c(2)	
	d	Other deductions (see instructions) Type ▶		13d	
Self-Employ-ment	14a	Net earnings (loss) from self-employment		14a	
	b	Gross farming or fishing income		14b	
	c	Gross nonfarm income		14c	
Credits	15a	Low-income housing credit (section 42(j)(5))		15a	
	b	Low-income housing credit (other)		15b	
	c	Qualified rehabilitation expenditures (rental real estate) (attach Form 3468)		15c	
	d	Other rental real estate credits (see instructions) Type ▶ _____		15d	
	e	Other rental credits (see instructions) Type ▶ _____		15e	
	f	Other credits (see instructions) Type ▶ _____		15f	
Foreign Transactions	16a	Name of country or U.S. possession ▶ _____			
	b	Gross income from all sources		16b	
	c	Gross income sourced at partner level		16c	
		Foreign gross income sourced at partnership level			
	d	Passive category ▶ _____ **e** General category ▶ _____ **f** Other ▶		16f	
		Deductions allocated and apportioned at partner level			
	g	Interest expense ▶ _____ **h** Other . . . . ▶		16h	
		Deductions allocated and apportioned at partnership level to foreign source income			
	i	Passive category ▶ _____ **j** General category ▶ _____ **k** Other ▶		16k	
	l	Total foreign taxes (check one): ▶ Paid ☐ Accrued ☐		16l	
	m	Reduction in taxes available for credit (attach statement)		16m	
	n	Other foreign tax information (attach statement)			
Alternative Minimum Tax (AMT) Items	17a	Post-1986 depreciation adjustment		17a	
	b	Adjusted gain or loss		17b	
	c	Depletion (other than oil and gas)		17c	
	d	Oil, gas, and geothermal properties—gross income		17d	
	e	Oil, gas, and geothermal properties—deductions		17e	
	f	Other AMT items (attach statement)		17f	
Other Information	18a	Tax-exempt interest income		18a	
	b	Other tax-exempt income		18b	
	c	Nondeductible expenses		18c	
	19a	Distributions of cash and marketable securities		19a	
	b	Distributions of other property		19b	
	20a	Investment income		20a	
	b	Investment expenses		20b	
	c	Other items and amounts (attach statement)			

Form **1065** (2012)

Form 1065 (2012)   Page **5**

Analysis of Net Income (Loss)

1	Net income (loss). Combine Schedule K, lines 1 through 11. From the result, subtract the sum of Schedule K, lines 12 through 13d, and 16l **1**					

2	Analysis by partner type:	(i) Corporate	(ii) Individual (active)	(iii) Individual (passive)	(iv) Partnership	(v) Exempt organization	(vi) Nominee/Other
a	General partners						
b	Limited partners						

Schedule L	**Balance Sheets per Books**	Beginning of tax year		End of tax year	
	Assets	(a)	(b)	(c)	(d)
1	Cash				
2a	Trade notes and accounts receivable . . .				
b	Less allowance for bad debts				
3	Inventories				
4	U.S. government obligations				
5	Tax-exempt securities				
6	Other current assets (attach statement) . .				
7a	Loans to partners (or persons related to partners)				
b	Mortgage and real estate loans				
8	Other investments (attach statement) . . .				
9a	Buildings and other depreciable assets . .				
b	Less accumulated depreciation				
10a	Depletable assets				
b	Less accumulated depletion				
11	Land (net of any amortization)				
12a	Intangible assets (amortizable only) . . .				
b	Less accumulated amortization				
13	Other assets (attach statement)				
14	Total assets				
	Liabilities and Capital				
15	Accounts payable				
16	Mortgages, notes, bonds payable in less than 1 year				
17	Other current liabilities (attach statement) .				
18	All nonrecourse loans				
19a	Loans from partners (or persons related to partners)				
b	Mortgages, notes, bonds payable in 1 year or more				
20	Other liabilities (attach statement)				
21	Partners' capital accounts				
22	Total liabilities and capital				

Schedule M-1	**Reconciliation of Income (Loss) per Books With Income (Loss) per Return**
	Note. Schedule M-3 may be required instead of Schedule M-1 (see instructions).

1	Net income (loss) per books		6	Income recorded on books this year not included on Schedule K, lines 1 through 11 (itemize):	
2	Income included on Schedule K, lines 1, 2, 3c, 5, 6a, 7, 8, 9a, 10, and 11, not recorded on books this year (itemize):		a	Tax-exempt interest $ _____	
3	Guaranteed payments (other than health insurance)		7	Deductions included on Schedule K, lines 1 through 13d, and 16l, not charged against book income this year (itemize):	
4	Expenses recorded on books this year not included on Schedule K, lines 1 through 13d, and 16l (itemize):		a	Depreciation $ _____	
a	Depreciation $ _____		8	Add lines 6 and 7	
b	Travel and entertainment $ _____		9	Income (loss) (Analysis of Net Income (Loss), line 1). Subtract line 8 from line 5 .	
5	Add lines 1 through 4				

Schedule M-2	**Analysis of Partners' Capital Accounts**

1	Balance at beginning of year . . .		6	Distributions: **a** Cash	
2	Capital contributed: **a** Cash . . .			**b** Property	
	b Property . .		7	Other decreases (itemize): _____	
3	Net income (loss) per books				
4	Other increases (itemize): _____		8	Add lines 6 and 7	
5	Add lines 1 through 4		9	Balance at end of year. Subtract line 8 from line 5	

Form **1065** (2012)

651112

☐ Final K-1   ☐ Amended K-1   OMB No. 1545-0099

Schedule K-1
(Form 1065)

20 **12**

Department of the Treasury
Internal Revenue Service

For calendar year 2012, or tax
year beginning _____, 2012
ending _____, 20 _____

Partner's Share of Income, Deductions,
Credits, etc.   ▶ See back of form and separate instructions.

Part I	**Information About the Partnership**

A Partnership's employer identification number

B Partnership's name, address, city, state, and ZIP code

C IRS Center where partnership filed return

D ☐ Check if this is a publicly traded partnership (PTP)

Part II	**Information About the Partner**

E Partner's identifying number

F Partner's name, address, city, state, and ZIP code

G ☐ General partner or LLC member-manager   ☐ Limited partner or other LLC member

H ☐ Domestic partner   ☐ Foreign partner

I1 What type of entity is this partner? (see instructions) _____

I2 If this partner is a retirement plan (IRA/SEP/Keogh/etc.), check here (see instructions) . . . . ☐

J Partner's share of profit, loss, and capital (see instructions):

	Beginning	Ending
Profit	%	%
Loss	%	%
Capital	%	%

K Partner's share of liabilities at year end:

Nonrecourse	$ _____
Qualified nonrecourse financing .	$ _____
Recourse	$ _____

L Partner's capital account analysis:

Beginning capital account . . .	$ _____
Capital contributed during the year	$ _____
Current year increase (decrease) .	$ _____
Withdrawals & distributions . .	$ (_____)
Ending capital account	$ _____

☐ Tax basis   ☐ GAAP   ☐ Section 704(b) book
☐ Other (explain)

M Did the partner contribute property with a built-in gain or loss?
☐ Yes   ☐ No
If "Yes," attach statement (see instructions)

Part III	**Partner's Share of Current Year Income, Deductions, Credits, and Other Items**

1	Ordinary business income (loss)		15	Credits
2	Net rental real estate income (loss)			
3	Other net rental income (loss)		16	Foreign transactions
4	Guaranteed payments			
5	Interest income			
6a	Ordinary dividends			
6b	Qualified dividends			
7	Royalties			
8	Net short-term capital gain (loss)			
9a	Net long-term capital gain (loss)		17	Alternative minimum tax (AMT) items
9b	Collectibles (28%) gain (loss)			
9c	Unrecaptured section 1250 gain			
10	Net section 1231 gain (loss)		18	Tax-exempt income and nondeductible expenses
11	Other income (loss)			
			19	Distributions
12	Section 179 deduction			
13	Other deductions		20	Other information
14	Self-employment earnings (loss)			

*See attached statement for additional information.

For IRS Use Only

For Paperwork Reduction Act Notice, see Instructions for Form 1065.   IRS.gov/form1065   Cat. No. 11394R   **Schedule K-1 (Form 1065) 2012**

2. Elections

To ensure consistency among the partners, the partnership is responsible for making elections that will impact the computation of its taxable income.[2] The election applies only with respect to partnership items. It does not impact the partner's tax items from sources other than the partnership.

The following decisions are made by the partnership:

- Accounting method;
- Inventory method;
- Depreciation method and whether to claim bonus depreciation;
- Election to amortize start-up expenses;
- Whether to report gain using the installment method;
- Election to deduct research and development expenses;
- Election to adjust the basis of partnership property under Section 754; and
- Election to defer gain from an involuntary conversion of partnership property.

A small number of elections are made by the individual partners. They include items such as elections related to income from discharge of indebtedness and the recapture of certain mining exploration expenditures.[3]

Practice Alert: If the partners are unaware that they are treated as a partnership for federal tax purposes, the partnership may fail to make a necessary election.

---

3. Separately Stated Items

While all partnership items are reported on the partnership's tax return, the partnership does not pay tax. Rather, the items pass through the partnership and are reported on the partner's individual income tax return.

Because the character of items may impact how they must be included on the partner's individual income tax return, some partnership items must be reported separately to the partners. The character of such items is determined as if each such item were realized directly from the source from which the partnership realized the item or as if the item had been incurred in the same manner as incurred by the partnership.[4]

Example: Millie's Form K-1 reflects her share of the partnership's gain as $100,000.

If the gain is ordinary, Millie will pay tax based on regular rates.

If the gain is a capital gain, Millie must net the gain with her other capital gains and losses to determine the amount of net capital gain or loss. If she

---

2. Code Sec. 703(b).
3. Id.
4. Code Sec. 702(b).

Determining Partner's Share of Partnership Items

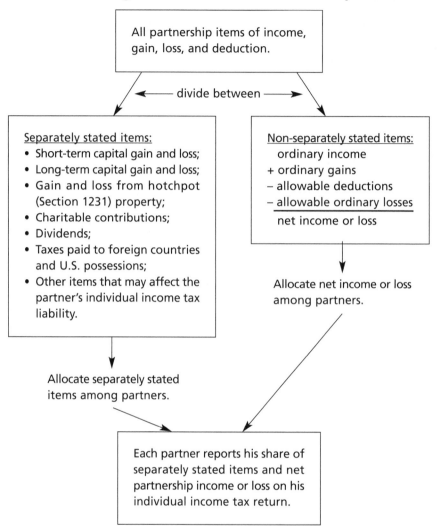

All partnership items of income, gain, loss, and deduction.

◄—— divide between ——►

Separately stated items:
- Short-term capital gain and loss;
- Long-term capital gain and loss;
- Gain and loss from hotchpot (Section 1231) property;
- Charitable contributions;
- Dividends;
- Taxes paid to foreign countries and U.S. possessions;
- Other items that may affect the partner's individual income tax liability.

Non-separately stated items:
  ordinary income
+ ordinary gains
− allowable deductions
− allowable ordinary losses
  net income or loss

Allocate net income or loss among partners.

Allocate separately stated items among partners.

Each partner reports his share of separately stated items and net partnership income or loss on his individual income tax return.

---

has no other capital gains or losses and the gain is a short-term capital gain, it will be taxed at her regular rates. If she has no other capital gains or losses and the gain is a long-term capital gain, it will be taxed at lower, preferential rates.

If the gain is a hotchpot (Section 1231) gain, it will be netted with other hotchpot gains and losses. If there is a net hotchpot gain, it will be treated as a long-term capital gain. If there is a net loss, the loss will be treated as ordinary.

Those items that must be separately stated when reported to the partners include:[5]

- Short-term capital gain and loss;
- Long-term capital gain and loss;

----

5. Code Sec. 702(a).

- Gain and loss from hotchpot (Section 1231) property;
- Charitable contributions;
- Dividends;
- Taxes paid to foreign countries and U.S. possessions; and
- Other items identified in the regulations that may affect the partner's individual income tax liability.

Those items that are not specially treated on an individual partner's income tax return can be netted together before being reported to the partners.

C. Application of Rules

Example 1. The partnership purchased a new stainless steel freezer for use in the business. To claim bonus depreciation, the partnership must make the election by filing a Form 4562, Depreciation and Amortization.

Example 2. John, a calendar year taxpayer, has a 10-percent interest in a partnership. In addition, during the year, he earned an $80,000 salary and sold Individual Acres, recognizing a $10,000 long-term capital gain.

The partnership, also a calendar year taxpayer, earned $100,000 from the sale of widgets. Its costs were as follows:

widget cleaner:	$5,000
widget holders:	4,000
salaries:	11,000

The partnership also sold Blueacre, land that it had been holding as investment property, for a $50,000 long-term capital gain and Greenacre, land it had been holding as investment property, for a $10,000 short-term capital loss.

The partnership does not need to separately state the income from the sale of widgets or the related expenses. Thus, the net income is:

Income:		$100,000
Expenses:		
widget cleaner:	$5,000	
widget holders:	4,000	
salaries:	11,000	
	$20,000	20,000
		$80,000

The partnership must separately state the $50,000 long-term capital gain from Blueacre and $10,000 short-term capital loss from Greenacre.

The partnership items are allocated as follows:

Item	Partnership Level	John's 10 percent share
Net income	$80,000	$8,000
Long-term capital gain	50,000	5,000
Short-term capital loss	10,000	1,000

Combined with his individual items, John must report:

- $88,000 of ordinary income ($80,000 of salary and $8,000 of net income from the partnership);
- $15,000 of long-term capital gain ($10,000 from sale of Individual Acres and $5,000 allocable share from the sale of Blueacre); and
- $1,000 of short-term capital loss (allocable share from the sale of Greenacre).

Example 3. Ted is a developer; he purchases land, subdivides the land, then sells the lots. He is also a partner in Investment Partnership. The partnership sold appreciated land it had held for five years as investment property. The character of the land is determined at the partnership level as long-term capital gain. The fact that the character would have been different if the land had been sold by Ted (ordinary gain) is irrelevant.

D. Cases and Materials

Rev. Rul. 68-79, *1968-1 C.B. 310*

In determining his gross income, a partner should, under section 702(a) of the Internal Revenue Code of 1954, take into account separately in his return, as long-term capital gain, his distributive share of the partnership's long-term capital gain arising from the sale by the partnership of stock held for more than six months as an investment, notwithstanding that the partner has a holding period for his partnership interest of not more than six months.

Advice has been requested whether a partner's distributive share of partnership capital gains resulting under the circumstances described below is long-term capital gain.

A, B and *C* were equal partners in *ABC* partnership. On June 1, 1966, the partnership acquired 300 shares of *X* corporation stock as an investment. On February 1, 1967, *A* sold his partnership interest to new partner *D*. On May 1, 1967, the partnership sold at a gain the 300 shares of *X* stock (at which time D's holding period for his partnership interest was not more than six months).

Section 1222(1) of the Internal Revenue Code of 1954 defines the term "short-term capital gain" as gain from the sale or exchange of a capital asset held for not more than six months, if and to the extent such gain is taken into account in computing gross income.

Section 1222(3) of the Code defines the term "long-term capital gain" as gain from the sale or exchange of a capital asset held for more than six months, if and to the extent that such gain is taken into account in computing gross income.

Section 702(a) of the Code provides that in determining his income tax, each partner shall take into account separately his distributive share of the partnership's gains and losses from sales or exchanges of capital assets held for more than six months.

Section 702(b) of the Code provides that the character of any item of income, gain, loss, deduction, or credit included in a partner's distributive share under paragraphs (1) through (8) of subsection (a) shall be determined as if such item were realized directly from the source from which realized by the partnership, or incurred in the same manner as incurred by the partnership.

The character of any item of income, gain, loss, deduction, or credit included in a partner's distributive share under paragraphs (1) through (8) of section 702(a) of the code is determined at the partnership level. Compare Revenue Ruling 67-188, C.B. 1967-1, 216.

Since the *ABC* partnership held the *X* stock for more than six months, the gain realized by the partnership is long-term capital gain.

Accordingly, in computing his gross income, *D* should take into account separately in his return, as long-term capital gain, his distributive share of the partnership's long-term capital gain arising from the sale by the partnership of *X* corporation stock held by it as an investment for more than six months, notwithstanding that D has a holding period for his partnership interest of not more than six months.

Demirjian v. Commissioner

457 F.2d 1 (3d Cir. 1972), aff'g 54 T.C. 1691 (1970)

The petitioning taxpayers, Anne and Mabel Dermirjian, have filed a timely petition for review of an adverse decision of the Tax Court affirming a finding of tax deficiencies for 1962 by the Commissioner of Internal Revenue. The tax deficiencies were based on the failure to report $54,835.00 in gain for the taxable year 1962. Plaintiffs maintain that the gain in question is covered by the nonrecognition provisions of Code Section 1033. As pointed out below, we agree with the ruling of the Tax Court that § 703 of the Internal Revenue Code requires that the nonrecognition of gain election and replacement under § 1033 be made by Kin-Bro Realty, a partnership, and that the replacements by plaintiffs individually were thus ineffective.

The facts, as stipulated in the proceedings before the Tax Court, show that Anne and Mabel Demirjian each owned 50% of the stock of Kin-Bro Realty Corporation, which had acquired title to a three-story office building in Newark, New Jersey, in October 1944. On November 3, 1960, the corporation was dissolved and its chief asset, the office building, was conveyed by deed to "Anne Demirjian ... and Mabel Demirjian ... partners trading as Kin-Bro Real Estate Company." Although no formal partnership agreement was executed, Anne and Mabel did file a trade name certificate indicating that they intended to conduct a real estate investment business at the Newark office building under the name of Kin-Bro Real Estate Company. The office building, which constituted Kin-Bro's sole operating asset, was conveyed to the Newark Housing Authority on September 12, 1962, after an involuntary condemnation proceeding. In the deed of conveyance the grantors are listed as "Anne Demirjian and Mabel Demirjian, partners trading as Kin-Bro Real Estate Company." The net proceeds of the sale were distributed to Anne and Mabel in amounts equal to approximately 50% of the total sale price. At this point, both Anne and Mabel apparently elected to replace the property with equivalent property in order to take advantage of the non-recognition of gain provision contained in § 1033 of the Internal Revenue Code. Normally gain resulting from the sale or exchange of investment real property is taxable, but § 1033 provides that if property is involuntarily converted and the proceeds are used to replace it with substantially equivalent property within one year, then gain is recognized only to the extent that the amount received due to the conversion exceeds the purchase price of the replacement property. The reinvestments, however, were made by Anne and Mabel as individuals and not through the partnership. On April 15, 1963, Anne invested $40,934.05 of her share of the proceeds in property which was similar to the condemned property. Mabel was unable to find suitable replacement property within the one-year replacement period, and, by letter of October 17, 1963, she made a written application to the District Director of Internal Revenue, Newark, New Jersey, for an extension of time in which to make such a replacement. In a letter dated January 16, 1964, the District Director stated:

> "In a letter dated October 17, 1963 received from Mr. Ralph Niebart and subsequent correspondence, an extension of time was requested for the purpose of replacing your share of the partnership property that was owned by Kin-Bro Real Estate Company (a partnership). The property was sold to the Housing Authority of the City of Newark on September 12, 1962 under threat of condemnation.

> "You have stated that although you have made a continued effort to replace the converted property, you have not been successful to date.

* * *

> "Based on the information submitted, together with the data already in our file, extension is hereby granted until December 31, 1964, within which to complete the replacement of the converted property."

On February 7, 1964, Mabel invested $45,711.17 in similar real estate. Neither Anne nor Mabel reported any portion of the gain realized on the condemnation sale in their initial returns for the 1962 tax year. In 1964 Anne and Mabel filed amended 1962 joint returns with their husbands, reporting the excess of their distributive share from the condemnation sale over the cost of their respective replacement property as long-term capital gains. The Commissioner of Internal Revenue disagreed with these computations and assessed deficiencies, reasoning that the § 1033 election for nonrecognition of gain and replacement with equivalent property could only be made by the partnership under the terms of § 703(b) of the Code. The Tax Court affirmed the Commissioner's finding of deficiencies and plaintiffs here appeal that decision.

* * *

Petitioners next contend that even if the office building was owned by the partnership, the election and replacement with equivalent property under 26 U.S.C. § 1033(a)(3) were properly made by them in their capacity as individual partners. We agree with the Tax Court's determination that 26 U.S.C. § 703(b) requires that the election and replacement under § 1033 be made by the partnership and that replacement by individual partners of property owned by the partnership does not qualify for nonrecognition of the gain. Section 703(b) provides, with exceptions not relevant here, that any election which affects the computation of taxable income derived from a partnership must be made by the partnership. The election for nonrecognition of gain on the involuntary conversion of property would affect such computation and is the type of election contemplated by § 703(b). The partnership provisions of the Internal Revenue Code treat a partnership as an aggregate of its members for purposes of taxing profits to the individual members and as an entity for purposes of computing and reporting income. In light of this entity approach to reporting income, Congress included § 703(b) to avoid the possible confusion which might result if each partner were to determine partnership income separately only on his own return for his own purposes. To avoid the possible confusion which could result from separate elections under § 1033(a), the election must be made by the partnership as an entity, and the failure of the partnership to so act results in the recognition of the gain on the sale of partnership property.

Petitioners' final contention is that the Commissioner is estopped from denying that a valid election and replacement were made under § 1033. Two separate grounds for estoppel are alleged. The first ground, that the petitioners have conformed their conduct to existing interpretations of the law and the Commissioner may not "invoke a retroactive interpretation to the taxpayer's detriment," is clearly without merit. The second alleged ground is that the Commissioner is estopped by the implicit approval of the individual partner's election and replacement by the District Director for Newark in his letter of January 16, 1964. Even if we were to accept the letter as a justifiable basis for detrimental reliance, petitioners have demonstrated no such reliance and, furthermore, the doctrine of estoppel does not prevent the Commissioner from correcting errors of law.

For the foregoing reasons, the September 1, 1970, orders of the Tax Court, in accordance with its opinion of that date, will be affirmed.

E. Problems

Tabby and Uganda are calendar year taxpayers. They are equal partners in the TU Partnership. The partnership agreement provides that allocations are to be made equally between the partners and that, when the partnership liquidates, distributions are to be made in accordance with capital account balances. The partnership had the following income and expenses during its taxable year that ended on January 31 of the current year:

Gross receipts from inventory sales	$200,000
Cost of goods sold	20,000
Salaries	50,000
Depreciation	8,000
Amortization	4,000
Utility expenses	6,000
Investment interest expense	4,000
Gain from the sale of equipment held for three years	
Section 1245 gain	10,000
Section 1231 gain	2,000
Dividends	7,000
Charitable contributions	1,000
Tax-exempt interest	1,000
Long-term capital gain on sale of Blackacre	6,000
Long-term capital gain on sale of XCo stock	4,000
Short-term capital loss on sale of Whiteacre	2,000
Short-term capital gain on sale of YCo stock	10,000

1. Which items must be separately stated? Why?

2. Which items are not separately stated?

3. When will Tabby and Uganda report the income?

4. Who will be liable for the taxes?

5. Would it matter if the gain on the sale of Blackacre would have been ordinary income if Tabby had sold it individually?

6. Application: Will the partnership hire an accountant to prepare the partnership's tax return? Who makes the decision? How do you know?

F. Advanced Problems — Looking Forward

Without conducting any research, consider the following questions:

1. After the partnership has determined the amount of non-separately stated items and separately stated items, how does the partnership allocate the amounts among the partners? Should allocations be based on partnership interests? Or something else?

2. Why would a partner be willing to be allocated less than his proportionate share of partnership items?

3. Why would a partner be willing to be allocated more than his proportionate share of partnership items?

4. If a partner contributed appreciated property to the partnership, how could the pre-contribution gain be allocated to the contributing partner when the property is sold by the partnership?

5. If a partner contributed depreciated property to the partnership, how could the pre-contribution loss be allocated to the contributing partner when the property is sold by the partnership?

6. Should there be a limit on the amount of deductions or losses a partner could claim? If so, what should that limit be?

7. How should the at risk limitation be applied? Should the limitation be applied at the partner level or the partnership level?

8. How should the passive activity loss limitation be applied? Should the limitation be applied at the partner level or the partnership level?

Chapter 10

Start-Up Costs

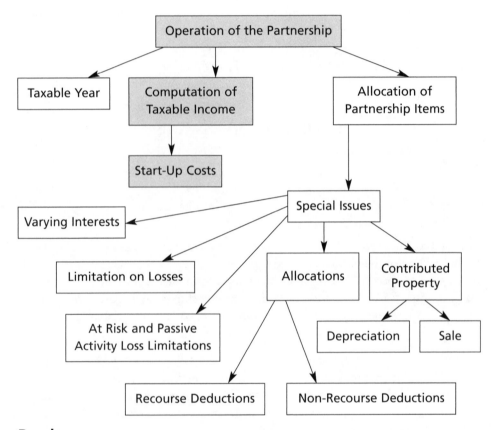

Read:

Code Section 709; 1.709-2.
Treas. Reg. § 1.709-1(a), (b)(1), (2).

A. Background

An individual taxpayer may elect to amortize start-up expenses.[1] In general, start-up expenses include expenses for:

---

1. Code Sec. 195.

- investigating the creation or acquisition of an active business;
- creating an active business; or
- for any activity engaged in for profit and for the production of income before the day on which the active business begins in anticipation of such activity becoming an active business.

To claim start-up expenses, the taxpayer must enter into the business after the expenses were incurred and elect to amortize the expenses.

If he makes the election, the taxpayer can claim a deduction for start-up expenses in the year he begins his business. First, the amount of the deduction is the lesser of two amounts: the total amount of start-up expenditures or $5,000 reduced by the amount by which the start-up expenditures exceed $50,000 (but not below zero). Then, any remaining start-up expenditures are amortized ratably over 180 months beginning in the month the taxpayer begins his business.[2]

B. Discussion of Rules

1. Determination of Expenses That Qualify

A partnership may elect to amortize the cost of organizational expenses.[3] To be an organizational expense, the expense must meet a three-part test.

First, the expense must be incident to the creation of the partnership.[4] To be incident to the creation of the partnership, the expense must have been incurred a reasonable time before the partnership began business and ending before the date its partnership tax return was due to be filed for the year the partnership began business, without taking into consideration any extensions. In contrast, an expense incurred for operating or starting operation of a partnership is not incident to the creation of partnership.[5]

Second, the expense must be one that is chargeable to capital account.[6]

Third, the expense must be of a character that, if expended incident to the creation of a partnership having an ascertainable life, would be amortizable over such life.[7] To satisfy this requirement, the expense should be for an item that would normally benefit the partnership throughout its entire life.[8]

Examples of organizational expenses include:[9]

- Legal fees for services incident to the organization of the partnership such as negotiation and preparation of a partnership agreement or operating agreement;

---

2. Code Sec. 195(b)(1).
3. Code Sec. 709(a), (b)(1).
4. Code Sec. 709(b)(3)(A).
5. Treas. Reg. § 1.709-2(a).
6. Code Sec. 709(b)(3)(B).
7. Code Sec. 709(b)(3)(C).
8. Treas. Reg. § 1.709-2(a).
9. Id.

- Accounting fees for services incident to the organization of the partnership; and
- Filing fees.

Examples of expenses that are not organizational expenses include:[10]

- Expenses connected with acquiring assets for the partnership or transferring assets to the partnership;
- Expenses connected with the admission or removal of partners or members other than at the time the partnership is first organized;
- Expenses connected with a contract relating to the operation of the partnership business; and
- Syndication expenses.

Syndication expenses are expenses connected with the issuing and marketing of interests in the partnership.[11] They include:

- brokerage fees;
- registration fees;
- legal fees of the underwriter or placement agent and the issuer for securities advice and for advice pertaining to the adequacy of tax disclosures in the prospectus or placement memorandum for securities law purposes;
- accounting fees for preparation of representations to be included in the offering materials;
- printing cost of the prospectus;
- printing cost of the placement memorandum; and
- printing cost of other selling and promotional material.

Because syndication expenses do not constitute organizational expenses, they must be capitalized.[12]

To be entitled to make the election to amortize organizational expenses, the partnership must have begun a business.[13] Whether or not a partnership has begun a business is a question of fact, based on all the facts and circumstances.

The mere signing of a partnership agreement is generally insufficient to establish that the partnership has engaged in business. Similarly, mere organizational activities, such as obtaining the certificate or articles of formation, is not sufficient to show the beginning of business. In contrast, if the partnership has the operating assets necessary for the type of business contemplated or otherwise starts the business operations for which it was organized, the partnership has begun business.[14]

2. Making the Election

A partnership is deemed to have made the election for the taxable year in which it begins business. If the partnership wants to forgo the election, it can do so by clearly

---

10. Id.
11. Treas. Reg. § 1.709-2(b).
12. Code Sec. 709(a); Treas. Reg. § 1.709-2(b).
13. Code Sec. 709(b)(1).
14. Treas. Reg. § 1.709-2(c).

electing to capitalize the organizational expenses on the return for the year in which it begins business.[15]

Once the election is made, whether the deemed election to amortize organizational expenses or the election to forgo amortization, it applies to all organizational expenses of the partnership. In addition, the election is irrevocable.[16]

3. Calculating the Amount of the Deduction

The amount the partnership can deduct is determined by a two-step process. First, the partnership can take an amount in the year it begins its business. The amount is the lesser of two amounts: the total amount of organizational expenses or $5,000 reduced by the amount by which the organizational expenses exceed $50,000 (but not below zero). Thus, if the partnership incurs more than $55,000 in organizational expenses, it is not entitled to any deduction under the first step. The expenses must be recovered entirely through the second step.[17] Conversely, if the total amount of organizational expenditures can be claimed under the first step no calculation need be done under the second step.

Under the second step, any remaining organizational expenses are amortized ratably over 180 months beginning in the month the partnership begins business.[18]

Practice Tip: In determining the organizational expenses that can be deducted and amortized, a cash basis method partnership may not amortize organizational expenses until it has actually paid them. [Treas. Reg. § 1.709-1(a).]

If a partnership goes out of business and is liquidated prior to the end of the amortization period, any remaining unamortized organizational expenses can be deducted as provided in Section 165 in the partnership's final taxable year. However, no deduction is allowed with respect to capitalized syndication expenses.[19]

C. Application of Rules

Example 1. The Triangle Partnership incurred $4,000 in organizational expenses and properly elected to amortize them. The partnership can deduct the entire $4,000 in the year it begins its business.

---

15. Treas. Reg. § 1.709-1(b)(2).
16. Treas. Reg. § 1.709-1(b)(3).
17. Code Sec. 709(b)(1)(A).
18. Code Sec. 709(b)(1)(B).
19. Code Sec. 709; Treas. Reg. 1.709-1(b)(3).

Example 2. The Square Partnership incurred $60,000 in organizational expenses and properly elected to amortize them. Under the first step, the partnership can deduct the lesser of two amounts: the total amount of organizational expenses or $5,000 reduced by the amount by which the organizational expenses exceed $50,000 (but not below zero). Because the organizational expenses exceed $50,000 by $10,000, the $5,000 is reduced to zero and the Square Partnership is not entitled to any deduction under the first step.

Under the second step, the Square Partnership may amortize the entire $60,000 of organizational expenses ratably over 180 months beginning in the month the partnership begins business.

Example 3. The Circle Partnership incurred $52,000 in organizational expenses and properly elected to amortize them. Under the first step, the partnership can deduct the lesser of two amounts: the total amount of organizational expenses or $5,000 reduced by the amount by which the organizational expenses exceed $50,000 (but not below zero). Because the organizational expenses exceed $50,000 by $2,000, the Circle Partnership may deduct $3,000 under the first step in the year the partnership begins business.

Under the second step, the Circle Partnership may amortize the remaining $49,000 ($52,000 less $3,000) of organizational expenses ratably over 180 months beginning in the month the partnership begins business.

D. Problems

1. Luxury Limited Partnership is a limited partnership that was formed this year to construct and operate luxury spa resorts. Logan was the developer for the project. He contributed $100,000 in exchange for a general partnership interest. Manny was responsible for selling the limited partnership interests to investors. To assist him in selling the interests, they prepared a prospectus describing the Luxury Limited Partnership interests.

To what extent would the following expenses qualify as organization expenses?

(a) Amounts associated with the formation of the partnership, including:
   (1) Amount paid to Logan for services he provided in organizing the partnership.
   (2) Amount paid to an attorney to draft the partnership agreement.
   (3) State filing fee for formation of the partnership.
   (4) Amount paid to accountant in conjunction with formation of the partnership.

(b) Amounts paid in conjunction with the sale of limited partnership interests, including:
   (1) Amount paid to Manny for his services in selling the limited partnership interests.
   (2) Amount paid to an attorney to prepare offering documents for limited partnership interests.
   (3) Amount paid for preparing and printing the prospectus.

2. The Orange Partnership incurred $5,000 in organizational expenses and properly elected to amortize them. What amount is Orange Partnership entitled to amortize in the first year? In the second year?

3. The Yellow Partnership incurred $80,000 in organizational expenses and properly elected to amortize them. What amount is Yellow Partnership entitled to amortize in the first year? In the second year?

4. The Green Partnership incurred $54,000 in organizational expenses and properly elected to amortize them. What amount is Green Partnership entitled to amortize in the first year? In the second year?

5. Application: Could you provide examples to the soon-to-be partners of the types of expenses that would qualify for amortization as start-up expenses?

Chapter 11

Allocation of Partnership Items

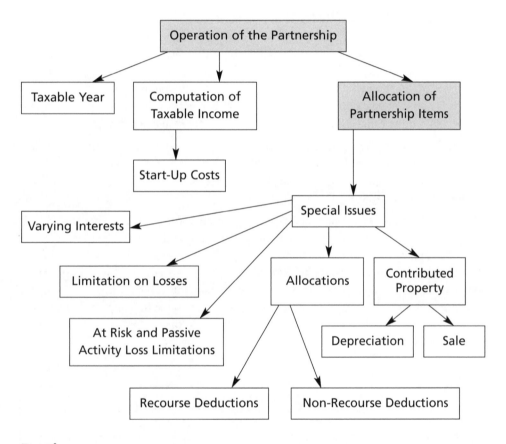

Read:

Code Sections 704(a),(b); 705(a).
Treas. Reg. §§ 1.704-1(a), -1(b)(1)(i), -1(b)(2)(iv)(b), -1(b)(3)(i), -1(b)(3)(ii); 1.705-1(a).

A. Background

Income generated from property owned by more than one taxpayer must be allocated among the owners. Similarly, losses generated from property owned by more than one taxpayer must be allocated among the owners. For example, if Jack and Jill are co-owners of rental property, generally each will report one half of the income and one half of the expenses from the property.

B. Discussion of Rules

1. Allocation of Partnership Items

A partnership can be viewed as an aggregate of the partners or as a separate entity. Recall that the Uniform Partnership Act follows the approach that a partnership is an aggregate of the partners. As such, all property contributed to or acquired by the partnership is partnership property.[1] However, each partner is a co-owner of partnership property with the other partners, holding it as tenants-in-partnership.[2]

The Revised Uniform Partnership Act (RUPA) follows the approach that a partnership is a separate entity.[3] Property acquired by the partnership, either through contribution or direct acquisition, is considered property of the partnership and not of the partners individually.[4]

Under either approach, partnership items generated from such property must be allocated among and reported by the partners. Thus, under the Code, the partnership is treated as an aggregate of the partners for purposes of reporting and paying tax on the partnership's income, gains, deductions, and losses. In general, partnership items are allocated among the partners based on the partnership agreement.[5] If the partnership agreement does not provide an allocation or there is no partnership agreement, the items will be allocated based on the partner's interest in the partnership.[6] The partners report their allocable share on their individual tax return.

Practice Note: An allocation and a distribution are different.
An allocation reflects the partner's distributive share of partnership items that must be reported on his individual income tax return, irrespective of whether the partnership makes a distribution to the partner.
A distribution is a withdrawal from the partnership by the partner of partnership assets. Generally, a distribution is not taxable.

---

1. UPA § 8(1).
2. UPA § 25(1).
3. RUPA § 201(a).
4. RUPA § 203.
5. Code Sec. 704(a); Treas. Reg. § 1.704-1(a).
6. Treas. Reg. § 1.704-1(b)(1)(i).

Partner's interest in the partnership. A partner's interest in the partnership is determined by considering all the facts and circumstances related to the economic arrangement of the partners.[7] Relevant factors to consider include:[8]

- The partners' relative contributions to the partnership;
- The partners' interests in economic profits and losses (if different from their interests in taxable income or loss);
- The partners' interests in cash flow and other non-liquidating distributions; and
- The partners' rights to distributions of capital upon liquidation.

> **Practice Note:** The default rule under RUPA is that the partners share profits equally, regardless of the relative capital contributions of the partners. This result may be inconsistent with the Code, which establishes a default rule that profits are shared based on the partners' relative interests in the partnership. For example, Kari and Laurie formed a partnership with Kari contributing $100 and Laurie contributing $900. Under RUPA, partnership items would be allocated equally between Kari and Laurie. Based on the partners' interests in the partnership, partnership items would be allocated 10 percent to Kari and 90 percent to Laurie.

2. Effect of Allocation on Basis

A partner's basis is increased for any income or gain that is allocated from the partnership to the partner.[9] It is also increased for any tax-exempt income allocated to the partner.[10]

A partner's basis is decreased for any expenses or losses that are allocated to the partner. It is also decreased for any expenses that are not deductible and not properly chargeable to capital account.[11] Examples of nondeductible, non-capital expenditures include illegal bribes and kickbacks, expenses relating to tax-exempt income, and disallowed losses between related parties. However, a partner's outside basis cannot be reduced below zero.[12]

---

7. Code Sec. 709; Treas. Reg. 1.709-1(b)(3).
8. Treas. Reg. § 1.704-1(b)(3)(i).
9. Code Sec. 705(a)(1)(A).
10. Code Sec. 705(a)(1)(B).
11. Code Sec. 705(a)(2).
12. Code Sec. 705(a)(2).

Practice Note: If the partner did not increase his basis by his distributive share of partnership income, he would be taxed again when he sold his partnership interest. Similarly, if he did not reduce his basis by his distributive share of partnership loss, he would be allowed the loss again when he sold his partnership interest.

For example, Max's basis in the partnership is $100,000 and his capital account is $100,000. His distributive share of partnership income for the taxable year is $20,000. He must report the $20,000 on his individual income tax return (and pay the applicable tax).

If Max failed to include his distributive share of partnership income in his basis and immediately sold his interest for $120,000, he would recognize $20,000 of gain (amount realized of $120,000 less basis of $100,000). This would be the result even though there has been no subsequent increase in the value of his partnership interest.

Alternatively, if he includes his distributive share of partnership income in his basis and immediately sells his partnership interest, he would not recognize any gain (amount realized of $120,000 less basis of $120,000). This result is the correct result.

Formula: To reflect the partner's share of partnership items in his outside basis, complete the following steps:

Step 1: Determine the partner's initial outside basis in the partnership.

Step 2: Increase the basis by the partner's allocable share of partnership taxable income and gain (both separately stated and non-separately stated).

Step 3: Increase the basis by the partner's allocable share of tax-exempt income.

Step 4: Decrease the basis by the partner's allocable share of expenses, depreciation, and losses (both separately stated and non-separately stated).

Step 5: Decrease the basis by the partner's allocable share of partnership expenditures that are neither deductible in computing partnership taxable income nor properly chargeable to capital account.

3. Effect of Allocation in Capital Account

A partner's capital account is increased for any book income or gain that is allocated from the partnership to the partner. It is also increased for any book tax exempt income allocated to the partner. The partner's capital account is decreased for any book deductible expenses, depreciation, losses, and nondeductible expenses that are allocated to the partner.

Formula: To reflect the partner's share of partnership items in his capital account, complete the following steps:

Step 1: Determine the partner's initial capital account.

Step 2: Increase the capital account by the partner's allocable share of partnership taxable book income and gain (both separately stated and non-separately stated).

Step 3: Increase the capital account by the partner's allocable share of book tax-exempt income.

Step 4: Decrease the capital account by the partner's allocable share of book expenses, depreciation, and losses (both separately stated and non-separately stated).

Step 5: Decrease the capital account by the partner's allocable share of partnership book expenditures that are neither deductible in computing partnership taxable income nor properly chargeable to capital account.

C. Application of Rules

Example 1. Laura and Matthew formed a general partnership. They each contributed $10,000. The partnership agreement does not address how the partnership will allocate partnership items. However, it does require that capital accounts be maintained in accordance with the regulations. In addition it provides that, when the partnership is liquidated, distributions must be made based on capital account balances.

Because the partnership agreement does not provide for an allocation, partnership items are allocated based on the partner's interest in the partnership. Because Laura and Matthew each contributed the same amount on formation and distributions will be made based on capital account balances, the facts indicate it is an equal partnership and the allocations will be made equally between Laura and Matthew.

Example 2. Nihna and Ollie are equal partners in the Grand Partnership and the partnership agreement provides that partnership items are allocated based on the partner's ownership interest.

Prior to allocation of partnership items for the year, Nihna's basis was $90,000 and her capital account was $100,000. Ollies's basis was $70,000 and his capital account was $100,000. For the year, the partnership had the following items:

Item	Amount
Net taxable income	$100,000
Long-term capital gain	400,000
Short-term capital loss	100,000

Because Nihna and Ollie are equal partners, the partnership items are allocated equally. Each partner would adjust his or her outside basis and his or her capital account as follows:

	Nihna		Ollie	
	Basis	Cap. Acct.	Basis	Cap. Acct.
Intial	90,000	100,000	70,000	100,000
Taxable income	50,000	50,000	50,000	50,000
LTCG	200,000	200,000	200,000	200,000
STCL	<50,000>	<50,000>	<50,000>	<50,000>
	290,000	300,000	270,000	300,000

Example 3. Oscar is a partner in the Little Partnership. He owns a one-quarter interest and the partnership agreement provides that partnership items are allocated based on the partner's ownership interest. Prior to allocation of partnership items for the year, his outside basis was $100,000 and his capital account was $100,000.

For the year, the partnership had $400,000, which it invested entirely in tax-exempt bonds. The bonds earned $40,000 of interest during the year. Oscar's share of the tax-exempt interest was $10,000. Thus, his basis is increased from $100,000 to $110,000 ($100,000 beginning basis plus $10,000 of tax-exempt interest). His capital account is increased from $100,000 to $110,000 ($100,000 beginning balance plus $10,000 of tax-exempt interest).

If he sold his partnership interest, he could sell it for his share of the partnership capital. The partnership has $440,000 of cash, and his one-quarter share would be $110,000. Note that this is also the amount reflected in his capital account. He would have no gain or loss to report (amount realized of $110,000 less outside basis of $110,000).

If his basis had not been adjusted for the tax-exempt interest, it would have been $100,000. His one-quarter share of the partnership capital would still have been $110,000, the amount reflected in his capital account. And, he would have had to report $10,000 of gain on the sale of his partnership interest (amount realized of $110,000 less outside basis of $100,000). Thus, even though the increase in partnership assets was due entirely to tax-exempt interest, Oscar would indirectly be paying tax on that interest. To prevent this result, his outside basis must be increased to reflect his share of partnership tax-exempt income.

D. Cases and Materials

Estate of Tobias v. Commissioner
T.C. Memo. 2001-37

These consolidated cases are before the Court to decide the motion for summary judgment filed by the Estate of James R. Tobias and Ms. V. Pauline Tobias, the cross-motion for summary judgment filed by Mr. Darwin R. Tobias, Sr., and Ms. Shirley I. Tobias, and the cross-motion for summary judgment filed by respondent. The principal issues for decision in these cases involve the allocation of income pursuant to section 704 from an animal farm business. All section references in this opinion are to the Internal Revenue Code as in effect during the years in issue, unless specified otherwise.

Respondent's determinations have the effect of allocating all of the income from the business for the years 1991 and 1993 to Mr. James R. Tobias and allocating 50 percent of the income from the same business for the years 1990, 1991, and 1993 to Mr. Darwin R. Tobias.

BACKGROUND

* * *

Circa 1960, James and Darwin orally agreed to operate an animal farm business as partners, but they never reduced their agreement to writing. Their agreement was general and did not include specific terms regarding how they would operate the business. For example, they never agreed to a specific division of labor. Over the years James spent a disproportionately greater amount of time and effort developing and expanding the business than his brother, Darwin. Each of the brothers had independent means of earning a living, and neither received a salary for his services to the business. It is not clear from the record whether they opened a bank account specifically for the business or whether they used an existing account, but it is clear that both of their signatures were required on checks drawn on the account.

The operation of the animal farm business took place primarily on land owned by James and his wife. Darwin also owned land that was farmed for the benefit of the animal farm business. In 1972, the brothers agreed that the business should pay rent for the use of each brother's personal land by the business. While Darwin often received his land rents, James frequently deferred his land rents until the business had the funds available to pay him.

In addition to using their land for business purposes, each brother occasionally made expenditures for the business with his own funds. Except for the reimbursement of some business expenses and the payment of land rents, neither brother received a distribution from the animal farm business. All profits were reinvested in the business.

In 1986, the brothers' relationship became acrimonious. James evicted Darwin from the business and prohibited him from coming onto the business premises. After his eviction, Darwin did not participate in the business or receive a distribution of any kind from the business. James continued to operate the animal farm business at least through December 31, 1993.

Following James' actions, on October 21, 1986, Darwin sued James in the Court of Common Pleas for Dauphin County, Pennsylvania (hereinafter State court), alleging that the business was an equally owned partnership. Darwin sought dissolution of the partnership and an accounting. See Tobias v. Tobias, No. 4583 (Ct. C.P. Dauphin County, Pa. July 7, 1992). On July 7, 1992, the State court issued its opinion holding that the animal farm business was a partnership under Pennsylvania State law (hereinafter the 1992 State court opinion). The State court found that Darwin had been "wrongfully excluded from the business" and was entitled to dissolution of the partnership and an accounting. In considering the question whether the partnership was an equal partnership, the State court found that James' contributions to the partnership far exceeded Darwin's contributions and that an inequity would be visited on James if the profits of the business were shared equally. The State court ordered that each partner be repaid his capital contributions before the profits of the partnership were divided equally between them. The order of the State court stated as follows:

> AND NOW, this 7 day of JULY, 1992, WE FIND that the business was operated on a partnership basis; the assets of the business are as set forth in this opinion. Plaintiff is entitled to dissolution of the partnership and an accounting. The profits will be shared equally after the partners are repaid their contribution as provided by the act.
>
> Unless an appeal is filed within thirty (30) days the court will appoint a Master to determine the asset valuation and disposition of assets.

The State court entered a second opinion on January 6, 1997, after 16 days of hearings, resolving differences between the brothers over an account of the business that had been filed by James and excepted to by Darwin (hereinafter the 1997 State court opinion). In the 1997 State court opinion, the State court determined that James had made capital contributions to the partnership of $1,001,558.60, that Darwin had made capital contributions to the partnership of $2,320, and that the partnership had $23,311.87 in its bank accounts. The court ordered payment of the outstanding liabilities of the partnership totaling $23,335.47. The court also ordered the sale of partnership equipment at a public auction, with all profits from the sale to be deposited into the partnership bank account. The partnership equipment included various pieces of restaurant equipment, such as a popcorn machine and an ice cream freezer, and various pieces of agricultural or farming equipment, such as a hay rake and a baler. Finally, the State court found that the partnership owned no land but that the value of certain fixtures and improvements to land occupied by the partnership was $144,234.

The State court ordered all partnership assets remaining after payment of partnership liabilities, including cash, to be distributed to James' estate "to repay on a dollar-for-dollar basis to the extent of such assets the contributions to capital made by James R. Tobias." The State court allocated none of the remaining partnership assets to Darwin. It is implicit in the order of the State court that the proceeds from the sale of the equipment would not equal James' disproportionately large capital contributions.

From 1965 until 1992, James treated the animal farm business as a sole proprietorship and reported the entire income from the business on his individual tax returns. After the State court found that the business was a partnership, James caused the partnership to file returns for the years 1990 through 1993. Darwin did not participate in the preparation or filing of the partnership returns.

* * *

None of the parties to the instant cases claims that there is a partnership agreement under which either partner's distributive share of income, gain, loss, deduction, or credit can be determined, as provided by section 704(a). This is consistent with the fact that James and Darwin did not enter into a written partnership agreement and the fact that their oral agreement was merely an informal, general agreement to operate an animal farm and did not contain any specific terms.

Because there is no partnership agreement in these cases, there is no need to address the estate's "alternative" argument that a 50–50 allocation of partnership income has substantial economic effect. See Brooks v. Commissioner, T.C. Memo. 1995-400; Mammoth Lakes Project Lakes Project v. Commissioner, T.C. Memo. 1991-4.

All of the parties to the instant cases take the position that the subject income must be allocated in accordance with each partner's interest in the partnership, as provided by section 704(b)(1). Accordingly, we must determine the interests of James and Darwin in the subject animal farm partnership.

The regulations promulgated under section 704 define the phrase "partner's interest in the partnership" as the "manner in which the partners have agreed to share the economic benefit or burden (if any) corresponding to the income, gain, loss, deduction, or credit (or item thereof) that is allocated." Sec. 1.704-1(b)(3)(i), Income Tax Regs. The regulations also provide that the determination of a partner's interest shall be made by taking into account all facts and circumstances relating to the economic arrangement of the partners. See sec. 1.704-1(b)(3)(i), Income Tax Regs., Specifically, section 1.704-1(b)(3)(ii), Income Tax Regs., provides that the following four factors shall be considered in determining a partner's interest in the partnership: (1) The partners' relative contributions to capital; (2) the partners' interests in economic profits and losses; (3) the partners' interests in cash-flow and other nonliquidating distributions; and (4) the rights of the partners to distributions of capital upon liquidation of the partnership. See Vecchio v. Commissioner, supra at 193; PNRC Ltd. Partnership v. Commissioner, T.C. Memo. 1993-335.

The first factor, the partners' relative capital contributions, was discussed in the 1997 State court opinion. The State court found that James' capital contributions totaled $1,001,568.60 and Darwin's contributions totaled $2,320. The parties to the instant cases do not challenge the findings of the State court regarding the capital contributions of each partner.

The 1997 State court opinion does not set forth the dates on which James made his contributions, but from our review of the 1992 and 1997 State court opinions, we conclude that a substantial percentage of James' contributions, at least $700,000, was made before the years in issue. According to the 1997 State court opinion, all of Darwin's contributions, in the aggregate amount of $2,320, were made before the years in issue.

The second factor to consider in determining a partner's interest in the partnership is the partner's interest in economic profits and losses. The 1992 State court opinion states that the partners would share the profits of the business after they were repaid their capital contributions.

The third factor to consider in determining a partner's interest in the partnership is the partner's interest in cash-flow and other nonliquidating distributions. Although all of the profits of the business were reinvested in the business, James and Darwin were reimbursed for various business expenses that they personally incurred. However, after his eviction in 1986, Darwin did not personally incur any business expenses because he did not participate in the business. Thus, for the years in issue, Darwin did not have any interest in the cash-flow or other nonliquidating distributions of the business.

The fourth factor to consider in determining a partner's interest in the partnership is the partner's right to distributions of capital upon liquidation of the partnership. This factor requires that we determine how the partnership would have been liquidated in each of the years in issue. This factor is directly related to the capital contributions of each partner. As discussed earlier, the State court determined that James' contributions,

$1,001,568.60, substantially exceeded Darwin's contributions, $2,320, and our review of the State court opinions suggests that James had contributed a substantial amount of the total, at least $700,000, before the years in issue.

Furthermore, the partnership returns filed by James report total assets for 1990 through 1993 of $171,769, $164,956, $166,836, and $200,135, respectively. This is corroborated by the 1997 State court opinion, which found that the value of the assets of the partnership was in approximately the same order of magnitude. Thus, the value of partnership assets did not approach the total of James' disproportionately large capital contributions for any of the years in issue. Accordingly, if the partnership had been liquidated at any time during the years in issue, all of the partnership assets would have been distributed to James. It is evident, therefore, that during each of the years in issue James bore the economic benefit of 100 percent of the income realized by the partnership. See sec. 1.704-1(b)(3), Income Tax Regs.

* * *

On the basis of the four factors listed in section 1.704-1(b)(3)(ii), Income Tax Regs., and all the facts and circumstances of these cases, we find that during each of the years in issue James had a 100-percent interest in the partnership income and Darwin had a zero interest in the partnership income. Accordingly, we agree with respondent and Darwin that 100 percent of the income of the partnership during the years in issue should be allocated to James.

On the basis of the foregoing,

Orders will be entered denying petitioners' motion for summary judgment filed in the case at docket No. 19756-97, granting petitioners' cross-motion for summary judgment filed in the case at docket No. 19757-97, and granting respondent's cross-motion for summary judgment filed in the case at docket No. 19756-97, and decisions will be entered for respondent in the case at docket No. 19756-97, and for petitioners in the case at docket No. 19757-97.

E. Problems

1. Tabby and Uganda are calendar year taxpayers. They are equal partners in the TU Partnership. The partnership agreement provides that allocations are to be made equally between the partners and that, when the partnership liquidates, distributions are to be made in accordance with capital account balances. The partnership had the following income and expenses during its taxable year that ended on January 31 of the current year:

Gross receipts from inventory sales	$200,000
Cost of goods sold	20,000
Salaries	50,000
Depreciation	8,000
Amortization	4,000

Utility expenses	6,000
Investment interest expense	4,000
Gain from the sale of equipment held for three years	
Section 1245 gain	10,000
Section 1231 gain	2,000
Dividends	7,000
Charitable contributions	1,000
Tax-exempt interest	1,000
Long-term capital gain on sale of Blackacre	6,000
Long-term capital gain on sale of XCo stock	4,000
Short-term capital loss on sale of Whiteacre	2,000
Short-term capital gain on sale of YCo stock	10,000

Assume this is the first year of partnership operations. At the beginning of the year, Tabby's basis in her partnership interest was $60,000, and Uganda's basis in his partnership interest was $40,000 and Tabby and Uganda's capital accounts were both $100,000.

(a) What will be the tax consequences of TU Partnership's first year operations to Tabby and Uganda?

(b) What will be the consequences of TU Partnership's first year operations to Tabby and Uganda's capital accounts?

---

2. Application:

(a) If there is no partnership agreement, what is the default rule in the jurisdiction in which you practice for how profits and losses are shared among the partners?

(b) How would you explain to the partners what the tax consequences of partnership allocations are? How would you explain to them how the default rule works?

(c) How would you explain to the partners the difference between an allocation and a distribution from the partnership?

(d) Draft language for a partnership agreement setting forth how partnership items should be allocated among the partners.

F. Advanced Problems—Looking Forward

Without conducting any research, consider the following questions:

1. How should partnership items be allocated among the partners if a partner was not a partner in the partnership for the entire year?

2. How should a distribution of cash from the partnership to a partner be treated?

3. How should a distribution of property from the partnership to the partner be treated? Would you have any concerns if that property had previously been contributed to the partnership by a different partner?

4. Why would a partner be willing to be allocated less than his proportionate share of partnership items based on his ownership interest?

5. Why would a partner be willing to be allocated more than his proportionate share of partnership items based on his ownership interest?

6. If a partner contributed appreciated property to the partnership, how could the pre-contribution gain be allocated to the contributing partner when the property is sold by the partnership?

7. If a partner contributed depreciated property to the partnership, how could the pre-contribution loss be allocated to the contributing partner when the property is sold by the partnership?

8. Should there be a limit on the amount of deductions or losses a partner could claim? If so, what should that limit be?

9. How should the at risk limitation be applied? Should the limitation be applied at the partner level or the partnership level?

10. How should the passive activity loss limitation be applied? Should the limitation be applied at the partner level or the partnership level?

Chapter 12

Varying Interests in the Partnership

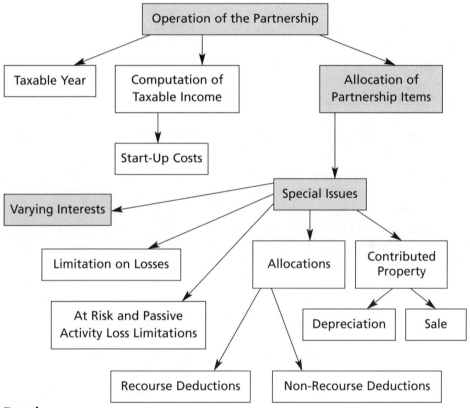

Read:

Code Section 706(c)(2)(B), (d)(1), (d)(2).
Treas. Reg. § 1.706-1(c)(4).

A. Discussion of Rules

A partner's interest in the partnership can change during the year for a number of reasons, including the entry of a new partner or a partner making a capital contribution. However, the partnership's taxable year does not close when there is a change. Rather, each partner's distributive share of partnership income or loss is determined by taking into account such varying interests in the partnership during the year.

> **Practice Tip:** The rules that apply to varying interests in a partnership are designed to disallow the allocation of an entire year's worth of deductions and losses to a partner who joins the partnership towards the end of the year.

To determine the amount allocated to each partner when their interests have varied over the year, either of two methods may be used. First, under the interim closing of the books method, income and deductions are traced back to the time they are paid or incurred. A partner is entitled to a share of items paid or incurred while he is a partner in the partnership.

In determining when items are paid by the partnership, a cash basis taxpayer must allocate certain items to when they were economically attributable, irrespective of when they are paid. In essence, it places a cash basis taxpayer on the accrual basis with respect to certain items. The items that must be so allocated are called "allocable cash basis items" and include interest, taxes, payments for services or for the use of property, and items specified by the Internal Revenue Service.[1]

If a cash basis item is allocable to a period before the year of payment, it is assigned entirely to the first day of the year. Then, the item is allocated among those partners who were partners at the time the deduction accrued based on their ownership interest at that time. If the payment is allocable to a period after the year of the payment, it is assigned entirely to the last day of the year.[2] If a partner would be entitled to an allocable share of the deduction but is no longer a partner in the partnership, that portion of the deduction must be capitalized and added to the basis of the partnership's assets.

Alternatively, under the proration method, all partnership items are prorated over the taxable year. Then, each partner's share of the items is determined by the number of days he is a partner in the partnership.

B. Application of Rules

Example 1. Angie, Brassie, and Charles are equal partners in the Change Partnership, a cash basis taxpayer. On July 1, Delilah joins the partnership, acquiring a one-quarter interest. On February 1, the partnership pays $3,000 for supplies and on August 1, the partnership pays $20,000 to settle a breach of contract suit.

---

1. Code Sec. 706(d)(2)(A), (d)(2)(B).
2. Code Sec. 706(d)(2).

If Change Partnership uses the interim closing of the books method, Angie, Brassie, and Charles are entitled to an allocation of one-third of all items received or paid during January through June. Thus, each of the three partners is entitled to be allocated $1,000 of the expense deduction with respect to the supplies.

Similarly, Angie, Brassie, Charles, and Delilah are entitled to an allocation of one-quarter of all items received or paid during July through December. Thus, each of the four partners is entitled to be allocated $5,000 of the deduction with respect to the settlement payment.

For the year, Angie, Brassie, and Charles each would be allocated a total of $6,000 ($1,000 from the supplies and $5,000 from the contract settlement) and Delilah would be allocated a total of $5,000 (from the contract settlement).

Example 2. Essex, Fannie, and Gerta are equal partners in the Alteration Partnership, a cash basis taxpayer. The partnership uses the interim closing of the books method. On November 1, Hillie joins the partnership, acquiring a one-quarter interest. On December 15, the partnership pays $50,000 in rent for the year.

Under the interim closing of the books method, Hillie would be allocated one-quarter of the rent. However, rent is an "allocable cash basis item." Accordingly, the partnership must allocate the rent to when it is economically attributable, irrespective of when it was paid; the rent is allocated ratably over the year. Allocation of the deduction would be as follows:

Partner	Ownership	Months	Computation	Partner Allocation
Essex	one-third	10	10/12 × 1/3 × 50,000	$13,888
	one-fourth	2	2/12 × 1/4 × 50,000	2,084
Fannie	one-third	10	10/12 × 1/3 × 50,000	13,889
	one-fourth	2	2/12 × 1/4 × 50,000	2,083
Gerta	one-third	10	10/12 × 1/3 × 50,000	13,889
	one-fourth	2	2/12 × 1/4 × 50,000	2,083
Hillie	one-fourth	2	2/12 × 1/4 × 50,000	2,084
Total				$50,000

For the year, Essex, Fannie, and Gerta each would be allocated $15,972 of the rent. Hillie would be allocated $2,084 of the rent.

Example 3. Ignatius, Julia, and Kirk are equal partners in the Transformation Partnership. Transformation Partnership uses the proration method. On December 1, Lonnie joins the partnership, acquiring a one-quarter interest. The partnership has a $40,000 net loss for the year.

The loss must be prorated among the partners based on their interest in Transformation Partnership. Allocation of the loss would be as follows:

Partner	Ownership	Months	Computation	Share of Loss
Ignatius	one-third	11	11/12 × 1/3 × $40,000	$12,222
	one-fourth	1	1/12 × 1/4 × $40,000	833
Julia	one-third	11	11/12 × 1/3 × $40,000	12,222
	one-fourth	1	1/12 × 1/4 × $40,000	833

Kirk	one-third	11	11/12 × 1/3 × $40,000	12,223
	one-fourth	1	1/12 × 1/4 × $40,000	833
Lonnie	one-fourth	1	1/12 × 1/4 × $40,000	834
Total				$40,000

For the year, Ignatius, Julia, and Kirk each would be allocated $13,055 of the loss. Lonnie would be allocated $834 of the loss.

C. Problems

1. Fletch and Gracie are equal partners in the Fun Partnership, an accrual basis taxpayer. On April 1, Fletch contributed additional cash to the partnership. After the contribution, Fletch owned three-fourths of the partnership and Gracie owned one-quarter of the partnership.

During the year, Fun Partnership earns $24,000 in profits. If the partnership uses the interim closing of the books method of allocation, how will the profits be allocated?

2. Henry and Ida Mae are equal partners in the Travel Partnership, a cash basis taxpayer. On April 1, Henry contributed additional cash to the partnership. After the contribution, Henry owned three-fourths of the partnership and Ida Mae owned one-quarter of the partnership.

(a) During the year, Travel Partnership earns $24,000 in profits. If the partnership uses the proration method of allocation, how will the profits be allocated?

(b) On January 1, Travel Partnership paid $24,000 in rent for the year. If the partnership uses the interim closing of the book method of allocation, how will the rent expense be allocated?

(c) Travel Partnership incurred a $20,000 expense on February 1 and paid the amount on November 1. If the partnership uses the interim closing of the book method of allocation, how will the expense be allocated?

(d) During the prior year, Travel Partnership incurred a $20,000 expense for rent, but paid the amount February 1 of the current year. If the partnership uses the interim closing of the book method of allocation, how will the rent expense be allocated?

3. Application:

(a) Who makes the decision as to which method, interim closing of the books or proration method, will be used by the partnership?

(b) Draft language for the partnership agreement that states which method will be used by the partnership.

Chapter 13

Limitation on Losses

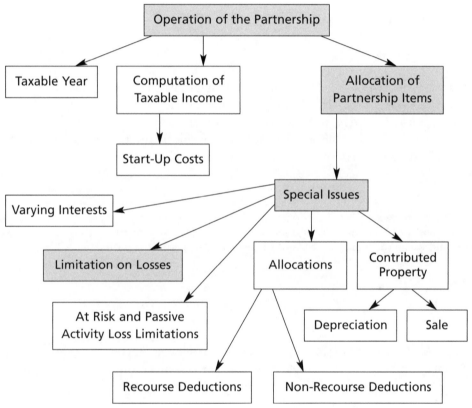

Read:

Code Section 704(d); 705(a)(2).

Treas. Reg. § 1.704-1(d).

A. Background

Basis reflects the taxpayer's tax investment in an item. For example, basis equals the cost of property. If the property is depreciable, the taxpayer can claim depreciation, reducing the asset's basis by the amount of depreciation allowed or allowable. However, when the basis has been reduced to zero, no further depreciation is allowed.

B. Discussion of Rules

1. Losses in Excess of Basis

A partner's basis in his partnership interest, to an extent, reflects his tax investment in the partnership. Just as when no additional depreciation is permitted when the basis of an asset reaches zero, no deductions (whether expenses, depreciation, losses, etc.) are permitted once the partner's basis in his partnership interest reaches zero.[1]

2. Carry Forward of Deferred Loss

Any loss that is not allowed because of an insufficiency of basis is deferred and carried forward until it can be used.[2] If necessary, the character of the loss allowed and the character of the loss deferred must be determined based on the composition of the loss.[3] The partner can deduct the proportion that each loss item bears to the total of all the partner's allocated partnership losses for the year. Losses that have been carried forward can be claimed by the partner when his basis rises above zero and continues to be above zero after current year losses are taken into consideration.

> **Practice Alert:** If a partner gifts his partnership interest or transfers his interest as part of his estate, it is unclear whether the new partner succeeds to any loss that was disallowed and carried forward by the transferor partner.

C. Application of Rules

Example 1. Omega's basis in the partnership is $10,000. At the end of the partnership's taxable year, she was allocated $12,000 of the partnership's ordinary loss. Omega may claim only $10,000 of the loss. Thus, her basis in the partnership is reduced to zero and she carries forward a $2,000 ordinary loss.

Example 2. Posh's basis in the partnership is $6,000. At the end of the partnership's taxable year, she was allocated $10,000 of the partnership's loss. Of the $10,000 of loss, $2,500 is a capital loss and $7,500 is an ordinary loss.

Posh may claim only $6,000 of loss, while $4,000 must be deferred. To determine the character of the loss allowed, a proportionate share of each character of loss must be allowed.

---

1. Code Secs. 705(a)(2); 704(d).
2. Code Sec. 704(d).
3. Treas. Reg. § 1.704-1(d)(4) Ex. 3.

$\dfrac{\$2,500}{\$10,000} \times \$6,000 = \$1,500$ capital loss is allowed

$\dfrac{\$7,500}{\$10,000} \times \$6,000 = \$4,500$ ordinary loss is allowed

To determine the character of the loss deferred, a proportionate share of each character must be deferred.

$\dfrac{\$2,500}{\$10,000} \times \$4,000 = \$1,000$ capital loss is deferred and carried forward

$\dfrac{\$7,500}{\$10,000} \times \$4,000 = \$3,000$ ordinary loss is deferred and carried forward

The $1,000 of capital loss and $3,000 of ordinary loss are carried forward, indefinitely, until they can be used.

In the subsequent year, Posh was allocated $10,000 of the partnership's net income. Her basis was increased to $10,000. In addition, she will be able to claim the $4,000 of loss carried forward, reducing her basis to $6,000.

D. Problems

1. Greg and Hank are equal partners. Greg's outside basis is $10,000. Hank's outside basis is $5,000.

(a) During the current year, the partnership has gross income of $40,000 and an ordinary $60,000 loss. What are Greg and Hank's basis at the end of the year?

(b) In the second year, the partnership has gross income of $50,000 and a $10,000 expense. What are Greg and Hank's basis at the end of the year?

(c) In the third year, the partnership has gross income of $10,000, an ordinary loss of $70,000 and a short-term capital loss of $40,000. What are Greg and Hank's basis at the end of the year?

2. Application:

(a) How will you explain to the partners what impact their outside basis can have on their ability to claim an allocable share of loss?

(b) How will each partner know what his outside basis is?

(c) If a partner anticipates having a low outside basis and being allocated losses, how might the partner increase his basis so that he can claim his allocable share of losses?

E. Advanced Problems — Looking Forward

Without conducting any research, consider the following questions:

1. Should a partner who sells his partnership interest be entitled to offset any gain from the sale with suspended losses?

2. Should a taxpayer who purchases a partnership interest be permitted to use the selling partner's suspended losses?

3. How should a distribution of cash from the partnership to a partner be treated?

4. How should a partner "draw" from a partnership be treated?

5. How should a distribution of property from the partnership to the partner be treated? Would you have any concerns if that property had previously been contributed to the partnership by a different partner?

6. Is the order in which adjustments are made to a partner's outside basis important? Why? In what order should the adjustments be made?

Chapter 14

At Risk and Passive Activity Loss Limitation

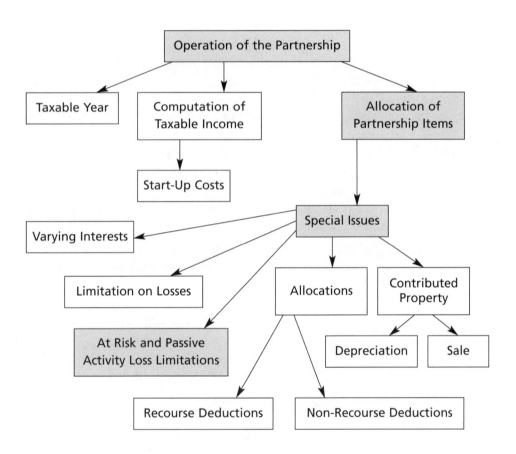

Read:

Code Sections 465(a)(1), (2), (b), (c)(1), (c)(2), (c)(3), (d), (e); 469(a), (b), (c), (d)(1), (e)(1)(A), (e)(3), (g)(1), (h)(1), (h)(2), (k); 772(a), (c)(2), (c), (d)(1), (f).
Temp. Reg. § 1.469-5T(a), (b)(2), (e).

A. Background

1. State Law

Under the default rules of the Uniform Partnership Act and the Revised Uniform Partnership Act, all partners have equal rights in the management and conduct of the partnership.[1] Under the Uniform Limited Partnership Act (2001), each general partner has equal rights in the management and conduct of the limited partnership's activities.[2]

2. At Risk Limitation

In response to the proliferation of tax shelters, Congress enacted the at risk limitation. The premise of the limitation mirrors similar limitations found in the Code. For example, the total amount of depreciation a taxpayer can claim cannot exceed what the taxpayer paid for the asset, its basis. The amount of loss a taxpayer can claim cannot exceed his remaining tax investment in the property, the property's adjusted basis. The maximum amount of loss a partner can claim from a partnership cannot exceed the partner's outside basis.

The at risk limitation similarly focuses on the taxpayer's investment. However, the provision focuses on the taxpayer's investment in an activity as opposed to a single asset. In general, the provision limits the amount of losses a taxpayer can claim from an activity to the amount the taxpayer is at risk.[3]

Loss. In this context, a "loss" is the extent to which deductions exceed income and gain from the activity.[4] Any loss that is disallowed may be carried forward to the following year.[5]

Example: Jaline is involved in a business activity. Her share of the activity's income is $1,000. Her share of the activity's deductions is $1,500. Accordingly, she has a net loss of $500 ($1,000 income, less $1,500 deduction) from the activity. The amount of the loss she may claim from the activity may be limited by the at risk provision.

Activity. The at risk limitation applies to any activity engaged in by the taxpayer in carrying on a business or for the production of income.[6]

---

1. UPA §18(e), RUPA §401(f).
2. ULPA §406(a).
3. Code Sec. 465(a)(1).
4. Code Sec. 465(d).
5. Code Sec. 465(a)(2).
6. Code Sec. 465(c).

Amount at risk. The at risk amount is intended to measure the amount a taxpayer could actually lose through an activity. A taxpayer's initial at risk amount for each activity is the total of:

- Cash contributed;
- The adjusted basis of property contributed by the taxpayer to the activity;
- The fair market value of property not contributed to the activity but used to secure a debt of the activity; and
- Any financing for which the taxpayer is personally liable.

In determining a taxpayer's at risk amount, he may include any "qualified non-recourse" financing. In general, qualified non-recourse financing is a non-recourse debt that is obtained from a commercial lender or the government,[7] is incurred with respect to holding real property, and is secured by the property.[8]

Formula: A taxpayer is initially at risk to the extent of the following amounts:
- Cash contributed;
- The adjusted basis of property contributed by the taxpayer to the activity;
- The fair market value of property not contributed to the activity but used to secure a debt of the activity;
- Any financing for which the taxpayer is personally liable; and
- Qualified non-recourse financing.

As the taxpayer continues his involvement in the activity, his initial amount at risk is increased by his share of income and additional contributions to the activity and decreased by his share of losses and distributions from the activity.[9]

Formula: A taxpayer's at risk amount is adjusted each year to reflect changes in the taxpayer's at risk amount in the activity. Specifically, the following adjustments are made to the taxpayer's at risk amount:

Initial amount or previous year's amount at risk
+ Share of income
+ Additional contributions
− Share of losses
− <u>Distributions</u>
At risk amount

---

7. In general, if the amount is borrowed from a related person, a person from whom the taxpayer acquired the real property, or a person who received a fee with respect to the investment, the amount generally is not qualified non-recourse financing. Code Sec. 465(b)(6). A loan from a related party may be treated as non-recourse financing if the loan is commercially reasonable and on the same terms as loans to unrelated people. Code Sec. 465(b)(6)(D)(ii).

8. Code Sec. 465(b). Qualified non-recourse financing does not include money borrowed from the seller or from a person who receives a fee with respect to the taxpayer's investment. Code Sec. 465(b)(6)(D).

9. Code Sec. 465(b)(5).

Example: Goldie invested $50,000 in a construction business. In the first year, the business generated a $30,000 loss (*i.e.*, the amount of the expenses and deductions from the business exceeded the income from the business by $30,000).

The construction business is an activity for purposes of the at risk limitation. Goldie's initial at risk amount is $50,000, the amount of her cash investment in the business.

Because her at risk amount is larger than the loss from the activity, Goldie may claim the $30,000 loss on her tax return. And, at the end of the first year of operations, her at risk amount is reduced by the $30,000 loss, or from $50,000 to $20,000.

In the second year, the business again generated a $30,000 loss. Because her at risk amount is only $20,000, the amount of loss she can claim on her tax return is $20,000. Her at risk limitation is reduced by the loss allowed, or from $20,000 to zero. She can carry forward the remaining $10,000 loss ($30,000 loss from the activity, less the $20,000 she was allowed to claim) until her at risk amount increases.

Practice Tip: A loss that is disallowed and carried forward because the taxpayer is not at risk is treated as a loss in the next year. There is no limit on the number of years a loss can be carried forward.

3. Passive Activity Loss Limitation

When Congress determined that the at risk limitation was insufficient to curb the use of tax shelters, it enacted the passive activity loss limitation. The provision takes a completely different approach. It focuses on classifying activities into different categories, rather than on the amount of a taxpayer's investment in a particular activity.

Activity. The taxpayer must determine the separate business activities in which he is engaged.[10] The regulations provide guidance regarding what constitutes an activity for purposes of the at risk limitations.[11]

Passive activities. The limitation applies to all passive activities. An activity in which the taxpayer is paid compensation for services (*e.g.*, salary, wages) is not a passive activity for that taxpayer.[12] Portfolio income and expenses (*e.g.*, interest, dividends, and

---

10. Code Sec. 469(c)(1).
11. Treas. Reg. §1.469-4.
12. Code Sec. 469(e)(3).

royalties) are not from a passive activity.[13] For all other activities, the determination of whether the activity is a passive activity depends on whether the taxpayer materially participated in the activity.[14]

Material participation. A taxpayer materially participates in an activity if he is involved in the activity on a regular, continuous, and substantial basis.[15] Some activities, such as a rental real estate activity or holding limited partnership interests, are treated as passive activities regardless of whether the taxpayer materially participates.[16]

Passive activity loss limitation. First, the taxpayer must determine the amount of net gain or loss from each separate passive activity. Next, the gains and losses from the separate passive activities are netted together.[17] If there is a net gain, the net gain is reported by the taxpayer. If there is a net loss, a net passive activity loss, the taxpayer is not entitled to claim the loss on his tax return.[18] Rather, the loss is deferred and carried forward.[19] Similarly, a credit from a passive activity is allowed only to the extent it offsets the tax liability of a passive activity. To the extent the credit is not allowed, it is deferred and carried forward.[20] Suspended losses are allowed in full in the year the taxpayer disposes of his interest in the activity.[21]

There are a few exceptions to the passive activity loss limitation. For example, if a taxpayer owns at least 10 percent of a rental real estate activity and actively participates in the activity, he may deduct up to $25,000 of losses from the rental real estate activity each year.[22]

Example: Hannah owned rental property. She collected the monthly rents, paid all the expenses, interviewed potential tenants, and handled any issues that arose regarding the property. In the first year, the rental business generated a loss of $30,000.

The rental real estate activity is a passive activity, regardless of whether Hannah materially participated in the activity. However, Hannah owns more than 10 percent of the activity and actively participated in the activity. Accordingly, under the exception, she may deduct up to $25,000 of losses from the rental real estate activity this year. Thus, she may claim $25,000 of the loss and the remaining $5,000 is carried forward.

---

13. Code Sec. 469(e)(1).
14. Code Sec. 469(c)(1).
15. Code Sec. 469(h)(1). The regulations provide seven tests for determining if a taxpayer is materially participating in an activity. See Temp. Reg. § 1.469-5T.
16. Code Sec. 469(c)(2), (c)(3), (c)(4), (h)(2). For exceptions to the per se passive rule for rental real estate, see Section 469(i), (c)(7). For exceptions to the per se passive rule for limited partnership interests, see Temp. Reg. § 1.469-5T(e)(2).
17. Portfolio income and losses are not considered passive income or losses. Code Sec. 469(e)(1).
18. Code Sec. 469(a)(1), (d)(1).
19. Code Sec. 469(b).
20. Code Sec. 469(a)(1), (b), (d)(2).
21. Code Sec. 469(g)(1)(A). This provision only applies to taxable dispositions.
22. Code Sec. 469(i). The exception is phased out for taxpayers with income over $100,000.

> **Practice Tip:** A loss from a passive activity that is disallowed and carried forward is treated as a passive activity loss in the next year. There is no limit on the number of years a passive activity loss can be carried forward.

B. Discussion of Rules

1. At Risk Limitation

The at risk rules are applied at the partner (*i.e.* individual) level, as opposed to the partnership level. In addition, they apply with respect to each separate activity in which the partnership is engaged.[23] Accordingly, a partner may not be able to claim all the losses allocated to him from the partnership.

Activities. The partner must determine the separate activities in which the partnership is engaged. In some circumstances separate partnership business activities must be aggregated to determine the activity to which the at risk limitation applies.[24]

Amount at risk. Next, the partner must determine the extent to which he is at risk for each activity. The partner's initial at risk amount is:[25]

- The amount of cash contributed to the activity;
- Plus the adjusted basis of any unencumbered property contributed to the activity;
- Plus liabilities for which the partner is personally liable;[26]
- Plus property pledged as security for a liability, but not used in the partnership activity (to the extent of the property's fair market value);
- Plus the partner's share of qualified non-recourse financing.[27]

Examples:
- If a general partner guarantees a partnership non-recourse liability, to the extent he is ultimately liable for the debt, his at risk amount is increased.[28]
- If a limited partner guarantees a partnership recourse liability but may

---

23. Code Sec. 465(a)(1), (c)(2)(A).
24. Code Sec. 465(c)(2)(A), (c)(2)(B), (c)(3)(A), (c)(3)(B), (c)(3)(C).
25. Code Sec. 465(b)(1).
26. Code Sec. 465(b)(3)(A), (b)(3)(B)(i); Treas. Reg. §1.465-8(a); Prop. Reg. §1.465-24(a)(2). Amounts for which the partner is protected against loss through guarantees, stop loss agreements, or similar arrangements are not included in the partner's at risk amount. Code Sec. 465(b)(4). Similarly, amounts borrowed from a person with an interest in the activity other than as a creditor or related person generally are not included in the partner's at risk amount. Code Sec. 465(b)(3).
27. The amount of qualified non-recourse financing is determined on the same basis that the partner's share of liabilities is determined. Code Sec. 465(b)(6)(C). In addition, the amount for which a partner may be treated as at risk cannot exceed the total amount of qualified non-recourse financing at the partnership level.
28. Abramson v. Commissioner, 86 T.C. 360 (1986).

seek reimbursement from the general partner, his at risk amount is not increased.[29]
- If a limited partner guarantees a partnership recourse liability but may not seek reimbursement from the general partner, his at risk amount is increased.[30]
- If a limited partner is allocated a portion of qualifying non-recourse financing, he is considered at risk to that extent.

The partner's at risk amount is determined annually. Each year, the prior year's at risk amount is increased by the partner's contributions and distributive share of income. It is decreased by the partner's share of losses and distributions.

Formula: A partner's at risk amount for his partnership activity is adjusted each year. Specifically, the following adjustments are made to the partner's at risk amount with respect to the activity:

> Initial amount or previous year's amount at risk
> + Distributive share of partnership income
> + Additional contributions
> − Distributive share of partnership losses
> − <u>Distributions</u>
> At risk amount

Limitation. To the extent a partner is not at risk with respect to the activity, he may not claim a loss on his tax return; instead, the loss is deferred. However, the partner's outside basis is reduced by the amount of the loss.[31]

If a partner's at risk amount falls below zero, the partner must include the amount by which the at risk amount has fallen below zero in his gross income.[32] If, in a subsequent year, the partner's at risk amount increases above zero, the partner may take a deduction for the previously included amount.[33]

A deferred loss can be carried forward until it can be used:[34] If the partner's at risk amount increases, the partner can claim deferred losses up to the amount of the increase.

If the partnership disposes of the activity, the partner may claim deferred losses up to the amount of any allocable share of gain generated by the activity. Alternatively, if the partner disposes of his interest in the partnership, any gain generated from the sale of the interest is treated as gain from the sale of the activity. The partner may claim deferred losses up to the amount of the gain.

---

29. Brand v. Commissioner, 81 T.C. 821 (1983).
30. Pritchett v. Commissioner, 827 F.2d 644 (9th Cir. 1987), *rev'g and remanding* 85 T.C. 580 (1985).
31. Prop. Reg. § 1.465-1(e).
32. Code Sec. 465(e)(1)(A).
33. Code Sec. 465(e)(1)(B).
34. Code Sec. 465(a)(1).

Ordering. The at risk limitation is applied after any limitations on losses due to a partner's insufficient outside basis (and before the passive activity loss limitation).

> **Practice Tip:** While a partner may have sufficient outside basis to claim a loss allocated to him from the partnership, the loss may be deferred under the at risk limitation rules.

2. Passive Activity Loss Limitation

The passive activity loss rules are applied at the partner (*i.e.* individual) level, as opposed to the partnership level. In addition, they apply with respect to each separate activity in which the partnership is engaged.[35] Accordingly, a partner may not be able to claim all the losses allocated to him from the partnership.

Activity. The partner must determine the separate business activities in which the partnership is engaged. The regulations provide substantial guidance regarding what constitutes an activity for purposes of the passive activity loss limitation.[36]

The partner then must determine which of those activities are passive activities. Compensation paid to a partner is not passive income.[37] The partner's share of portfolio income and expenses (*e.g.*, interest, dividends, and royalties) is not from a passive activity.[38] For all other activities, the determination of whether the activity is a passive activity depends on whether the partner materially participated in the activity.[39]

Material participation. A general partner materially participates if he is involved in the activity on a regular, continuous, and substantial basis.[40] Some activities, such as a rental real estate activity, are treated as passive activities regardless of whether the partner materially participates.[41] However, if the partner owns at least 10 percent of a rental real estate activity and the partner actively participates in the activity, he can deduct up to $25,000 of losses each year from the activity.[42] If the partner is a limited partner, he cannot come within this exception.[43]

A limited partner is considered as not materially participating in any partnership

---

35. Code Sec. 469(a)(2).
36. Temp. Reg. § 1.469-4T.
37. Code Sec. 469(e)(3).
38. Code Sec. 469(e)(1).
39. Code Sec. 469(c)(1).
40. Code Sec. 469(h)(1). The regulations provide seven tests for determining if a taxpayer is materially participating in an activity. See Temp. Reg. § 1.469-5T.
41. Code Sec. 469(h)(2). For exceptions to the per se passive rule for rental real estate, see Section 469(i), (c)(7). For exceptions to the per se passive rule for limited partnership interests, see Temp. Reg. § 1.469-5T(e)(2).
42. The allowable deduction is phased out for taxpayers with income over $100,000. Code Sec. 469(i).
43. Code Sec. 469(i)(6)(C).

activities. However, the activity may be treated as not a passive activity if the limited partner meets any of the following:[44]

- The partner participates in the activity for more than 500 hours during the taxable year;
- The partner materially participated in the activity for any five tax years during the ten years preceding the taxable year; or
- The activity is a personal service activity and the limited partner materially participated in the activity for any three tax years preceding the taxable year.

If the partnership holds a working interest in oil or gas property and the partner's liability is not limited, the activity is not considered a passive activity with respect to that partner.[45]

If the partner is both a general and a limited partner and he meets any of the seven tests for material participation, he is treated as materially participating with respect to both the general and the limited partnership interest.[46]

Passive activity loss limitation. First, the partner must determine the amount of net gain or loss from each separate passive activity, both those engaged in through the partnership and those engaged in individually. Next, the gains and losses from the separate passive activities are netted together.[47] If there is a net gain, the net gain is reported by the taxpayer-partner. If there is a net loss, a net passive activity loss, the taxpayer-partner is not entitled to claim the loss on his tax return.[48] Rather, the loss is deferred and carried forward.[49] Similarly, a credit from a passive activity is allowed only to the extent it offsets the tax liability of a passive activity. To the extent the credit is not allowed, it is deferred and carried forward.[50]

Any deferred loss can be carried forward until the partner has passive activity income.[51] Alternatively, if the partnership disposes of the activity, the income from the disposition will be treated as passive if the activity is considered passive during that year.[52] If the income is passive, the partner may offset the income by the deferred passive losses from the activity.[53]

Ordering. The limitation on losses due to insufficient basis and the at risk limitation are applied before the passive activity loss limitation is applied. Thus, the passive activity loss limitation is applied only to those losses allowed after application of the basis limitation and at risk rules.[54] In addition, any loss carried forward is characterized as passive or non-passive based on the partner's level of participation in the year.[55]

---

44. Temp. Reg. § 1.469-5T(e)(1), (e)(2).
45. Code Sec. 469(c)(3)(A). A limited partner will qualify under this exception only if he is also a general partner whose liability is not limited. Temp. Reg. § 1.469-1T(e)(4)(v)(A)(1).
46. Temp. Reg. § 1.469-5T(e)(1), (3).
47. Portfolio income and losses are not considered passive income or losses. Code Sec. 469(e)(1).
48. Code Sec. 469(a)(1), (d)(1).
49. Code Sec. 469(b).
50. Code Sec. 469(a)(1), (b), (d)(2).
51. Code Sec. 469(b).
52. Code Sec. 469(g)(1).
53. Temp. Reg. § 1.469-2T(c)(2)(i)(A)(2).
54. Temp. Reg. § 1.469-2T(d)(6).
55. Treas. Reg. § 1.469-2(d)(8).

Determination of Amount of Loss Allowed a Partner on His Individual Return

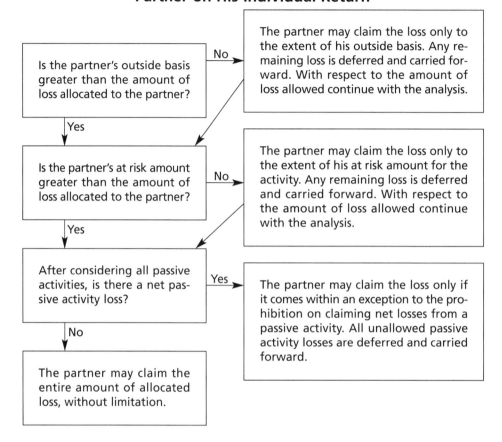

Practice Tip: While a partner may have sufficient outside basis to claim a loss allocated to him from the partnership, the loss may be deferred under the passive activity loss limitation rules.

Practice Tip: In determining if a partner may claim a loss from the partnership on his individual income tax return, the limitations are applied in the following order:
1. A loss is not allowed to the extent it exceeds a partner's outside basis.
2. A loss is not allowed to the extent a partner is not at risk.
3. A loss is not allowed to the extent it is a net passive activity loss.

Electing large partnerships. Certain large partnerships may use simplified reporting rules that reduce the number of separately stated items that are reported.[56] A partnership may make the election to use the simplified method if it has 100 or more partners in the preceding taxable year.[57] If the election is made, each partner takes into account his allocable share of:[58]

- Taxable income or loss from passive loss limitation activities;
- Taxable income or loss from other activities;
- Net capital gain or loss allocated between passive loss limitation and other activities;
- Tax-exempt interest;
- Net alternative minimum tax adjustment separately computed for passive loss limitation activities and other activities;
- Certain tax credits;
- Foreign income taxes; and
- Other items, as identified in the regulations.

A passive loss limitation activity is any partnership activity that involves the conduct of a business and any rental activity.[59] Note that a limited partner's distributive share of an electing large partnership's taxable income or loss from the passive loss limitation activity is treated as being from a single passive activity; the amount from separate passive activities is not separately reported.[60] Amounts that are not from passive loss limitation activities are treated as portfolio income.[61] However, if the partner is a general partner, the partner's share of items is taken into account separately to the extent necessary to comply with the passive activity loss rules.[62]

Publicly traded partnerships. A publicly traded partnership is generally taxed as a corporation.[63] However, if 90 percent of the gross income is "qualifying income," the publicly traded partnership is not taxed as a corporation.[64] Qualifying income generally includes passive investment income such as dividends, interest, real property rents, and natural resources royalties.[65] If the partnership is taxed as a partnership, the net income that passes through to the partners is treated as portfolio income. Any passive losses may be deducted only against passive income from the same publicly traded partnership. Unused losses are carried forward until the partnership has passive income or until the partner completely disposes of his interest in the partnership.

---

56. See Code Secs. 771 through 777.
57. Code Secs. 771; 775(a). In general, a service partnership may not make the election to be treated as an electing large partnership. Code Sec. 775(b).
58. Code Sec. 772(a).
59. Code Sec. 772(d)(1).
60. Code Sec. 772(c)(2).
61. Code Sec. 772(c)(3)(A).
62. Code Sec. 772(f).
63. Code Sec. 7704(a). A publicly traded partnership is a partnership whose interests are traded on an established securities market or are readily tradable on a secondary market. Code Sec. 7704(b).
64. Code Sec. 7704(c).
65. Code Sec. 7704(d).

C. Application of Rules

Example 1. At risk limitation. Amanda and Bruce each contributed $100,000 to the Square Partnership, a partnership engaged in the consulting business, in exchange for a 50-percent general partnership interest. Square Partnership obtained a $300,000 non-recourse loan and used the proceeds in the operation of its business.

Amanda and Bruce each have a $250,000 outside basis, $100,000 of cash contributed plus $150,000 share of the non-recourse liability. The consulting business is an activity of the partnership for purposes of the at risk limitation. Each partner's at risk amount is $100,000, the amount of cash each partner contributed.

In the first year of operations, the partnership had $300,000 of losses, which were divided equally between Amanda and Bruce. Each partner has sufficient basis to claim the loss ($250,000 basis less $150,000 of loss). However, because each partner is at risk only to the extent of $100,000, each may deduct only $100,000 on his and her individual income tax return. The remaining $50,000 of loss is deferred and carried forward. Note that both Amanda's and Bruce's basis are reduced to $100,000 ($250,000 initial basis, less $150,000 allocable share of loss).

Example 2. Passive activity loss limitation. Candace and Danny are general partners in the Circle Partnership. Each has an outside basis of $100,000. The partnership owns stock in Triangle Co. and also owns and operates a grocery store. Danny spends a substantial amount of time working at the grocery store. Candace does not devote any time to partnership activities.

In the first year of operations, the partnership has $100,000 of operating losses and a $20,000 loss from the sale of Triangle Co. stock. All losses are divided equally between Candace and Danny.

The grocery store business is an activity of the partnership for purposes of the passive activity loss limitation. Danny actively participated in the activity and Candace did not. Thus, the $50,000 of loss allocated to Danny is not a passive activity loss, but the $50,000 of loss allocated to Candace is a passive activity loss.

The loss from the sale of Triangle Co. stock is not a passive loss (it is from portfolio assets). Thus, the $10,000 loss allocated to each of Candace and Danny is not a passive activity loss.

Unless Candace has passive income from another source, she may not claim the $50,000 passive loss from the grocery store activity that was allocated to her from the partnership. She may claim the $10,000 of loss from the sale of Triangle Co. stock that was allocated to her. Her outside basis is reduced from $100,000 to $40,000 (basis of $100,000 reduced by the $50,000 of passive loss and $10,000 of portfolio loss).

Danny may claim the $50,000 (non-passive) loss from the grocery store activity that was allocated to him. He may also claim the $10,000 of loss from the sale of Triangle Co. stock that was allocated to him. His outside basis is reduced from $100,000 to

$40,000 (basis of $100,000 reduced by the $50,000 of loss from the grocery activity and $10,000 of portfolio loss).

D. Cases and Materials

Hubert Enterprises, Inc. v. Commissioner

2007-1 USTC 50,494 (6th Cir. 2007),
aff'g in part and rev'g in part 125 T.C. 72 (2005)

Petitioners-appellants Hubert Enterprises, Inc., and its subsidiaries (collectively "HEI") and Hubert Holding Company ("HHC") challenge the Tax Court's denial of their petition for a redetermination of deficiencies assessed against them by the Internal Revenue Service. Petitioners' appeal turns on two aspects of the Tax Court's decision. HEI challenges the Tax Court's determination that certain advances of capital made by HEI to another entity constituted a constructive dividend, precluding HEI's deduction of those amounts—either as an ordinary business loss or as a bad debt—even though those sums were not repaid. HHC challenges the Tax Court's determination that amendments made to the operating agreement for a limited liability company of which HHC was a member did not place HHC "at risk" within the meaning of I.R.C. § 465 for the recourse debt of that company and the resulting denial of a deduction for that amount. For the reasons that follow, we affirm the Tax Court's decision denying HEI's petition for a redetermination, vacate the Tax Court's decision as to HHC, and remand the case for further proceedings consistent with this opinion.

* * *

II.

HHC is a parent corporation of affiliated companies; its consolidated income tax returns for fiscal years 2000 and 2001 are also at issue in this appeal. In August of 1999, HEI transferred ownership of all of its subsidiaries to HHC in exchange for 100% of HHC's stock. HBW, Inc., a subsidiary of HEI and subsequently HHC, owned 99 of the 100 membership units of Leasing Company LLC ("LCL"), a limited liability company organized under the laws of Wyoming. LCL's original operating agreement was amended and restated on March 28, 2001. Included in the amendments was new section 7.7 (known as a "DRO") that obligated the members of LCL, upon liquidation of their membership interests, to satisfy any negative balances in their capital accounts.

HHC sought deductions under § 465 of the Internal Revenue Code, claiming that the amendment to the LCL operating agreement rendered it "at risk," as that term is defined under § 465, with respect to LCL's recourse debt. According to HHC, the situation may arise where the effect of the DRO would be to obligate the members of LCL to contribute capital equal in amount to each member's *pro rata* share of LCL's recourse indebtedness. The IRS disallowed those deductions, and the Tax Court ruled in favor of the Commissioner on this issue.

I.R.C. § 465 provides that taxpayers engaged in certain activities—including the leasing activities of LCL—may deduct losses incurred as a result of those activities to the extent they are "at risk" as defined by the statute. §465(a). A taxpayer is "at risk" for any capital contributions made. *See* §465(b)(1)(A). In addition, a taxpayer is "at risk" under §465 with respect to amounts borrowed in order to carry on the activity to the extent he or she is personally liable for the repayment of those amounts. §465(b)(2). The parties point to *Emershaw v. Commissioner* as establishing the standard for determining whether a taxpayer is personally liable for purposes of §465. 949 F.2d 841 (6th Cir. 1991). Under the *Emershaw* standard, a taxpayer is personally liable if, in the worst case, he or she will be the "payor of last resort." *Id.* at 849–51; *see also Pledger v. United States,* 236 F.3d 315, 319 (6th Cir. 2000).

In its opinion the Tax Court did not explicitly reach this issue, instead determining that to the extent the DRO provision created liability, that liability was contingent on an LCL member's liquidation of its interest, and because HHC did not liquidate its interest in LCL during the taxable years at issue, it could not be considered "at risk." The Commissioner acknowledges that the Tax Court did not explicitly engage in the worst-case analysis called for by the payor of last resort test. Thus, the Tax Court's opinion failed to address whether or not economic circumstances beyond the control of LCL members might force liquidation of their interests, thus causing the DRO to operate in a manner that might cause LCL members to become liable for a portion of LCL's obligations.

Under the circumstances, we deem it prudent to vacate the decision of the Tax Court with respect to the effect of the DRO and the extent to which it placed HHC "at risk" for a portion of LCL's recourse obligations. Furthermore, we remand this case in order to allow the parties to develop the factual record before the Tax Court more fully and determine whether or not the DRO rendered HHC the "payor of last resort" as required by our precedent.

III.

For the foregoing reasons, we affirm the decision of the Tax Court denying HEI a deduction for sums advanced to ALSL under the Grid Note, vacate the decision of the Tax Court as to the effect of the DRO on HHC's "at risk" amount under I.R.C. §465, and remand the case to the Tax Court for further proceedings consistent with this opinion.

E. Problems

1. Tracey contributed $10,000 to the Development Partnership in exchange for a 10-percent limited partnership interest. The partnership engaged in property development. The partnership obtained a $100,000 non-recourse liability, and, under Section 752, the liability was allocated based on how the partners share profits. Thus, for purposes of determining her basis, her share of the liability was $10,000.

(a) In the first year of operations, the Development Partnership had a loss of $110,000. The loss was allocated among the partners based on their ownership interest. Thus, $11,000 of loss was allocated to Tracey. What is the result to Tracey at the end of the first year?

(b) In the second year of operations, the Development Partnership had a gain of $100,000, $10,000 of which was allocated to Tracey. What is the result to Tracey at the end of the second year?

---

2. Evelyn was a general partner and Felicity was a limited partner in the Shopping Center Partnership. Each had an outside basis of $200,000. The partnership owned a portfolio of stock and bonds. It also owned and operated a shopping center. Evelyn spent a substantial amount of time overseeing operation of the shopping center. Felicity did not devote any time to partnership activities.

(a) In the first year of operations, the partnership had $200,000 of operating losses and $40,000 of losses from its portfolio of stocks and bonds. All losses were divided equally between Evelyn and Felicity. What are the results to Evelyn and Felicity at the end of the first year?

(b) In the second year of operations, the partnership had $300,000 of operating profits and $40,000 of losses from its portfolio. All income and losses were divided equally between Evelyn and Felicity. What are the results to Evelyn and Felicity at the end of the second year?

(c) What result in (a), above, if Felicity also had $100,000 of passive income allocated to her from another partnership in which she held an interest?

---

3. Application:

(a) How will the partner know in which activities the partnership is engaged?

(b) How will the partner know what his initial amount at risk is?

(c) How will the partner be able to keep track of his at risk amount while he is a partner in the partnership?

(d) If the partner wants to make sure he materially participates in a partnership activity:
   (1) How would he do that?
   (2) What types of records would you advise him to keep?
   (3) Who decides which partners are allowed to participate in each activity?
   (4) Can the participation of a partner be limited? Who decides?
   (5) Draft language for a partnership agreement that sets forth the extent to which the partners are permitted to participate in partnership activities.

Chapter 15

Allocation of Recourse Deductions

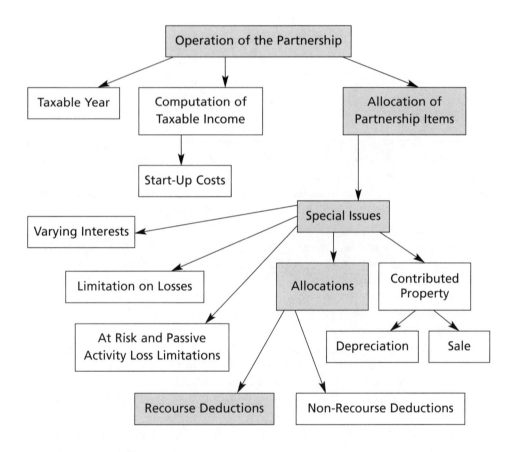

Read:

Code Section 704(a), (b).
Treas. Reg. § 1.704-1(a), -1(b)(1)(i), -1(b)(1)(vii), -1(b)(2)(i), -1(b)(2)(ii)(a)-(d),
-1(b)(2)(ii)(h), -1(b)(2)(ii)(i), -1(b)(2)(iii)(a)-(c), -1(b)(2)(iv)(a)-(c), -1(b)(2)(iv)(d)(1),
-1(b)(2)(iv)(d)(2), -1(b)(2)(iv)(e)(1), -1(b)(2)(iv)(h), -1(b)(2)(iv)(n),
-1(b)(3)(i)-(iii), -1(b)(5) Ex. (1), (2), (3), (5), (6), (7) & (15)(i), (ii); 1.752-1(a)(1).

A. Background

In the Supreme Court case *Horst v. Helvering*,[1] the taxpayer clipped interest coupons from a bond and gave them to his son. The issue before the court was who was the correct taxpayer to include the coupon interest in income, the dad or the son. The Supreme Court turned to the fruit and tree analysis it had first utilized in *Lucas v. Earl*[2] and stated that the fruit could not be attributed to a different tree from that upon which it grew. Using this axiom, it held that, because the father held the tree (the bond), he should be taxed on the fruit (the interest coupons).[3] In other words, the person who controls the capital that generated the income is the person who should pay tax on the income. To allow otherwise would be to allow taxpayers to shift income between themselves and to the taxpayer with the lowest marginal rate, potentially avoiding or improperly reducing the overall tax liability.

B. Discussion of Rules

In some situations, the partnership rules provide a means for a shifting of the income, gain, deductions, or losses that was prohibited in *Lucas v. Earl* and *Horst v. Helvering*. Specifically, through an allocation of partnership items—including an allocation not based on the partners' respective interests in the partnership—such a shifting can occur. It is this flexibility that makes partnerships popular for tax planning.

Example: Able and Bob form an equal general partnership. They each contribute $50 to the partnership. If the partnership made allocations based on their interest in the partnership, each partner would receive an allocation of one-half of all partnership items. However, Able and Bob agree upon a special allocation. All net income will be allocated to Able and all net losses will be allocated to Bob.

In the first year of partnership operations, the partnership has net income of $25. Based on the partners' agreement, the net income is allocated entirely to Able. In general, Able must report $25 of income on his individual income tax return, increase his outside basis by $25, and increase his capital account by $25.

In the second year of partnership operations, the partnership has a net loss of $25. Based on the partners' agreement, the net loss is allocated entirely to Bob. In general, Bob must report $25 of loss on his individual income tax return, decrease his outside basis by $25, and decrease his capital account by $25.

---

1. 311 U.S. 112 (1940).
2. 281 U.S. 111 (1930).
3. The holding in Horst is sometimes interpreted as requiring the taxpayer who controls the income (rather than the property that generated the income) to report the income.

For an allocation to be respected, it must have substantial economic effect. This requirement is broken down into two parts. First, the allocation must have economic effect. Second, the economic effect must be substantial. The test is applied to all allocations from the partnership, whether a separately-stated or a net amount.[4] In addition, it is applied on an annual basis.[5]

Practice Note: For an allocation to be respected, the allocation must—
• Have economic effect; and
• The economic effect must be substantial.

---

1. Economic Effect

For the allocation to have economic effect, it must be consistent with what the partners have agreed to from an economic perspective. In other words, the partner receiving the allocation must bear the tax burden and receive the economic benefit of the allocation.[6] To understand how this requirement is applied, some basic partnership concepts must be understood.

a. Underlying Concepts

Maintenance of capital accounts. The regulations provide rules for maintaining capital accounts.[7] If these rules are followed, the capital accounts will reflect the partner's economic situation in the partnership and his economic situation as compared to the other partners.

Example: The partnership agreement of the Clue Partnership provides that capital accounts are to be maintained in accordance with Treas. Reg. §1.704-1(b)(2)(iv)(*b*). The capital accounts and ownership interests in the partnership are as follows:

Partner	Capital Account	Percentage Ownership
Ms. Scarlet	$10,000	10 percent
Col. Mustard	50,000	50 percent
Mr. Green	5,000	5 percent
Prof. Plum	20,000	20 percent
Mrs. White	10,000	10 percent
Mrs. Peacock	5,000	5 percent
Total	$100,000	100 percent

---

4. Treas. Reg. §1.704-1(b)(1)(i).
5. Treas. Reg. §1.704-1(b)(2)(i).
6. Treas. Reg. §1.704-1(b)(2)(ii)(*a*).
7. Treas. Reg. §1.704-1(b)(2)(iv)(*b*).

Pursuant to the rules set forth in the regulations, a partner's capital account is increased by:

- The amount of cash contributed by the partner;
- The value of property contributed by the partner, reduced by any liabilities the property is subject to; and
- Any allocations of income or gain to the partner.

The partner's capital account is decreased by:

- The amount of cash withdrawn by the partner from the partnership;
- The value of property distributed by the partnership to the partner, reduced by any liabilities the property is subject to; and
- Any allocations of deductions or loss to the partner.

Example: Wesley contributed $10,000 and land worth $100,000, subject to a recourse liability of $40,000, to a partnership in exchange for a general partnership interest. In the first year of partnership operations he was allocated $20,000 of net income. At the end of the first year, his capital account would be as follows.

Cash:	$10,000
Net value of land:	60,000*
Allocation of income:	20,000
End of year balance:	$90,000

* Fair market value of $100,000, less liability of $40,000, resulting in a contribution of equity in the amount of $60,000.

In the second year of partnership operations, Wesley was allocated $10,000 of net loss and he withdrew $5,000 from the partnership. At the end of the second year, his capital account would be as follows:

Beginning balance:	$90,000
Cash withdrawal:	<5,000>
Allocation of loss:	<10,000>
End of year balance:	$75,000

Practice Tip: For the rules on how to maintain capital accounts, see Treas. Reg. § 1.704-1(b)(2)(iv)(*b*).

Practice Tip: It is imperative that the parties determine the correct fair market value of items contributed by, or distributed to, a partner. If the value is incorrectly determined, capital accounts will be incorrect and previous allocations based on the incorrect capital accounts will have to be reallocated based on the corrected values.

Liquidating distributions based on capital account balances. If capital accounts are maintained according to the rules set forth in the regulations, they reflect the partner's economic situation in the partnership and his economic situation as compared to the other partners. Thus, if the partnership were to liquidate, each partner would expect to receive from the partnership the amount reflected in his capital account.

Example: From the previous example of the Clue Partnership, if capital accounts were maintained in accordance with Treas. Reg. § 1.704-1(b)(2)(iv)(*b*), and the partnership were to liquidate its $100,000 of assets, the partners would expect to receive liquidating distributions in the following amounts:

Partner	Capital Account	Distribution
Ms. Scarlet	$10,000	$10,000
Col. Mustard	50,000	50,000
Mr. Green	5,000	5,000
Prof. Plum	20,000	20,000
Mrs. White	10,000	10,000
Mrs. Peacock	5,000	5,000
Total	$100,000	$100,000

Restoration of negative capital account balance. A partner's capital account reflects his investment in the partnership relative to the other partners. It also reflects what he is entitled to receive upon distribution. Thus, a negative capital account reflects the fact that the partner has received more from the partnership than what he had a right to receive on liquidation. In essence, he has received a loan from the partnership. If he is not obligated to restore the negative capital account, a portion of partnership assets have been shifted away from other partners and to this partner.

Example: Candy and Dorna formed an equal general partnership, each contributing $50 to the partnership. They agreed that all net income would be allocated to Candy and all net losses allocated to Dorna. At the time of formation, the partnership balance sheet would appear as follows:

Asset	Basis	FMV	Partner	Basis	Cap. Acct.
Cash	$100	$100	Candy	$50	$50
	$100	$100	Dorna	$50	$50
				$100	$100

In year 1, the partnership has a net loss of $75, which is allocated to Dorna. Dorna's basis can be reduced only to zero ($50 reduced by the $75 loss, limited by her outside basis) and her capital account is reduced to <$25> ($50 less net loss of $75). After the first year, the balance sheet would appear as follows:

Asset	Basis	FMV	Partner	Basis	Cap. Acct.
Cash	$25	$25	Candy	$50	$50
	$25	$25	Dorna	$0	<25>
				$50	$25

If the partnership were to liquidate, Candy would expect to receive $50 from the partnership. However, the partnership has only $25 of cash. Dorna's negative capital account reflects the fact that she has received more from the partnership than she contributed.

If Dorna is not obligated to restore her negative capital account balance, $25 that properly belongs to Candy has been shifted to Dorna.

If Dorna is obligated to restore her negative capital account balance, she must contribute $25 to the partnership. The partnership would then have $50 available to distribute to Candy in liquidation of her partnership interest. As Dorna's capital account would be zero (<$25> increased by the $25 contribution), she would not be entitled to any liquidating distribution.

b. General Test for Economic Effect

For an allocation to be respected, the partner receiving the allocation must bear the tax burden and receive the economic benefit of the allocation. For this result to occur, a three-part test must be satisfied:[8]

- The partnership must maintain capital accounts in accordance with Treas. Reg. §1.704-1(b)(2)(iv)(*b*);
- All partners must have an obligation to restore negative capital account balances upon liquidation before the later of the end of the taxable year of liquidation of the partner's interest or 90 days after the date of the liquidation; and
- Liquidating distributions must be made in accordance with capital account balances.

> **Practice Tip:** For general partnerships, the requirements of the general test for economic effect should be incorporated into the partnership agreement.

c. Alternate Test for Economic Effect

If the partner is a limited partner or a member of a limited liability company, the partner (or member) likely will be unwilling to enter into a partnership agreement (or operating agreement) that requires him to make additional contributions to the partnership (or LLC) (*i.e.*, restore a negative capital account balance). Thus, the partnership will not be able to meet the general test for economic effect.

Through the alternate test for economic effect, the regulations address this issue simply by not allowing the limited partner's capital account to become negative beyond any amount the partner has agreed to contribute to the partnership.

For this approach to work, and result in the least chance possible that the partner's capital account will go below zero, adjustments to the partner's capital account must

---

8. Treas. Reg. §1.704-1(b)(2)(ii)(*b*), -1(b)(2)(ii)(*c*).

be anticipated prior to considering any allocations to the partner. Thus, certain temporary adjustments must be made for any allocations that are reasonably expected to occur. Some of the adjustments that must be anticipated include:

- Allocations due to reasonably expected changes in interests in the partnership in future years; and
- Any distributions that are expected to be made to the partner, less any increases due to reasonably expected allocations of income.

If, by chance, the partner's capital account does go negative, the partnership must allocate items of income to the partner until his capital account is no longer negative. The obligation to allocate income items to the partner is called a qualified income offset.

For an allocation to be respected under the alternate economic effect test, a four-part test must be satisfied:[9]

- The partnership must maintain capital accounts in accordance with Treas. Reg. § 1.704-1(b)(2)(iv)(*b*);
- Liquidating distributions must be made in accordance with capital account balances;
- The allocation of recourse deductions cannot cause or increase a deficit in the partner's capital account in excess of any limited amount the partner is obligated to restore; and
- The partnership agreement must contain a qualified income offset.

Practice Tip: For a limited partnership or a limited liability company, the requirements for the alternate test for economic effect should be incorporated into the partnership agreement or LLC operating agreement.

Tests to Determine If an Allocation Has Economic Effect: For an allocation to have economic effect, one of the following tests must be met.

General Test:
- Partners' capital accounts must be maintained according to the regulations;
- Liquidating distributions must be made in accordance with positive capital account balances; and
- If, following a liquidation, a partner has a deficit balance in his capital account, he must be unconditionally obligated to restore the amount of such deficit balance.

Alternate Test:
- Partners' capital accounts must be maintained according to the regulations;
- Liquidating distributions must be made in accordance with positive capital account balances;

---

9. Treas. Reg. § 1.704-1(b)(2)(ii)(*d*).

- The allocation of recourse deductions cannot cause or increase a deficit in the partner's capital account in excess of any limited amount the partner is obligated to restore; and
- The partnership agreement contains a qualified income offset.

---

d. Failure to Meet General or Alternate Test

Economic effect equivalence. If the allocation fails to meet either the general test or the alternate test, the allocation can still be respected if the allocation would have been the same if the above criteria had been met. In other words, even though the partnership failed to include such provisions in its agreement, the partner who was allocated gain or income increased his investment in the partnership and a partner who was allocated a deduction or loss decreased his investment in the partnership.[10]

Allocation in accordance with the partners' interest in the partnership. If the allocation fails to have substantial economic effect and the economic effect equivalence test is not applicable, the allocations will be reallocated in accordance with the partners' respective interests in the partnership.[11] In other words, allocations will be made based on the manner in which the partners have agreed to share the economic benefit or burden that corresponds with the allocation.

A partner's interest in the partnership is determined by considering all the facts and circumstances related to the economic arrangement of the partners.[12] Relevant factors to consider include:[13]

- The partners' relative contributions to the partnership;
- The interests of the partners in the economic profits and loss (if different from their interests in taxable income or loss);
- The interest of the partners in cash flow and other nonliquidating distributions; and
- The rights of the partners to distributions of capital upon liquidation.

There is an exception to using the factors to determine the partner's interest in the partnership. Specifically, if the reason the partnership allocation fails the substantial economic effect test is because it lacked a deficit makeup obligation, the partner's interest in the partnership is determined using a comparative liquidation test. The manner in which distributions would be made if all partnership property were sold at book value and the partnership were liquidated immediately following the end of the taxable year to which the allocation relates is compared with the manner in which distributions would be made if all partnership property were sold at book value and the partnership were liquidated immediately following the end of the prior table year (and certain other adjustments are made).[14]

---

10. Treas. Reg. § 1.704-1(b)(2)(ii)(*i*).
11. Treas. Reg. § 1.704-1(b)(3).
12. Treas. Reg. § 1.704-1(b)(3)(i).
13. Treas. Reg. § 1.704-1(b)(3)(ii).
14. Treas. Reg. § 1.704-1(b)(3)(iii).

2. Substantiality

In addition to having economic effect, the effect must be substantial.[15] The economic effect will be considered substantial if the allocation substantially alters the way the partners share items economically and not just the way the allocation affects them for tax purposes. In other words, it must affect substantially the dollar amounts that the partners will receive from the partnership, independent of tax consequences.

In general, the allocation is not substantial if at the time the allocation is agreed upon, its inclusion causes the after-tax economic position of at least one partner to be enhanced while there is a strong likelihood that the after-tax economic position of no partner will be diminished. Accordingly, the allocation contained in the partnership agreement is compared to an allocation made in accordance with the partners' interests in the partnership, and, in determining the after-tax consequences to the partner, both the partner's partnership items and individual items are considered.[16]

General Rule for Substantiality: The economic effect of an allocation is *not* substantial if:

- The after-tax economic consequences of at least one partner may, in present value terms, be enhanced compared to such consequences if the allocation were not contained in the partnership agreement; and
- There is a strong likelihood that the after-tax economic consequences of no partner will, in present value terms, be substantially diminished compared to such consequences if the allocation were not contained in the partnership agreement.

Shifting tax consequences test. Under the shifting allocation test, allocations during just one year are considered. First, at the time the allocation is agreed upon, there must be a strong likelihood that the net change in the respective partners' capital accounts for the year with the special allocation would not differ substantially from the net change that would occur without the special allocation. Second, the total tax liability of the partners (determined by including their individual tax attributes) will be less with the special allocation than without the special allocation. If this result in fact occurs, it is presumed that there was a strong likelihood that that would be the result.[17]

Transitory allocation test. Under the transitory allocation test, allocations over two or more years are considered. First, at the time the allocation is agreed upon, there must be a strong likelihood that the net change in the respective partners' capital accounts over a span of years with the special allocation would not differ substantially from the net change that would occur without the special allocation. Second, the total tax liability of the partners (determined by including their individual tax attributes)

---

15. Treas. Reg. § 1.704-1(b)(2)(iii).

16. The tax attributes of a de minimis partner does not have to be taken into consideration. A de minimis partner is any partner that owns directly or indirectly less than 10 percent of the capital and profits of a partnership and is allocated less than 10 percent of each partnership item of income, gain, loss, deduction and credit. Treas. Reg. § 1.704-1(b)(2)(iii)(e).

17. Treas. Reg. § 1.704-1(b)(2)(iii)(*b*).

over the same span of years will be less with the special allocation than without the special allocation.[18]

Practice Note: An allocation and a subsequent offsetting allocation will not be considered transitory if there is a strong likelihood that the offsetting allocation will not, in large part, be made within five years of the original allocation [Treas. Reg. § 1.704-1(b)(2)(iii)(c)].

Failure to pass substantiality tests. If the special allocation is considered not substantial, the allocation will be disregarded and the partnership items will be reallocated based on the partners' interests in the partnership.[19]

Note that the regulations provide that the adjusted basis of property is presumed to be its fair market value. Thus, to the extent the basis is reduced for deprecation, the value of the property is reduced. Upon sale of the property, using this presumption, there will not be a presumption of gain. As there will not be any gain, there can never be a strong likelihood that the economic effect of an allocation of deprecation will be offset by a subsequent gain on disposition.[20]

Substantiality:

Shifting: Special allocations that impact one year are considered.

Transitory: Special allocations that impact two or more years are considered.

---

3. Areas of Special Concern

a. Depreciation Recapture

When property subject to depreciation has been sold, the gain on disposition will be the difference between the selling price and the basis, as adjusted for depreciation taken. To the extent of the gain that is due solely to the depreciation that was taken, the character of the gain will be ordinary. This portion of the gain is often referred to as depreciation recapture. The character of the remainder of the gain will depend on the use of the property. Because depreciation recapture only affects the character of the gain, and not the amount of the gain, an allocation based on such character will only alter the tax results of the partners. Accordingly, an allocation of gain based on its characterization as recapture gain will not have substantial economic effect.

The regulations provide some guidance as to how the gain from the sale of depreciable property should be allocated. The objective is to match an allocation of recap-

---

18. Treas. Reg. § 1.704-1(b)(2)(iii)(c).
19. Treas. Reg. § 1.704-1(b)(3).
20. Treas. Reg. § 1.704-1(b)(2)(iii)(c).

Allocations of Recourse Deductions

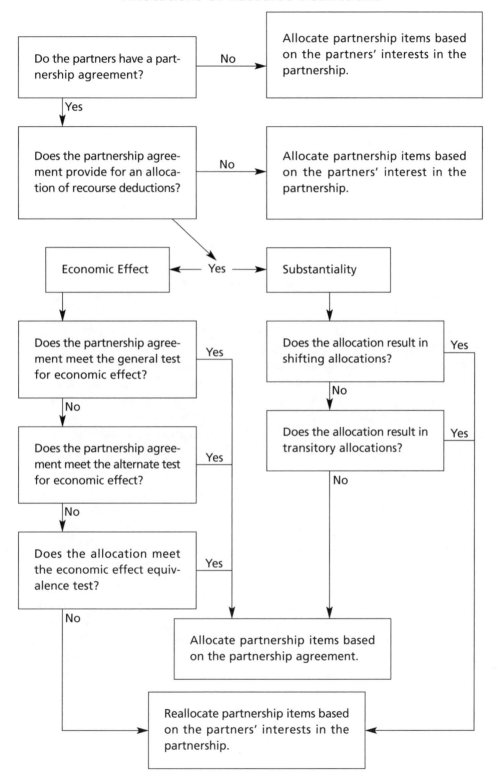

ture gain to a previous allocation of depreciation. A partner's share of recapture gain generally is equal to the lesser of:

- The partner's share of the total gain from the disposition of the property; or
- The total amount of depreciation previously allocated to the partner with respect to the property.

The partner's allocation of recapture gain may be limited by that partner's share of total gain.

b. Allocation of Credits

Partnership credits are not reflected in a partner's capital account. Thus, a special allocation of partnership credits cannot have substantial economic effect. Accordingly, generally, all allocations of credits must be made in accordance with the partners' interests in the partnership.[21]

C. Application of Rules

Example 1. Economic effect — general rule. Lisa and Maurice each contributed $40,000 and formed a general partnership. The partnership used the cash to purchase depreciable equipment. The partnership agreement provided that Lisa and Maurice would share profits and losses equally, but that all depreciation would be allocated to Lisa. The agreement also provided that capital accounts would be maintained in accordance with the regulations, but that, upon liquidation, distributions would be made equally between the partners (and not in accordance with capital account balances). The agreement does not require that a partner restore a negative capital account balance.

If the first year of operation, operating income exactly equaled operating expenses. In addition, the partnership was entitled to $20,000 in deprecation, which was allocated entirely to Lisa. At the end of the first year, the balance sheet would be as follows:

Asset	Basis	FMV	Partner	Basis	Cap. Acct.
Equipment	$60,000	$60,000	Lisa	$20,000	$20,000
	$60,000	$60,000	Maurice	$40,000	$40,000
				$60,000	$60,000

If the partnership liquidated at the end of the year, pursuant to the partnership agreement Lisa and Maurice would each receive $30,000. Under this method of distribution, Lisa did not bear the full risk of the economic loss corresponding to the deduction she received. Thus, the special allocation of depreciation to Lisa lacks economic substance and will be disregarded. The depreciation deduction must be reallocated based on the partners' interests in the partnership.

Because the Lisa and Maurice made equal contributions to the partnership, shared equally in operating income and losses, and shared equally in liquidating distributions,

---

21. Treas. Reg. § 1.704-1(b)(4)(ii).

they both had a 50-percent interest in the partnership. Accordingly, depreciation will be re-allocated equally between Lisa and Maurice.[22]

Example 2. Economic effect — alternate economic effect test. Nellie and Oscoda each contributed $40,000 and formed a limited partnership with Nellie as the limited partner and Oscoda as the general partner. The partnership used the cash to purchase depreciable equipment. The partnership agreement provided that Nellie and Oscoda would share profits and losses equally, but that all depreciation would be allocated to Nellie. The agreement also provided that capital accounts would be maintained in accordance with the regulations, that a general partner must restore a negative capital account balance, and that liquidating distributions would be made in accordance with capital account balances. The agreement did not require that a limited partner restore a negative capital account balance, but it did contain a qualified income offset.

If the first year of operation, operating income exactly equaled operating expenses and the partnership was entitled to $20,000 in deprecation. No items were reasonably expected to cause or increase a deficit balance in Nellie's capital account. The depreciation was allocated entirely to Nellie. At the end of the first year, the balance sheet would be as follows:

Asset	Basis	FMV	Partner	Basis	Cap. Acct.
Equipment	$60,000	$60,000	Nellie	$20,000	$20,000
	$60,000	$60,000	Oscoda	40,000	40,000
				$60,000	$60,000

In the second year of operation, operating income exactly equaled operating expenses and the partnership was entitled to $25,000 in depreciation. The depreciation was allocated entirely to Nellie. At the end of the second year, the balance sheet would appear as follows:

Asset	Basis	FMV	Partner	Basis	Cap. Acct.
Equipment	$35,000	$35,000	Nellie	$-0-	<$5,000>
	$35,000	$35,000	Oscoda	$40,000	40,000
				$40,000	$35,000

The special allocation of $25,000 of depreciation to Nellie satisfies the alternate economic effect test only to the extent of $20,000. Thus, only $20,000 of depreciation can be allocated to Nellie and the remaining $5,000 must be re-allocated in accordance with the partners' interests in the partnership.

The partner's interest in the partnership is determined using a comparative liquidation test. If the equipment were sold for book value at the end of the prior year, it would have been sold for $60,000 and the proceeds allocated $20,000 to Nellie and $40,000 to Oscoda. If the equipment had been sold at book value at the end of the current taxable year, it would have been sold for $35,000 and the proceeds allocated entirely to Oscoda. Because his capital account was $40,000, but he would receive only $35,000, he bears the burden of the $5,000 of depreciation. Accordingly, the $5,000 of depreciation is re-allocated to him.[23] The balance sheet would appear as follows:[24]

---

22. Treas. Reg. § 1.704-1(b)(5) Ex. (1)(i).
23. Treas. Reg. § 1.704-1(b)(3)(iii).
24. Treas. Reg. § 1.704-1(b)(5) Ex. (1)(iii), (iv), Ex. 15(i), (ii).

Asset	Basis	FMV	Partner	Basis	Cap. Acct.
Equipment	$35,000	$35,000	Nellie	$-0-	-0-
	$35,000	$35,000	Oscoda	$35,000	35,000
				$35,000	$35,000

Example 3. Economic effect equivalence. Paula and Quasar formed a partnership. Paula contributed $40,000 and Quasar contributed $60,000. The partnership agreement provided that profits and losses would be allocated 40 percent to Paula and 60 percent to Quasar. The agreement failed to provide that capital accounts would be maintained in accordance with the regulations, that liquidating distributions would be made in accordance with capital account balances, or that a partner has an obligation to restore a deficit balance in his capital account. However, Paula and Quasar are ultimately liable under state law for a right of contribution of 40 percent and 60 percent, respectively.

Because the agreement does not meet the general test or the alternate test for economic effect, the allocation does not have economic effect. However, because the allocations are the same allocations that would have been made if the general or alternative test had been met, the allocations will be respected.[25]

Example 4. Substantiality—transitory allocations. Raymond and Stella were equal general partners in a partnership that invested in stock and tax-exempt bonds. Over the next several years, Raymond expected to be in the 50-percent marginal tax bracket, and Stella expected to be in the 10-percent marginal tax bracket. There was a strong likelihood that in each of the next several years the partnership would realize $500 of tax-exempt interest and $500 of dividend income.

Raymond and Stella agreed to share equally in gains and losses from the sale of the partnership's stock. They also agreed that, rather than share dividend income and tax-exempt interest equally, they would allocate the tax-exempt income 80 percent to Raymond and 20 percent to Stella and 100 percent of the dividend income to Stella.

The partnership agreement provided that capital accounts would be maintained in accordance with the regulations, that liquidating distributions would be made in accordance with capital account balances, and that all partners have an obligation to restore a negative capital account balance.

The allocation of dividend income and tax-exempt interest has economic effect.

Without the allocation (based on 50 percent ownership interests):

Partner	Taxable Interest	Tax-Exempt Interest	Net Amount
Raymond	$250	$250	$375*
Stella	$250	$250	$475**

 * $375 = $250 of taxable dividends, less taxes of $250 × .50 ($125), plus $250 of tax-exempt interest

** $475 = $250 of taxable interest, less taxes of $250 × .10 ($25), plus $250 of tax-exempt interest

---

25. Treas. Reg. § 1.704-1(b)(5), Ex. (4)(ii).

With the allocation:

Partner	Taxable Interest	Tax-Exempt Interest	Net Amount
Raymond	-0-	$400	$400
Stella	$500	$100	$550*

* $550 = $500 of taxable dividends, less taxes of $500 x .10 ($50), plus $100 of tax-exempt interest

Thus, at the time the allocation became part of the partnership agreement, both Raymond and Stella are expected to enhance their after-tax economic consequences as a result of the allocation and neither will diminish their after-tax economic consequences as a result of the allocations. The allocation is not substantial and must be reallocated in accordance with the partners' interests in the partnership.[26]

Example 5. Substantiality—shifting allocations. Trigger, Ursaline, and Venda were equal general partners in a partnership that owned rental property and reasonably expected to receive about $90,000 in rent each year. The partnership agreement provided that capital accounts would be maintained in accordance with the regulations, that liquidating distributions would be made in accordance with capital account balances, and that all partners have an obligation to restore a negative capital account balance.

At the beginning of the year, Trigger knew for certain that he had a $90,000 net operating loss deduction from activities not related to the partnership that would expire if not used. Ursaline and Venda were in the highest marginal tax brackets.

The partners agreed to allocate 100 percent of partnership income in the current year to Trigger. In the two subsequent years, the partnership income would be allocated equally between Ursaline and Venda. In the following years, the income would be allocated equally between Trigger, Ursaline, and Venda.

The special allocation has economic effect.

Without the allocation:

Partner	Trigger	Ursaline	Venda
First year	$30,000	$30,000	$30,000
Second year	30,000	30,000	30,000
Third year	30,000	30,000	30,000
Total	$90,000	$90,000	$90,000

With the allocation:

Partner	Trigger	Ursaline	Venda
First year	$90,000	-0-	-0-
Second year	-0-	$45,000	$45,000
Third year	-0-	$45,000	$45,000
Total	$90,000	$90,000	$90,000

At the time the allocation was agreed upon, there was a strong likelihood that the net change in each partners' capital accounts over the three years with the special alloca-

---

26. Treas. Reg. § 1.704-1(b)(5) Ex. (5)(i).

tion would not differ substantially from the net change that would occur without the special allocation. The net change in the partner's capital accounts, with or without the allocation, will be an increase of $90,000.

Second, the total tax liability of the partners (determined by including their individual tax attributes) over the same span of years will be less with the special allocation than without the special allocation. While each partner will be allocated a total of $90,000 of partnership income over the three years, with the special allocation of all income to Trigger in the first year he will be able to offset his $90,000 of income with his $90,000 net operating loss. Thus, the total tax liability of the partners will be less with the special allocation. Accordingly, the economic effect of the allocation is not substantial.[27]

Example 6. Allocation of depreciation recapture. Will and Xendie each contributed $5,000 and became equal general partners. The partnership used the cash to purchase depreciable equipment.

The partnership agreement provided that capital accounts would be maintained in accordance with the regulations, that liquidating distributions would be made in accordance with capital account balances, and that all partners have an obligation to restore a negative capital account balance.

The partners agreed that 90 percent of the depreciation would be allocated to Will and 10 percent would be allocated to Xendie. When the equipment was sold, the gain would be allocated in such a way so as to equalize the partners' capital accounts. Any remaining gain would be allocated equally between Will and Xendie.

In the first year, operating income exactly equaled operating expenses and the partnership was entitled to $1,000 of depreciation. The depreciation was allocated $900 to Will and $100 to Xendie. The balance sheet would appear as follows:

Asset	Basis	FMV	Partner	Basis	Cap. Acct.
Equipment	$9,000	$9,000	Will	$4,100	$4,100
	$9,000	$9,000	Xendie	$4,900	4,900
				$9,000	$9,000

If the partnership sold the property at the beginning of the second year for $10,400 (for the sake of simplicity, without taking into consideration any depreciation the might be allowed for the second year), it would have $1,400 of gain (amount realized of $10,400, less adjusted basis of $9,000). Of that gain, $1,000 is characterized as ordinary recapture gain and $400 is characterized as hotchpot (section 1231) gain.

Based on the partnership agreement, the first $800 of gain is allocated to Will to equalize their capital accounts. The remaining $600 of gain is allocated equally between them. Thus, a total of $1,100 of gain will be allocated to Will ($800 plus $300) and $300 will be allocated to Xendie. Each partner's share of the gain that is characterized as depreciation recapture gain is the lesser of:

- The partner's share of the total gain from the disposition of the property; or

---

27. Treas. Reg. § 1.704-1(b)(5) Ex. (9).

- The total amount of depreciation previously allocated to the partner with respect to the property.

For Will, his total share of gain from disposition of the equipment is $1,100. The total amount of depreciation previously allocated to him was $900. The lesser of the two amounts is $900. For Xendie, her total share of gain from the disposition of the equipment is $300. The total amount of depreciation previously allocated to her was $100. The lesser of the two amounts is $100. Accordingly, the character of the gain allocated to Will and Xendie would be as follows:[28]

Partner	Recapture	Hotchpot	Total Gain
Will	$900	$200	$1,100
Xendie	100	200	300
Total	$1,000	$400	$1,400

D. Cases and Materials

Conroe Office Building, Ltd. v. Commissioner
T.C. Memo 1991-224

On March 10, 1987, respondent issued a Notice of Final Partnership Administrative Adjustment (FPAA) in regard to **Conroe** Office Building, Ltd. (hereinafter referred to as **Conroe,** the partnership), for the calendar years 1983 and 1984. Some issues raised by the pleadings have been disposed of by agreement of the parties leaving for decision the following:

* * *

(4) whether the special allocation of partnership losses claimed on the Forms K-1 attached to **Conroe's** returns of income should be disregarded.

FINDINGS OF FACT

* * *

Article 5.01 of the Limited Partnership Agreement and Amended Limited Partnership Agreement provides that the amount of net profits and net losses of the partnership to be allocated to and charged against each partner shall be determined by the percentage set opposite his name in exhibit A attached to the agreement. Nowhere in either agreement is it specified how the percentage was determined.

During a 1982 meeting of "a quorum" of the partnership, it was unanimously agreed that the Pasadena E.N.T. Clinic Defined Benefit Pension Fund (Pasadena Pension Fund) would shift its pro rata share of partnership losses to its vested beneficiaries and Joe Izen, M.D., and that the Peter DiSclafani, D.D.S., P.C. Pension Fund (D.D.S. Pension Fund) would shift its pro rata share of partnership losses to its vested beneficiaries who were its partners.

---

28. Treas. Reg. § 1.1245-1(e)(2)(iii) Ex. 1.

The following tables list the percentage of profit, loss, and ownership of capital as reported on the Forms K-1 attached to the 1983 and 1984 partnership returns: [chart omitted]

* * *

ISSUE 4: SPECIAL ALLOCATION

In general, a partner's distributive share of income, gain, loss, deduction, or credit shall be determined by the terms of the partnership agreement. Sec. 704(a). The partnership agreement includes any modifications that are made until the time required for the filing of the partnership return which are agreed to by all the partners or which are adopted in such other manner as may be provided by the partnership agreement. Sec. 761(c). The limited partnership agreement could be amended or modified by the partners only by written instrument executed by partners owning collectively at least a 95 percent interest of the partnership.

During a 1982 meeting of the partnership, it was unanimously agreed by "a quorum" of partners that the Pasadena Pension Fund would shift its pro rata share of partnership losses to Joe Izen, M.D. and its vested beneficiaries and that the D.D.S. Pension Fund would shift its pro rata share of partnership losses to its vested beneficiaries who were its partners. Petitioners have not established that the modification in the allocation was agreed to by *all* the partners or partners collectively owning at least a 95 percent interest. There is nothing in this record to show what amount of interest in the partnership constituted "a quorum."

Modification of the Limited Partnership Agreement required a written instrument executed by partners owning collectively at least a 95 percent interest of the partnership. Regardless of whether the minutes of the meeting could qualify as such a written instrument, petitioners have not established that partners owning collectively at least a 95 percent interest of the partnership were present at the meeting to approve the modification. Accordingly, the modification in the allocation is not considered part of the partnership agreement under section 761(c). See *Kresser v. Commissioner*, 54 T.C. 1621 (1970).

All allocation of partnership items must be according to the Amended Limited Partnership Agreement and the special allocation referred to in the minutes of the meeting held in 1982 has no effect. Because we find that the modification was not part of the partnership agreement, we do not reach the question of whether the special allocation would have substantial economic effect.

Decision will be entered under Rule 155.

E. Problems

1. Alice and Ben formed a partnership. Alice contributed $100,000 in exchange for a general partnership interest, and Ben contributed $100,000 for a limited partnership interest.

The partnership purchased an office building on leased land for $200,000. The partnership is entitled to $50,000 of depreciation each year (ignoring any conventions). The partnership agreement allocates all items of income and expenses equally; all depreciation is allocated to Ben.

(a) For the allocation of the depreciation to be respected, what must the partnership agreement include? Must the agreement be a written agreement?

(b) The partnership agreement provides that capital accounts will be maintained in accordance with the regulations and that liquidating distributions will be made in accordance with capital account balances. Alice has an unconditional obligation to restore a negative capital account balance. The agreement includes a qualified income offset with respect to Ben.

(1) In the first year, before taking into consideration the depreciation, partnership income equals its expenses.

(a) Construct a balance sheet reflecting the situations of the partnership and the partners at the end of the first year.

(b) If at the end of the year the partnership sold the building for $150,000 and liquidated, how would the proceeds from the sale be distributed? (Assume that there are no selling costs).

(c) Alternatively, if at the end of the year the partnership sold the building for $200,000 and liquidated, how would the proceeds from the sale be distributed? (Assume that there are no selling costs).

(d) Alternatively, if at the end of the year the partnership sold the building for $100,000 and liquidated, how would the proceeds from the sale be distributed? (Assume that there are no selling costs.)

(2) The partnership elected not to sell the building in the first year. In the second year, before taking into consideration the depreciation, partnership income equals its expenses.

(a) Construct a balance sheet reflecting the situations of the partnership and the partners at the end of the second year.

(b) What is the impact on the allocation of depreciation to Ben if the partnership expects to distribute $50,000 to Ben at the beginning of year three?

(c) What is the impact on the allocation of depreciation to Ben if the partnership expects to distribute $50,000 to Ben at the beginning of year three only if the building has increased in value to $250,000?

(3) The partnership makes no distributions to Ben in the second year. In the third year, the partnership has $20,000 of income, $20,000 of expenses, and $50,000 of depreciation from the building.

(a) What is the impact of the allocation of depreciation in year three?

(b) Alternatively, in the third year Ben contributed a promissory note for $75,000 to the partnership. What is the impact on the allocation of depreciation?

(c) Alternatively, the partnership distributed $30,000 to Ben at the beginning of year three. What is the impact of the distribution on the allocation of depreciation and other partnership items?

(d) Alternatively, the partnership agreement does not require that liquidating distributions be made in accordance with capital account balances, that Alice has an unconditional obligation to restore a negative capital account balance, or provide for a qualified income offset with respect to Ben. However, the agreement does provide that all depreciation be allocated to Ben each year. How would the depreciation be allocated during the first three years.

2. Cathy and Dennis formed an equal general partnership to sell state-of-the art cook-ware throughout the world. The partnership agreement provided that capital accounts will be maintained in accordance with the regulations, that liquidating distributions will be made in accordance with capital account balances, and both partners have an obligation to restore negative capital account balances.

Cathy is a resident of the United States and is responsible for marketing outside the United States. Dennis is a nonresident alien who is not subject to income tax from sales generated in the United States; he is responsible for marketing in the United States.

(a) The partnership agreement provides that all income from sales in the United States will be allocated to Dennis and all income from sales outside the United States will be allocated to Cathy. At the time they enter into the agreement, they are uncertain about how many sales they will have inside and outside the United States. Will the allocation have substantial economic effect?

(b) Alternatively, the partnership agreement provides that all income from sales in the United States will be allocated to Dennis and all income from sales outside the United States will be allocated to Cathy. At the time they enter into the agreement, they are relatively certain that sales outside the United States will equal sales in the United States. Will the allocation have substantial economic effect?

---

3. Edna and Fred form a limited partnership to purchase and lease a computer for $2,000,000. Edna has a substantial amount of income from other sources outside the partnership. Fred is currently a student and anticipates attending medical school. He earns a minimal amount of income and does not expect his income to increase until he completes medical school in six years. Edna contributed $1,900,000 in exchange for a limited partnership interest. Fred contributed $100,000 in exchange for a general partnership interest.

The partnership agreement provided that capital accounts will be maintained in accordance with the regulations, that liquidating distributions will be made in accordance with capital account balances, that Fred has an obligation to restore a negative capital account balance. The agreement also contained a qualified income offset with respect to Edna.

The agreement also provided that depreciation deductions will be allocated entirely to Edna for the first six year. Then, beginning in year seven, Edna will be allocated income until the amount of income equals the total of the previously claimed depreciation deductions. Thereafter, Edna and Fred will share income and loss equally. Does the allocation have substantial economic effect?

---

4. Application:

(a) How would you explain special allocations to the partners?

(b) When might you advise the partners to have a special allocation?

(c) Draft language for the partnership agreement that would satisfy the general test for economic effect.

(d) Draft language for the partnership agreement that would satisfy the alternate test for economic effect.

F. Advanced Problems — Looking Forward

Without conducting any research, consider the following questions:

1. Recall that a recourse debt is one for which the partner bears the risk of loss under the doomsday scenario. Often, this risk of loss was evidenced by a negative capital account and the obligation to restore the account to zero. Is there a connection between an allocation of recourse deductions and allocation of recourse debt?

2. What if the liability that gave rise to the deduction was not a recourse liability? Will the partner receiving the allocation have to bear the tax burden? If not, how will such allocation have substantial economic effect?

Chapter 16

Allocation of Non-Recourse Deductions

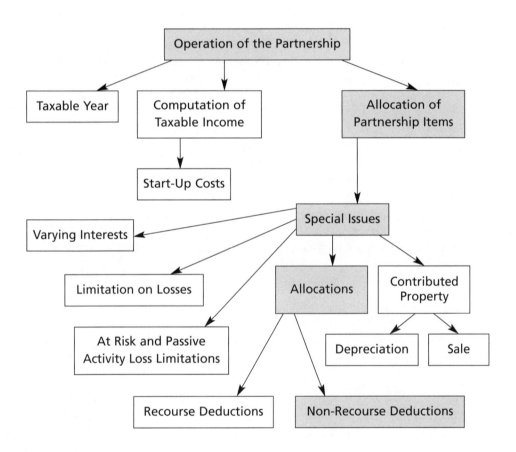

Read:

Code Section 704(a), (b).
Treas. Reg. § 1.704-2(b), (c), (d)(1), (d)(3), (e), (f)(1)-(3), (g), (h)(1), (j), (m) Ex. 1(i)-(iv); 1.752-1(a)(2).

A. Background

Debt. In general, a recourse liability is one for which the borrower is personally liable. A non-recourse liability is one for which the borrower is not personally liable. Most often, a non-recourse loan is secured by the property purchased with the borrowed funds. When the liability is a non-recourse liability, the lender bears the risk of loss.

Obtaining a loan (either recourse or non-recourse) does not create income to the borrower. Furthermore, if the loan was acquired upon acquisition of the property securing the loan, the amount of the loan is included in the property's basis.[1] If depreciable, the basis will be adjusted for depreciation allowed.

Example: In Year 1, Amy purchased an apartment building for $50,000. She used $20,000 from her own funds and obtained a $30,000 non-recourse loan, secured by the apartment building. Amy was not required to make any principal payments on the non-recourse loan until Year 5. She was allowed to claim $10,000 of depreciation each year. At the end of Year 3, Amy had claimed a total of $30,000 in depreciation.

Year	Depreciation	Adjusted Basis of Building
1	$10,000	$40,000
2	10,000	30,000
3	10,000	20,000
Total:	$30,000	

If she abandoned the property and the fair market value of the property was equal to its adjusted basis, the lender would bear the $10,000 loss (the difference between the $30,000 outstanding loan balance and the $20,000 value of the building).

Role of debt in amount realized. If, as part of the disposition of property, a third party agrees to pay a liability of the taxpayer, the amount of the debt relief is included in the amount realized.[2] In essence, because the buyer is assuming the debt, it is as if the buyer transferred cash to the taxpayer and the taxpayer used the cash to pay off the debt.

Similarly, when a taxpayer abandons property subject to a non-recourse debt or sells the property for the amount of the debt, the taxpayer is treated as having received an amount equal to the non-recourse debt.[3] Accordingly, the minimum amount of gain a taxpayer will realize on the disposition of encumbered property is the amount of the loan, less the adjusted basis. This gain is often referred to as *Tufts* gain, after the Supreme Court opinion in *Commissioner v. Tufts*,[4] or phantom gain.

---

1. Woodsam Associates, Inc. v. Commissioner, 198 F.2d 357 (2nd Cir. 1952), *aff'g* 16 T.C. 649 (1951).
2. Tufts v. Commissioner, 461 U.S. 300 (1983); Crane v. Commissioner, 331 U.S. 1 (1947); Old Colony Trust Co. v. Commissioner, 279 U.S. 716 (1929).
3. Crane v. Commissioner, 331 U.S. 1 (1947).
4. 461 U.S. 300 (1983).

> **Practice Note:** *Tufts* gain (phantom gain) is the excess of the non-recourse debt over the adjusted basis of the property that secures the debt. It may also represent the amount of deductions generated by the property that exceeds the taxpayer's actual investment in the property.

Example: In Year 1, Amy purchased an apartment building for $50,000. She used $20,000 from her own funds and obtained a $30,000 non-recourse loan, secured by the apartment building. Amy was not required to make any principal payments on the non-recourse loan until Year 5. She was allowed to claim $10,000 of depreciation each year. At the end of Year 3, Amy had claimed a total of $30,000 in depreciation.

Year	Depreciation	Adjusted Basis of Building
1	$10,000	$40,000
2	10,000	30,000
3	10,000	20,000
Total:	$30,000	

Notice that the total depreciation deductions she claimed exceeded her $20,000 investment in the property by $10,000. And, if she abandoned the property and the fair market value of the property was equal to its adjusted basis, the lender would bear the $10,000 loss (the difference between the $30,000 outstanding loan balance and the $20,000 value of the building).

If Amy were allowed to abandon the building without including the amount of the debt in her amount realized, she would get the benefit of $10,000 of depreciation without any cost to her.

In contrast, by requiring the non-recourse liability to be included in the amount realized when she abandons the building, she has $10,000 of gain (amount realized of $30,000 non-recourse debt, less adjusted basis of $20,000). In this way, Amy must recognize the $10,000 of depreciation she was previously allowed to claim and that exceeded her investment in the property.

B. Discussion of Rules

1. Non-Recourse Liability

A non-recourse deduction is a deduction that is financed by a non-recourse liability of the partnership. Recall that a partnership liability is a recourse liability to the extent that any partner bears the economic risk of loss for that liability or would be obligated to contribute to the partnership to satisfy the liability.[5] The amount of part-

---

5. Treas. Reg. § 1.752-2(a).

nership liability that has not been characterized as a recourse liability, the amount for which no partner bears the economic risk of loss, is a non-recourse liability.[6]

2. Relevance of *Tufts*, or Phantom, Gain

The allocation of deductions that arise out of property encumbered by a non-recourse liability cannot be addressed in the same manner as the allocation of deductions that arise out of property encumbered by a recourse liability. Allocation of the latter is based on the premise that the allocation reflects the economic risk of loss of the partners; one or more of the partners will be liable to pay the outstanding balance of the loan.

In contrast, because the non-recourse lender, and not any of the partners, bears the economic risk of loss for the loan proceeds, an allocation of deductions that arises out of property encumbered by a non-recourse liability does not reflect an economic risk of loss of the partners. Accordingly, the allocation will not pass the test of substantial economic effect.

However, the fact that a partner is not liable for repayment of the loan proceeds is only part of the consequences associated with a non-recourse liability. From a tax perspective, upon disposition, the least amount of gain the partnership must recognize is the amount of the non-recourse debt, less the adjusted basis of the property that secures the debt (*Tufts* or phantom gain). If the *Tufts* gain is allocated to a partner to the extent the partner was allocated deductions from the property, the partner who received the tax benefit of the deduction will bear the tax burden on disposition of the property.

Example: In Year 1, the partnership purchased an apartment building for $50,000. It was financed entirely with a $50,000 non-recourse loan, secured by the apartment building. The partnership was not required to make any principal payments on the non-recourse loan until Year 5. It was allowed to claim $10,000 of depreciation each year. The partnership allocated all depreciation deductions to Amy, a partner in partnership. At the end of Year 3, Amy had claimed a total of $30,000 in depreciation.

Year	Depreciation	Adjusted Basis of Building
1	$10,000	$40,000
2	10,000	30,000
3	10,000	20,000
Total:	$30,000	

Notice that the total depreciation deductions Amy has been able to claim exceeds the partnership's investment in the property by $30,000.

From the perspective of the lender, if the partnership abandons the property and the fair market value of the property was equal to its adjusted basis, the lender would bear the $30,000 loss (the difference between the $50,000 outstanding loan balance and the $20,000 value of the building).

From the perspective of the partnership, if the property is abandoned or sold for the amount of the outstanding liability, the partnership will recognize

---

6. Treas. Reg. §§ 1.752-1(a)(2), 1.704-2(b)(2).

$30,000 of gain (amount realized of $50,000 non-recourse debt, less adjusted basis of $20,000). Note that the gain is due entirely to the depreciation claimed with respect to the property. Amy will bear the burden of the $30,000 depreciation deductions she received if she is required to report the correlative $30,000 gain on disposition of the property.

3. Safe Harbor Requirements

The partners can agree to an allocation of non-recourse deductions. However, for the allocation to be respected, the partnership agreement must include four safe harbor requirements. In general, the safe harbor requirements are centered around the concept that the partner who received the deductions generated by the non-recourse debt should be allocated the *Tufts* (or phantom) gain upon disposition of the property.

> **Practice Tip:** The gain sometimes is referred to as phantom gain because there is no cash associated with the gain. It is a gain for tax purposes only.

The safe harbor requirements include several technical terms that must be understood before the requirements can be understood.

a. *Underlying Concepts*

Partnership minimum gain. In general, partnership minimum gain (PMG) is the excess of the non-recourse liability over the adjusted basis of the encumbered property.[7] In other words, partnership minimum gain includes the amount of potential *Tufts* gain or phantom gain. Similarly, a net increase in partnership minimum gain for the year reflects a net increase in potential *Tufts* (or phantom) gain for the year.

Partnership minimum gain can arise through three methods, two of them are based solely on *Tufts*, or phantom, gain. First, partnership minimum gain may be created through deductions associated with the property that secures the non-recourse liability, most often depreciation deductions.

> **Example:** In Year 1, the partnership purchased an apartment building for $50,000. It was financed entirely with a $50,000 non-recourse loan, secured by the apartment building. The partnership was not required to make any principal payments on the non-recourse loan until Year 5. It was allowed to claim $10,000 of depreciation each year. The partnership allocated all depreciation deductions to Amy, a partner in the partnership.
>
> At the end of Year 1, Amy had claimed $10,000 in depreciation and the adjusted basis of the building was $40,000. The amount of partnership minimum gain (or *Tufts* or phantom gain) was $10,000.

---

7. Treas. Reg. § 1.704-2(d)(1).

At the end of Year 2, Amy had claimed an additional $10,000 in depreciation and the adjusted basis of the building was $30,000. The total amount of partnership minimum gain (or *Tufts* or phantom gain) was $20,000. The increase in partnership minimum gain for the year was $10,000.

At the end of Year 3, Amy had claimed an additional $10,000 in depreciation and the adjusted basis of the building was $20,000. The total amount of partnership minimum gain (or *Tufts* or phantom gain) was $30,000. The increase in partnership minimum gain for the year was $10,000.

In summary:

Year	Depreciation	Adjusted Basis	Increase in PMG	Total PMG
1	$10,000	$40,000	$10,000	$10,000
2	10,000	30,000	10,000	20,000
3	10,000	20,000	10,000	30,000

In determining the excess of the non-recourse liability over the property's adjusted basis, there potentially may be two different adjusted bases that may be used. The "adjusted tax basis" refers to the partner's basis in the property at the time it was contributed to the partnership, adjusted by depreciation deductions. "Adjusted book basis" refers to the fair market value of the property at the time it was contributed to the partnership, adjusted by book depreciation deductions. If the adjusted tax basis differs from the adjusted book basis, the adjusted book basis is used for purposes of computing minimum gain.[8] There also may be a difference between the two basis when there has been a revaluation of the partnership property.[9]

Practice Note: When computing partnership minimum gain, if the adjusted basis for tax purposes differs from the adjusted basis for book purposes, the gain is determined by using the adjusted basis for book purposes.

Second, partnership minimum gain may be created when the amount of non-recourse liability is increased.

Example: In Year 1, the partnership purchased an apartment building for $50,000. It was allowed to claim $10,000 of depreciation each year. In Year 3, when the adjusted basis of the building was $20,000, the partnership obtained a $50,000 non-recourse loan, secured by the building.

Upon obtaining the non-recourse liability, the non-recourse debt, $50,000, exceeded the building's adjusted basis, $20,000, by $30,000. Thus, the partnership now has $30,000 of partnership minimum gain.

Finally, a partner's share of partnership minimum gain is increased when a partner receives a distribution of proceeds from a non-recourse loan allocable to an in-

---

8. Treas. Reg. § 1.704-2(d)(3).
9. Treas. Reg. § 1.704-2(d)(4).

crease in partnership minimum gain. The reason why there is partnership minimum gain in such a situation can be best understood by considering the ramifications of such a distribution.

A distribution of loan proceeds may cause a deficit balance in the partner's capital account. If the partnership has a qualified income offset, the partnership then would be required to allocate items of income or gain to the partner until his account was brought back to zero. However, by creating partnership minimum gain to the extent of the distribution, the partner can be allocated a correlative portion of the gain upon disposition of the property securing the non-recourse liability. It follows that, in anticipation of the future allocation of gain, under the alternate economic effect test the partner can be treated as having an obligation to restore a negative capital account balance to the extent of his share of partnership minimum gain.[10]

Example: In Year 1, the partnership purchased an apartment building for $50,000. It was allowed to claim $10,000 of depreciation each year. In Year 3, when the adjusted basis of the building was $20,000, the partnership obtained a $50,000 non-recourse loan, secured by the building.

Upon obtaining the non-recourse liability, the non-recourse debt, $50,000, exceeded the building's adjusted basis, $20,000, by $30,000. Thus, the partnership now has $30,000 of partnership minimum gain.

The partnership distributed $30,000 of non-recourse loan proceeds to Ben, a limited partner in the partnership. If his capital account was zero before the distribution, it will be <$30,000> after the distribution.

Note that the non-recourse loan proceeds are no longer part of the partnership property, no partner has an obligation to repay the loan, and, because the proceeds did not generate any deductions, there is no correlation between an allowable depreciation deduction and potential future gain. In addition, Ben is not obligated to restore a negative capital account balance. Under the qualified income offset, the partnership would be obligated to begin allocating income and gain to Ben.

However, Ben's share of partnership minimum gain is increased through the distribution of loan proceeds allocable to an increase in partnership minimum gain. Because of the allocation of partnership minimum gain, Ben will be treated as having an obligation to contribute $30,000 to the partnership.

If the partnership immediately sold the property for the amount of the debt, the partnership would have $30,000 of gain ($50,000 non-recourse debt, less $20,000 adjusted basis). Based on the minimum gain chargeback all $30,000 will be allocated to Ben, bringing his capital account from <$30,000> to zero.

Thus, by increasing the partner's share of partnership minimum gain when there has been a distribution of non-recourse loan proceeds allocable to an increase in partnership minimum gain, the qualified income offset is not triggered and Ben will be responsible for the tax liability associated with the distribution upon disposition of the property securing the debt.

---

10. Treas. Reg. § 1.704-2(g)(1), flush language.

> **Practice Note:** A net increase in partnership minimum gain may be attributable to:
> - Depreciation deductions in excess of repayments of the principal balance of the liability;
> - Non-recourse refinancing in excess of basis; or
> - A conversion of a partnership recourse liability to a non-recourse liability.
>
> A net decrease in partnership minimum gain may be attributable to:
> - Taxable disposition of the property securing the non-recourse liability;
> - Repayments of the principal balance of the liability in excess of depreciation deductions claimed for the year; or
> - A conversion of a partnership non-recourse liability to a recourse liability.

Non-recourse deduction. A non-recourse deduction is equal to the net increase in partnership minimum gain, less distributions of proceeds of a non-recourse liability that are allocable to an increase in partnership minimum gain.[11]

> **Example:** In Year 1, the partnership purchased an apartment building for $50,000. It was financed entirely with a $50,000 non-recourse loan, secured by the apartment building. The partnership was not required to make any principal payments on the non-recourse loan until Year 5. It was allowed to claim $10,000 of depreciation each year. Each year the depreciation deductions will create a $10,000 increase in partnership minimum gain. Accordingly, each year the partnership has $10,000 in non-recourse deductions.

> **Practice Note:** Non-recourse deductions are deemed to consist first of depreciation deductions with respect to the property subject to the non-recourse liability to the extent of any increase in partnership minimum gain attributable to the property. Next, non-recourse deductions are deemed to consist of a ratable share of the partnership's other items of loss, deduction, and nondeductible, non-capitalizable expenditures for the year. [Treas. Reg. § 1.704-2(c)]

Minimum gain chargeback. When there is a decrease in a partner's share of partnership minimum gain, a corresponding amount of gain must be allocated, or charged-back, to that partner.[12] Two different events may cause a decrease in a partner's share of partnership minimum gain.

First, the property subject to the non-recourse debt may be sold, triggering gain at least in the amount of the *Tufts* gain. Second, a decrease can occur when the amount

---

11. Treas. Reg. § 1.704-2(c).
12. Treas. Reg. § 1.704-2(f)(1).

of non-recourse debt is reduced, either by repayment of any portion of the liability or by conversion of any portion of a non-recourse debt into a recourse debt.

Example: In Year 1, the partnership purchased an apartment building for $50,000. It was financed entirely with a $50,000 non-recourse loan, secured by the apartment building. The partnership was not required to make any principal payments on the non-recourse loan until Year 5. It was allowed to claim $10,000 of depreciation each year. The partnership allocated all depreciation deductions to Amy, a partner in the partnership. Amy's initial capital account was $100,000.

At the end of Year 1, Amy had claimed $10,000 in depreciation and the adjusted basis of the building was $40,000. The amount of non-recourse deduction (*i.e.*, the increase in the amount of partnership minimum gain or *Tufts* or phantom gain) was $10,000. Her capital account was reduced by $10,000 to $90,000.

At the end of Year 2, Amy claimed an additional $10,000 in depreciation and the adjusted basis of the building was $30,000. The total amount of partnership minimum gain (or *Tufts* or phantom gain) was $20,000. The amount of non-recourse deduction (*i.e.*, the increase in the amount of partnership minimum gain or *Tufts* or phantom gain) was $10,000. Her capital account was reduced by $10,000 to $80,000.

At the end of Year 3, Amy claimed an additional $10,000 in depreciation and the adjusted basis of the building was $20,000. The total amount of partnership minimum gain (or *Tufts* or phantom gain) was $30,000. The amount of non-recourse deduction (*i.e.*, the increase in the amount of partnership minimum gain or *Tufts* or phantom gain) was $10,000. Her capital account was reduced by $10,000 to $70,000.

In summary:

Year	Depreciation	Building Adj Bas.	NR ded.	Total PMG
1	$10,000	$40,000	$10,000	$10,000
2	10,000	30,000	10,000	20,000
3	10,000	20,000	10,000	30,000

At the beginning of Year 4 (ignoring any applicable depreciation for the year) the partnership then sold the building for the amount of the non-recourse debt, $50,000. It recognized $30,000 of gain (amount realized of $50,000, less adjusted basis of $20,000). After the sale, because the partnership no longer has any partnership minimum gain, there has been a $30,000 decrease in partnership minimum gain ($30,000 partnership minimum gain to zero partnership minimum gain). This decrease triggers a minimum gain chargeback to Amy, the partner who was allocated the correlative non-recourse deductions. Her capital account is increased by the $30,000 of gain from $70,000 to $100,000.

There are some exceptions to the requirement of a minimum gain chargeback. First, the outstanding balance of the non-recourse liability may be reduced by funds contributed by the partner to the partnership to pay down a non-recourse liability. Because the partner's capital account will be increased by the amount of the contribution, to this extent the reduction in the partner's share of partnership minimum gain will not trigger any qualified income offset. Similarly, to this extent, there is no need to allocate income to the partner through a minimum gain chargeback.[13]

Second, if any portion of the non-recourse debt is converted to recourse debt, the partner may bear the economic risk of loss for the debt. To such an extent, there is no need for a minimum gain chargeback.[14]

Finally, there is no minimum gain chargeback if it would cause a distortion in the economic arrangement of the partners and there is sufficient other income to correct the distortion.[15]

Practice Note: Because the partner will be allocated gain equal to the amount of non-recourse deductions that have been allocated to him (in general, his share of partnership minimum gain), under the alternate economic effect test he is treated as having an obligation to restore a negative capital account balance to the extent of his share of partnership minimum gain. [Treas. Reg. § 1.704-2(g)(1), flush language.]

Partner's share of partnership minimum gain. The partnership's total partnership minimum gain is allocated among the partners. Each partner's share of partnership minimum gain is important:

- For determining the extent to which a partner is treated as having an obligation to restore a negative capital account balance (so as to not trigger a qualified income offset);
- To determine the amount of *Tufts*, or phantom, gain that must be allocated to the partner; and
- As will be seen in a later chapter, to determine the partner's share of a non-recourse liability.

A partner's share of partnership minimum gain is the sum of the non-recourse deductions allocated to the partner throughout the life of the partnership and the partner's share of distributions of non-recourse liability proceeds allocable to an increase in minimum gain, less the partner's share of any prior net decreases in partnership minimum gain.[16]

A partner's minimum gain chargeback is equal to his share of the net decrease in partnership minimum gain. In general, a partner's share of the net decrease is the amount of the total net decrease, multiplied by the partner's percentage share of the partnership minimum gain at the end of the immediately preceding taxable year.[17] The allocation consists first of gains recognized from disposition of the property subject to a

---

13. Treas. Reg. § 1.704-2(f)(3).
14. Treas. Reg. § 1.704-2(f)(2).
15. Treas. Reg. § 1.704-2(f)(4).
16. Treas. Reg. § 1.704-2(g)(1).
17. Treas. Reg. § 1.704-2(g)(2).

non-recourse liability. Second, it consists of a ratable share of other items of partnership income and gain for the year.[18]

Practice Note: A minimum gain chargeback must be made before any other allocations of partnership items for the year. [Treas. Reg. § 1.704-2(j)] If the partnership does not have sufficient items of income or gain to satisfy the chargeback, such items must be allocated in the subsequent years to cure the deficiency as soon as possible. [Treas. Reg. § 1.704-2(f)(6), (j)(1)]

Summary of Definitions:

  Non-recourse debt
 − Book adjusted basis
  Partnership minimum gain (*Tufts* gain or phantom income)

  Net increase in PMG
 − Distributions made during the year of proceeds of non-recourse liability that are allocable to an increase in PMG
  Non-recourse deductions

  Non-recourse deduction allocations
 + distributions of non-recourse liability proceeds allocable to increase in PMG
  Partner's share of PMG

Minimum gain chargeback: if there is a net decrease in PMG, each partner must be allocated items of income/gain equal to that partner's share of the net decrease in PMG unless the decrease is due to:
 • The liability becoming recourse to that partner; or
 • A contribution to capital that is used to repay the non-recourse liability.

A partner's share of the net decrease in PMG = (total net decrease) x (partner's percentage share of PMG at the end of prior year).

---

b. Safe Harbor Requirements

The allocation of deductions and losses attributable to non-recourse liabilities will be deemed to have been made in accordance with the partner's interest in the partnership and, therefore will be respected, if the safe harbor requirements set forth in the regulations are met.[19]

The first requirement is that the partnership agreement must meet either the general economic effect test or the alternate economic effect test.[20]

The second requirement is that, beginning in the first taxable year in which the partnership has non-recourse deductions, allocation of non-recourse deductions must be

---

18. Treas. Reg. § 1.704-2(f)(6).
19. Treas. Reg. § 1.704-2(e).
20. Treas. Reg. § 1.704-2(e)(1).

reasonably consistent with allocations of some other significant partnership item attributable to the property securing the non-recourse liabilities of the partnership (other than allocation of minimum gain). Such other allocations must have substantial economic effect.[21]

The third requirement is that, in the first year in which the partnership has non-recourse deductions or makes a distribution of proceeds of a non-recourse liability allocable to an increase in partnership minimum gain, the partnership agreement must contain a minimum gain chargeback.[22]

The fourth requirement is that all other material allocations and capital account adjustments under the partnership agreement must comply with the basic Section 704(b) regulations.[23]

Safe Harbor Requirements for Allocation of Non-Recourse Deductions:

- The economic effect test must be met (either the general or the alternate);
- Beginning in the year the partnership has non-recourse deductions, the allocation must be reasonably consistent with other allocations (which have substantial economic effect) attributable to the property securing the non-recourse debt;
- There must be a minimum gain chargeback provision; and
- Allocations of other material items must have substantial economic effect.

If the allocation of non-recourse deductions does not meet the safe harbor requirements, it will be reallocated in accordance with the partner's interest in the partnership.[24]

C. Application of Rules

Example 1. Lorelei, the limited partner, and Garth, the general partner, formed a limited partnership to acquire and operate a shopping mall. Lorelei contributed $180,000 and Garth contributed $20,000. The partnership obtained an $800,000 non-recourse loan and purchased the mall (on leased land) for $1,000,000. The non-recourse loan was secured only by the mall, and no principal payments were due for five years.

The partnership agreement provided that capital accounts would be maintained according to the regulations, liquidating distributions would be make according to capital account balances and that Garth would be required to restore any deficit balance in his capital account. Lorelei was not required to restore any deficit balance in her account, but the agreement contained a qualified income offset with respect to her. The partnership agreement also contained a minimum gain chargeback. Finally, the part-

---

21. Treas. Reg. § 1.704-2(e)(2).
22. Treas. Reg. § 1.704-2(e)(3).
23. Treas. Reg. § 1.704-2(e)(4).
24. Treas. Reg. §§ 1.704-1(b)(3), -2(b)(1).

nership agreement provided that, except as otherwise required by its qualified income offset and minimum gain chargeback provisions, all partnership items would be allocated 90 percent to Lorelei and 10 percent to Garth, except non-recourse deductions which would be allocated 80 percent to Lorelei and 20 percent to Garth, until the first time when the partnership had recognized items of income and gain that exceeded the items of loss and deduction it had recognized over its life. Then, all partnership items would be allocated equally between Garth and Lorelei.

At the end of each partnership taxable year, no items are reasonably expected to cause or increase a deficit balance in Lorelei's capital account.

In each of the partnership's first two taxable years, it generates rental income equal to its expenses and a depreciation deduction of $100,000. There is no increase in partnership minimum gain in the first two years.

Year	Depreciation	Building AB	Non-Rec. Ded.	Total PMG
1	$100,000	$900,000	$-0-	$-0-
2	100,000	800,000	-0-	-0-

Because there is no partnership minimum gain in the first two years, the allocation is an allocation of recourse deductions. Furthermore, the allocation of the losses 90 percent to Lorelei and 10 percent to Garth has substantial economic effect. The partners' capital accounts would appear as follows:

	Lorelei	Garth
Capital account on formation:	$180,000	$20,000
Depreciation from year one:	<90,000>	<10,000>
Depreciation from year two:	<90,000>	<10,000>
Capital account at end of year 2:	$-0-	$-0-

In the partnership's third taxable year, income again equals expenses, and the partnership has $100,000 of depreciation.

Year	Depreciation	Adjusted Basis	Non-Rec. Ded.	Total PMG
3	$100,000	$700,000	$100,000	$100,000

There is a $100,000 increase in partnership minimum gain in the third year. Thus, there is a $100,000 non-recourse deduction.

Allocation of non-recourse deductions, 80 percent to Lorelei and 20 percent to Garth, is consistent with the allocation of other significant items related to the building. The other items are allocated in a manner that has substantial economic effect. The partnership agreement contains a minimum gain chargeback. And, other material allocations and capital account adjustments under the partnership agreement comply with the basic Section 704(b) regulations. The partners' capital accounts would appear as follows:

	Lorelei	Garth
Capital account at end of year 2:	$-0-	$-0-
Depreciation in year three:	<80,000>	<20,000>
Capital account at end of year 3:	<$80,000>	<$20,000>

The total partnership minimum gain is $100,000. Lorelei's share of partnership minimum gain is $80,000 and Garth's share is $20,000. Note that Lorelei is treated as having an obligation to restore a deficit capital account balance of $80,000 (the amount of her partnership minimum gain).[25] Thus, even though she is a limited partner and does not have an obligation to restore a negative capital account, her negative capital account balance does not trigger the qualified income offset.

Example 2. Failing the safe harbor requirements. The facts are the same as above, except the partnership agreement provided that all non-recourse deductions of the partnership would be allocated 99 percent to Lorelei and one percent to Garth. And, at the time the partnership agreement is entered into, there is a reasonable likelihood that over the partnership life it will realize amounts of income and gain significantly in excess of amounts of loss and deductions, other than non-recourse deductions.

The analysis is the same for the first two years. In the partnership's third taxable year, because there was a $100,000 increase in partnership minimum gain, there was a $100,000 non-recourse deduction.

Allocation of the non-recourse deduction (99 percent to Lorelei and one percent to Garth) is not consistent with the allocation of other significant items related to the building (recourse deductions allocated 90 percent to Lorelei and 10 percent to Garth and, eventually, equally between the partners). Thus, the allocation of non-recourse deductions fails the safe harbor and does not have substantial economic effect. The allocation must be disregarded and the non-recourse deductions reallocated accordingly to the partners' overall economic interests in the partnership.[26]

Example 3. Conversion of non-recourse debt to recourse debt. Marlene, the limited partner, and Nester, the general partner, formed a limited partnership to acquire and operate a book store. Marlene contributed $180,000 and Nester contributed $20,000. The partnership obtained an $800,000 non-recourse loan and purchased the building (on leased land) for $1,000,000. The non-recourse loan was secured only by the building, and no principal payments were due for five years.

The partnership agreement provided that capital accounts would be maintained according to the regulations, liquidating distributions would be made according to capital account balances and Nester would be required to restore any deficit balance in his capital account. Marlene was not required to restore any deficit balance in her account, but the agreement contained a qualified income offset with respect to her. The partnership agreement also contained a minimum gain chargeback. Finally, the partnership agreement provided that, except as otherwise required by its qualified income offset and minimum gain chargeback provisions, all partnership items would be allocated 90 percent to Marlene and 10 percent to Nester, except non-recourse deductions which would be allocated 80 percent to Marlene and 20 percent to Nester, until the first time when the partnership had recognized items of income and gain that exceeded the items of loss and deduction it had recognized over its life. Then, all partnership items would be allocated equally between Marlene and Nester.

---

25. Treas. Reg. §§ 1.704-2(m), Ex. 1(i).
26. Treas. Reg. § 1.704-2(m) Ex. 1(iii).

At the end of each partnership taxable year, no items are reasonably expected to cause or increase a deficit balance in Marlene's capital account.

In each of the partnership's first two taxable years, it generates rental income equal to its expenses and a depreciation deduction of $100,000. There is no increase in partnership minimum gain in the first two years.

Year	Depreciation	Building AB	Non-Rec. Ded.	Total PMG
1	$100,000	$900,000	$-0-	$-0-
2	100,000	800,000	-0-	-0-

Because there is no partnership minimum gain in the first two years, the allocation is an allocation of recourse deductions. Furthermore, the allocation of the depreciation 90 percent to Marlene and 10 percent to Nester has substantial economic effect. The partners' capital accounts would appear as follows:

	Marlene	Nester
Capital account on formation:	$180,000	$20,000
Depreciation from year one:	<90,000>	<10,000>
Depreciation from year two:	<90,000>	<10,000>
Capital account at end of year 2:	$-0-	$-0-

In the partnership's third taxable year, income again equals expenses, and the partnership has $100,000 of depreciation.

Year	Depreciation	Adjusted Basis	Non-Rec. Ded.	Total PMG
3	$100,000	$700,000	$100,000	$100,000

There is a $100,000 increase in partnership minimum gain in the third year. Thus, there is a $100,000 non-recourse deduction.

Allocation of non-recourse deductions is consistent with the allocation of other significant items related to the building. The other items are allocated in a manner that has substantial economic effect. The partnership agreement contains a minimum gain chargeback. And, other material allocations and capital account adjustments under the partnership agreement comply with the basic Section 704(b) regulations. The partners' capital accounts would appear as follows:

	Marlene	Nester
Capital account at end of year 2:	$-0-	$-0-
Depreciation in year three:	<80,000>	<20,000>
Capital account at end of year 3:	<$80,000>	<$20,000>

The total partnership minimum gain is $100,000. Marlene's share of partnership minimum gain is $80,000 and Nester's share is $20,000.

In the partnership's fourth taxable year Marlene contributed $160,000 and Nester contributed $40,000. The $200,000 was used to reduce the debt from $800,000 to $600,000.

Year	Depreciation	Adjusted Basis	Non-Rec. Ded.	Total PMG
4	$100,000	$600,000	$-0-	$-0-

There is a $100,000 decrease in partnership minimum gain in the fourth year. Marlene's share of the decrease is $80,000 and Nester's is $20,000. However, because the decrease was due to a capital contribution used to repay the non-recourse liability, the partners are not subject to a minimum gain chargeback.[27]

D. Problems

1. Jack and Jill formed a limited partnership. Jack contributed $90,000 in exchange for a limited partnership interest and Jill contributed $10,000 in exchange for a general partnership interest. The partnership agreement allocated all depreciation 90 percent to Jack and 10 percent to Jill and allocated all non-recourse deductions 80 percent to Jack and 20 percent to Jill. When the partnership had recognized items of income and gain that exceeded the items of loss and deduction it had recognized over its life, all partnership items would be allocated equally between Jack and Jill.

The partnership purchased a building for $300,000, using the $100,000 cash contributed by the partners and financing the remaining $200,000 with a non-recourse debt, secured by the building. No payments were due on the loan for five years. Ignoring all conventions, in each year the partnership was entitled to $50,000 of depreciation. During each year, before considering depreciation, partnership income equaled its expenses.

(a) For the allocation of the depreciation to be respected, what must the partnership agreement include?

(b) The partnership agreement provided that capital accounts would be maintained in accordance with the regulations, that Jill had an obligation to restore a negative capital account, and that liquidating distributions would be made in accordance with capital account balances. With respect to Jack, the partnership agreement had a qualified income offset. The partnership agreement also contained a minimum gain chargeback. It provided that any excess non-recourse debt would be allocated equally between the partners.

In each year, before taking into consideration the depreciation, partnership income equaled its expenses.
(1) In the first year:
    (a) Is the debt a non-recourse debt?
    (b) Is the depreciation a non-recourse deduction?
    (c) Construct a balance sheet reflecting the situations of the partnership and the partners at the end of the first year.
(2) In the second year:
    (a) Is the depreciation a non-recourse deduction?
    (b) Construct a balance sheet reflecting the situations of the partnership and the partners at the end of the second year.
(3) In the third year:
    (a) Is the depreciation a non-recourse deduction?
    (b) What are the partner's capital accounts at the end of the third year?

---

27. Treas. Reg. §§ 1.704-2(f)(3); 1.704-2(m) Ex. 1(iv).

   (c) Alternatively, if the partnership agreement provided that non-recourse de-
        ductions would be allocated 99 percent to Jack and one percent to Jill,
        would the allocation be respected?
(4) In the fourth year:
   (a) Is the depreciation a non-recourse deduction?
   (b) If Jack contributed $90,000 and Jill contributed $10,000, and the partner-
        ship used the $100,000 to pay down the liability to $100,000, would the re-
        duction in the debt trigger a minimum gain chargeback?
   (c) Alternatively, if the partnership converted the liability from a non-re-
        course to a recourse liability, would the conversion trigger a minimum
        gain chargeback?
   (d) Alternatively, the partnership incurred an additional $100,000 in non-re-
        course debt, secured by the building. It distributed the proceeds, $60,000
        to Jack and $40,000 to Jill. What are the consequences to the partners?

---

2. Application:

(a) How would you explain non-recourse deductions to the partners?

(b) When might you advise the partners to have a special allocation (an allocation not
     based on the partners' interests in the partnership) of non-recourse deductions?

(c) How would you explain to the partners whether an allocation of non-recourse de-
     ductions has substantial economic effect?

(d) Draft language for the partnership agreement that would satisfy the safe harbor
     test for an allocation of non-recourse deductions.

(e) Can you explain to the partners the connection between an allocation of non-re-
     course deductions and an allocation of non-recourse debt?

Chapter 17

Allocations of Depreciation from Property Contributed to the Partnership by a Partner

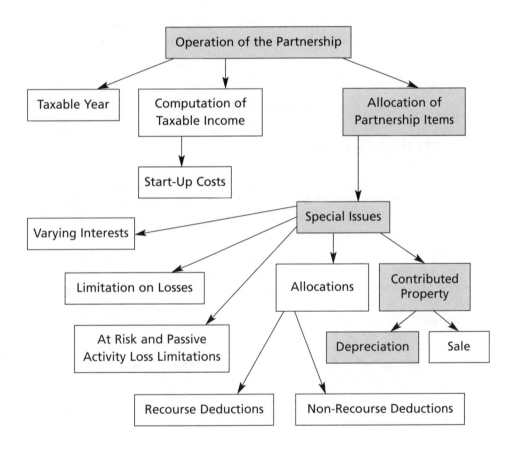

Read:

Code Section 704(c)(1)(A).

Treas. Reg. § 1.704-3(a)(1), -3(a)(2), -3(a)(3), -3(b)(1), -3(b)(2) Ex. 1(i), (ii), -3(c)(1)-(3), -3(d)(1)-(4), -3(d)(7) Ex. 1, -3(e)(1).

A. Background

Acquisition of partnership interest. A taxpayer is not required to recognize gain or loss from the transfer of property to a partnership in which the taxpayer is a partner. Rather, any gain or loss is deferred. In addition, his basis in the partnership interest is the amount of money and the adjusted basis of the property at the time of the contribution.[1]

Expense and depreciation. An expense has a life or benefit that lasts less than one year. As long as the expense is an ordinary and necessary expense that was paid or incurred in the partnership's business or for the production of income, the partnership is allowed a current deduction.

In contrast, a capital expenditure has a life or benefit that extends beyond one year. If the asset wears out over time, the cost of the asset is recovered through depreciation (for tangible property) or amortization (for intangible property) using the appropriate recovery method. In general, the amount of depreciation allowed is based on the cost of the property, the property's useful life, and the recovery method.

B. Discussion of Rules

1. Allocation of Depreciation

When partners are forming a partnership, they evaluate their respective economic positions based on the fair market value (less any liabilities the property is taken subject to) of the property contributed to the partnership.

Example: Ossie and Glory formed a general partnership. Ossie contributed $200,000 and Glory contributed equipment with a fair market value of $200,000. Because they contributed assets of equal value, generally they will be equal partners.

The tax treatment of the item may differ from the treatment for economic purposes. More specifically, for tax purposes, depreciation is determined based on the adjusted basis of the property. If the property had been purchased by the partnership, the cost of the property is recovered through depreciation or amortization and there will be no disparity between the depreciation determined for tax purposes and the depreciation determined for economic, or book, purposes. However, if the property had been contributed to the partnership by a partner, the partnership assumes the basis of the property and the partner's recovery method. Accordingly, there likely will be a disparity between the depreciation determined for tax purposes and the depreciation determined for economic, or book, purposes.

---

1. Code Sec. 722. The basis is increased by the amount (if any) of gain recognized under Section 721(b).

Recovery Method for Property Used in a Trade or Business or for the Production of Income

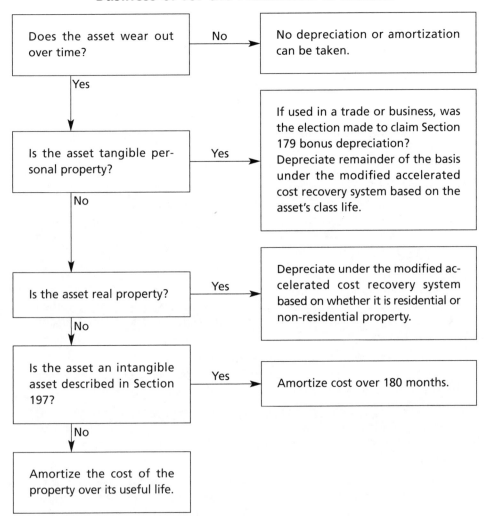

Example: Ossie and Glory formed an equal general partnership. Ossie contributed $200,000 and Glory contributed equipment with a fair market value of $200,000 and adjusted basis of $100,000. There are four years remaining on the life of the equipment. Assume for purposes of simplicity that the remaining basis is recovered using the straightline method (with no conventions).

From an economic perspective, the value of the property, $200,000, is recovered over the next four years, or $50,000 each year. As a 50-percent partner, Ossie will expect to receive an allocation of one-half of the depreciation, or $25,000 each year.

At the time of contribution, Glory's adjusted basis in the equipment was $100,000. For tax purposes, the adjusted basis is recovered over the next four years, or $25,000 each year. As a 50-percent partner, Ossie would be entitled to $12,500.

> There is a disparity between how much depreciation Ossie expects from an economic perspective, $25,000, and how much she would be allocated for tax purposes, $12,500.

To address the disparity that will exist when tax and economic, or book, depreciation are not the same, the regulations provide that the noncontributing partner is allocated the same amount of depreciation for tax purposes as he is allocated for economic, or book, purposes. Any remaining amount of depreciation is allocated to the contributing partner.[2] When computing the amount of depreciation, the same method and recovery period must be used for computing tax and economic, or book, depreciation.

Example: Ossie and Glory formed an equal general partnership. Ossie contributed $200,000 and Glory contributed equipment with a fair market value of $200,000 and adjusted basis of $100,000. There are four years remaining on the life of the equipment. Assume for purposes of simplicity that the remaining basis is recovered using the straightline method (with no conventions).

From an economic perspective, the value of the property, $200,000, is recovered over the next four years, or $50,000 each year. As a 50-percent partner, Ossie will expect to receive an allocation of one-half of the depreciation, or $25,000 each year.

At the time of contribution, Glory's adjusted basis in the equipment was $100,000. For tax purposes, the adjusted basis is recovered over the next four years, or $25,000 each year.

As the non-contributing partner, Ossie is allocated the same amount of depreciation for tax purposes as she is allocated for economic, or book, purposes, or $25,000. There is no remaining amount of depreciation to be allocated to the contributing partner, Glory.

Note that this result makes sense. As a partner with an indirect one-half ownership interest in the equipment, Ossie was entitled to depreciation with respect to one-half of the equipment. Glory, as the contributing partner, was able to claim depreciation prior to contribution. To the extent he previously claimed depreciation with respect to the equipment, he has claimed depreciation with respect to his indirect one-half ownership interest.

Assume that Glory had previously purchased the equipment for $200,000 and that he was entitled to claim $25,000 of depreciation each year (ignoring any conventions). If he contributed the property in the fifth year, the total amount of depreciation claimed by Ossie and Glory would be as follows:

Year	Glory	Ossie	Basis in property
1	$25,000	—	$175,000
2	25,000	—	150,000
3	25,000	—	125,000
4	25,000	—	100,000

---

2. Code Sec. 704(c)(1)(A); Treas. Reg. § 1.704-3(b)(1).

—equipment contributed to partnership—

5	—	$25,000	75,000
6	—	25,000	50,000
7	—	25,000	25,000
8	—	25,000	-0-
Total: $100,000		$100,000	

When the equipment is fully depreciated, both Ossie and Glory will have claimed one-half of the total cost of the property, $200,000, as depreciation, or $100,000 each.

Formula For Allocating Tax Depreciation Among the Partners Under The Traditional Method:
1. Determine the total amount of tax depreciation.
2. Determine the total amount of book depreciation.
3. Determine how the book depreciation would be allocated among the partners.
4. Allocate to the noncontributing partners tax depreciation in an amount equal to the amount of book depreciation.
5. Allocate any remaining tax depreciation to the contributing partner.

Exception for small disparity. If the amount of built-in gain or loss is small, the allocation required by Section 704(c) can be disregarded. The disparity is small if the total fair market value of all property contributed by a partner during the taxable year does not differ from the total adjusted basis of the property by more than 15 percent of the adjusted basis and the total gross disparity does not exceed $20,000.[3]

Example: Paul purchased equipment for $90,000. When the equipment had increased in value to $100,000, he contributed it to a partnership in exchange for a 50-percent general partnership interest. Quix contributed $100,000 cash.

Fifteen percent of the adjusted basis of the equipment is $13,500 (15% × 90,000). The fair market value of the equipment, $100,000, does not differ from the basis of the property, $90,000, by more than $13,500. And, the total disparity does not exceed $20,000. Accordingly, the disparity between basis and fair market value is a small disparity and may be disregarded.

---

2. Ceiling Rule

In certain circumstances, the amount of tax depreciation will be less than the amount of economic, or book, depreciation. When this result occurs, the regulations provide that the maximum amount of depreciation that can be allocated to the noncontributing partner is the amount of tax depreciation. The rule is referred to as the ceiling rule.

---

3. Treas. Reg. § 1.704-3(e)(1).

Under the traditional method, no adjustments are made to address the disparity between the amount of tax depreciation that is available to be allocated to the noncontributing partners and the amount of economic, or book, depreciation.

Example: Ossie and Glory formed an equal general partnership. Ossie contributed $200,000 and Glory contributed equipment with a fair market value of $200,000 and adjusted basis of $75,000. There are three years remaining on the life of the equipment. Assume for purposes of simplicity that the remaining basis is recovered using the straightline method (with no conventions).

From an economic perspective, the value of the property, $200,000, is recovered over the next three years, or $66,667 each year. As a 50-percent partner, Ossie will expect to receive an allocation of one-half of the depreciation, or $33,333 each year.

At the time of contribution, Glory's adjusted basis in the equipment was $75,000. For tax purposes, the adjusted basis is recovered over the next three years, or $25,000 each year.

As the non-contributing partner, Ossie should be allocated the same amount of depreciation for tax purposes as she is allocated for economic, or book, purposes, or $33,333. However, there is only $25,000 of tax depreciation available to be allocated to Ossie.

Note that this result creates a disparity. As a partner with an indirect one-half ownership interest in the equipment, Ossie should be entitled to depreciation with respect to one-half of the equipment. Glory, as the contributing partner, was able to claim depreciation prior to contribution. To the extent he previously claimed depreciation with respect to the equipment, he has claimed more than his one-half of the depreciation.

Assume that Glory had previously purchased the equipment for $200,000 and that he was entitled to claim $25,000 of depreciation each year (ignoring any conventions). If he contributed the property in the sixth year, the total amount of depreciation claimed by Ossie and Glory would be as follows:

Year	Glory	Ossie	Basis in property
1	$25,000	—	$175,000
2	25,000	—	150,000
3	25,000	—	125,000
4	25,000	—	100,000
5	25,000	—	75,000
—equipment contributed to partnership—			
6	—	$25,000	50,000
7	—	25,000	25,000
8	—	25,000	-0-
Total:	$125,000	$75,000	

When the ceiling rule applies there is an insufficient amount of tax depreciation available to be allocated to the non-contributing partner. Under the traditional method, this disparity is not corrected.[4] However, the shortfall can be corrected through one

---

4. Treas. Reg. § 1.704-3(b)(1).

of two methods, the traditional method with curative allocations or the remedial method.

a. Traditional Method with Curative Allocations

Under the traditional method with curative allocations, the partnership can allocate depreciation in the amount of the shortfall to the noncontributing partner from a different asset. Alternatively, the partnership can reduce the amount of ordinary income allocated to the noncontributing partner in an amount equal to the amount of the shortfall.[5] The curative allocation only impacts the partner's outside basis.

> **Practice Tip:** Curative allocations impact the partner's outside basis. They do not impact the partner's capital account.

b. Remedial Allocations

Under the remedial method, the partnership creates the necessary amount of depreciation to make up the shortfall caused by the ceiling rule. In addition, it creates an offsetting amount of ordinary income that is allocated to the contributing partner. The remedial allocation only impacts the partner's outside basis.[6]

If the remedial method is used, the economic, or book, depreciation is calculated in a different manner. The economic, or book, basis is divided into two portions, the first portion is equal to the tax basis and the second portion is equal to the remainder. With respect to the first portion, the amount equal to tax basis, depreciation is computed in the same manner as it is computed for tax purposes. With respect to the second portion, the remainder amount, depreciation is computed using the applicable recovery period and method that would be used if the partnership had just acquired the property.[7]

> **Practice Tip:** Remedial allocations impact the partner's outside basis. They do not impact the partner's capital account.

C. Application of Rules

Example 1. Contribution of depreciable property. Lendi contributed equipment with a basis of $6,000 and a fair market value of $9,000 to a partnership in exchange for a 50-percent partnership interest. The remaining useful life of the equipment was three

---

5. Treas. Reg. § 1.704-3(c).
6. Treas. Reg. § 1.704-3(d).
7. Treas. Reg. § 1.704-3(d)(2).

Allocation of Depreciation from Contributed Property

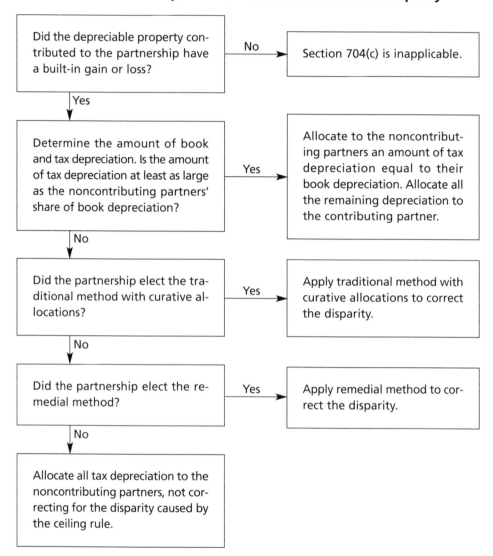

years. Margie contributed $9,000 cash in exchange for a 50-percent partnership interest. At the time of formation, the balance sheet would appear as follows:

Asset	Basis	FMV	Partner	Basis	Cap. Acct.
Cash	$9,000	$9,000	Lendi	$6,000	$9,000
Equipment	6,000	9,000	Margie	9,000	9,000
	$15,000	$18,000		$15,000	$18,000

The amount of tax depreciation is $2,000 ($6,000 recovered over three years). The amount of book deprecation is $3,000 ($9,000 recovered over three years). Margie would be allocated $1,500 of depreciation for book purposes. Accordingly, as the noncontributing partner, she is allocated $1,500 of tax depreciation and Lendi is allocated the remainder, or $500. Thus, the depreciation is allocated as follows:

	Lendi		Margie	
Tax	Book	Tax	Book	
<$500>	<$1,500>	<$1,500>	<$1,500>	

After the allocation of depreciation, the balance sheet would appear as follows:

Asset	Basis	FMV	Partner	Basis	Cap. Acct.
Cash	$9,000	$9,000	Lendi	$5,500	$7,500
Equipment	4,000	6,000	Margie	7,500	7,500
	$13,000	$15,000		$13,000	$15,000

Example 2. Ceiling rule—traditional method. Peter contributed equipment with a basis of $4,000 and a fair market value of $10,000 to a partnership in exchange for a 50-percent partnership interest. The remaining useful life of the equipment was two years. Quinton contributed $10,000 cash in exchange for a 50-percent partnership interest. With respect to Section 704(c) the partnership used the traditional method of allocation. At the time of formation, the balance sheet would appear as follows:

Asset	Basis	FMV	Partner	Basis	Cap. Acct.
Cash	$10,000	$10,000	Peter	$4,000	$10,000
Equipment	4,000	10,000	Quinton	10,000	10,000
	$14,000	$20,000		$14,000	$20,000

The amount of tax depreciation is $2,000 ($4,000 recovered over two years). The amount of book deprecation is $5,000 ($10,000 recovered over two years). Quinton would be allocated $2,500 of depreciation for book purposes. As the non-contributing partner, he should be allocated $2,500 of depreciation for tax purposes. However, there is only $2,000 of tax depreciation to allocate to Quinton. Because the partnership uses the traditional method of allocation, the partnership will not correct the disparity. The depreciation is allocated as follows:

	Peter		Quinton	
Tax	Book	Tax	Book	
$-0-	<$2,500>	<$2,000>	<$2,500>	

After the allocation of depreciation, the balance sheet would appear as follows:

Asset	Basis	FMV	Partner	Basis	Cap. Acct.
Cash	$10,000	$10,000	Peter	$4,000	$7,500
Equipment	2,000	5,000	Quinton	8,000	7,500
	$12,000	$15,000		$12,000	$15,000

Example 3. Ceiling rule—traditional method with curative allocations. Rochelle contributed equipment with a basis of $4,000 and a fair market value of $10,000 to a partnership in exchange for a 50-percent partnership interest. The remaining useful life of the equipment was two years. Sandy contributed $10,000 cash in exchange for a 50-percent partnership interest. With respect to Section 704(c) the partnership used the traditional method with curative allocations. At the time of formation, the balance sheet would appear as follows:

Asset	Basis	FMV	Partner	Basis	Cap. Acct.
Cash	$10,000	$10,000	Rochelle	$4,000	$10,000
Equipment	4,000	10,000	Sandy	10,000	10,000
	$14,000	$20,000		$14,000	$20,000

During the year, the partnership earned $20,000 of income.

The amount of tax depreciation is $2,000 ($4,000 recovered over two years). The amount of book deprecation is $5,000 ($10,000 recovered over two years). Sandy would be allocated $2,500 of depreciation for book purposes. As the non-contributing partner, she should be allocated $2,500 of depreciation for tax purposes. However, there is only $2,000 of tax depreciation to allocate to Sandy. Because the partnership uses the traditional method with curative allocations, it can correct the disparity.

Generally, the partnership income would be allocated equally between Rochelle and Sandy, or $10,000 each. However, the partnership can use the ordinary income to correct the disparity caused by the ceiling rule. It can allocate $500 less of the partnership income to Sandy (to account for the fact that she received $500 less of a depreciation deduction). Thus, the income, for tax purposes, would be allocated $10,500 to Rochelle and $9,500 to Sandy. The curative allocation does not impact their capital accounts; they are each allocated $10,000 of income. The allocations would appear as follows:

	Rochelle		Sandy	
	Tax	Book	Tax	Book
Depreciation	$-0-	<$2,500>	<$2,000>	<$2,500>
Income	10,500	10,000	9,500	10,000

After the allocation of income and depreciation, the balance sheet would appear as follows:

Asset	Basis	FMV	Partner	Basis	Cap. Acct.
Cash	$30,000	$30,000	Rochelle	$14,500	$17,500
Equipment	2,000	5,000	Sandy	17,500	17,500
	$32,000	$35,000		$32,000	$35,000

Example 4. Ceiling rule—remedial method. Trish contributed equipment with a basis of $4,000 and a fair market value of $10,000 to a partnership in exchange for a 50-percent partnership interest. The remaining useful life of the equipment was four years. Ursula contributed $10,000 cash in exchange for a 50-percent partnership interest. With respect to Section 704(c) the partnership used the remedial method. At the time of formation, the balance sheet would appear as follows:

Asset	Basis	FMV	Partner	Basis	Cap. Acct.
Cash	$10,000	$10,000	Trish	$4,000	$10,000
Equipment	4,000	10,000	Ursula	10,000	10,000
	$14,000	$20,000		$14,000	$20,000

Under the remedial method, book depreciation is calculated by dividing the book basis into two portions. The first portion is equal to the tax basis, $4,000, and the second portion is equal to the remainder, $6,000. With respect to the first portion, depreciation is computed in the same manner as it is computed for tax purposes, or $1,000 each year. With respect to the second portion, depreciation is computed using the applicable recovery period and method which would be used if the partnership had just acquired the property. Assume that, if the partnership had just acquired the property, it could recover the cost over ten years, using the straightline method (assuming no conventions). Accordingly, the second portion is $600 ($6,000 divided by ten years). Thus, there is a total of $1,600 of book depreciation for the year ($1,000 under the first portion and $600 under the second portion), which is allocated equally between Trish and Ursula, or $800 each. Ursula, as the non-contributing partner, is allocated $800 of tax depreciation and Trish is allocated the remainder, or $200. No remedial allocations are needed yet. The depreciation is allocated as follows:

	Trish		Ursula	
	Tax	Book	Tax	Book
	<$200>	<$800>	<$800>	<$800>

The results are the same for the following three years. In the fifth year, the first portion of the book depreciation has been fully recovered. Accordingly, an amount is recovered only under the second portion. Thus, there is a total of $600 of book depreciation for the year, which is allocated equally between Trish and Ursula, or $300 each. However, there is no tax depreciation to allocate to Urusla. Because the partnership uses the remedial method it can correct the disparity by creating an additional $300 of depreciation to allocate to Ursula and creating an offsetting $300 allocation of income to allocate to Trish. The allocations created under the remedial method do not impact the partners' capital accounts. The allocations are as follows:[8]

	Trish		Ursula	
	Tax	Book	Tax	Book
Depreciation	—	<$300>	—	<$300>
Remedial	$300	—	<$300>	

D. Problems

1. Hans and Irene formed a partnership. Hans contributed equipment with a fair market value of $20,000 and a remaining useful life of four years. Irene contributed $20,000 cash.

(a) What are the tax consequences if the basis of the equipment was $12,000? The partnership had no other income or expenses during the year. Prepare a balance sheet to reflect the situation of the partners at the end of the year.

(b) Alternatively, what are the tax consequences if the basis of the equipment was $8,000 and the partnership used the traditional method? The partnership had no other income or expenses during the year. Prepare a balance sheet to reflect the situation of the partners at the end of the year.

---

8. Treas. Reg. § 1.704-3(d)(7) Ex. 1.

(c) Alternatively, what are the tax consequences if the basis of the equipment was $8,000 and the partnership used the traditional method with curative allocations? The partnership had $10,000 of other income during the year. Prepare a balance sheet to reflect the situation of the partners at the end of the year.

(d) Alternatively, the basis of the equipment was $8,000 and the partnership used the remedial method. If the partnership had just acquired the property, it could recover the cost over ten years, using the straightline method (assuming no conventions) what are the tax consequences:

(1) In the first year.

(2) In the fifth year.

---

2. Application:

(a) How would you explain to the partners the disparity between tax depreciation and book depreciation?

(b) Which curative method, if any, will you advise the partners to elect? Why? What information might you need to help you decide? Who gets to make the decision as to which method, if any, will be used? How do you know?

E. Advanced Problems — Looking Forward

Without conducting any research, consider the following question:

What impact will depreciation have on the amount of built-in gain or loss that should be allocated to the contributing partner upon sale of the property?

Chapter 18

Allocations Related to the Sale of Contributed Property

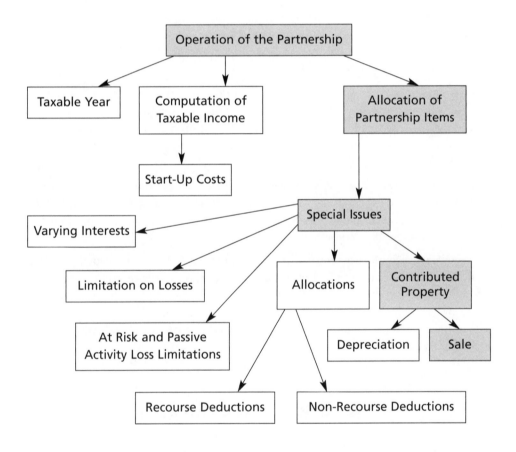

Read:

Code Section 704(c)(1)(A), (c)(1)(C); 724; 751(c), (d).

Treas. Reg. § 1.704-3(a)(1)-(3), -3(a)(10)(i), -3(b)(1), -3(b)(2) Ex. 1(i),
 -3(c)(2), -3(c)(3)(i), -3(c)(3)(ii), -3(c)(3)(iii)(A), -3(d)(1), -3(d)(3), -3(d)(4), -3(d)(7).
Ex. 2, -3(d)(7) Ex. 3, -3(e)(1).

A. Background

Shifting of gain or loss between taxpayers. As a general rule, gain or loss from the disposition of property belongs to the person who owns the property. For example, in *Salvatore v. Commissioner,*[1] Mrs. Salvatore entered into an agreement to sell an oil and gas station to Texaco. However, after she entered into the sale agreement, she transferred one-half of the property to her five children. The sale was then completed by Mrs. Salvatore and her five children as the sellers. Mrs. Salvatore reported one-half of the gain and her five children reported one-half of the gain.

The Internal Revenue Service argued that, even though the form of the transaction was a sale from Mrs. Salvatore and her children to Texaco, the substance of the transaction was a sale of the entire property by Mrs. Salvatore. The transfers to her children should be disregarded and Mrs. Salvatore should report all of the gain. The Tax Court agreed with the Internal Revenue Service.

Acquisition of partnership interest. A taxpayer is not required to recognize gain or loss from the transfer of property to a partnership in which the taxpayer is a partner. Rather, any gain or loss is deferred. In addition, his basis in the partnership interest is the amount of money and the adjusted basis of the property at the time of the contribution.[2]

Expense and depreciation. An expense has a life or benefit that lasts less than one year. As long as the expense is an ordinary and necessary expense that was paid or incurred in the partnership's business or for the production of income, the partnership is allowed a current deduction.

In contrast, a capital expenditure has a life or benefit that extends beyond one year. If the asset wears out over time, the cost of the asset is recovered through depreciation (for tangible property) or amortization (for intangible property) using the appropriate recovery method. In general, the amount of depreciation allowed is based on the cost of the property, the property's useful life, and the recovery method. Depreciation is computed for both tax and book purposes.

B. Discussion of Rules

1. Allocation of Gain or Loss From Sale of Contributed Property

Pre-contribution gain or loss. Prior to contribution of property to a partnership, the partner is the owner of the property. Thus, any gain or loss that arises in the property

---

1. T.C. Memo. 1970-30, *aff'd,* 434 F2d 600 (3d Cir. 1970).
2. Code Sec. 722. The basis is increased by the amount (if any) of gain recognized under Section 721(b).

prior to contribution belongs to the partner individually and must be allocated to, and reported by, the contributing partner. It cannot be shifted to the other partners.[3]

Example: Lexi purchased land for $10,000. When the land had increased in value to $50,000, she contributed it to a partnership in exchange for a 50-percent general partnership interest. Mark contributed $50,000 cash in exchange for a 50-percent general partnership interest. The partnership agreement provided that allocations would be made based on ownership interests.

Eight years later, the partnership sold the land for $50,000, realizing a tax gain of $40,000 (amount realized of $50,000, less adjusted basis of $10,000). It did not recognize any book gain (amount realized of $50,000, less book basis of $50,000).

All of the $40,000 of tax gain represents Lexi's pre-contribution gain. Thus, even though the partnership agreement provides that allocations are made based on ownership interests, the $40,000 of gain must be allocated solely to Lexi.

Practice Tip: Note that the tax allocation associated with the built-in gain or loss does not have a correlative economic allocation or adjustment to the partner's capital account. There has been no change at the partnership level.

The amount of built-in gain or loss is the difference between the book value and the adjusted tax basis of the property.[4]

Example: Nikki purchased equipment for $10,000. When the equipment had an adjusted basis of $7,000 and fair market value of $8,000, she contributed it to a partnership in exchange for a 50-percent general partnership interest. Opus contributed $8,000 cash in exchange for a 50-percent general partnership interest. The partnership agreement provided that allocations would be made based on ownership interests.

Eight years later, when the equipment had an adjusted basis of $5,000 and book value of $6,000, the partnership sold the equipment for $6,000. The partnership realized a tax gain of $1,000 (amount realized of $6,000, less adjusted basis of $5,000). It did not recognize any book gain (amount realized of $6,000, less book basis of $6,000).

The amount of built-in gain is the different between the book value, $6,000, and the adjusted basis, $5,000. Accordingly, all of the $1,000 of tax gain represents Nikki's pre-contribution gain. Thus, even though the partnership agreement provides that allocations are made based on ownership interests, the $1,000 of gain must be allocated solely to Nikki.

---

3. Code Sec. 704(c)(1)(A); Treas. Reg. § 1.704-3(a)(1).
4. Treas. Reg. § 1.704-3(a)(3)(ii).

> **Practice Tip:** The allocation of pre-contribution gain or loss cannot be addressed through a special allocation. Because the tax gain or loss associated with the built-in gain or loss does not have a correlative capital account adjustment, a special allocation of the tax gain or loss would not have substantial economic effect.

Definitions:

The property has a built-in gain when, at the time the property is contributed to the partnership, the fair market value (book value) is greater than the adjusted basis.

The property has a built-in loss when, at the time the property is contributed to the partnership, the adjusted basis is greater than the fair market value (book value).[5]

Post-contribution gain or loss. After contribution of the property, the partnership is the owner of the property. Any gain or loss that arises after contribution must be allocated among and reported by the partners. The amount of post-contribution gain or loss is measured by the difference between the selling price and the property's book value. Unlike pre-contribution gain or loss, post-contribution gain or loss is reflected in the partners' capital accounts.

> **Example:** Lexi purchased land for $10,000. When the land had increased in value to $50,000, she contributed it to a partnership in exchange for a 50-percent general partnership interest. Mark contributed $50,000 cash in exchange for a 50-percent general partnership interest. The partnership agreement provided that allocations would be made based on ownership interests.
>
> Eight years later, the partnership sold the land for $60,000, realizing a tax gain of $50,000 (amount realized of $60,000, less adjusted basis of $10,000). It recognized $10,000 of book gain (amount realized of $60,000, less book basis of $50,000).
>
> The $40,000 of tax gain represents Lexi's pre-contribution gain. Thus, even though the partnership agreement provides that allocations are made based on ownership interests, $40,000 of gain must be allocated solely to Lexi. The remaining $10,000 of gain is post-contribution gain that is allocated equally between Lexi and Mark. Similarly, the $10,000 of book gain is allocated equally between Lexi and Mark.
>
> | | Lexi | | Mark | |
> |--------|----------|----------|----------|----------|
> | | Tax | Book | Tax | Book |
> | | $45,000 | $5,000 | $5,000 | $5,000 |

Exception for small disparity. If the amount of built-in gain or loss is small, the allocation required by Section 704(c) can be disregarded. The disparity is small if the

---

5. Treas. Reg. § 1.704-3(a)(3)(ii).

total fair market value of all property contributed by a partner during the taxable year does not differ from the total adjusted basis of the property by more than 15 percent of the adjusted basis and the total gross disparity does not exceed $20,000.[6]

Example: Paul purchased land for $90,000. When the land had increased in value to $100,000, he contributed it to a partnership in exchange for a 50-percent general partnership interest. Quix contributed $100,000 cash.

Fifteen percent of the adjusted basis of the land is $13,500 (15% x 90,000). The fair market value of the land, $100,000, does not differ from the basis of the property, $90,000, by more than $13,500. And, the total disparity does not exceed $20,000. Accordingly, the disparity between basis and fair market value is a small disparity and may be disregarded.

Anti-abuse rule for property with built-in loss. If a partner contributes property with a built-in loss, special rules apply.[7] First, the built-in loss is taken into consideration only when considering allocations to the contributing partner. Second, except when provided for in the regulations, when considering allocations to the noncontributing partners, the property is treated as if its basis was its fair market value at the time of contribution.

Reverse Section 704(c). While a Section 704(c) issue may arise when a partner contributes property to a partnership, it is not the only time a partnership may have to address built-in gain or loss in partnership assets. When a new partner joins an existing partnership, there may be gain or loss in the assets at the time he joins. This pre-existing gain or loss should be allocated to the old (existing) partners, and not the new partner. Then, any gain or loss that occurs after the new partner joins should be allocated among all the partners.

To address this issue, the partners can use one of two methods. First, it can provide for a special allocation of the gain or loss at the time the new partner joins the old (existing) partners.[8]

Example: Blair and Cindy were equal partners in the Epsilon Partnership. The partnership had previously purchased Blackacre for $100,000. Its current fair market value was $200,000. Deidre joined the partnership by contributing $100,000 cash in exchange for a one-third interest.

At the time Deidre joined the partnership, Blackacre had $100,000 of built-in gain that occurred while only Blair and Cindy were partners. When Blackacre is sold, tax gain will equal book, or economic, gain. Of this gain the built-in gain at the time Deidre joined the partnership should be specially allocated to Blair and Cindy. Any gain attributable to the time after Deidre joined the partnership should be allocated among the three partners.

For example, if Blackacre was later sold for $290,000, the tax (and book) gain would be $190,000. Of this gain, $100,000 should be specially allocated

---

6. Treas. Reg. § 1.704-3(e)(1).
7. Code Sec. 704(c)(1)(C).
8. Treas. Reg. § 1.704-1(b)(5) Ex. (14)(iv).

equally between Blair and Cindy. The remaining $90,000 should be allo-
cated equally among Blair, Cindy, and Deidre. Thus, Blair and Cindy each
will recognize $80,000 and Deidre will recognize $30,000 of gain (both tax
and book).

Alternatively, the partnership can restate its assets at their fair market value at the time
the new partner joins the partnership. The built-in gain or loss reflected in the reval-
ued assets will be allocated to the old (existing) partners.[9]

Example: Blair and Cindy were equal partners in the Epsilon Partnership.
The partnership had previously purchased Blackacre for $100,000. Its current
fair market value was $200,000. Deidre joined the partnership by con-
tributing $100,000 cash in exchange for a one-third interest.

At the time Deidre joined the partnership, Blackacre had $100,000 of built-in
gain that occurred while only Blair and Cindy were partners. The Epsilon partnership elected to restate its assets at their fair market value. The balance
sheet then would reflect Blackacre with a basis of $100,000 and fair market value
of $200,000. The $100,000 of gain is treated as built-in gain, allocable to Blair
and Cindy. When Blackacre is sold, the book, or economic, gain will reflect the
gain that occurred after Deidre joined the partnership. It should be allocated
between the three partners. The difference between the book and tax gain represents the built-in gain and is allocated to Blair and Cindy.

For example, if Blackacre was later sold for $290,000, the tax gain would be
$190,000 and the book, or economic, gain would be $90,000. The difference
between the book and tax gain, $100,000, represents the built-in gain and is
allocated to Blair and Cindy. The book gain should be allocated between the
three partners. Thus, Blair and Cindy each will recognize $80,000 and Deidre
will recognize $30,000 of tax gain. They each will have $30,000 of book, or
economic, gain.

---

2. Ceiling Rule

In certain circumstances, the sale of a contributed partnership asset may not generate sufficient gain or loss to allocate the pre-contribution gain or loss to the contributing partner. When this result occurs, the regulations provide that the maximum amount
of built-in gain or loss that can be allocated to the partner is the amount of tax gain or
loss generated by the sale of the asset. The rule is referred to as the ceiling rule.

When the ceiling rule applies to property with a built-in gain, the property has depreciated in value from the time of contribution to the partnership. Thus, the partners have experienced an economic loss. When the ceiling rule applies to property

---

9. Treas. Reg. § 1.704-1(b)(4)(i), -1(b)(5) Ex. (14)(i).

with a built-in loss, the property has increased in value from the time of contribution to the partnership. Thus, the partners have experienced an economic increase.

Example: Lexi purchased land for $10,000. When the land had increased in value to $50,000, she contributed it to a partnership in exchange for a 50-percent general partnership interest. Mark contributed $50,000 cash in exchange for a 50-percent general partnership interest. The partnership agreement provided that allocations would be made based on ownership interests.

Eight years later, the partnership sold the land for $40,000, realizing a tax gain of $30,000 (amount realized of $40,000, less adjusted basis of $10,000). It recognized $10,000 of book loss (amount realized of $40,000, less book basis of $50,000).

Even though Lexi should be allocated $40,000 of tax gain, there is only $30,000 available to allocate to her. All $30,000 of gain must be allocated solely to Lexi. There has been an economic loss at the partnership level. This $10,000 loss is allocated equally between Lexi and Mark.

Lexi		Mark	
Tax	Book	Tax	Book
$30,000	<$5,000>	—	<$5,000>

When there is a shortfall due to the ceiling rule, there will be a disparity between the partner's built-in gain or loss and the tax gain or loss. Under the traditional method, the disparity is not corrected.[10] However, the shortfall can be corrected through either of two methods, the traditional method with curative allocations or the remedial method.[11]

Anti-abuse rule. Each method is subject to an anti-abuse rule. The allocation method will not be respected if the contribution of property and allocation of associated gain or loss is made with a view to shifting the tax consequences of the built-in gain or loss among the partners so as to substantially reduce the present value of their aggregate tax liability.[12]

Choice of method. Only one method may be used for any one piece of property contributed with a built-in gain or loss. However, the partnership may use different methods for different properties, as long as the combination of methods is reasonable based on the facts and circumstances.[13]

a. Traditional Method With Curative Allocations

When the ceiling rule applies because the sale of a contributed partnership asset did not generate sufficient gain or loss to allocate the pre-contribution gain or loss to the

---

10. Treas. Reg. § 1.704-3(b)(1).
11. Treas. Reg. § 1.704-3(a)(1), -3(b), -3(c), -3(d). The regulations also provide that any reasonable method may be used, as long as it is consistent with the purposes of Section 704(c). Treas. Reg. § 1.704-3(a)(1).
12. Treas. Reg. § 1.704-3(a)(10).
13. Treas. Reg. § 1.704-3(a)(2).

contributing partner, there will be a disparity between the partner's outside basis and capital account in the amount of the shortfall. Under the traditional method with curative allocations, this disparity can be corrected at the time of sale by allocating gain or loss (as appropriate) from items other than the sale of the property.[14] Because the shortfall is a tax shortfall, the curative allocation only impacts the partner's outside basis; it does not impact the partner's capital account.

For the curative allocation to be respected, it must:[15]

- Not exceed the amount necessary to correct the disparity caused by the ceiling rule; and
- Be of the same character and have the same tax consequences as the contributed property.

A curative allocation may be made only if the partnership has income or loss in a sufficient amount and in the right character. Accordingly, in some situations, it will not be possible for the partnership to make the necessary curative allocations. Thus, the partnership may make an allocation in a year subsequent to the year the property was sold, as long as the allocation is made within a reasonable amount of time and the partnership agreement provided for curative allocations in the year the property was contributed to the partnership.[16]

Practice Tip: Curative allocations impact the partner's outside basis. They do not impact the partner's capital account.

---

b. Remedial Method

When the ceiling rule applies because the sale of a contributed partnership asset did not generate sufficient gain or loss to allocate the pre-contribution gain or loss to the contributing partner, there will be a disparity between the partner's outside basis and capital account in the amount of the shortfall. Under the remedial method, the partnership creates the necessary amount of gain or loss (of the correct character) to make up the shortfall caused by the ceiling rule. In addition, it creates an offsetting gain or loss to allocate to the non-contributing partners.[17] Because the shortfall is a tax shortfall, the remedial allocation only impacts the partner's outside basis; it does not impact the partner's capital account.[18]

---

14. Treas. Reg. § 1.704-3(c).
15. Treas. Reg. § 1.704-3(c)(3).
16. Treas. Reg. § 1.704-3(c)(3)(ii).
17. Treas. Reg. § 1.704-3(d)(1).
18. Treas. Reg. § 1.704-3(d)(4)(ii).

Application of Section 704(c)

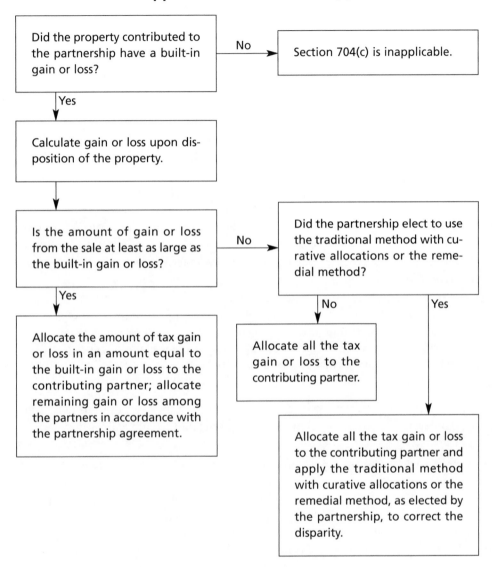

Practice Tip: Remedial allocations impact the partner's outside basis. They do not impact the partner's capital account.

3. Characterization Issues

Congress was concerned that partner-taxpayers would attempt to change the character of gain or loss from the sale of property by contributing the property to a partnership and having the partnership sell the property (generally converting ordinary income into capital gain and capital losses into ordinary losses).

Example: A taxpayer may be in the business of developing lots for sale. Any gain from the sale of such lots would be ordinary income, taxed at regular rates.

The taxpayer may attempt to convert the ordinary gain into long-term capital gain by contributing the property to a partnership and having the partnership hold the property for investment purposes, then sell it to recognize long-term capital gain.

To curb this abuse, Congress identified three types of property and set forth specific characterization rules that apply to each specific category. The three categories are: unrealized receivables, inventory items, and capital loss property.

Unrealized receivables. Unrealized receivables include, to the extent not previously included in income, any right to payment for services rendered. It also includes the right to payment for goods delivered to the extent the proceeds would be treated as amounts received from the sale or exchange of property other than a capital asset. It also includes any gain that would be characterized as ordinary income under the depreciation recapture provisions.[19]

Example: Collections Partnership holds only accounts receivable. If the partnership is a cash method taxpayer, the accounts receivable are unrealized receivables. In contrast, if the partnership is an accrual method taxpayer, the accounts receivable are not unrealized receivables.

Any gain or loss recognized by the partnership from the sale or disposition of unrealized receivables contributed by a partner to the partnership will be characterized as ordinary.[20]

Inventory items. Inventory includes those assets held for sale to customers and any items that are not characterized as a capital or hotchpot (Section 1231) item.[21] For five years from the time of contribution of inventory by a partner to the partnership, any gain or loss recognized by the partnership from the sale will be characterized as ordinary.[22] At the end of the five year period, the character of the gain or loss is determined under the regular rules, *i.e.*, at the partnership level.

Capital loss property. Capital loss property includes any capital asset held by the contributing partner that had a built-in loss immediately before the partner contributed the property to the partnership. For five years from the time of contribution to the partnership, the loss, up to the amount of the built-in loss, will retain its character as a capital loss. Any additional loss is characterized at the partnership level.[23] At the end of the five year period, the character of the loss (or gain) is determined under the regular rules, *i.e.*, at the partnership level.

---

19. Code Secs. 724(a), (d)(1); 751(c).
20. Code Sec. 724(a).
21. Code Secs. 724(b), (d)(2); 751(d).
22. Code Sec. 724(b).
23. Code Sec. Code Sec. 724(c).

Practice Tip:
- Section 704(c) prevents the shifting of income between taxpayers.
- Section 724 prevents the conversion of the character of gain or loss from ordinary to capital or vise versa.

If the partnership exchanges the unrealized receivable, inventory, or capital loss property for other property in a like-kind exchange, the characterization rules apply to the property received in the exchange to the same extent they applied to the property transferred.[24] When determining the five-year time period, the five years begins as of the date the original property was contributed to the partnership. The only exception is if the property received is stock in a corporation acquired in an exchange governed by Section 351.[25]

Application of Section 724

Was the property sold by the partnership previously contributed by a partner?	**No** →	Section 724 is not applicable.

↓ **Yes**

At the time of contribution, was the property characterized as accounts receivable in the hands of the partner?	**Yes** →	Gain or loss always will be characterized as ordinary.

↓ **No**

At the time of contribution, was the property characterized as inventory in the hands of the partner?	**Yes** →	Gain or loss will be characterized as ordinary if sold within five years of contribution. If sold after five years, characterization is determined at the partnership level.

↓ **No**

At the time of contribution, was the property characterized as a capital asset that had a built-in loss in the hands of the partner?	**Yes** →	To the extent of the built-in loss, the loss will be characterized as capital if sold within five years of contribution. Any excess loss, or loss (or gain) if sold after five years, is characterized at the partnership level.

↓ **No**

Characterize the gain or loss at the partnership level.

---

24. Code Sec. 724(d)(3)(A).
25. Code Sec. 724(d)(3)(B).

C. Application of Rules

Example 1. Built-in gain. Sandy contributed land with a basis of $2,000 and a fair market value of $10,000 to a partnership in exchange for a 50-percent partnership interest. Thomas contributed $10,000 cash in exchange for a 50-percent partnership interest. At formation the balance sheet would appear as follows:

Asset	Basis	FMV	Partner	Basis	Cap. Acct.
Cash	$10,000	$10,000	Sandy	$2,000	$10,000
Land	2,000	10,000	Thomas	10,000	10,000
	$12,000	$20,000		$12,000	$20,000

The partnership agreement provided that all partnership items would be allocated equally between the partners.

Six years later, when the land was worth $16,000, the partnership sold the land. The amount of tax gain was $14,000. Of this gain, $8,000 is pre-contribution gain and must be allocated to Sandy. The remaining tax gain, $6,000, is post-contribution gain and is allocated equally between Sandy and Thomas, or $3,000 each. Thus, Sandy is allocated a total of $11,000 gain ($8,000 pre-contribution, plus $3,000 post-contribution) and Thomas is allocated a total of $3,000 (post-contribution) gain. Each of their bases is increased by the amount of the allocation.

From an economic perspective, the property has increased in value $6,000 from the time of contribution ($10,000 at the time of contribution to $16,000 at the time of sale). This economic appreciation is allocated equally between the partners. Each partner's capital account is increased by $3,000.

After the sale, the balance sheet would appear as follows:

Asset	Basis	FMV	Partner	Basis	Cap. Acct.
Cash	$26,000	$26,000	Sandy	$13,000	$13,000
	$26,000	$26,000	Thomas	13,000	13,000
				$26,000	$26,000

Example 2. Built-in loss. Nora contributed stock with a basis of $20,000 and a fair market value of $10,000 to a partnership in exchange for a 50-percent partnership interest. Olson contributed $10,000 cash in exchange for a 50-percent partnership interest. At formation the balance sheet would appear as follows:

Asset	Basis	FMV	Partner	Basis	Cap. Acct.
Cash	$10,000	$10,000	Nora	$20,000	$10,000
Stock	20,000	10,000	Olson	10,000	10,000
	$30,000	$20,000		$30,000	$20,000

The partnership agreement provided that all partnership items would be allocated equally between the partners.

Seven years later, when the stock was worth $6,000, the partnership sold the stock. The amount of tax loss was $14,000. Of this loss, $10,000 is pre-contribution loss and must be allocated to Nora. The remaining tax loss, $4,000, is post-contribution loss and is allocated equally between Nora and Olson, or $2,000 each. Thus, Nora is allocated a total loss of $12,000 ($10,000 pre-contribution, plus $2,000 post-contribution) and Olson is allocated a $2,000 (post-contribution) loss. Each of their bases is decreased by the amount of the allocation.

From an economic perspective, the property has decreased in value $4,000 from the time of contribution ($10,000 at the time of contribution to $6,000 at the time of sale). This economic depreciation is allocated equally between the partners. Each partner's capital account is decreased by $2,000. After the sale, the balance sheet would appear as follows:

Asset	Basis	FMV	Partner	Basis	Cap. Acct.
Cash	$16,000	$16,000	Nora	$8,000	$8,000
	$16,000	$16,000	Olson	8,000	8,000
				$16,000	$16,000

Example 3. Ceiling rule—traditional method. Peter contributed stock with a basis of $20,000 and a fair market value of $10,000 to a partnership in exchange for a 50-percent partnership interest. Quint contributed $10,000 cash in exchange for a 50-percent partnership interest. With respect to Section 704(c), the partnership uses the traditional method of allocation. At formation the balance sheet would appear as follows:

Asset	Basis	FMV	Partner	Basis	Cap. Acct.
Cash	$10,000	$10,000	Peter	$20,000	$10,000
Stock	20,000	10,000	Quint	10,000	10,000
	$30,000	$20,000		$30,000	$20,000

The partnership agreement provided that all partnership items would be allocated equally between the partners.

Seven years later, when the stock was worth $15,000, the partnership sold the stock. While the built-in loss upon contribution was $10,000, the sale of the stock generated a tax loss of $5,000, an insufficient amount of loss to allocate to Peter to account for the built-in loss. Nevertheless, the ceiling rule provides that the maximum amount of built-in loss that can be allocated to Peter is the amount of tax loss generated by the sale, or $5,000. Peter's basis is decreased by the $5,000 loss. No loss is allocated to Quint.

When the ceiling rule applies to property with a built-in loss, the property has increased in value from the time of contribution to the partnership to the time of sale. Thus, the partners have experienced an economic increase. The amount of book gain is $5,000 (amount realized of $15,000, less book basis of $10,000). The book gain is allocated equally between Peter and Quint, or $2,500 each.

Because the partnership uses the traditional method of allocation and the ceiling rule applies, the partnership's balance sheet will reflect the fact that not all of the built-in loss was allocated to Peter on sale of the stock. After sale of the stock, the balance sheet would appear as follows:

Asset	Basis	FMV	Partner	Basis	Cap. Acct.
Cash	$25,000	$25,000	Peter[26]	$15,000	$12,500
	$25,000	$25,000	Quint	10,000	12,500
				$25,000	$25,000

Example 4. Ceiling rule—traditional method with curative allocations. Rochelle contributed XCo stock with a basis of $20,000 and a fair market value of $10,000 to a partnership in exchange for a 50-percent partnership interest. Sandy contributed YCo stock with a basis of $10,000 and a fair market value of $10,000 in exchange for a 50-percent partnership interest. With respect to Section 704(c), the partnership uses the traditional method with curative allocation. At formation the balance sheet would appear as follows:

Asset	Basis	FMV	Partner	Basis	Cap. Acct.
YCo stock	$10,000	$10,000	Rochelle	$20,000	$10,000
XCo stock	20,000	10,000	Sandy	10,000	10,000
	$30,000	$20,000		$30,000	$20,000

Seven years later, when the XCo stock was worth $15,000, the partnership sold the stock. While the built-in loss upon contribution was $10,000, the sale of the stock generated a tax loss of $5,000, an insufficient amount of loss to allocate to Rochelle to account for the built-in loss. The ceiling rule provides that the maximum amount of built-in loss that can be allocated to Rochelle is the amount of tax loss generated by the sale, or $5,000.

When the ceiling rule applies to property with a built-in loss, the property has increased in value from the time of contribution to the partnership. Thus, the partners have experienced an economic increase. This increase is reflected in their capital accounts. The amount of book gain from the sale of XCo stock is $5,000 (amount realized of $15,000, less book basis of $10,000). The book gain is allocated equally between Rochelle and Sandy, or $2,500 each.

In that same year, when the YCo stock was worth $2,000, the partnership sold the stock generating an $8,000 loss. There was no built-in gain or loss in the stock, so it is allocated equally between the partners, or $4,000 each. The partnership also had a book loss of $8,000 (amount realized of $2,000, less book basis of $10,000). The loss is allocated equally between Rochelle and Sandy, or $4,000 each.

Under the traditional method with curative allocations, the disparity caused by the ceiling rule to Rochelle can be corrected at the time of sale by allocating loss from items other than the sale of the XCo stock.[27] A curative allocation may be made because, with the sale of the YCo stock, the partnership had loss in a sufficient

---

26. Because the partnership has only cash, there is no more gain or loss for the partners to recognize. However, Peter has an outside basis of $15,000 and capital account of $12,500. If he sold his interest for $12,500, he would recognize a $2,500 loss. This is the remaining portion of his built-in loss. Stated another way, it is the original $10,000 built-in loss, reduced by the $5,000 loss allocated to him upon sale of the stock, reduced by his share of the partnership-level increase in value of $2,500, leaving $2,500 of loss.

27. The total built-in loss was $10,000 of capital loss. The amount of tax loss from the sale allocated to Rochelle was $5,000. Her share of economic gain was $2,500. Thus, there is a disparity of $2,500 of loss.

amount and in the right character. Thus, $2,500 of loss from the sale of YCo stock is allocated away from Sandy and to Rochelle. The curative allocation only impacts Rochelle's outside basis; it does not impact her capital account. The allocations are as follows:

	Rochelle		Sandy	
	Tax	Book	Tax	Book
XCo stock	<$5,000>	$2,500	—	$2,500
YCo stock	<6,500>	<4,000>	<$1,500>	<4,000>

After sale of the stock, the balance sheet would appear as follows:

Asset	Basis	FMV	Partner	Basis	Cap. Acct.
Cash	$17,000	$17,000	Rochelle	$8,500	$8,500
	$17,000	$17,000	Sandy	8,500	8,500
				$17,000	$17,000

Example 5. Ceiling rule—remedial method. Trish contributed stock with a basis of $20,000 and a fair market value of $10,000 to a partnership in exchange for a 50-percent partnership interest. Ursula contributed $10,000 cash in exchange for a 50-percent partnership interest. With respect to Section 704(c), the partnership uses the remedial method. At formation the balance sheet would appear as follows:

Asset	Basis	FMV	Partner	Basis	Cap. Acct.
Cash	$10,000	$10,000	Trish	$20,000	$10,000
Stock	20,000	10,000	Ursula	10,000	10,000
	$30,000	$20,000		$30,000	$20,000

Seven years later, when the stock was worth $15,000, the partnership sold the stock. While the built-in loss upon contribution was $10,000, the sale of the stock generated a tax loss of $5,000, an insufficient amount of loss to allocate to Trish to account for the built-in loss. Nevertheless, the ceiling rule provides that the maximum amount of built-in loss that can be allocated to Trish is the amount of tax loss generated by the sale, or $5,000. No loss is allocated to Ursula.

When the ceiling rule applies to property with a built-in loss, the property has increased in value from the time of contribution to the partnership to the time of sale. Thus, the partners have experienced an economic increase. This increase is reflected in their capital accounts. The amount of book gain is $5,000 (amount realized of $15,000, less book basis of $10,000). The book gain is allocated equally between Trish and Ursula, or $2,500 each.

Under the remedial method, the partnership creates the necessary amount of loss (of the correct character) to make up the shortfall caused by the ceiling rule. Thus, the partnership creates a $2,500 capital loss to allocate to Trish. In addition, it creates an offsetting $2,500 capital gain to allocate to Ursula.[28] The remedial allocation only impacts the partner's outside basis; it does not impact the partner's capital account.

---

28. The remedial method creates an allocation in the amount of the shortfall. It is the original $10,000 loss, reduced by the $5,000 loss allocated to Trish upon sale of the stock, reduced by her share of the partnership-level increase in value of $2,500, leaving $2,500 of loss.

The allocations are as follows:

	Trish		Ursula	
	Tax	Book	Tax	Book
Stock	<$5,000>	$2,500	—	$2,500
Remedial allocation	<2,500>		$2,500	

After sale of the stock, the balance sheet would appear as follows:

Asset	Basis	FMV	Partner	Basis	Cap. Acct.
Cash	$25,000	$25,000	Trish	$12,500	$12,500
	$25,000	$25,000	Ursula	12,500	12,500
				$25,000	$25,000

Example 6. Built-in gain — depreciable property. Viola contributed equipment with a basis of $4,000 and a fair market value of $10,000 to a partnership in exchange for a 50-percent partnership interest. Wesley contributed $10,000 cash in exchange for a 50-percent partnership interest. The partnership agreement provided that all partnership items would be allocated equally between the partners.

Two years later, when the equipment had a basis of $2,000 and book value of $5,000, the partnership sold the equipment for $10,000, generating $8,000 of tax gain. Of this gain, $3,000 is pre-contribution gain (book value, less tax basis) and must be allocated to Viola. The remaining tax gain, $5,000, is post-contribution gain and is allocated equally between Viola and Wesley, or $2,500 each. Thus, Viola is allocated a total of $5,500 ($3,000 of pre-contribution gain, plus $2,500 of post contribution gain) and Wesley is allocated $2,500 (post-contribution) gain.

From an economic perspective, the property has increased in value $5,000 from the time of contribution, taking into consideration depreciation (book value of $5,000 to $10,000 at the time of sale). Each partner's capital account is increased by $2,500.

Example 7. Character of loss. Jim contributed Whiteacre with a basis of $10,000 and a fair market value of $8,000 to a partnership in exchange for a partnership interest. At the time of contribution, Jim had held Whiteacre for investment purposes. The partnership held the property as part of its inventory.

Three years later, the partnership sold Whiteacre for $5,000, realizing a $5,000 tax loss.

Because the property was contributed to the partnership with a built-in loss and sold within five years from the time of contribution to the partnership, the loss, up to the amount of the built-in loss, retains its character as a capital loss. Thus, $2,000 of the loss is a capital loss. The additional loss, $3,000, is characterized at the partnership level as an ordinary loss.

D. Problems

1. Cindy and David formed an equal partnership. Cindy contributed land with a fair market value of $50,000 and David contributed $50,000 cash. The partnership agreement provided that all partnership items would be shared equally.

(a) Cindy had purchased the land for $30,000. Five years later, the partnership sold the land for $60,000. How is the gain allocated between the partners? Construct a balance sheet to reflect the situation of the partners and partnership after the sale.

(b) Alternatively, Cindy had purchased the land for $70,000. Five years later, the partnership sold the land for $40,000. How is the loss allocated between the partners? Construct a balance sheet to reflect the situation of the partners and partnership after the sale.

(c) Alternatively, Cindy had purchased the land for $30,000. Five years later, the partnership sold the land for $40,000. For purposes of Section 704(c) the partnership elected to use the traditional method. How is the gain allocated between the partners? Construct a balance sheet to reflect the situation of the partners and partnership after the sale.

(d) Alternatively, Cindy had purchased the land for $30,000. Five years later, the partnership sold the land for $40,000. During that year, the partnership also sold stock it had held for five years. The partnership had purchased the stock for $100,000 and sold it for $130,000. For purposes of Section 704(c) the partnership elected to use the traditional method with curative allocations. How is the gain from the land and stock allocated between the partners? What is the impact of the sale of the land and stock on the partners' capital accounts?

(e) Alternatively, Cindy had purchased the land for $30,000. Five years later, the partnership sold the land for $40,000. For purposes of Section 704(c) the partnership elected to use the remedial method. What allocations are made to Cindy and David? What is the impact of the sale on the partners' capital accounts?

---

2. Emmie and Florence formed an equal partnership. Emmie contributed equipment with an adjusted basis of $50,000 and a fair market value of $100,000. Florence contributed $100,000 cash. The partnership agreement provided that all partnership items would be shared equally.

Three years later, when the adjusted basis of the equipment was $20,000 and the book value was $40,000, the partnership sold it for $50,000. How is the gain allocated between the partners? What is the impact of the sale on the partners' capital accounts?

---

3. Marlene contributed accounts receivable to a partnership in exchange for a general partnership interest. The accounts receivable had a basis of zero and a fair market value of $5,000.

(a) Four years later, the partnership sold the accounts receivable for $5,000. What is the character of the gain?

(b) Alternatively, six years later, the partnership sold the accounts receivable for $5,000. What is the character of the gain?

---

4. Gil contributed an inventory of widgets to the partnership in exchange for a general partnership interest. Each widget had a basis of $10 and a fair market value of $30. The partnership held the widgets for investment purposes.

(a) Four years later, the partnership sold the widgets for $40 each. What is the character of the gain?

(b) Alternatively, six years later, the partnership sold the widgets for $40 each. What is the character of the gain?

---

5. Harris contributed Greenacre, property he held for investment, to Development Partnership in exchange for a limited partnership interest. It had a basis of $100,000 and a fair market value of $30,000. The partnership held Greenacre as part of its inventory.

(a) One year later, Development Partnership sold Greenacre for $20,000. What is the character of the loss?

(b) Alternatively, six years later, Development Partnership sold Greenacre for $20,000. What is the character of the loss?

---

6. Application:

(a) How would you explain to the partners the concept of built-in gain or loss?

(b) Which curative method, if any, will you advise the partners to elect? Why? What information might you need to help you decide? Who gets to make the decision as to which method, if any, will be used? How do you know?

E. Advanced Problems — Looking Forward

Without conducting any research, consider the following questions:

1. The sale of partnership property that had previously been contributed to the partnership by a partner will trigger the application of Section 704(c). Should the partnership be able to avoid this result by, instead of selling the property, distributing the property to a partner?

2. If a partner contributes appreciated property to a partnership and the partnership distributes partnership property (other than the property he contributed) or cash to the partner, might the transaction actually be a sale of the property by the partner to the partnership? If so, how close in time should the contribution and subsequent distribution be? Could an argument be made that it is not, actually, a sale by the partner?

Overview Problem—Putting It All Together

Stacey, Bill, and Olivia formed a general partnership to operate the coffee shop. Stacey, Bill, and Olivia own 20 percent, 50 percent, 30 percent, respectively. This past year it performed fairly well. The following is a summary of the partnership's income, expenses, and depreciation:

Income from sales:		$150,000
Expenses:		
Coffee:	$30,000	
Cups:	10,000	
Sugar:	1,000	
Milk:	3,000	
Salaries:	40,000	
Interest:	4,000	
Depreciation:	12,000	
	100,000	100,000
Profit:		$50,000

In addition, the partnership sold a piece of land for $50,000. The land had been contributed by Bill to the partnership when its fair market value was $40,000. He had originally purchased the land for $20,000.

Stacey has a substantial amount of income from investments that she owns individually. Bill has a modest amount of income he made from working at the coffee shop. Olivia has a net loss that will be carried forward from the previous year.

While things have been going well for the partnership, the partners have decided it was time to be more proactive in planning the management and operation of the shop and in planning for tax consequences. The partners set a time for a partnership meeting to discuss the taxable year of the partnership, how the partnership items will be allocated, when (and how) the items will be subject to tax, who will be responsible for running the day-to-day operations of the coffee shop, and any other item a partner thinks is important. You have been invited to the meeting to advise them.

1. With respect to the partnership's taxable year:
    (a) Will all the partners want the partnership to have the same taxable year?
    (b) What information must you obtain from the partners to determine what the partnership's taxable year will be?
    (c) How might you advise the partners?
2. Will all the partners be in favor of the partnership claiming bonus depreciation? If not, how will the partnership decide whether to make the election?
3. With respect to when and how the partnership items will be taxed to the partners:
    (a) Will all the partners want an allocation based on their interests in the partnership?
    (b) Would there be any need to have a special allocation?
    (c) How would you explain to the partners how a special allocation works?

(d) How would the partnership decide if the partnership agreement will incorporate special allocations?

(e) What might you advise the partners?

(f) How would you know if an allocation were of recourse deductions or non-recourse deductions?

(g) What language would you use in the partnership agreement with respect to an allocation of recourse deductions? Of non-recourse deductions?

(h) Will any of the depreciation have to be allocated under Section 704(c)?

(i) Has the partnership elected to correct any disparity that may be caused by Section 704(c)? If not, would you recommend a method? Why or why not?

(j) Can you explain to the partners the tax consequences of an allocation of losses in excess of basis?

4. With respect to participation of the partners:

(a) Will the partners all be participating in operating the coffee shop?

(b) Is it important to determine which partners will participate? Why?

5. With respect to a sale of partnership items:

(a) Does the partnership anticipate selling any of its assets?

(b) What information would you need to know before you could determine the tax consequences of a sale?

Practitioner's Checklist

Taxable Year and Computation of Taxable Income:

☐ Use the taxable year of each of the partners to determine the taxable year of the partnership. (Determine if the partnership will elect a different taxable year and steps needed to establish a different taxable year.) Taxable year:

_____

☐ Determine how decisions will be made with respect to elections (i.e., amortization of start-up costs, bonus depreciation, inventory method, etc.).

Start-up Costs:

☐ Obtain documentation of costs the partners incurred to begin the business (i.e., start-up costs).

☐ Identify any syndication costs and remove from start-up cost total.

☐ Confirm partners want to amortize start-up costs.

Accounting Method:

☐ Accounting method the partnership will use (cash, accrual, other). _____

☐ If a partner's interest in the partnership is altered during the year, method the partnership will use (interim closing of the books or proration method).

_____

Allocations:

- ☐ Each partners interest in the partnership. _____

- ☐ Determine how each partner will be apprised of his basis in the partnership and confirm each understands he is not entitled to claim losses on his tax return in excess of his basis in the partnership.

- ☐ How will partnership items be allocated (including allocation of recourse deductions, non-recourse deductions, and credits). _____

- ☐ For purposes of Section 704(c), method the partnership will use (traditional method, curative method, or remedial method). _____

At-risk and Passive Activity Loss:

- ☐ To what extent is each partner at risk?

- ☐ To what extent will each partner participate in each partnership activity?

Items to include in the partnership or operating agreement:

- ☐ Statement of ownership interests.

- ☐ How decisions will be made (i.e., one partner given authority, majority vote, etc.).

- ☐ Whether the partnership will use the interim closing of the books or proration method.

- ☐ Language to satisfy the safe harbor for the economic effect test for recourse deductions (general or alternate or both).

- ☐ Language to satisfy the safe harbor for allocations of non-recourse deductions.

- ☐ Any agreed upon special allocations.

- ☐ For purposes of Section 704(c), identify the method the partnership will use, traditional method, curative method, or remedial method.

V.

Effect of Liabilities—Revisited

Overview Problem

Stacey, Bill, and Olivia own and operate the coffee shop. Stacey has a 20 percent general interest, Bill has a 50 percent limited interest, and Olivia has a 30 percent limited interest. The partners intend to allocate a disproportionately large portion of the partnership deductions to Bill and Olivia.

After the partnership was formed, the partners found an appropriate location from which to operate the coffee shop. The property owner was willing to either lease the space or sell them the building. The partners are in agreement that they want to purchase the building. However, because the partnership does not have the funds, it will have to obtain a loan. If it could, the partnership would obtain a non-recourse loan to finance the purchase. If it could not obtain a non-recourse loan, the partnership would obtain a recourse loan. Either way, to assist in obtaining the loan, if necessary, Olivia has agreed to personally guaranty the liability. However, if she does so, she wants to be "compensated" by the partnership through a special allocation of additional deductions. As a last resort, Olivia has agreed to purchase the property herself, financed entirely with borrowed funds, then contribute the property subject to the liability to the partnership.

They have come to you for advice about the tax consequences of the various financing options on the partners and the partnership.

Effect of Liabilities

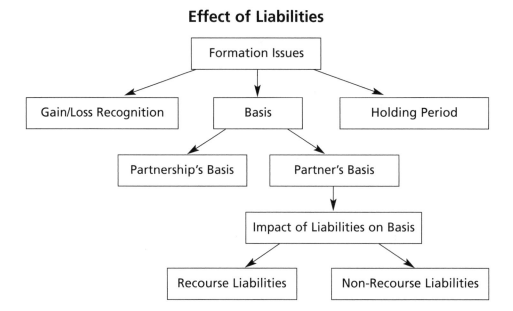

Chapter 19

Recourse Liabilities

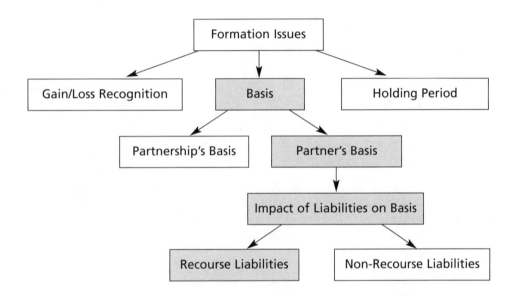

Read:

Code Section 752(a)-(c).
Treas. Reg. Treas. Reg. §§ 1.704-1(b)(2)(iv)(a), -1(b)(2)(iv)(b), -1(b)(2)(iv)(c), -1(b)(2)(iv)(d)(1), -1(b)(2)(iv)(d)(2); 1.752-1(a)(1), -1(a)(2), -1(a)(4)(i), -1(b)-(f), -1(g) Ex. 1; 1.752-2(a), -2(b), -2(f) Ex. 1, 4, -2(h)(1)-(4), -2(j)(1)-(3).

A. Background

1. Debt

When a partner contributes property subject to a liability to a partnership, the amount of the debt relief (the debt assumed by the partnership) is part of the partner's amount realized (*i.e.*, what the partner is receiving in exchange for the property being contributed to the partnership). In essence, because the partnership is assuming the debt, it is as if the partnership transferred cash to the partner and the partner used the cash to pay off the debt. As such, the assumption of the debt is treated as a distribution of cash from the partnership to the partner.

If the partnership acquires debt in conjunction with the purchase of property, the partnership's basis in the property is the cost of the property. The source of the money used to purchase the asset is irrelevant.

Whether a partnership assumes a debt on property transferred to the partnership by a partner or incurs the debt directly, the partnership is liable for repayment. In addition, under the Uniform Partnership Act or Revised Uniform Partnership Act, each general partner is secondarily liable for payment of the debt.

2. Definition of Liability

The regulations provide a specific definition of what constitutes a liability. An obligation is a liability to the extent that incurring the obligation—[1]

- Creates or increases the basis of the obligor's assets;
- Gives rise to an immediate deduction to the obligor; or
- Gives rise to an expense that is not deductible and not properly chargeable to capital.

If a cash basis taxpayer contributes accounts payable to a partnership, the accounts payable are not treated as a liability for purposes of Section 752.[2]

3. Allocation of Partnership Items

Partnership items must be allocated among and reported by the partners. In general, partnership items are allocated among the partners based on the partnership agreement.[3] If the partnership agreement does not provide an allocation or there is no partnership agreement, the items will be allocated based on the partner's interest in the partnership.[4] The partners report their allocable share on their individual tax return.

In some situations, the partnership rules provide a means for a shifting of the income, gain, deductions, or losses that was prohibited in *Lucas v. Earl* and *Horst v. Helvering*. Specifically, through a special allocation of partnership items—an allocation not based on the partners' respective interests in the partnership—such a shifting can occur.

For an allocation to be respected, it must have substantial economic effect. This requirement is broken down into two parts. First, the allocation must have economic effect. Second, the economic effect must be substantial. The test is applied to all allocations

---

1. Treas. Reg. § 1.752-1(a)(4)(i).
2. Rev. Rul. 88-77, 1988-2 C.B. 129.
3. Code Sec. 704(a); Treas. Reg. § 1.704-1(a).
4. Treas. Reg. § 1.704-1(b)(1)(i).

from the partnership, whether a separately stated or a net amount.[5] In addition, it is applied on an annual basis.[6]

Tests to Determine If an Allocation Has Economic Effect: For an allocation to have economic effect, one of the following tests must be met.

General Test:
- Partners' capital accounts must be maintained according to the regulations;
- Liquidating distributions must be made in accordance with positive capital account balances; and
- If, following a liquidation, a partner has a deficit balance in his capital account, he must be unconditionally obligated to restore the amount of such deficit balance.

Alternate Test:
- Partners' capital accounts must be maintained according to the regulations;
- Liquidating distributions must be made in accordance with positive capital account balances;
- The allocation of recourse deductions cannot cause or increase a deficit in the partner's capital account in excess of any limited amount the partner is obligated to restore; and
- The partnership agreement contains a qualified income offset.

Obligation to restore negative capital account balance. Recall that capital accounts reflect a partner's economic interest in the partnership. The account is increased by cash and the net value of property contributed to the partnership and partnership gain or income allocated to the partner. Similarly, it is decreased by the amount of cash and the net value of property distributed to the partner from the partnership and partnership expenses and losses allocated to the partner.[7]

The partnership agreement may require the partner to restore a negative capital account balance. In the alternative, it may prohibit a partner from having a negative capital account balance, and, in the event the partner unexpectedly has a negative balance, the partner must be allocated items of income or gain until his account is no longer negative.

Practice Note: Because it can not only create an obligation to make a payment to the partnership but also impact a partner's outside basis, the partnership agreement should clearly state whether a partner is obligated to restore a negative capital account balance.

---

5. Treas. Reg. § 1.704-1(b)(1)(i).
6. Treas. Reg. § 1.704-1(b)(2)(i).
7. Treas. Reg. § 1.704-1(b)(2)(iv)(b).

B. Overview of Rules

When the partnership acquires debt, either directly or through property contributed by a partner subject to a debt, the debt generally becomes the responsibility of the general partners. To the extent a partner has increased his share of responsibility for a partnership liability, he is treated as having advanced to the partnership his portion of the funds needed to repay the debt. Because a partner's outside basis reflects all contributions, including expected contributions for liabilities, the partner's outside basis is increased by the amount of the liability for which the partner is responsible.[8]

> **Practice Note:** The extent to which a limited partner is liable to make additional contributions to the partnership, or is in any way personally liable for a partnership debt, may affect his outside basis. Thus, the partnership agreement or other relevant documentation should clearly state the extent to which a limited partner is liable for a debt of the partnership or has an obligation to contribute to the partnership in the future.

A partner's outside basis depends, in part, on the partner's share of partnership liabilities. In turn, the partner's share of partnership liabilities depends on whether the liability is a recourse or non-recourse liability and on related facts, such as whether a partner has guaranteed the debt or is entitled to be reimbursed for amounts paid with respect to the debt.

Recall that a partnership liability is a recourse liability to the extent that any partner bears the economic risk of loss for that liability or would be obligated to contribute to the partnership to satisfy the liability.[9] To ascertain whether a partner bears the economic risk of loss, the regulations create a doomsday scenario and then consider which partners would have to contribute to the partnership to satisfy the liability. Note that whether a partner is required to contribute to the partnership to satisfy a liability is based on economic, or book, value, not on tax values. Specifically, a partner bears the economic risk of loss if:[10]

- The partnership constructively liquidated;
- As a result of the liquidation, the partner would be obligated to make a payment because the liability became due and payable; and
- The partner would not be entitled to reimbursement from another partner.

Whether a partner has an obligation to make a contribution to the partnership is

---

8. Code Sec. 752(a).
9. Treas. Reg. § 1.752-2(a).
10. Treas. Reg. § 1.752-2(b)(1).

based on all the facts and circumstances.[11] All obligations are taken into consideration, including the following:[12]

- Guarantees.
- Any obligations imposed by the partnership agreement, including the obligation to restore a negative capital account balance.
- Any obligations imposed by state law, including the obligation to restore a negative capital account balance.
- Whether a partner is entitled to be reimbursed or indemnified by another partner. There is a presumption that any partner required to reimburse another partner does so, even if the partner does not have the funds to make the payment (unless there is a plan to circumvent or avoid the payment). However, if an obligation is subject to a contingency that makes it unlikely it would ever be paid, the obligation is disregarded.

Steps in Constructive Liquidation: To determine the partner's economic risk of loss, the regulations create a doomsday scenario based on the following steps:

Step 1: All of the partnership liabilities become due and payable.

Step 2: Any separate property pledged by a partner to secure a partnership liability is transferred to the creditor in full or partial satisfaction of the liability.

Step 3: Any asset subject to a non-recourse debt is sold for the amount of the debt.

Step 4: All remaining partnership assets (including cash) become worthless.

Step 5: Considering fair market, or book, value, the partnership sells the remaining assets in a taxable transaction for nothing.

Step 6: Any resulting gain or loss is allocated among the partners based on how they have agreed to share profits and losses. Their capital accounts are adjusted accordingly.

Step 7: The partnership liquidates.

Taking into account all relevant agreements or laws, as a result of the liquidation is a partner obligated to make a payment to the partnership so that the partnership can discharge a liability that has become due and payable?

---

11. Treas. Reg. § 1.752-2(b)(3). In determining the extent to which a partner bears the risk of loss, obligations of related parties are also taken into consideration. A related person includes a person related to a partner as defined in Section 267(b) or 707(b)(1), except that 80 percent is substituted for 50 percent; brother and sisters are excluded; and section 267(e)(1) and 267(f)(1)(A) are disregarded. Treas. Reg. § 1.752-4(b)(1).

If the obligation to make a payment is not required to be satisfied within a reasonable time after the liability becomes due, or the obligation to make a contribution to the partnership is not required to be satisfied before the later of the end of the year in which the partnership interest is liquidated or 90 days after the liquidation, then the liability is only taken into account to the extent of its value. Treas. Reg. § 1.752-2(g)(1).

12. Treas. Reg. § 1.752-2(b).

> **Practice Tip:** To the extent a partner is not allowed to have a negative capital account, he generally will not have an obligation to make a payment to the partnership so that the partnership can discharge a liability that has become due and payable. Thus, in determining his outside basis, generally he will not be allocated any portion of the recourse debt beyond the amount of his capital account after allocating losses in the doomsday scenario.

Tiered partnerships. A partnership may be a partner in a second partnership. As a partner in the second partnership, it may be allocated a portion of the second partnership's liabilities. Those liabilities also are treated as liabilities of the first partnership and must be allocated under Section 752.

> **Example:** Redly and Greenie both contributed $10,000 to become equal partners in Primary Partnership, a general partnership. The partnership agreement provided that the partners share profits and losses equally and that excess non-recourse liabilities are shared equally.
>
> Primary Partnership owned a one-quarter interest in Secondary Partnership, a general partnership. Secondary Partnership incurred a $100,000 recourse liability that was allocated equally between its four partners, with $25,000 being allocated to Primary Partnership.
>
> In determining Redly and Greenie's basis, each partner must take into consideration the $25,000 liability allocated from Secondary Partnership to Primary Partnership. As equal partners, Redly and Greenie each are allocated half of the $25,000 recourse liability, or $12,500. Thus, both partners have a basis of $22,500 ($10,000 cash plus $12,500 share of the recourse liability).

C. Application of Rules

Example 1. Recourse debt incurred by general partnership. Mindy and Nelson formed a general partnership. Mindy contributed $100 and Nelson contributed $900. However, they agreed to share profits and losses equally. The partnership agreement provided that, upon liquidation, all partners must restore negative capital account balances. The partnership purchased a building for $10,000. It paid $1,000 in cash and obtained a $9,000 recourse loan for the remaining purchase price.

Mindy and Nelson's basis depends, in part, on their share of partnership liabilities. The partnership's $9,000 liability is a recourse liability to the extent that any partner bears the economic risk of loss for that liability or would be obligated to contribute to the partnership to satisfy the liability. To ascertain whether Mindy or Nelson bears the economic risk of loss, the partnership must go though the constructive liquidation of the doomsday scenario.

First, the partnership is constructively liquidated. As part of the liquidation, the $9,000 obligation becomes due. Considering fair market, or book, value, the partnership sells the building for nothing. The tax consequences from the sale are as follows:

Amount realized:	0
Book basis:	$10,000
Loss:	<$10,000>

The $10,000 book loss is allocated equally between Mindy and Nelson, or <$5,000> each. The impact to Mindy and Nelson's capital accounts would be as follows:

	Mindy	Nelson
Capital account on formation:	$100	$900
Loss from sale of building:	<$5,000>	<$5,000>
Balance:	<$4,900>	<$4,100>

The partnership liquidates. Since a negative capital account represents the amount a partner must contribute to the partnership upon liquidation, Mindy would have an obligation to contribute $4,900 and Nelson would have an obligation to contribute $4,100 to the partnership. The total amount contributed, $9,000, would be used to satisfy the $9,000 debt.

The liability is a recourse liability because one or more partners bears the economic risk of loss. Specifically, Mindy bears an economic risk of loss of $4,900 and Nelson bears an economic risk of loss of $4,100. Their basis would be determined as follows.

	Mindy	Nelson
Cash:	100	900
Increase in liabilities:	4,900	4,100
Basis:	5,000	5,000

After purchase of the building, the balance sheet would appear as follows:

Asset	Adj. Basis	FMV	Liabilities:		$9,000
Building	$10,000	$10,000		Adj. Basis	Cap. Acct.
			Mindy	$5,000	$100
			Nelson	5,000	900
Total:	$10,000	$10,000		$10,000	$10,000

Example 2. Recourse debt incurred by general partnership. Tex and Ursula formed a general partnership. They both contributed $20,000 cash. The partnership agreement provided that profits and losses would be divided 60 percent to Tex and 40 percent to Ursula and that, upon liquidation, all partners must restore negative capital account balances. The partnership purchased a building for $50,000. It paid $40,000 in cash and obtained a $10,000 recourse loan for the remaining purchase price.

Tex and Ursula's basis depends, in part, on their share of partnership liabilities. The partnership's $10,000 liability is a recourse liability to the extent that any partner bears the economic risk of loss for that liability or would be obligated to contribute to the partnership to satisfy the liability. To ascertain whether Ted or Ursula bears the economic risk of loss, the partnership must go though the constructive liquidation of the doomsday scenario.

First, the partnership is constructively liquidated. As part of the liquidation, the $10,000 obligation becomes due. Considering fair market, or book, value, the partnership sells the building for nothing. The tax consequences from the sale are as follows:

Amount realized:	0
Book basis:	$50,000
Loss:	<$50,000>

The $50,000 book loss is allocated 60 percent to Tex and 40 percent to Ursula, or $30,000 to Tex and $20,000 to Ursula. The impact to Tex and Ursula's capital accounts would be as follows:

	Tex	Ursula
Capital account on formation:	$20,000	$20,000
Loss from sale of building:	<$30,000>	<$20,000>
Balance:	<$10,000>	-0-

The partnership liquidates. Since a negative capital account represents the amount a partner must contribute to the partnership upon liquidation, Tex would have an obligation to contribute $10,000 and Ursula would not have an obligation to contribute to the partnership. The total amount, the $10,000 contributed by Tex, would be used to satisfy the $10,000 debt.

The liability is a recourse liability because one or more partners bears the economic risk of loss. Specifically, Tex bears an economic risk of loss of $10,000. The partners' basis would be determined as follows.

	Tex	Ursula
Cash:	$20,000	$20,000
Increase in liabilities:	10,000	-0-
Basis:	$30,000	$20,000

After purchase of the building, the balance sheet would appear as follows:[13]

Asset	Adj. Basis	FMV	Liabilities:		$10,000
Building	$50,000	$50,000		Adj. Basis	Cap. Acct.
			Tex	$30,000	$20,000
			Ursula	20,000	20,000
Total:	$50,000	$50,000		$50,000	$50,000

Example 3. Recourse debt incurred by general partnership. Willie and Xander formed a general partnership. Willie contributed $30,000 and Xander contributed $10,000. The partnership agreement provided that profits and losses would be divided equally between the partners and that, upon liquidation, all partners must restore negative capital account balances. The partnership purchased a building for $50,000. It paid $40,000 in cash and obtained a $10,000 recourse loan for the remaining purchase price.

Willie and Xander's basis depends, in part, on their share of partnership liabilities. The partnership's $10,000 liability is a recourse liability to the extent that any partner

---

13. See Treas. Reg. § 1.752-2(f) Ex. 1 and 2.

bears the economic risk of loss for that liability or would be obligated to contribute to the partnership to satisfy the liability. To ascertain whether Willie or Xander bears the economic risk of loss, the partnership must go though the constructive liquidation of the doomsday scenario.

First, the partnership is constructively liquidated. As part of the liquidation, the $10,000 obligation becomes due. Considering fair market, or book, value, the partnership sells the building for nothing. The tax consequences from the sale are as follows:

Amount realized: 0
Book basis: $50,000
Loss: <$50,000>

The $50,000 book loss is allocated equally between Willie and Xander, or $25,000 each. The impact to the partners' capital accounts would be as follows:

	Willie	Xander
Capital account on formation	$30,000	$10,000
Loss from sale of building:	<$25,000>	<$25,000>
Balance:	$5,000	<$15,000>

The partnership liquidates. Since a negative capital account represents the amount a partner must contribute to the partnership upon liquidation, Xander has an obligation to contribute $15,000 to the partnership. However, only $10,000 of that amount would be used to satisfy the $10,000 debt; the remaining $5,000 would be distributed to Willie in satisfaction of his capital account balance. Thus, the liability is a recourse liability because one or more partners bears the economic risk of loss. Specifically, Xander bears the economic risk of loss of the $10,000 liability and Willie and Xander's basis would be determined as follows.

	Willie	Xander
Cash:	$30,000	$10,000
Increase in liabilities:	0	10,000
Basis:	$30,000	$20,000

After purchase of the building, the balance sheet would appear as follows:

Asset	Adj. Basis	FMV	Liabilities:		$10,000
Building	$50,000	$50,000		Adj. Basis	Cap. Acct.
			Willie	$30,000	$30,000
			Xander	20,000	10,000
Total:	$50,000	$50,000		$50,000	$50,000

Example 4. Individual debt incurred by limited partnership. Yeti and Zeke formed an equal limited partnership. Yeti contributed $10,000 in exchange for a general partnership interest and Zeke contributed $10,000 in exchange for a limited partnership interest. The partnership agreement provided that profits and losses would be divided equally between the partners and that, upon liquidation, only Yeti had an obligation to restore a negative capital account balance. With respect to Zeke, the partnership agreement contained a qualified income offset. The partnership purchased a building

for $50,000. It paid $20,000 in cash and obtained a $30,000 recourse loan for the remaining purchase price.

Yeti and Zeke's basis depends, in part, on their share of partnership liabilities. The partnership's $30,000 liability is a recourse liability to the extent that any partner bears the economic risk of loss for that liability or would be obligated to contribute to the partnership to satisfy the liability. To ascertain whether Yeti or Zeke bears the economic risk of loss, the partnership must go though the constructive liquidation of the doomsday scenario.

First, the partnership is constructively liquidated. As part of the liquidation, the $30,000 obligation becomes due. Considering fair market, or book, value, the partnership sells the building for nothing. The tax consequences from the sale are as follows:

Amount realized:	0
Book basis:	$50,000
Loss:	<$50,000>

The $50,000 book loss is allocated equally between Yeti and Zeke, or <$25,000> each. The impact to the partners' capital accounts would be as follows:

	Yeti	Zeke
Capital account on formation:	$10,000	$10,000
Loss from sale of building:	<25,000>	<25,000>
Balance:	<$15,000>	<$15,000>

The allocation of $25,000 of loss to Zeke satisfies the alternate economic effect test only to the extent of $10,000. Thus, only $10,000 of loss can be allocated to Zeke. The remaining $15,000 must be re-allocated to Yeti, in accordance with the partners' interests in the partnership. Thus, the impact to the partners' capital accounts would be as follows:

	Yeti	Zeke
Capital account on formation:	$10,000	$10,000
Loss from sale of building:	<40,000>	<10,000>
Balance:	<$30,000>	-0-

The partnership liquidates. Since a negative capital account represents the amount a partner must contribute to the partnership upon liquidation, Yeti would have an obligation to contribute $30,000 to the partnership. This $30,000 could then be used to satisfy the $30,000 debt.

The liability is a recourse liability because one or more partners bears the economic risk of loss. Specifically, Yeti bears the economic risk of loss. The partners' basis would be determined as follows.

	Yeti	Zeke
Cash:	$10,000	$10,000
Increase in liabilities:	30,000	-0-
Basis:	$40,000	$10,000

After purchase of the building, the balance sheet would appear as follows:[14]

---

14. See Treas. Reg. § 1.752-2(f) Ex. 3.

Asset	Adj. Basis	FMV	Liabilities:		$30,000
Building:	$50,000	$50,000		Adj. Basis	Cap. Acct.
Total:	$50,000	$50,000	Yeti	$40,000	$10,000
			Zeke	10,000	10,000
				$50,000	$50,000

Example 5. Recourse debt incurred by limited partnership. AnnaMarie and Barnie formed a limited partnership. AnnaMarie contributed $10,000 in exchange for a limited partnership interest and Barnie contributed $40,000 in exchange for a general partnership interest. The partnership agreement provided that profits and losses would be divided equally between the partners and that, upon liquidation, Barnie must restore a negative capital account balance. AnnaMarie is not required to restore a negative capital account; however, with respect to her, the partnership agreement contained a qualified income offset. The partnership purchased land for $90,000. It paid $50,000 in cash and obtained a $40,000 recourse loan for the remaining purchase price.

AnnaMarie and Barnie's basis depends, in part, on their share of partnership liabilities. The partnership's $40,000 liability is a recourse liability to the extent that any partner bears the economic risk of loss for that liability or would be obligated to contribute to the partnership to satisfy the liability. To ascertain whether AnnaMarie or Barnie bears the economic risk of loss, the partnership must go though the constructive liquidation of the doomsday scenario.

First, the partnership is constructively liquidated. As part of the liquidation, the $40,000 obligation becomes due. Considering fair market, or book, value, the partnership sells the land for nothing. The tax consequences from the sale are as follows:

Amount realized:	0
Book basis:	$90,000
Loss:	<$90,000>

The $90,000 book loss is allocated equally between AnnaMarie and Barnie, <$45,000> each. The impact to AnnaMarie and Barnie's capital accounts would be as follows:

	AnnaMarie	Barnie
Capital account on formation:	$10,000	$40,000
Loss from sale of building:	<45,000>	<45,000>
Balance:	<$35,000>	<$5,000>

The allocation of $45,000 of loss to AnnaMarie satisfies the alternate economic effect test only to the extent of $10,000. Thus, only $10,000 of loss can be allocated to AnnaMarie. The remaining $35,000 must be re-allocated to Barnie, in accordance with the partners' interests in the partnership.

With the loss reallocated, the capital account would appear as follows:

	AnnaMarie	Barnie
Capital account on formation:	$10,000	$40,000
Loss from sale of building:	<10,000>	<80,000>
Balance:	-0-	<$40,000>

The partnership liquidates. Since a negative capital account represents the amount a partner must contribute to the partnership upon liquidation, Barnie would have an obligation to contribute $40,000. The total amount contributed, $40,000, would be used to satisfy the $40,000 debt.

The liability is a recourse liability because one or more partners bears the economic risk of loss. Specifically, Barnie bears an economic risk of loss of $40,000. Their basis would be determined as follows.

	AnnaMarie	Barnie
Cash:	$10,000	$40,000
Increase in liabilities:	-0-	40,000
Basis:	10,000	$80,000

After purchase of the land, the balance sheet would appear as follows:

Asset	Adj. Basis	FMV	Liabilities:		$40,000
Land	$90,000	$90,000		Adj. Basis	Cap. Acct.
			AnneMarie	$10,000	$10,000
			Barnie	80,000	40,000
Total:	$90,000	$90,000		$90,000	$90,000

D. Problems

1. Kendal, Lance, and Marianne formed the Junction Partnership. The partnership agreement provided that capital accounts would be maintained in accordance with the regulations.

(a) The Junction Partnership was a general partnership and Kendal, Lance, and Marianne each contributed $10,000. The partnership agreement also provided that profits and losses would be divided equally between the partners and that, upon liquidation, all partners must restore negative capital account balances.

The Junction Partnership purchased land for $90,000. It paid $30,000 in cash and obtained a $60,000 recourse loan for the remaining purchase price. What is each partner's basis in the partnership? Prepare a balance sheet for the partnership.

(b) The Junction Partnership was a general partnership and Kendal, Lance, and Marianne each contributed $10,000. The partnership agreement also provided that profits and losses would be allocated 10 percent to Kendal, 20 percent to Lance, and 70 percent to Marianne and that, upon liquidation, all partners must restore negative capital account balances.

The Junction Partnership purchased land for $90,000. It paid $30,000 in cash and obtained a $60,000 recourse loan for the remaining purchase price. What is each partner's basis in the partnership? Prepare a balance sheet for the partnership.

(c) The Junction Partnership was a general partnership and Kendal contributed $10,000, Lance contributed $20,000, and Marianne contributed $30,000. The partnership agreement also provided that profits and losses would be divided equally between the partners and that, upon liquidation, all partners must restore negative capital account balances.

The Junction Partnership purchased land for $90,000. It paid $60,000 in cash and obtained a $30,000 recourse loan for the remaining purchase price. What is each partner's basis in the partnership? Prepare a balance sheet for the partnership.

(d) The Junction Partnership was a limited partnership and Kendal contributed $10,000 and Lance contributed $20,000 for limited partnership interests and Marianne contributed $30,000 for a general partnership interest. The partnership agreement also provided that profits and losses would be divided equally between the partners and that, upon liquidation, Marianne must restore a negative capital account balance. Kendal and Lance are not required to restore a negative capital account; however, with respect to them, the partnership agreement contains a qualified income offset.

The Junction Partnership purchased land for $90,000. It paid $60,000 in cash and obtained a $30,000 recourse loan for the remaining purchase price. What is each partner's basis in the partnership? Prepare a balance sheet for the partnership.

(e) The Junction Partnership was a limited partnership and Kendal contributed $10,000 and Lance contributed $20,000 for limited partnership interests and Marianne contributed $30,000 for a general partnership interest. The partnership agreement also provided that profits and losses would be divided equally between the partners and that, upon liquidation, Marianne must restore a negative capital account balance. Kendal and Lance are not required to restore a negative capital account; however, with respect to them, the partnership agreement contains a qualified income offset.

The Junction Partnership purchased land for $90,000. It paid $60,000 in cash and obtained a $30,000 recourse loan for the remaining purchase price. Kendal pledged $10,000 of YCo stock as security for the liability. All income, gain, or loss from the stock is allocated to Kendal. What is each partner's basis in the partnership?

(f) The Junction Partnership was a limited partnership and Kendal contributed $10,000 and Lance contributed $20,000 for limited partnership interests and Marianne contributed $30,000 for a general partnership interest. The partnership agreement also provided that profits and losses would be divided equally between the partners and that, upon liquidation, Marianne must restore a negative capital account balance. Kendal and Lance are not required to restore a negative capital account; however, with respect to them, the partnership agreement contains a qualified income offset.

The Junction Partnership purchased land for $90,000. It paid $60,000 in cash and obtained a $30,000 recourse loan for the remaining purchase price. Kendal contributed a $10,000 promissory note as security for the liability. What is each partner's basis in the partnership?

(g) The Junction Partnership was a limited partnership and Kendal and Lance contributed $10,000 each for limited partnership interests and Marianne contributed $20,000 for a general partnership interest. The partnership agreement also provided that profits and losses would be divided equally between the partners and that, upon liquidation, Marianne must restore a negative capital account balance. Kendal and

Lance are not required to restore a negative capital account; however, with respect to them, the partnership agreement contains a qualified income offset.

The Junction Partnership purchased land for $90,000. It paid $40,000 in cash and obtained a $50,000 recourse loan for the remaining purchase price. Kendal executed a personal guaranty for the $50,000 liability. What is each partner's basis in the partnership? Prepare a balance sheet for the partnership.

---

2. Application:

(a) Can you explain to the partners the relationship between the economic risk of loss analysis used for determining whether allocations of partnership items will be respected and the method for allocating recourse debt?

(b) If a partnership incurs a recourse liability, how will a partner know what his basis in his partnership interest is? Why might that information be important for him to know?

Chapter 20

Non-Recourse Liabilities

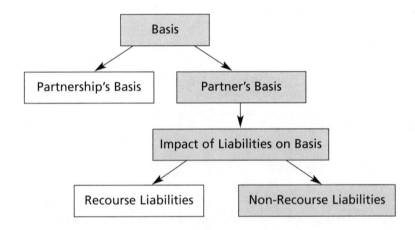

Read:

Code Section 752(a)-(c).
Treas. Reg. §§ 1.752-1(a)(2); 1.752-3(a), -3(c) Ex 1, 2.

A. Background

In general, a recourse liability is one for which the borrower is personally liable. A non-recourse liability is one for which the borrower is not personally liable. Most often, a non-recourse loan is secured by the property purchased with the borrowed funds.

Pursuant to the regulations, a partnership liability is a non-recourse liability to the extent that no partner bears the economic risk of loss for that liability.[1] Accordingly, the constructive liquidation of the doomsday scenario can be used to determine which liabilities are recourse liabilities. Any remaining liabilities will be non-recourse liabilities. Noteworthy, because no partner will bear the economic risk of loss for the liability, such risk cannot be used to allocate the liability among the partners.

---

1. Treas. Reg. § 1.752-1(a)(2).

> **Practice Note:** Because a recourse liability may have a substantially different impact on a partner's basis in the partnership than a non-recourse liability, the documents should clearly identify the partnership debt as recourse or non-recourse.

Safe Harbor Requirements for Allocation of Non-Recourse Deductions:
- The economic effect test must be met (either the general or the alternative);
- Beginning in the year the partnership has non-recourse deductions, the allocation must be reasonably consistent with other allocations (which have substantial economic effect) attributable to the property securing the non-recourse debt;
- There must be a minimum gain chargeback provision; and
- Allocations of other material items must have substantial economic effect.

Summary of Definitions:

> Non-recourse debt
> – <u>Book adjusted basis</u>
> Partnership minimum gain (*Tufts* gain or phantom income)
>
> Net increase in PMG
> – <u>Distributions made during the year of proceeds of non-recourse liability that are allocable to an increase in PMG</u>
> Non-recourse deductions
>
> Non-recourse deduction allocations
> + <u>distributions of non-recourse liability proceeds allocable to increase in PMG</u>
> Partner's share of PMG

<u>Minimum gain chargeback</u>: if there is a net decrease in PMG, each partner must be allocated items of income/gain equal to that partner's share of the net decrease in PMG unless the decrease is due to:
- The liability becoming recourse to that partner; or
- A contribution to capital that is used to repay the non-recourse liability.

A partner's share of the net decrease in PMG = (total net decrease) x (partner's percentage share of PMG at the end of prior year)

B. Overview of Rules

Partnership non-recourse debt is allocated using a three-tiered system.

First tier. Under the first tier, the partner is allocated a portion of the non-recourse debt equal to his share of partnership minimum gain.

Recall that, because of the basis limitation rules of Section 704(d), a partner only may claim a deduction if the partner has a sufficient amount of basis. Accordingly, to ensure that a partner who has been allocated a non-recourse deduction will have sufficient basis to claim the non-recourse deduction, the partner will be allocated a portion of the debt that corresponds to the amount of non-recourse deduction. This amount is also reflected in the partner's increase in partnership minimum gain for the year.[2]

Example: Jean is a limited partner in the JK Partnership. The JK Partnership purchased a building for $100,000, financed entirely with non-recourse debt. Ignoring all conventions, assume the partnership is entitled to claim $5,000 of depreciation each year. Pursuant to the partnership agreement, Jean is allocated $2,000 of that depreciation each year. Her outside basis is zero.

Because Jean is a limited partner and the debt is non-recourse, no amount of the debt would be allocated to her under the doomsday scenario and her basis would not be increased.

In the first year, the JK Partnership's partnership minimum gain increased by $5,000 (the amount by which the non-recourse debt, $100,000, exceeded the building's adjusted basis, $95,000). Thus, the depreciation is a non-recourse deduction.

Pursuant to the partnership agreement, Jean was allocated $2,000 of the depreciation. If her basis were not adjusted as provided for under the regulations, with a zero basis she would not be able to claim the depreciation. It would be disallowed and carried forward.

If the partnership later sold the building, Jean would be allocated $2,000 of the gain, based on her share of partnership minimum gain. Her basis would be increased from zero to $2,000 and, at that time, she would be able to claim the suspended depreciation.

In contrast, by allocating a portion of the liability to Jean equal to the amount of her share of partnership minimum gain, Jean would be able to claim the $2,000 of depreciation in the year it was allocated to her. Her basis would be increased by her share of partnership minimum gain from zero to $2,000. Then, upon allocation of depreciation to her, Jean's basis would be reduced from $2,000 to zero. No amount of the depreciation would be suspended.

Second tier. The second tier is applicable only when property has been contributed by a partner to the partnership (or otherwise has built-in gain or loss). The focus is on the built-in gain in the property. Under the second tier, the partner is allocated a portion of the non-recourse debt equal to the minimum amount of built-in gain that would be allocated to the contributing partner upon sale of the property. Because the property can never be disposed of for less than the amount of the non-recourse debt, the minimum amount of tax gain that will be allocated to the contributing partner will always be the excess of the liability over the adjusted basis.

Recall that, because of the basis limitation rules of Section 704(d), a partner may only claim a deduction if the partner has a sufficient amount of basis. By allocating to the contributing partner a portion of the debt equal to the amount of built-in tax gain, to that extent, the partner will have basis in his partnership interest that will allow him

---

2. Treas. Reg. § 1.752-3(a)(1).

to claim a non-recourse deduction.[3] These deductions eventually will be offset by the built-in tax gain.

> **Practice Note:** The amount of built-in gain, or potential Section 704(c) gain, will never be characterized as partnership minimum gain. Partnership minimum gain is the excess of the non-recourse liability over the fair market value, or book value, of the property. Because the property is incorporated into the partnership's balance sheet upon contribution at its fair market value, there is no partnership minimum gain at that time, only built-in gain. The fair market value, or book value, will always represent the point at which built-in gain ends and partnership minimum gain begins.

An allocation of built-in gain may also apply in a reverse Section 704(c) situation. If a partner joined a pre-existing partnership, there will likely be gain or loss in the partnership assets. The partnership may elect to restate the fair market value of all assets to reflect their current fair market values. The difference between the property's adjusted basis and fair market value at the time the new partner joins the partnership is treated the same as built-in gain or loss at the time of contribution of an asset.[4]

Third tier. The third tier allocates the amount of the debt that is remaining after the first and second tier allocations. Sometimes this amount is referred to as the "excess" amount.

> **Practice Note:**
> Total amount of non-recourse debt
> – Amount of debt allocated under the first tier
> – Amount of debt allocated under the second tier
> Amount of debt allocated under the third tier (excess amount)

In general, the excess amount is allocated based on how the partners share profits, or based on their ownership interests. If the partners have agreed to a special allocation of profits associated with partnership assets, an allocation will be respected as long as it is reasonably consistent with an allocation (having substantial economic effect) of any significant item of partnership income or gain.[5] Alternatively, the partners may allocate excess non-recourse liability in a manner in which it is reasonably expected that the deductions attributable to the liability will be allocated.[6] Alternatively, if the non-recourse debt secures property contributed by a partner to the partnership, the part-

---

3. Treas. Reg. § 1.752-3(a)(2).
4. Treas. Reg. §§ 1.704-1(b)(2)(iv)(f); 1.752-3(a)(2).
5. Treas. Reg. § 1.752-3(a)(3).
6. Treas. Reg. § 1.752-3(b).

Effect of Liabilities

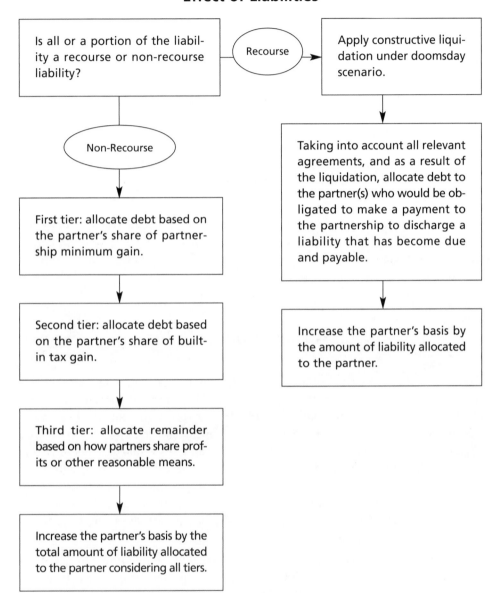

ners may allocate excess non-recourse liability to the contributing partner to the extent the built-in gain on the property will be greater than the phantom, or *Tufts,* gain.

Each year, the partners may select a different method for allocating excess non-recourse deductions.[7] If the partners fail to identify how the excess non-recourse liability will be allocated, the allocation will be made consistent with the partners' interest in the partnership.[8]

---

7. Treas. Reg. § 1.752-3(b).
8. Treas. Reg. § 1.752-3(a)(3).

> **Practice Note:** Because the partners may determine how excess non-recourse liabilities are allocated, the partnership agreement should clearly state the allocation method.

Formula: A partner's share of a non-recourse debt is the sum of—
- The partner's share of partnership minimum gain; plus
- If the liability secures property contributed by the partner, the amount of gain that would be generated and allocated to the contributing partner if the partnership sold the property for the amount of the debt; plus
- The partner's share of any remaining, or excess, non-recourse liabilities.

Part recourse, part non-recourse debt. If the liability is in part a recourse liability and in part a non-recourse liability, the debt must be bifurcated into its two portions. The portion that is recourse is allocated under the recourse rules and the portion that is non-recourse is allocated under the non-recourse rules.

C. Application of Rules

Example 1. Non-recourse debt and partnership minimum gain. Ellen and Francine formed a limited partnership with Ellen as the limited partner and Francine as the general partner. The partnership agreement provided that capital accounts would be maintained in accordance with the regulations, that Francine has an obligation to restore a negative capital account, and that liquidating distributions would be made in accordance with capital account balances. With respect to Ellen, the partnership agreement contained a qualified income offset. The partnership agreement also contained a minimum gain chargeback provision and provided that any excess non-recourse debt would be allocated equally between the partners. Finally, the partnership agreement allocated all profits and losses equally.

The partnership purchased a building for $10,000 financed entirely by a $10,000 non-recourse loan, secured by the building. No payments were due on the loan for five years. In the first year, the partnership was entitled to $1,000 of depreciation. The partnership agreement provided that all depreciation would be allocated to Francine until the first time the partnership has recognized items of income and gain that exceed the items of loss and deduction it has recognized over its life. Then, all further depreciation deductions will be allocated equally between Ellen and Francine.

Because the debt is a non-recourse debt, neither Ellen nor Francine bears the economic risk of loss. The constructive liquidation of the doomsday scenario confirms this.

At the end of the first year, the non-recourse debt is $10,000 and the adjusted basis of the building was $9,000 (cost of $10,000, less $1,000 of depreciation). Thus, the $1,000 depreciation deduction is a non-recourse deduction and there is $1,000 of partnership minimum gain, allocable entirely to Francine.

Under the first tier, a partner is allocated a portion of the debt equal to his share of partnership minimum gain. Thus, of the $10,000 debt, $1,000 is allocated to Francine under the first tier.

The second tier is applicable only when property has been contributed by a partner to the partnership (or otherwise has built-in gain or loss). Because the partnership purchased the property, there is no allocation under the second tier.

Under the third tier, the partners can agree on how to allocate the excess amount. The partners agreed that this excess amount, $9,000, would be allocated equally between the partners, or $4,500 each. The allocation will be respected because it is reasonably consistent with an allocation (having substantial economic effect) of any significant item of partnership income or gain.

Thus the debt is allocated as follows:

	Francine	Ellen
1st tier	$1,000	$-0-
2nd tier	-0-	-0-
3rd tier	4,500	4,500
Total	$5,500	$4,500

Example 2. Non-recourse debt and built-in gain. Gretel and Hansel formed an equal partnership. Gretel contributed $10,000 and Hansel contributed land with a fair market value of $15,000, subject to a non-recourse liability of $5,000, and a basis of $3,000. Pursuant to the partnership agreement, the partnership uses the traditional method to allocate Section 704(c) gain and allocates all excess non-recourse liabilities equally.

Because the debt is a non-recourse debt, neither Gretel nor Hansel bears the economic risk of loss. The constructive liquidation of the doomsday scenario confirms this. In addition, their basis depends, in part, on their share of the non-recourse liability.

Under the first tier, a partner is allocated a portion of the debt equal to his share of partnership minimum gain. Because the amount of the liability, $5,000, does not exceed the book value, or fair market value, of the land, $15,000, there is no partnership minimum gain. Thus, there is no allocation under the first tier.

The second tier is applicable only when property has been contributed by a partner to the partnership (or otherwise has built-in gain or loss). It takes into consideration the minimum amount of tax built-in gain that will be allocated to the partner upon sale of the property. Because the property can never be disposed of for less than the amount of the non-recourse liability, the minimum amount of gain is the excess of the liability over the adjusted basis, or $2,000 (the excess of $5,000 over $3,000). Accordingly, $2,000 of the liability is allocated to Hansel, the contributing partner.

Under the third tier, the partners can agree on how to allocate the excess amount. The partners agreed that this excess amount, $3,000, would be allocated equally between the partners, or $1,500 each. The allocation will be respected because it is reasonably consistent with an allocation (having substantial economic effect) of any significant item of partnership income or gain.

Thus the debt is allocated as follows:

	Gretel	Hansel
1st tier	$-0-	$-0-
2nd tier	-0-	2,000
3rd tier	1,500	1,500
Total	$1,500	$3,500

The net change in liability for Hansel was <$1,500> ($5,000 decrease in individual liability, $3,500 increase in share of partnership liabilities).

D. Cases and Materials

Rev. Rul. 95-41, 1995-1 C.B. 132

ISSUES: How does § 704(c) of the Internal Revenue Code affect the allocation of nonrecourse liabilities under § 1.752-3(a) of the Income Tax Regulations?

FACTS: *A* and *B* form a partnership, *PRS,* and agree that each will be allocated a 50 percent share of all partnership items. *A* contributes depreciable property subject to a nonrecourse liability of $6,000, with an adjusted tax basis of $4,000 and a fair market value of $10,000. *B* contributes $4,000 cash.

LAW: Section 1.752-3(a) provides that a partner's share of the nonrecourse liabilities of a partnership equals the sum of the amounts specified in § 1.752-3(a)(2)-(3).

Section 1.752-3(a)(1) provides that the partner's share of the nonrecourse liabilities of a partnership includes the partner's share of partnership minimum gain determined in accordance with the rules of § 704(b) and the regulations thereunder. See § 1.704-2.

Section 1.752-3(a)(2) provides that the partner's share of the nonrecourse liabilities of the partnership includes the amount of any taxable gain that would be allocated to the partner under § 704(c) (or in the same manner as § 704(c) in connection with a revaluation of partnership property) if the partnership disposed of (in a taxable transaction) all partnership property subject to one or more nonrecourse liabilities of the partnership in full satisfaction of the liabilities and for no other consideration.

Section 1.752-3(a)(3) provides that the partner's share of the nonrecourse liabilities of the partnership includes the partner's share of the excess nonrecourse liabilities (those not allocated under § 1.752-3(a)(1) and (a)(2)) of the partnership as determined in accordance with the partner's share of partnership profits. The partner's interest in partnership profits is determined by taking into account all facts and circumstances relating to the economic arrangement of the partners. The partnership agreement may specify the partners' interests in partnership profits for purposes of allocating excess nonrecourse liabilities, provided the interests so specified are reasonably consistent with allocations (that have substantial economic effect under the § 704(b) regulations) of some other significant item of partnership income or gain. Alternatively, excess nonrecourse liabilities may be allocated among the partners in accordance with the manner in which it is reasonably expected that the deductions attributable to those nonrecourse liabilities will be allocated.

Section 704(c)(1)(A) provides that income, gain, loss, and deduction with respect to property contributed to the partnership by a partner shall be shared among the partners so as to take account of the variation between the adjusted tax basis of the property to the partnership and its fair market value at the time of contribution.

Section 1.704-3(a)(3)(i) provides that the book value of contributed property is equal to its fair market value at the time of contribution and is subsequently adjusted for cost recovery and other events that affect the basis of the property.

Section 1.704-3(a)(3)(ii) provides that the built-in gain on § 704(c) property is the excess of the property's book value over the contributing partner's adjusted tax basis in the property upon contribution. The built-in gain is thereafter reduced by decreases in the difference between the property's book value and adjusted tax basis.

ANALYSIS:

Upon A's contribution of the depreciable property to PRS, there is $6,000 of § 704(c) built-in gain (the excess of the book value of the property ($10,000) over A's adjusted tax basis in the property at the time of contribution ($4,000)). As a result of the contribution, A's individual liabilities decreased by $6,000 (the amount of the nonrecourse liability which PRS is treated as having assumed). A's share of the partnership's nonrecourse liabilities is determined under § 1.752-3.

(1) First Tier Allocations:

Under § 1.752-3(a)(1), a partner's share of the nonrecourse liabilities of PRS includes the partner's share of partnership minimum gain determined in accordance with the rules of § 704(b) and the regulations thereunder. Section 1.704-2(d)(1) provides that partnership minimum gain is determined by computing, for each partnership nonrecourse liability, any gain the partnership would realize if it disposed of the property subject to that liability for no consideration other than full satisfaction of the liability, and then aggregating the separately computed gains. Pursuant to § 1.704-2(d)(3), partnership minimum gain is determined with reference to the contributed property's book value rather than its adjusted tax basis.

In contrast, § 704(c) requires that allocations take into account the difference between the contributed property's adjusted tax basis and its fair market value. Thus, because partnership minimum gain is computed using the contributed property's book value rather than its tax basis, allocations of nonrecourse liabilities under § 1.752-3(a)(1) are not affected by § 704(c). Moreover, because the book value of the property at the time of contribution ($10,000) exceeds the amount of the nonrecourse liability ($6,000), there is no partnership minimum gain immediately after the contribution, and neither A nor B receive an allocation of nonrecourse liabilities under § 1.752-3(a)(1) immediately after the contribution.

(2) Second Tier Allocations:

Under § 1.752-3(a)(2), a partner's share of the nonrecourse liabilities of the partnership includes the amount of taxable gain that would be allocated to the contributing partner under § 704(c) if the partnership, in a taxable transaction, disposed of the contributed property in full satisfaction of the nonrecourse liability and for no other consideration. If PRS sold the contributed property in full satisfaction of the liability and for no other consideration, *PRS* would recognize a taxable gain of $2,000 on the sale ($6,000 amount of the nonrecourse liability less $4,000 adjusted tax basis of the property). Under §704(c) and §1.704-3(b)(1), all of this taxable gain would be allocated to *A*. The hypothetical sale also would result in a book loss of $4,000 to *PRS* (excess of $10,000 book value of property over $6,000 amount of the nonrecourse liability). Under the terms of the partnership agreement, this book loss would be allocated equally between *A* and *B*. Because *B* would receive a $2,000 book loss but no corresponding tax loss, the hypothetical sale would result in a $2,000 disparity between *B's* book and tax allocations.

If *PRS* used the traditional method of making §704(c) allocations described in §1.704-3(b), *A* would be allocated a total of $2,000 of taxable gain from the hypothetical sale of the contributed property. Therefore, *A* would be allocated $2,000 of nonrecourse liabilities under §1.752-3(a)(2) immediately after the contribution.

If *PRS* adopted the remedial allocation method described in §1.704-3(d), *PRS* would be required to make a remedial allocation of $2,000 of tax loss to *B* in connection with the hypothetical sale to eliminate the $2,000 disparity between *B's* book and tax allocations. *PRS* also would be required to make an offsetting remedial allocation of tax gain to *A* of $2,000. Thus, *A* would be allocated a total of $4,000 of tax gain ($2,000 actual gain plus the $2,000 allocation of remedial gain) from the hypothetical sale of the contributed property. Therefore, if the partnership adopted the remedial allocation method, *A* would be allocated $4,000 of nonrecourse liabilities under §1.752-3(a)(2) immediately after the contribution.

If *PRS* used the traditional method with curative allocations described in §1.704-3(c), *PRS* would be permitted to make reasonable curative allocations to reduce or eliminate the difference between the book and tax allocations to *B* that resulted from the hypothetical sale. However, *PRS's* ability to make curative allocations would depend on the existence of other partnership items and could not be determined solely from the hypothetical sale of the contributed property. Because any potential curative allocations could not be determined solely from the hypothetical sale of the contributed property, curative allocations are not taken into account in allocating nonrecourse liabilities under §1.752-3(a)(2). Therefore, if *PRS* used the traditional method with curative allocations, *A* would be allocated $2,000 of nonrecourse liabilities under §1.752-3(a)(2) immediately after the contribution.

(3) Third Tier Allocations:

Following the allocation under §1.752-3(a)(2), *PRS* has excess nonrecourse liabilities that must be allocated between *A* and *B*. Section 1.752-3(a)(3) provides several alternatives for allocating excess nonrecourse liabilities.

(a) First, *PRS* may choose to allocate excess nonrecourse liabilities in accordance with the partners' shares of partnership profits. The partners' interests in partnership profits are determined by taking into account all the facts and circumstances relating to the economic arrangement of the partners. The partners' agreement to share the profits of the partnership equally is one fact to be considered in making this determination. Another fact to be considered is a partner's share of §704(c) built-in gain to the extent that the gain was not taken into account in making an allocation of nonrecourse liabilities under § 1.752-3(a)(2). This built-in gain is one factor because, under the principles of § 704(c), this excess built-in gain, if recognized, will be allocated to A. A's share of § 704(c) built-in gain that is not taken into account in making allocations under § 1.752-3(a)(2) is, therefore, one factor, but not the only factor, to be considered in determining A's interest in partnership profits.

The amount of the § 704(c) built-in gain that is not considered in making allocations under § 1.752-3(a)(2) must be given an appropriate weight in light of all other items of partnership profit. For example, if it is reasonable to expect that PRS will have items of partnership profit over the life of the partnership that will be allocated to B, PRS may not allocate all of the excess nonrecourse liabilities to A. Rather, the remaining nonrecourse liabilities must be allocated between A and B in proportion to their interests in total partnership profits.

(b) Second, the PRS partnership agreement may specify the partners' interest in partnership profits for purposes of allocating excess nonrecourse liabilities, provided that the interests specified are reasonably consistent with allocations (that have substantial economic effect under the § 704(b) regulations) of some other significant item of partnership income or gain. The partnership agreement provides that each partner will be allocated a 50 percent share of all partnership items. Assuming that such allocations have substantial economic effect, PRS can choose to allocate the excess nonrecourse liabilities 50 percent to each partner. Section 804(c) allocations, however, do not have substantial economic effect under the § 704(b) regulations. See § 1.704-1(b)(2)(iv)(d). Accordingly, under this alternative, § 704(c) allocations cannot be used as a basis for allocating excess nonrecourse liabilities.

(c) Finally, PRS may choose to allocate the excess nonrecourse liabilities in accordance with the manner in which it is reasonably expected that the deductions attributable to the excess nonrecourse liabilities will be allocated. Because A and B have agreed to allocate all partnership items 50 percent to each partner, A and B each will be entitled to allocations of book depreciation of $5,000 over the life of the contributed property. The contributed property, however, has an adjusted tax basis of $4,000 and, regardless of the method used by the partnership under § 704(c), the entire $4,000 of tax depreciation over the life of the contributed property must be allocated to B. Therefore, PRS must allocate all of the excess nonrecourse liabilities to B if it chooses to allocate the excess nonrecourse liabilities in accordance with the manner that the deductions attributable to the excess nonrecourse liabilities will be allocated.

HOLDINGS: (1) Allocations of nonrecourse liabilities under § 1.752-3(a)(1) are not affected by § 704(c).

(2) Allocations of nonrecourse liabilities under § 1.752-3(a)(2) take into account remedial allocations of gain that would be made to the contributing partner under § 1.704-3(d). Allocations of nonrecourse liabilities under § 1.752-3(a)(2) do not take into account curative allocations under § 1.704-3(c).

(3) Allocations of nonrecourse liabilities under § 1.752-3(a)(3) are affected by § 704(c) in the following manner:

- (a) If the partnership determines the partners' interests in partnership profits based on all of the facts and circumstances relating to the economic arrangement of the partners, § 704(c) built-in gain that was not taken into account under § 1.752-3(a)(2) is one factor, but not the only factor, to be considered under § 1.752-3(a)(3).

- (b) If the partnership chooses to allocate excess nonrecourse liabilities in a manner reasonably consistent with allocations (that have substantial economic effect under the § 704(b) regulations) of some other significant item of partnership income or gain, § 704(c) does not affect the allocation of nonrecourse liabilities under § 1.752-3(a)(3) because § 704(c) allocations do not have substantial economic effect.

- (c) If the partnership chooses to allocate excess nonrecourse liabilities in accordance with the manner in which it is reasonably expected that the deductions attributable to the nonrecourse liabilities will be allocated, the partnership must take into account the allocations required by § 704(c) in determining the manner in which the deductions attributable to the nonrecourse liabilities will be allocated.

E. Problems

1. Jack and Jill formed a limited partnership. Jack contributed $90,000 in exchange for a limited partnership interest and Jill contributed $10,000 in exchange for a general partnership interest. The partnership agreement provided that capital accounts would be maintained in accordance with the regulations, that Jill had an obligation to restore a negative capital account, and that liquidating distributions would be made in accordance with capital account balances. With respect to Jack, the partnership agreement had a qualified income offset. The partnership agreement also contained a minimum gain chargeback provision. It provided that any excess non-recourse debt be allocated equally between the partners. Finally, the partnership agreement allocated all depreciation 90 percent to Jack and 10 percent to Jill and allocated all non-recourse deductions 80 percent to Jack and 20 percent to Jill until the first time the partnership recognized items of income and gain that exceeded the items of loss and deduction it had recognized over its life. Then, all further depreciation deductions would be allocated equally between Jack and Jill.

The partnership purchased a building for $300,000, using the $100,000 cash contributed by the partners and financing the remaining $200,000 with a non-recourse debt, secured by the building. No payments were due on the loan for five years. Ignoring all conventions, in each year the partnership was entitled to $50,000 of depreciation. In each year, before taking into consideration the depreciation, partnership income was equal to its expenses.

(a) What is each partner's basis at the end of the first year? Create a balance sheet to reflect the situation of the partners and partnership.

(b) What is each partner's basis at the end of the second year? Create a balance sheet to reflect the situation of the partners and partnership.

(c) What is each partner's basis at the end of the third year? Create a balance sheet to reflect the situation of the partners and partnership.

(d) Alternatively, if the partnership agreement provided that excess non-recourse debt be allocated 80 percent to Jack and 20 percent to Jill, what is each partner's basis at the end of the third year?

---

2. Harry and Wes formed a general partnership. Harry contributed $50,000. Wes contributed land with a fair market value of $75,000 and basis of $10,000. The land was subject to a $25,000 non-recourse debt and the debt was assumed by the partnership.

The partnership agreement provided that capital accounts would be maintained in accordance with the regulations, that the partners have an obligation to restore a negative capital account, and that liquidating distributions would be made in accordance with capital account balances. The partnership agreement also contained a minimum gain chargeback provision. It provided that any excess non-recourse debt would be allocated equally between the partners.

What is each partner's basis as of the formation of the partnership? Create a balance sheet to reflect the situation of the partners and partnership.

---

3. Application:

(a) Will you try to explain to the partners the method by which non-recourse debt is allocated? Why or why not?

(b) Draft language for the partnership agreement allocating excess (third tier) non-recourse debt.

Overview Problem—Putting It All Together

Stacey, Bill, and Olivia own and operate the coffee shop. Stacey has a 20 percent general partnership interest, Bill has a 50 percent limited partnership interest, and Olivia has a 30 percent limited partnership interest. The partners intend to allocate a disproportionately large portion of the partnership deductions to Bill and Olivia.

After the partnership was formed, the partners found an appropriate location from which to operate the coffee shop. The property owner was willing to either lease the space or sell them the building. The partners are in agreement that they want to purchase the building. However, because the partnership does not have the funds, it will have to obtain a loan. If it could, the partnership would obtain a non-recourse loan to finance the purchase. If it could not obtain a non-recourse loan, the partnership would obtain a recourse loan. Either way, to assist in obtaining the loan, if necessary, Olivia has agreed to personally guaranty the liability. However, if she does so, she wants to be "compensated" by the partnership through a special allocation of additional deductions. As a last resort, Olivia has agreed to purchase the property herself, financed entirely with borrowed funds, then contribute the property subject to the liability to the partnership.

They have come to you for advice about the tax consequences of the various financing options on the partners in the partnership.

1. If the partnership is able to obtain a non-recourse loan:

    (a) To carry out the intent of the partners, what provisions do you need to make sure are in the partnership agreement?

    (b) What problems do you foresee?

    (c) If Olivia is called upon to guaranty the debt, what impact (if any) will that fact have?

2. If the partnership is able to obtain a recourse loan:

    (a) To carry out the intent of the partners, what provisions do you need to make sure are in the partnership agreement?

    (b) What problems do you foresee?

    (c) If Olivia is called upon to guaranty the debt, what impact (if any) will that fact have?

3. If Olivia purchases the property, then contributes it subject to the liability to the partnership, what problems do you foresee? What other information would you want to know to be able to advise the partners on this option?

VI.

Transfer of a Partnership Interest

Overview Problem

Stacey, Bill, and Olivia have operated the coffee shop for a number of years. While Olivia has really enjoyed being a partner in the partnership, she has decided that it is time for her to do something different. She has always wanted to design woman's apparel. With the financial security the partnership has given her, she is ready to leave the partnership and give designing a try. However, she also wants to make sure that Stacey and Bill have someone to take over the responsibilities she has been handling. After some intense discussions with Charles, she decides he could take on her responsibilities and that she would like to sell her partnership interest to him.

Currently, the partnership has the following items:

	Adj. Basis	FMV
Cash	$50,000	$50,000
Acct. Rev.	-0-	40,000
Coffee bean inventory	30,000	30,000
Misc. supplies	25,000	25,000
Espresso machine	2,000	10,000
Building	100,000	100,000

The partners held a partnership meeting to discuss Olivia's leaving and Charles's joining the partnership. Even though Stacey and Bill will be sad to see her go, they understand her desire to try something new.

The partners need to determine the consequences of Olivia leaving and Charles joining the partnership. You have been invited to the meeting to advise them.

Transfer of a Partnership Interest

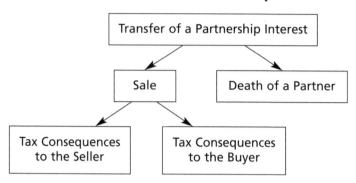

Chapter 21

Tax Consequences to Transferring Partner

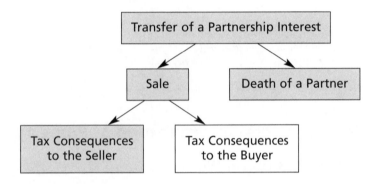

Read:

Code Sections 1(h)(5)(B), (h)(9), (h)(10)(D); 741; 751(a), (c), (d); 752(d).
Treas. Reg. §§ 1.1(h)-1(a), -1(b)(1), -1(b)(2), -1(b)(3), -1(c), -1(f) Ex. 1; 1.741-1;
1.751-1(a), -1(c)(1)-(3), -1(d)(2), -1(g) Ex. 1; 1.1223-3(a), -3(c).

A. Background

1. State Law Consequences of the Transfer of an Interest in a Partnership

Under the Uniform Partnership Act, in general, a partner's leaving the partnership may cause the partnership to dissolve and terminate.[1] Under the Revised Uniform Partnership Act (RUPA), a partner's leaving the partnership is referred to as dissociation.[2] A partner has the power to dissociate from a partnership at any time. However, the partner does not always have the right to dissociate. In some situations, a partner's dissociation is considered wrongful and he will be liable for damages caused by his departure.[3]

---

1. UPA §29-31.
2. RUPA §601.
3. RUPA §602.

> **Practice Tip:** A partnership may intend to be in existence for:
> - A term of years;
> - The length of time necessary to complete a specific undertaking; or
> - Until the partners decide to discontinue operating as a partnership (at-will).

Under the RUPA, a partner's dissociation from a partnership may cause the partnership to dissolve and terminate.[4] For example, a partner's voluntarily leaving an at-will partnership will cause a dissolution of the partnership.[5] The death of a partner is a dissociation[6] and may result in the termination of the partnership.[7]

> **Practice Alert:** An event that causes dissolution of a partnership under state law may not be considered dissolution of a partnership for federal tax purposes. [See Code Sec. 708(b) and Chapters 31 and 32.]

2. Tax Consequences on Disposition of Property

a. Gain or Loss on Disposition

Gross income includes income from all sources derived.[8] One of the items enumerated in section 61(a) is gain derived from dealings in property.[9] The amount of gain is the excess of the amount realized over the adjusted basis.[10] Unless otherwise provided, the gain realized must be recognized, *i.e.*, reported on the taxpayer's income tax return.[11]

The amount of loss from a disposition of property is the excess of the adjusted basis over the amount realized. The taxpayer can recognize, *i.e.*, report the loss on his tax return, if it was incurred while engaged in a business or in a transaction entered into for profit.[12]

> **Example:** Allison owns land with a basis of $100 and a fair market value of $500. Blake owns equipment with a basis of $700 and fair market value of $500. Allison sells the land for $500 and Blake sells the equipment for $500.
>
> Upon disposition of the land, Allison would realize gain as follows:

---

4. RUPA § 801.
5. RUPA § 801(1).
6. RUPA § 601(7)(i).
7. RUPA § 801(2).
8. Code Sec. 61.
9. Code Sec. 61(a)(3).
10. Code Sec. 1001(a).
11. Code Sec. 1001(c).
12. Code Sec. 165(a), (c)(1), (c)(2).

Amount realized = $500
Adjusted basis =   100
Gain realized = $400

As provided by sections 61(a)(3) and 1001(c), Allison must recognize the $400 gain.

Upon disposition of the equipment, Blake would realize a loss as follows:

Amount realized = $500
Adjusted basis =   700
Loss realized =   <$200>

If Blake held the equipment in his business or through a transaction entered into for profit, he can recognize the $200 loss.

b. Character of Gain or Loss

The net gain from capital assets that have been held more than a year, net long-term capital gain, is taxed at preferential rates. The net gain from capital assets that have been held for a year or less, net short-term capital gain, is taxed at regular rates. Net capital losses, whether long-term or short-term, are allowed only to the extent of $3,000 each year, with any excess carried forward.

Determination of Which Assets are Capital Assets: In general, capital assets include all property except:[13]
- Inventory;
- Real property held primarily for sale to customers in the course of the taxpayer's business;
- Depreciable property used in the taxpayer's business;
- Real property used in the taxpayer's business;
- Certain copyrights;
- Accounts receivable acquired in the ordinary course of the taxpayer's business; and
- Supplies used in the taxpayer's business.

Ordinary income is taxed at the taxpayer's regular tax rates. There is no limit on the amount of ordinary loss a taxpayer can claim.

13. See Code Sec. 1221(a).

Summary of Tax Results:

	Ordinary	Capital
Gain	Taxed at regular rates.[14]	• Net long-term gain—taxed at preferential rates. • Net short-term gain—taxed at regular rates.[15]
Loss	In general, if otherwise allowable, no limitation on the amount of loss that can be claimed.	• To the extent it exceeds capital gains, the amount allowed is limited to $3,000.[16] • Any excess loss can be carried forward, retaining its character as long-term or short-term capital loss.[17]

---

c. Preferential Capital Gain Rates

The tax rate applicable to net long-term capital gains depends on the nature of the asset sold and the taxpayer's tax bracket. The rate will be one of the following:[18]

- 28 percent;
- 25 percent;
- 15 percent;
- Zero percent; or
- The tax rate applied to the taxpayer's ordinary income.

If the taxpayer is in a tax bracket higher than 28 percent and the item sold is either "collectibles" or "Section 1202 gain," the maximum tax rate will be 28 percent.[19] If the taxpayer would otherwise be in a lower tax bracket, the lower rate will apply. Collectibles gain is gain from the sale or exchange of any rug, antique, metal, gem, stamp, coin, or other collectible that has been held as a capital asset for more than one year.[20] "Section 1202" gain generally is 50 percent of the gain from the sale or exchange of certain stock described in Section 1202.[21]

Example: Jamaal, who was in the 35 percent tax bracket, sold an antique rug he had purchased three years earlier for investment purposes. He recognized a long-term capital gain of $30,000. Because the gain was from a collectible and Jamaal would otherwise have been in a higher tax bracket, the gain from the rug will be taxed at the 28 percent rate. His remaining income will be taxed at the 35 percent rate.

Alternatively, assume Jamaal had been in the 15 percent tax bracket when he sold the antique rug. He still recognized a long-term capital gain of $30,000.

---

14. There is one exception—dividends. Dividends, while ordinary income, are taxed at preferential rates. See Code Sec. 1(h)(11).
15. See Code Sec. 1(h).
16. See Code Sec. 1211(b).
17. See Code Sec. 1212(b).
18. Code Sec. 1(h).
19. Code Sec. 1(h)(1), (h)(4).
20. Code Sec. 1(h)(5).
21. Code Sec. 1(h)(7).

Because he was not in a tax bracket higher than 28 percent, the gain will be taxed at the 15 percent rate, the same as his other income.

If the gain is "unrecaptured Section 1250 gain," it is taxed at a maximum rate of 25 percent.[22] In general, unrecaptured Section 1250 gain is long-term capital gain attributable to depreciation allowed with respect to real estate held for more than one year.[23]

Example: Brian sold a building that he had used in his business for two years for $100,000. At the time of the sale, the adjusted basis in the building was $75,000 and he had claimed $25,000 of depreciation; he recognized $25,000 of gain. Because the gain from the sale was attributable to the depreciation taken by Brian prior to sale, the gain is characterized as unrecaptured Section 1250 gain and is taxed at a rate not higher than 25 percent.

Adjusted net capital gain is taxed at a maximum rate of 15 percent.[24] Adjusted net capital gain is the gain remaining after considering the previous two categories of gain, *i.e.*, the net capital gain reduced by the amount of gain from collectibles, Section 1202 gain, and unrecaptured Section 1250 gain.[25] If the gain would otherwise have been taxed at the 15 percent rate, then the adjusted net capital gain is taxed at a maximum rate of zero percent.

Example: Erik is in the 35 percent tax bracket. He sold stock in GainCo and recognized a long-term capital gain of $20,000. Erik sold no other assets during the year. Because he had no collectibles, Section 1202, or unrecaptured Section 1250 gain, the adjusted net capital gain is $20,000. It will be taxed at the 15 percent rate. All other income will be taxed at the 35 percent rate.

Alternatively, if Erik had been in the 15 percent tax bracket, the gain would otherwise have been taxed at the 15 percent rate. Thus, it will be taxed at the zero percent rate and all other income will be taxed at the 15 percent rate.

---

d. Installment Sales

Certain gain realized from the disposition of property may be reported using the installment method.[26] The installment method is available if at least one payment is received in a year subsequent to the year of disposition.[27] In addition, in general, all gains are eligible to be reported using the installment method except gains from the sale of inventory and depreciation recapture.[28]

---

22. Code Sec. 1(h)(1)(D).
23. Code Sec. 1(h)(7).
24. Code Sec. 1(h)(1)(C).
25. Code Sec. 1(h)(3).
26. Code Sec. 453(a).
27. Code Sec. 453(b)(1).
28. Code Sec. 453(b)(2)(B), (i).

e. Bequests and Inheritances

There are no federal income tax consequences on the transfer of property from an estate to the beneficiaries.[29] And, the beneficiary can exclude the bequest from income.[30] If the beneficiary-taxpayer subsequently disposes of the property, he generally determines his gain or loss by using a basis equal to the fair market value of the property as of the date of the decedent's death.[31]

Example: When his aunt passed away, Sam received Yellowacre from her estate. While his aunt had paid $10,000 for the parcel, its fair market value was $50,000 when she passed away.

Sam does not have to include the value of Yellowacre in his gross income and his basis is $50,000.

B. Discussion of Rules

1. Sale of a Partnership Interest — General Rule

Character of gain. In general, the disposition of a partnership interest is treated as a disposition of a capital asset. Any gain is a capital gain and any loss is a capital loss.[32]

Holding period of partnership interest. Recall that the holding period of the partnership interest may depend on the assets contributed to the partnership. The partner's holding period in the asset contributed to the partnership tacks onto his holding period of his partnership interest if the asset is a capital asset or hotchpot (Section 1231) asset. The holding period does not tack if the partner contributes cash or ordinary income assets; the holding period begins the day following contribution.[33] If a partner contributes assets whose holding period tacks and those that do not, the holding period will be divided between the two.[34] For purposes of this determination, Section 1245 recapture gain is not treated as a capital or hotchpot (Section 1231) asset. The length of time the partnership interest was held determines whether the gain or loss on disposition is long-term or short-term.

Example: Clinton became a partner in the Style Partnership five years ago by contributing $100,000 in exchange for a 10-percent general partnership interest. The partnership owns only cash and land held for investment.

This year Clinton sold his partnership interest to Stacey for $150,000. At the time of the sale, his outside basis was $75,000. Clinton realizes and recognizes

---

29. However, the estate tax may apply.
30. Code Sec. 102(a).
31. Code Sec. 1015. If the estate elects an alternate valuation date, the basis is equal to the value as of the alternate date.
32. Code Sec. 741.
33. Code Sec. 1223(1).
34. Treas. Reg. § 1.1223-3(a)(2).

$75,000 of gain (amount realized of $150,000, less adjusted basis of $75,000). The gain will be long-term capital gain.

The characterization provisions apply to the partner's total gain or loss on disposition. Note that the amount realized includes any debt relief[35] and the adjusted basis includes any adjustments to the partner's outside basis that reflect his pro rata distribution of partnership items up to the time of sale.[36]

Practice Note: When a partner sells a portion of his interest in a partnership, generally the partnership taxable year does not end [Code Sec. 706(c)]. At the end of the partnership's taxable year, the partner's allocable share of partnership items is determined by taking into consideration his varying interest in the partnership during the year. [Code Sec. 706(c)(2)(B), (d). See Chapter 12.] The portion of the basis allocable to the portion of the interest sold must be adjusted to reflect the allocable portion of the partner's distributive share [Treas. Reg. § 1.705-1(a)(1)].

When a partner sells his entire interest in the partnership, the partnership's taxable year with respect to that partner closes [Code Sec. 706(c)(2)(A)]. The partner's basis must be adjusted for items allocated to him from the partnership's short taxable year [Treas. Reg. §§ 1.705-1(a); 1.706-1(c)(2)(ii)].

---

2. Exceptions to the General Rule

a. Hot Assets

While the general rule is that gain from the disposition of a partnership interest is capital gain, this result allowed taxpayers to convert what would have been ordinary income into capital gain.

Example: Jack became a partner in the Consulting Partnership five years ago by contributing $100,000 in exchange for a 10-percent general partnership interest. The partnership is a cash basis taxpayer that holds only accounts receivable. Jack's proportionate share of the partnership accounts receivable is $10,000. His outside basis currently is $100,000.

If Jack waits until the partnership collects the accounts receivable, he would be required to report $10,000 of ordinary income.

In contrast, under the general rule, if Jack sold his partnership interest for $110,000 a year after he purchased it, but before the accounts receivable had been collected, he would realize and recognize $10,000 of gain (amount re-

---

35. Code Sec. 752(d).
36. Code Sec. 705.

alized of $110,000, less adjusted basis of $100,000). Under the general rule, the gain would be long-term capital gain. Effectively, Jack would have been able to convert what would have been ordinary income into long-term capital gain. Section 751(a) prohibits this result.

The statutory provisions return to an aggregate approach, in part, to determine the character of gain or loss when a partner sells all or a portion of his partnership interest. To determine the portion of the gain or loss that must be rechacterized as ordinary, first determine whether the partnership has any unrealized receivables or inventory items.

Practice Tip: Sometimes, unrealized receivables and inventory are referred to as "hot assets."

Unrealized receivables. Unrealized receivables include, to the extent not previously included in income, any right to payment for services rendered. They also include the right to payment for goods delivered to the extent the proceeds would be treated as amounts received from the sale or exchange of property other than a capital asset. They also include any gain that would be characterized as ordinary income under the depreciation recapture provisions.[37]

Example: Collections Partnership holds only accounts receivable. If the partnership is a cash method taxpayer, the accounts receivable are unrealized receivables. In contrast, if the partnership is an accrual method taxpayer, the accounts receivable are not unrealized receivables.

Inventory items. Inventory includes those assets held for sale to customers and any items held by the partnership that are not characterized as a capital or hotchpot (Section 1231) item.[38]

If an item comes within the definition of both unrealized receivables and inventory items, it is considered only once.

Example: Developer Partnership is a cash basis partnership that develops lots for sale to customers. Its balance sheet appears as follows:

Asset	Adj. Basis	FMV	Partners	Adj. Basis	Cap. Acct.
Cash	$3,000	$3,000	Arthur	$10,000	$20,000
Acct. Rec.	-0-	14,000	Brindle	10,000	20,000
Lots for sale	10,000	20,000		$20,000	$40,000
Land	7,000	3,000			
Total:	$20,000	$40,000			

---

37. Code Sec. 751(c).

38. Code Sec. 751(d). It also includes any property that, if held by the selling partner, would be inventory. Code Sec. 751(d)(3).

The accounts receivable come within the definition of unrealized receivables. Both the lots held for sale and the accounts receivable come within the definition of inventory. However, the accounts receivable are considered only once.

In contrast, if the partnership were an accrual basis method taxpayer, its balance sheet would appear as follows:

Asset	Adj. Basis	FMV	Partners	Adj. Basis	Cap. Acct.
Cash	$3,000	$3,000	Arthur	$17,000	$20,000
Acct. Rec.	14,000	14,000	Brindle	17,000	20,000
Lots for sale	10,000	20,000		$34,000	$40,000
Land	7,000	3,000			
Total:	$34,000	$40,000			

The accounts receivable do not come within the definition of unrealized receivables. The lots held for sale and the accounts receivable both come within the definition of inventory.

Determination of gain or loss allocable to unrealized receivables and inventory items. To determine how much gain or loss must be recharacterized as ordinary, determine how much gain or loss the partner would have if all unrealized receivables and inventory items were sold for their fair market value and an allocable share allocated to the selling partner.[39] In determining the amount of gain or loss allocable to the partner, take into consideration any special allocations and any allocations required by Section 704(c) (addressing built-in gains and losses), including any remedial allocations. To that extent, the gain or loss is characterized as ordinary income or loss.

Finally, determine the amount necessary so that, when added to the amount of ordinary income, it results in the amount of gain or loss the partner has on disposition of the partnership interest (*i.e.*, the amount of the gain or loss on disposition, less the amount of gain or loss from unrealized receivables or inventory items). This amount continues to be characterized as capital gain or loss.

Practice Note: Because Section 751(a) requires a netting of the ordinary income amounts and the gain or loss on disposition, it is possible to have ordinary income and a capital loss or an ordinary loss and a capital gain.

Practice Tip: A partner selling any part of an interest in a partnership that has any Section 751(a) property at the time of sale must submit with his income tax return for the taxable year in which the sale occurs a statement setting forth the following information [Treas. Reg. § 1.751-1(a)(3)]:
- The date of the sale;
- The amount of any gain or loss attributable to the Section 751 property; and
- The amount of any gain or loss attributable to capital gain or loss on the sale of the partnership interest.

---

39. Treas. Reg. § 1.751-1(a)(2).

b. Lukewarm Assets

Not all capital gains are taxed at the same tax rate. Rather, collectibles and unrecaptured Section 1250 gain are taxed at preferential rates. Similarly, the capital gain from the disposition of a partnership interest may be taxed at various rates, depending on the assets held by the partnership.[40]

Practice Tip: Sometimes, collectibles and unrecaptured Section 1250 gain are referred to as "lukewarm assets."

If the partner held the partnership interest for more than one year, and the partnership holds appreciated collectibles, the regulations use an aggregate approach and look through the partnership. The portion of the gain that would be allocated to the partner if the collectibles were sold for fair market value (taking into consideration Section 704(c)) is taxed as capital gain from a collectible.[41]

The same analysis is used if the partner held the partnership interest for more than one year and the partnership holds unrecaptured Section 1250 gain. The portion of the gain that would be allocated to the partner if the property were sold for fair market value is taxed as gain from an unrecaptured Section 1250 asset.[42]

The remaining amount of capital gain, the total capital gain less the amount allocated to appreciated collectibles and unrecaptured Section 1250 gain, is the adjusted net capital gain.[43]

3. Allocation of Basis and Holding Period

When a partner sells only a portion of his partnership interest, the basis and holding period must be allocated between the portion sold and the portion retained.

Example: Maybell is a partner in a partnership. At a time when her basis was $4,000, she sold one-quarter of her interest. The basis in the portion of the interest she sold was $1,000 (one-quarter of $4,000).

Practice Tip: If a partner is both a general partner and a limited partner, he is treated as having a unitary basis in his partnership interest [Rev. Rul. 84-52, 1984-1 C.B. 157].

---

40. Treas. Reg. § 1.1(h)-1.
41. Treas. Reg. § 1.1(h)-1(b)(2)(ii).
42. Treas. Reg. § 1.1(h)-1(b)(3)(ii).
43. Treas. Reg. § 1.1(h)-1(c).

A partner may have a divided holding period in his partnership interest.[44] Thus, upon disposition of the partnership interest, a portion of the capital gain may be long-term and a portion may be short-term. Allocation of the holding period is based on the relative portions of the interest that have been held long term and short term.[45]

Example: Ness purchased a one-quarter interest in the partnership five years ago for $2,000. Earlier this year, she acquired an additional one-quarter interest in the partnership for $6,000. Ness sold her one-half interest in the partnership this year for $12,000, recognizing $4,000 of capital gain (amount realized of $12,000, less adjusted basis of $8,000).

Of the one-half interest sold by Ness, one-quarter was held long-term and one-quarter was held short-term. Thus, of the $4,000 of capital gain, one-half is characterized as long-term and one-half as short-term.

---

4. Sale Using the Installment Method

A partner may sell his partnership interest using the installment method. Once again, the partnership provisions return to an aggregate approach in determining the applicability of reporting under the installment method. Specifically, to the extent of gain from unrealized receivables, inventory, or depreciation recapture (generally, to the extent of gain from the hot assets), the partner may not use the installment method. Rather, such gain must be reported in the year of disposition.[46]

Determining Character of Gain on Disposition of a Portion or All of a Partner's Interest in a Partnership:

Step 1: Determine the partner's adjusted basis as of the day of the sale by taking into consideration any allocations to the partner. Determine the amount realized, including any debt relief.

Step 2: Determine the partner's total amount of gain or loss on disposition of the partnership interest.

Step 3: To the extent the partnership has any unrealized receivables or inventory items, determine how much gain or loss the partner would have if these items were sold for their fair market value and an allocable share allocated to the selling partner, taking into consideration any special allocations and any allocations required by Section 704(c). To this extent, the gain or loss is characterized as ordinary income or loss.

---

44. Treas. Reg. § 1.1223-3(a).
45. Treas. Reg. § 1.1223-3(c)(1).
46. Rev. Rul. 89-108, 1989-2 C.B. 100.

Step 4:   Determine the amount that, when added to the amount of ordinary income, results in the amount of gain or loss the partner has on disposition of the partnership interest (*i.e.*, the amount of the gain or loss on disposition, less the amount of gain or loss from unrealized receivables or inventory items). This amount is characterized as capital gain or loss.

Step 5:   To the extent the partnership has any collectibles or unrecognized Section 1250 gain, determine how much gain or loss the partner would have if the assets were sold for their fair market value and an allocable share allocated to the selling partner; apply the relevant tax rate to each category of gain. Tax any remaining gain, the adjusted net capital gain, at the relevant applicable rate.

Sale of Partnership Interest

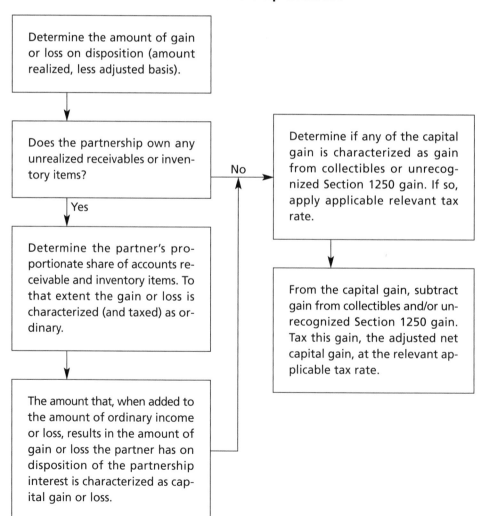

Determine the amount of gain or loss on disposition (amount realized, less adjusted basis).

Does the partnership own any unrealized receivables or inventory items?

No

Yes

Determine if any of the capital gain is characterized as gain from collectibles or unrecognized Section 1250 gain. If so, apply applicable relevant tax rate.

Determine the partner's proportionate share of accounts receivable and inventory items. To that extent the gain or loss is characterized (and taxed) as ordinary.

From the capital gain, subtract gain from collectibles and/or unrecognized Section 1250 gain. Tax this gain, the adjusted net capital gain, at the relevant applicable tax rate.

The amount that, when added to the amount of ordinary income or loss, results in the amount of gain or loss the partner has on disposition of the partnership interest is characterized as capital gain or loss.

5. Like-Kind Exchange

A partnership interest may be sold or exchanged for a different partnership interest. However, the exchange does not qualify under the like-kind exchange provisions.[47]

6. Tiered Partnerships

One of the assets a partnership may own is an interest in a second partnership. Congress was concerned that a taxpayer could attempt to avoid the requirement of recognizing ordinary income under Section 751(a) by placing any hot assets in the second partnership. Because the interest in the second partnership has not been sold, arguably, a taxpayer could avoid reporting any ordinary income.

To prevent this result, the Code requires that the assets of the second partnership be treated as owned proportionately by the original partnership. Thus, when a partner sells a partnership interest, the characterization of income or loss as ordinary under Section 751(a) applies to a proportionate share of any hot assets held by the second partnership.[48]

Example: Alex is a general partner in Primary Partnership. Primary Partnership owns Blackacre (land held for investment), cash, and a general partnership interest in Secondary Partnership. Secondary Partnership owns accounts receivable. Alex sells his partnership interest in Primary Partnership for $200. At the time of the sale, his basis was $50. Thus, Alex realizes $150 gain from the disposition of the interest.

While the general rule is that gain from the disposition of a partnership interest is capital gain, it is recharacterized as ordinary to the extent of the partner's share of gain or loss from the partnership's unrealized receivables or inventory. While Primary Partnership does not own any unrealized receivables or inventory directly, it does own unrealized receivables indirectly through its interest in Secondary Partnership.

Primary Partnership is treated as owning a proportionate share of the accounts receivable owned by Secondary Partnership. Thus, Alex must recharacterize the gain as ordinary to the extent of his proportionate share of the accounts receivable he owns indirectly in Secondary Partnership.

---

47. Code Sec. 1031(a)(2)(D); Treas. Reg. §1.1031(a)-1(a)(1).
48. Code Sec. 751(f).

7. Death of a Partner

a. In General

Closing of taxable year. In general, the death of a partner does not close the partnership's taxable year.[49] However, the partnership taxable year closes with respect to the partner.[50]

The death of a partner closes his individual taxable year.[51] His final income tax return must include his allocable share of partnership items for the short taxable year. In addition, if the partnership's prior taxable year's allocations had not yet been included, they must be included in the partner's final tax return.[52]

Built-in loss. If the deceased-partner had contributed property to the partnership with a built-in loss, the loss is eliminated when the partnership interest is transferred.[53]

b. Transfer of the Partnership Interest

When a partner passes away, the partnership interest generally becomes property of his estate. The estate may have options as to how to dispose of the interest.

First, the estate may be able to sell the partnership interest. In some circumstances, if required by the partnership agreement or buy-sell agreement, it may be required to sell the interest. The tax consequences of the sale are the same as they would have been if the partner had sold the interest during his lifetime.

Second, the interest may be transferred to a beneficiary of the decedent-partner's estate. The beneficiary takes the partnership interest with a basis equal to its fair market value as of the date of death,[54] increased by the successor's share of partnership liabilities, and decreased by any income in respect of decedent items.

Practice Tip: A partnership does not terminate if a partner owning 50 percent of the partnership passes away and his interest is transferred as part of his estate. A transfer by gift or inheritance is not considered a sale or exchange for purposes of the termination provisions in Section 708(b)(1)(B) [Treas. Reg. § 1.708-1(b)(2)].

Practice Tip: If one partner in a two-partner partnership passes away, the partnership does not terminate for tax purposes as long as the deceased partner's successor in interest has a share in the profits and losses of the partnership [Treas. Reg. § 1.708-1(b)(1)(i)].

---

49. Code Sec. 706(c)(1).
50. Code Sec. 706(c)(2).
51. Code Sec. 443(a)(2).
52. Code Sec. 706(a).
53. Code Sec. 704(c)(1)(C)(ii).
54. If the estate elects an alternative valuation date, the basis is equal to the value as of the alternate date.

Income in respect of a decedent. The beneficiary-partner will be required to report certain income items that had not been taxed to the decedent-partner. These items also will be required to have the same character they would have had in the hands of the decedent-partner.[55]

Basis elections. If the partnership has made a Section 754 election, the beneficiary's basis in the partnership assets will be adjusted as provided for in Section 743(b).[56] If the partnership's assets have substantially depreciated,[57] it will be required to make the adjustment.[58] If the partnership has not made the election, the beneficiary-partner may elect a basis adjustment for any property distributed to him within two years.[59]

Finally, the partnership may liquidate the deceased partner's interest. If the interest is liquidated, amounts classified under Section 736(a) are treated as income in respect of a decedent.[60] Amounts classified in Section 736(b) are treated as a payment for the partner's interest in partnership property.[61]

C. Application of Rules

Example 1. Sale of interest with hot assets. Russ and Sue are equal partners in the Consulting Partnership. Sue had joined the partnership four years earlier.

The partnership is a cash basis, general partnership that provides consulting services. At the end of the year, Sue sold her interest to Terri in exchange for $15,000 cash. At the time of the sale, the balance sheet appeared as follows:

Asset	Adj. Basis	FMV	Liabilities		$2,000
Cash	$3,000	$3,000	Partners	Adj. Basis	Cap. Acct.
Acct. Rec.	-0-	14,000	Russ	10,000	$15,000
Land	10,000	10,000	Sue	10,000	15,000
Land	7,000	5,000		$20,000	$32,000
Total:	$20,000	$32,000			

None of the assets were transferred to the partnership by a partner.

Upon sale of her partnership interest, Sue received $16,000, $15,000 cash and $1,000 of debt relief. Sue's basis was $10,000. Thus, Sue had $6,000 of gain she had to recognize.

The accounts receivable are unrealized receivables. If the partnership had sold the accounts receivable for their fair market value, it would have gain recognized of $14,000

---

55. See Code Secs. 451(a); 691(a)(1), (a)(3); 1014(c). See, *e.g.*, Woodhall v. Commissioner, 454 F.2d 226 (9th Cir. 1972), *aff'g* T.C. Memo. 1969-279.

56. See discussion in Chapter 22.

57. The assets have substantially depreciated if the adjusted basis of its assets exceeds the fair market value of the assets by more than $250,000. Code Sec. 743(d)(1).

58. Code Sec. 743(a), (d). See also Chapter 22.

59. Code Sec. 732(b). See discussion in Chapter 23.

60. Code Sec. 753. See also Quick's Trust v. Commissioner, 54 T.C. 1336 (1970), *aff'd*, 444 F.2d 90 (8th Cir. 1971).

61. See discussion of distributions in liquidation of a partner's interest in Chapter 28.

(amount realized of $14,000, less zero basis). One-half, or $7,000, would have been allocated to Sue. To this extent Sue must recognize ordinary income.

The amount that, when added to the amount of ordinary income of $7,000, results in the amount of gain Sue has on disposition of the partnership interest, $6,000, is a loss of $1,000. The loss is characterized as a long-term capital loss. In sum, Sue must recognize $7,000 of ordinary income and a $1,000 long-term capital loss.[62]

Example 2. Sale of interest with hot assets and Section 704(c) property. Ubrix and Venus are equal partners in the Services Partnership. Ubrix had joined the partnership a little over one year earlier and had contributed the accounts receivable to the partnership.

The partnership is a cash basis, general partnership that provides consulting services. At the end of the year, Ubrix sold her interest to Whalen in exchange for $11,000 cash. At the time of the sale, the balance sheet appeared as follows:

Asset	Adj. Basis	FMV	Partners	Adj. Basis	Cap. Acct.
Cash	$3,000	$3,000	Ubrix	2,000	$11,000
Acct. Rec.	-0-	14,000	Venus	8,000	11,000
Land	7,000	5,000		$10,000	$22,000
Total:	$10,000	$22,000			

Upon sale of her partnership interest, Ubrix received $11,000 and her basis was $2,000. Thus, Ubrix had $9,000 of gain she had to recognize.

The accounts receivable are unrealized receivables. If the partnership had sold the accounts receivable for their fair market value, it would have gain recognized of $14,000 (amount realized of $14,000, less zero basis). Because the accounts receivable had been contributed by Ubrix, all of the gain would be allocated to her. To this extent, Ubrix must recognize ordinary income.

The amount that, when added to the amount of ordinary income of $14,000, results in the amount of gain Ubrix has on disposition of the partnership interest, $9,000, is a loss of $5,000. The loss is characterized as a long-term capital loss. In sum, Ubrix must recognize $14,000 of ordinary income and a $5,000 long-term capital loss.

Example 3. Sale of interest with lukewarm assets. Xander and Yanni are equal partners in the Investments Partnership. Xander had joined the partnership a little over one year earlier.

The partnership is a cash basis, general partnership that invests in various assets. It holds the coins as a collectible. At the end of the year, Xander sold his interest to Zulu in exchange for $15,000 cash. At the time of the sale, the balance sheet appeared as follows:

Asset	Adj. Basis	FMV	Liabilities:		$2,000
Cash	$13,000	$13,000	Partners	Adj. Basis	Cap. Acct.
Acct. Rec.	-0-	14,000	Xander	$10,000	$15,000
Coins	1,000	3,000	Yanni	10,000	15,000
Land	6,000	2,000		$20,000	$32,000
Total:	$20,000	$32,000			

---

62. See Treas. Reg. § 1.751-1(g) Ex. 1.

None of the assets were transferred to the partnership by a partner.

Upon the sale of his partnership interest, Xander received $16,000 ($15,000 cash, plus $1,000 of debt relief) and his basis was $10,000. Thus, Xander had $6,000 of gain he had to recognize.

The accounts receivable are unrealized receivables. If the partnership had sold the accounts receivable for their fair market value, it would have gain recognized of $14,000 (amount realized of $14,000, less zero basis). One-half, or $7,000, would have been allocated to Xander. To this extent Xander must recognize ordinary income.

The amount that, when added to the amount of ordinary income of $7,000, results in the amount of gain Xander has on disposition of the partnership interest, $6,000, is a loss of $1,000.

If the partnership had sold the coins, a collectible, for their fair market value, it would have gain recognized of $2,000 (amount realized of $3,000, less $1,000 basis). One-half, or $1,000, would have been allocated to Xander. To this extent Xander has capital gain from collectibles.

The amount that, when added to the amount of gain from collectibles, $1,000, results in the amount of capital loss Xander has on disposition of the partnership interest, $1,000 loss, is a capital loss of $2,000. Thus, Xander has $2,000 of adjusted net long-term capital loss.

In sum, from the sale of his partnership interest, Xander must report $7,000 of ordinary income, $1,000 capital gain from collectibles, and $2,000 of net long-term capital loss.[63]

Example 4. Death of a partner. Keesha, a calendar year taxpayer, was a partner in a calendar year partnership. She passed away on February 1. Her final income tax return must include her allocable share of partnership items for the year prior to her death and her allocable share of partnership items attributable to January of the year of her death.

D. Cases and Materials

Glazer v. Commissioner
44 T.C. 541 (1965)

* * *

The only issue remaining for decision is whether the gain to the petitioners arising from the purported sale of their interests in a partnership is to be treated as ordinary income or capital gain. All of the facts have been stipulated.

Petitioners Herman Glazer (hereinafter referred to as Herman) and Mollie Glazer, husband and wife, petitioner Forrest B. Fleisher (hereinafter sometimes referred to as For-

---

63. See Treas. Reg. § 1.1(h)-1(f) Ex. 1.

rest), and David Fleisher (hereinafter sometimes referred to as David) and petitioner Frances E. Fleisher, husband and wife, were all individuals residing in Philadelphia, Pa., during the year 1959. David was Forrest's father. The Herman Glazers and David Fleishers filed their respective joint income tax returns and Forrest E. Fleisher his individual income tax return with the district director of internal revenue in Philadelphia for the calendar year 1959. Since that time David has died and Frances E. Fleisher has been appointed executrix.

In 1957 Lowell Hills, a partnership, was formed for the purpose of constructing and selling 94 single-family dwellings on a 30-acre tract of land in Upper Merion Township, Pa. The respective partnership interests were described in the stipulation of facts as follows:

> 5. Herman and Forrest were the active partners in the above venture. Herman was entitled to 75% of the profits of the Lowell Hills partnership. The balance of the profits accrued to the partnership Fleisher and Fleisher, which was owned two-thirds by Forrest and one-third by his father, David. Forrest had the right to represent, sign for and bind his father in all transactions pertaining to the Lowell Hills partnership.

When Lowell Hills acquired the tract of land part of it had already been subdivided. The partnership subdivided the balance and proceeded with the planned construction of the 94 single-family dwellings. The first sale by Lowell Hills occurred in 1958. In that year, 46 lots and homes were sold. Between January 1, 1959, and July 21, 1959, 24 additional lots and homes were sold. The profits therefrom were properly reported as ordinary income. As of July 21, 1959, agreements of sale had been entered into for each of the 24 remaining lots and homes and construction of these homes was approximately 80 percent completed on that date.

On July 21, 1959, Herman and Forrest (acting for himself and David), as sellers, entered into an agreement with Marvin J. Levin, purporting to sell to him their partnership interests in Lowell Hills for an aggregate amount of $172,000. The parties have stipulated that "if the twenty-four remaining lots and homes had not been under agreements of sales, the sales price of the alleged partnership interest would have been $6,000 less." Levin was an attorney for Lowell Hills, and had no experience or training in the building construction field. He thereafter not only prepared the Glazers' 1959 returns but appeared as counsel for petitioners herein.

* * *

By its terms, section 741 explicitly removes from its operative scope the situations covered by section 751, and section 751(a) declares that—

> any money * * * received by a transferor partner in exchange for * * * his interest in the partnership attributable to—
>
> (1) unrealized receivables of the partnership * * *
>
> * * * *
>
> shall be considered as an amount realized from the sale or exchange of property other than a capital asset.

The purpose of these provisions as stated in the committee reports was "to prevent the conversion of potential ordinary income into capital gain by virtue of transfers of partnership interests." S. Rept. No. 1622, 83d Cong., 2d Sess., p. 98; H. Rept. No. 1337, 83d Cong., 2d Sess., p. 70.

Under these provisions the money received by a selling partner to the extent attributable to unrealized receivables in respect of goods delivered, or to be delivered, is to be treated as received from the sale of property other than a capital asset. This is because the proceeds of the sale of such property by the partnership itself would be treated as the sale of property other than a capital asset; and the statute was intended to require that such proceeds retain the same character in the hands of the selling partners to the extent that the selling price of their partnership interests reflected such proceeds.

In terms of the present case the partnership was in the business of selling houses, and the sales of its houses were concededly properly classified as ordinary rather than capital transactions. Accordingly, to the extent the amounts receivable from the sales of the partnership's 24 remaining houses were reflected in the amounts receivable by the selling partners, the transaction may not be classified as a sale of a capital asset. In short, the amounts receivable from the sale of the 24 remaining houses fall within the term "unrealized receivables" in section 751, and therefore are denied capital gains treatment under section 741.

Petitioners do not contest the point that the agreements for the sales of the 24 houses were "unrealized receivables" within the meaning of section 751. But they argue that the money "attributable to" the unrealized receivables was only $6,000 because the parties have stipulated that if the 24 remaining lots and homes had not been under agreements of sale, the sales price would have been $6,000 less. We hold that no such limitation may fairly be read into the statutory provisions, and if such limitation were to be given effect it would defeat the very purpose of the legislation.

Stated in its simplest terms, the amount "attributable to" the unrealized receivables of a partnership is that portion of the sales price received in exchange therefor. The regulations, sec. 1.751-1(c)(3), provide that in determining the amount of the sales price attributable to unrealized receivables any arm's-length agreement between buyer and seller will generally establish the amount or value. In the absence of such an agreement full account is to be taken of the estimated cost of completing performance of the contract or agreement, and of the time between the sale and the date of payment. In the present case the existence of an arm's-length agreement is questionable, but in any event it appears that the only partnership assets of value were "unrealized receivables" so that the entire purchase price must be allocated thereto. Cf. *John Winthrop Wolcott*, 39 T.C. 538.

Petitioners misconstrue the meaning of the phrase "attributable to" as used in section 751(a), in making the argument that only $6,000 was *attributable* to unrealized receivables. While it is undoubtedly true that the partnership interests were more valuable because the lots and homes were under agreements of sale, the increase in the value of the partnership is not the amount "attributable to" the unrealized receivables, under the provisions of section 751.

Had petitioners retained their partnership interests there is no question that they would have realized ordinary income upon collection of amounts receivable under the agreements of sale for the 24 lots and homes. Furthermore, had construction been completed on all the houses so that all that remained for the partners to do was to collect their money at the time of the sale of their partnership interests it is clear that the entire amounts received would be attributable to unrealized receivables. The statute was written to apply in the same manner to unrealized receivables arising out of both completed and uncompleted contracts and results should be arrived at in the same manner in both situations. Where houses are sold, although not yet completed, the cost of the lots and the cost of construction of the houses, to the extent not previously deducted as expense, would go into the basis of the unrealized receivables, and would not be totally disregarded. Sec. 1.751-1(c)(2), Income Tax Regs. Petitioners could not have disposed of anything more than bare legal title to the lots and houses since they had already been sold. The only thing of substance that petitioners had to sell was their right to receive the income from the sales upon completion of construction. Under section 751 gains resulting from amounts received therefor are to be taxed as ordinary income. *John Winthrop Wolcott, supra.*

Decisions will be entered for the respondent.

Ledoux v. Commissioner
77 T.C. 293 (1981), aff'd 695 F.2d 1320 (11th Cir. 1983)

* * *

After concessions, the sole issue remaining for our decision is whether any portion of the amount received by petitioner John W. Ledoux pursuant to an agreement for the sale of a partnership interest was attributable to an unrealized receivable of the partnership and thus was required to be characterized as ordinary income under section 751, I.R.C. 1954.

FINDINGS OF FACT

* * *

Pari-mutuel wagering at greyhound dogracing tracks was legalized in the State of Florida in 1935. Prior to July 1955, the Sanford-Orlando Kennel Club, Inc. (hereinafter referred to as the corporation), held a greyhound racing permit issued by the Florida State Racing Commission to operate a racetrack in Seminole County, Fla. The corporation owned certain land in Seminole County, Fla., and improvements thereon including a grandstand, kennels, track, and other facilities and equipment necessary to operate a racetrack and to handle pari-mutuel pools. The sole shareholders of the corporation were a Mr. Anderson and a Mr. Davey. Also prior to July 1955, the corporation had entered into an operating agreement with the Sanford-Orlando Kennel Club, a copartnership composed of Messrs. Anderson and Davey, as the partners. Under the agreement, the copartnership was to operate the track and the corporation was to receive 30 percent of the net profits from the dog track operation.

Due to problems in managing the dog track, the Sanford-Orlando Kennel Club copartnership entered into a written agreement (dog track agreement) on July 9, 1955, with Jerry Collins, an experienced operator of dogracing tracks, and his son, Jack Collins. Pursuant to the dog track agreement, the Collinses acquired the right "to manage and operate the Greyhound Racing Track, owned by the Sanford-Orlando Kennel Club, Inc.," for a period of 20 years commencing on October 1, 1955. In return, the Collinses agreed to pay to the copartnership the first $200,000 of net annual profit from track operations.

* * *

During the period from October 1, 1955, to September 30, 1972, the Collins-Ledoux partnership operated the greyhound racetrack pursuant to and in accordance with the July 9, 1955, agreement, as amended. Petitioner John W. Ledoux was a manager of the operations of the racetrack for the Collins-Ledoux partnership. Petitioner received compensation for his services in the form of salary, which was charged as an expense of the track operation. Along with his salary, petitioner received a share of the net profits of the Collins-Ledoux partnership. Petitioner's duties included, among other things, the directing of promotional, advertising, and development activities on behalf of the Collins-Ledoux partnership.

* * *

The partnership's actions with respect to operation and management of the dog track were eminently successful. During the period from 1955 to 1972, the gross income from track operations increased from $3.6 million to $23.6 million, and the net income to the Collins-Ledoux partnership increased from $72,000 to over $550,000. The increases in gross and net income were attributable to the work of the partnership, including petitioner, and to the general economic growth in the Central Florida area. Accordingly, the fair value of the right to operate the greyhound racetrack in Seminole County, Fla., pursuant to the racing permit held by the corporation and pursuant to the dog track agreement, increased significantly during the period from 1955 to 1972.

* * *

After the 1972 racing season two of the partners, Jerry Collins and Jack Collins, decided to purchase petitioner's 25-percent partnership interest. They agreed to allow Ledoux to propose a fair selling price for his interest. Ledoux set a price based on a price-earnings multiple of 5 times his share of the partnership's 1972 earnings. This resulted in a total value for his 25-percent interest of $800,000. There was no valuation or appraisal of specific assets at the time, and the sales price included his interest in all of the assets of the partnership.

At the closing, there was no discussion about values of, or allocation to, any specific assets. In fact, no part of the sales price was allocated to any specific partnership asset. At the time of the sale, the partnership assets consisted of an escrow deposit; certain prepaid expenses; a stock investment in Sanford-Seminole Development Co.; investment in land, buildings, and equipment; improvements on the corporation's property used in connection with the operation of the dog track; and rights arising out of the dog track agreement.

* * *

OPINION

The sole issue presented is whether a portion of the amount received by petitioner on the sale of his 25-percent partnership interest is taxable as ordinary income and not as capital gain. More specifically, we must decide whether any portion of the sales price is attributable to "unrealized receivables" of the partnership.

Generally, gain or loss on the sale or exchange of a partnership interest is treated as capital gain or loss. Sec. 741. Prior to 1954, a partner could escape ordinary income tax treatment on his portion of the partnership's unrealized receivables by selling or exchanging his interest in the partnership and treating the gain or loss therefrom as capital gain or loss. To curb such abuses, section 751 was enacted to deal with the problem of the so-called "collapsible partnership." See S. Rept. 1622, 83d Cong., 2d Sess. 98 (1954).

* * *

Petitioner contends that the dog track agreement gave the Collins-Ledoux partnership the right to manage and operate the dog track. According to petitioner, the agreement did not give the partnership any contractual rights to receive future payments and did not impose any obligation on the partnership to perform services. Rather, the agreement merely gave the partnership the right to occupy and use all of the corporation's properties (including the racetrack facilities and the racing permit) in operating its dog track business; if the partnership exercised such right, it would be obligated to make annual payments to the corporation based upon specified percentages of the annual mutuel handle. Thus, because the dog track agreement was in the nature of a leasehold agreement rather than an employment contract, it did not create the type of "unrealized receivables" referred to in section 751.

Respondent, on the other hand, contends that the partnership operated the racetrack for the corporation and was paid a portion of the profits for its efforts. As such, the agreement was in the nature of a management employment contract. When petitioner sold his partnership interest to the Collinses in 1972, the main right that he sold was a contract right to receive income in the future for yet-to-be-rendered personal services. This, respondent asserts, is supported by the fact that petitioner determined the sales price for his partnership interest by capitalizing his 1972 annual income (approximately $160,000) by a factor of 5. Therefore, respondent contends that the portion of the gain realized by petitioner that is attributable to the management contract should be characterized as an amount received for unrealized receivables of the partnership. Consequently, such gain should be characterized as ordinary income under section 751.

The legislative history is not wholly clear with respect to the types of assets that Congress intended to place under the umbrella of "unrealized receivables." The House report states:

> The term "unrealized receivables or fees" is used to apply to any rights to income which have not been included in gross income under the method of accounting employed by the partnership. The provision is applicable mainly to cash basis partnerships which have acquired a contractual or other legal right to income for goods or services. * * * [H. Rept. 1337, 83d Cong., 2d Sess. 71 (1954).]

Essentially the same language appears in the report of the Senate committee. S. Rept. 1622, 83d Cong., 2d Sess. 98 (1954). In addition, the regulations elaborate on the meaning of "unrealized receivables" as used in section 751. Section 1.751-1(c), Income Tax Regs., provides:

> Sec. 1.751-1(c) *Unrealized receivables.* (1) The term "unrealized receivables", * * * means any rights (contractual or otherwise) to payment for—
>
> > (i) Goods delivered or to be delivered (to the extent that such payment would be treated as received for property other than a capital asset), or

(ii) Services rendered or to be rendered, to the extent that income arising from such rights to payment was not previously includible in income under the method of accounting employed by the partnership. Such rights must have arisen under contracts or agreements in existence at the time of sale or distribution, although the partnership may not be able to enforce payment until a later time. For example, the term includes trade accounts receivable of a cash method taxpayer, and rights to payment for work or goods begun but incomplete at the time of the sale or distribution.

* * * *

(3) In determining the amount of the sale price attributable to such unrealized receivables, or their value in a distribution treated as a sale or exchange, any arm's length agreement between the buyer and the seller, or between the partnership and the distributee partner, will generally establish the amount or value. In the absence of such an agreement, full account shall be taken not only of the estimated cost of completing performance of the contract or agreement, but also of the time between the sale or distribution and the time of payment.

The language of the legislative history and the regulations indicates that the term "unrealized receivables" includes any contractual or other right to payment for goods delivered or to be delivered or services rendered or to be rendered. Therefore, an analysis of the nature of the rights under the dog track agreement, in the context of the aforementioned legal framework, becomes appropriate. A number of cases have dealt with the meaning of "unrealized receivables" and thereby have helped to define the scope of the term. Courts that have considered the term "unrealized receivables" generally have said that it should be given a broad interpretation. Cf. *Corn Products Co. v. Commissioner*, 350 U.S. 46, 52 (1955) (the term "capital asset" is to be construed narrowly, but exclusions from the definition thereof are to be broadly and liberally construed). For instance, in *Logan v. Commissioner*, 51 T.C. 482, 486 (1968), we held that a partnership's right in quantum meruit to payment for work in progress constituted an unrealized receivable even though there was no express agreement between the partnership and its clients requiring payment.

In *Roth v. Commissioner*, 321 F.2d 607 (9th Cir. 1963), affg. 38 T.C. 171 (1962), the Ninth Circuit dealt with the sale of an interest in a partnership which produced a movie and then gave a 10-year distribution right to Paramount Pictures Corp. in return for a percentage of the gross receipts. The selling partner claimed that his right to a portion of the payments expected under the partnership's contract with Paramount did not constitute an unrealized receivable. The court rejected this view, however, reasoning that Congress "meant to exclude from capital gains treatment any receipts which would have been treated as ordinary income to the partner if no transfer of the partnership interest had occurred." 321 F.3d at 611. Therefore, the partnership's right to payments under the distribution contract was in the nature of an unrealized receivable.

A third example of the broad interpretation given to the term "unrealized receivable" is *United States v. Eidson*, 310 F.2d 111 (5th Cir. 1962), revg. an unreported opinion (W.D. Tex. 1961). The court there considered the nature of a management contract which was similar to the one at issue in the instant case. The case arose in the context of a sale by a partnership of all of its rights to operate and manage a mutual insurance company. The selling partnership received $170,000 for the rights it held under the management contract, and the Government asserted that the total amount should be treated as ordinary income. The Court of Appeals agreed with the Government's view on the ground that what was being assigned was not a capital asset whose value had accrued over a period of years; rather, the right to operate the company and receive profits therefrom during the remaining life of the contract was the real subject of the assignment. 310 F.2d at 116. The Fifth Circuit found the Supreme Court's holding in *Commissioner v. P.G. Lake, Inc.*, 356 U.S. 260 (1958), to be conclusive:

> The substance of what was assigned was the right to receive future income. The substance of what was received was the present value of income which the recipient would otherwise obtain in the future. In short, consideration was paid for the right to receive future income, not for an increase in the value of the income-producing property. [356 U.S. at 266, cited in 310 F.2d at 115.]

In *United States v. Woolsey*, 326 F.2d 287 (5th Cir. 1963), revg. 208 F. Supp. 325 (S.D. Tex. 1962), the Fifth Circuit again faced a situation similar to the one that we face herein. The Fifth Circuit considered whether proceeds received by taxpayers on the sale of their partnership interests were to be treated as ordinary income or capital gain. There, the court was faced with the sale of interests in a partnership which held, as one of its assets, a 25-year contract to manage a mutual insurance company. As in the instant case, the contract gave the partners the right to render services for the term of the contract and to earn ordinary income in the future. In holding that the partnership's management contract constituted an unrealized receivable, the court stated:

> When we look at the underlying right assigned in this case, we cannot escape the conclusion that so much of the consideration which relates to the right to earn ordinary income in the future under the "management contract," taxable to the assignee as ordinary income, is likewise taxable to the assignor as ordinary income although such income must be earned. Section 751 has defined "unrealized receivables" to include any rights, contractual or otherwise, to ordinary income from "services rendered, *or to be rendered*," (emphasis added) to the extent that the same were not previously includable in income by the partnership, with the result that capital gains rates cannot be applied to the rights to income under the facts of this case, which would constitute ordinary income had the same been received in due course by the partnership. * * * It is our conclusion that such portion of the consideration received by the taxpayers in this case as properly should be allocated to the present value of their right to earn ordinary income in the future under the "management contract" is subject to taxation as ordinary income. * * * [326 F.2d at 291.]

Petitioner attempts to distinguish *United States v. Woolsey, supra*, and *United States v. Eidson, supra*, from the instant case by arguing that those cases involved a sale or termination of contracts to manage mutual insurance companies in Texas and that the management contracts therein were in the nature of employment agreements. After closely scrutinizing the facts in those cases, we conclude that petitioner's position has no merit. The fact that the *Woolsey* case involved sale of 100 percent of the partnership interests, as opposed to a sale of only a 25-percent partnership interest herein, is of no consequence. In addition, the fact that *Eidson* involved the surrender of the partnership's contract right to manage the insurance company, as opposed to the continued partnership operation in the instant case, also is not a material factual distinction.

The dog track agreement at issue in the instant case is similar to the management contract considered by the Fifth Circuit in *Woolsey*. Each gives the respective partnership the right to operate a business for a period of years and to earn ordinary income in return for payments of specified amounts to the corporation that holds the State charter. Therefore, based on our analysis of the statutory language, the legislative history, and the regulations and relevant case law, we are compelled to find that the dog track agreement gave the petitioner an interest that amounted to an "unrealized receivable" within the meaning of section 751(c).

Petitioner further contends that the dog track agreement does not represent an unrealized receivable because it does not require or obligate the partnership to perform personal services in the future. The agreement only gives, the argument continues, the Collins-Ledoux partnership the right to engage in a business.

We find this argument to be unpersuasive. The words of section 751(c), providing that the term "unrealized receivable" includes the right to payment for "services rendered, or to be rendered," do not preclude that section's application to a situation where, as here, the performance of services is not required by the agreement. As the Fifth Circuit said in *United States v. Eidson, supra.*:

> The fact that * * * income would not be received by the [partnership] unless they performed the services which the contract required of them, that is, actively managed the affairs of the insurance company in a manner that would produce a profit after all of the necessary expenditures, does not, it seems clear, affect the nature of this payment. It affects only the amount. That is, the fact that the taxpayers would have to spend their time and energies in performing services for which the compensation would be received merely affects the price at which they would be willing to assign or transfer the contract. * * * [310 F.2d at 115.]

Consequently, a portion of the consideration received by Ledoux on the sale of his partnership interest is subject to taxation as ordinary income.

Having established that the dog track agreement qualifies as an unrealized receivable, we next consider whether all or only part of petitioner's gain in excess of the amount attributable to his share of tangible partnership assets should be treated as ordinary income. Petitioner argues that this excess gain was attributable to goodwill or the value of a going concern.

With respect to goodwill, we note that petitioner's attorney drafted, and petitioner signed, the agreement for sale of partnership interest, dated October 17, 1972, which contains the following statement in paragraph 7:

> 7. In the determination of the purchase price set forth in this agreement, the parties acknowledge no consideration has been given to any item of goodwill.

The meaning of the words "no consideration" is not entirely free from doubt. They could mean that no thought was given to an allocation of any of the sales price to goodwill, or they could indicate that the parties agreed that no part of the purchase price was allocated to goodwill. The testimony of the attorney who prepared the document indicates, however, that he did consider the implications of the sale of goodwill and even did research on the subject. He testified that he believed, albeit incorrectly, that, if goodwill were part of the purchase price, his client would not be entitled to capital gains treatment.

Petitioner attempts to justify this misstatement of the tax implications of an allocation to goodwill not by asserting mistake, but by pointing out that his attorney "is not a tax lawyer but is primarily involved with commercial law and real estate." We find as a fact that petitioner agreed at arm's length with the purchasers of his partnership interest that no part of the purchase price should be attributable to goodwill. The Tax Court long has adhered to the view that, absent "strong proof," a taxpayer cannot challenge an express allocation in an arm's-length sales contract to which he had agreed. See, e.g., *Major v. Commissioner*, 76 T.C. 239, 249 (1981), appeal pending (7th Cir., July 7, 1981); *Lucas v. Commissioner*, 58 T.C. 1022, 1032 (1972). In *Spector v. Commissioner*, 641 F.2d 376 (5th Cir. 1981), revg. 71 T.C. 1017 (1979) the Fifth Circuit, to which an appeal in this case will lie, appeared to step away from its prior adherence to the "strong proof" standard and move toward the stricter standard enunciated in *Commissioner v. Danielson*, 378 F.2d 771, 775 (3d Cir. 1967), remanding 44 T.C. 549 (1965), cert. denied 389 U.S. 858 (1967). However, in this case, we need not measure the length of the step since we hold that petitioner has failed to introduce sufficient evidence to satisfy even the more lenient "strong proof" standard.

We next turn to petitioner's contention that part or all of the purchase price received in excess of the value of tangible assets is attributable to value of a going concern. In *VGS Corp. v. Commissioner*, 68 T.C. 563 (1977), we stated that—

> Going-concern value is, in essence, the additional element of value which attaches to property by reason of its existence as an integral part of a going concern. * * * [The] ability of a business to continue to function and generate income without interruption as a consequence of the change in ownership, is a vital part of the value of a going concern. * * * [68 T.C. at 591–592; citations omitted.]

However, in the instant case, the ability of the dogracing track to continue to function after the sale of Ledoux's partnership interest was due to the remaining partners' retention of rights to operate under the dog track agreement. Without such agreement, there would have been no continuing right to operate a business and no right to continue to earn income. Thus, the amount paid in excess of the value of Ledoux's share of the tangible assets was not for the intangible value of the business as a going concern but rather for Ledoux's rights under the dog track agreement.

Finally, we turn to petitioner's claim that a determination of the value of rights arising from the dog track agreement has never been made and no evidence of the value of such rights was submitted in this case. We note that the $800,000 purchase price was proposed by petitioner and was accepted by Jack Collins and Jerry Collins in an arm's-length agreement of sale evidenced in the memorandum of agreement of July 19, 1972, and the agreement for sale of partnership interest of October 17, 1972. In addition, the October 17, 1972, sales agreement, written by petitioner's attorney, provided in paragraph 1 that the "Seller [Ledoux] sells to buyer [Jerry Collins and Jack Collins] all of his interest in [the partnership] * * * including but not limited to, *the seller's right to income* and to acquire the capital stock of The Sanford-Orlando Kennel Club, Inc." (Emphasis added.) Section 1.751-1(c)(3), Income Tax Regs., provides that an arm's-length agreement between the buyer and the seller generally will establish the value attributable to unrealized receivables.

Based on the provision in the agreement that no part of the consideration was attributable to goodwill, it is clear to us that the parties were aware that they could, if they so desired, have provided that no part of the consideration was attributable to the dog track agreement. No such provision was made. Furthermore, the agreement clearly stated that one of the assets purchased was Ledoux's rights to future income. Considering that petitioner calculated the purchase price by capitalizing future earnings expected under the dog track agreement, we conclude that the portion of Ledoux's gain in excess of the amount attributable to tangible assets was attributable to an unrealized receivable as reflected by the dog track agreement.

Decision will be entered for the respondent.

E. Problems

1. Mary Beth, Nancy, and Othello are the original equal partners of Manufacturing Partnership. The partnership is a cash method, calendar year general partnership that manufactures and sells widgets. All of the assets had been purchased by the partnership.

Five years after formation of the partnership, on January 1st, Mary Beth sold her one-third interest in the partnership to Patrick. Consider the tax consequences to Mary Beth on her sale in each of the following alternative situations:

(a) Mary Beth sold her interest for $150,000 cash. At the time of the sale, the balance sheet of Manufacturing Partnership was as follows:

Asset	Adj. Basis	FMV	Partners	Adj. Basis	Cap. Acct.
Cash	$85,000	$85,000	Mary Beth	$100,000	$150,000
Acct. Rec.	-0-	45,000	Nancy	100,000	150,000
Inventory	15,000	30,000	Othello	100,000	150,000
Stock	200,000	290,000		$300,000	$450,000
Total:	$300,000	$450,000			

(b) Mary Beth sold her interest for $250,000 cash. At the time of the sale, the balance sheet was as follows:

Asset	Adj. Basis	FMV	Partners	Adj. Basis	Cap. Acct.
Cash	$375,000	$375,000	Mary Beth	$240,000	$250,000
Acct. Rec.	-0-	45,000	Nancy	240,000	250,000
Inventory	15,000	30,000	Othello	240,000	250,000
Stock	330,000	300,000		$720,000	$750,000
Total:	$720,000	$750,000			

(c) Mary Beth sold her interest for $200,000 cash. At the time of sale, the balance sheet was as follows:

Asset	Adj. Basis	FMV	Liablity:		$150,000
Cash	$375,000	$375,000	Partners	Adj. Basis	Cap. Acct.
Acct. Rec.	-0-	45,000	Mary Beth	$240,000	$200,000
Inventory	15,000	30,000	Nancy	240,000	200,000
Stock	330,000	300,000	Othello	240,000	200,000
Total:	$720,000	$750,000		$720,000	$750,000

(d) Mary Beth sold her interest for $150,000 cash. Manufacturing Partnership is an accrual method partnership. At the time of sale the balance sheet was as follows:

Asset	Adj. Basis	FMV	Partners	Adj. Basis	Cap. Acct.
Cash	$85,000	$85,000	Mary Beth	$115,000	$150,000
Acct. Rec.	45,000	45,000	Nancy	115,000	150,000
Inventory	15,000	30,000	Othello	115,000	150,000
Stock	200,000	290,000		$345,000	$450,000
Total:	$345,000	$450,000			

(e) How would your analysis change, if at all, if the partnership had entered into a contract to perform consulting services for the next five years in exchange for $60,000?

---

2. Application:

(a) Could you explain to a selling partner what the tax consequences of the sale of his partnership interest would be?

(b) Draft a template of a statement the selling partner could attach to his return for the year he sells his partnership interest.

(c) Based on the law of the state in which you practice, when does a partner's leaving a partnership cause a termination of the partnership?

(d) What language might you include in the partnership agreement to address:

(1) When a partner may leave a partnership.

(2) When a partnership is terminated for state law purposes.

(3) When a partnership is terminated for federal tax purposes.

F. Advanced Problems — Looking Forward

Without conducting any research, consider the following question:

If the selling partner is taxed on his share of unrealized receivables and inventory (hot assets), what should the buying partner's position be with respect to those items when he joins the partnership?

Chapter 22

Tax Consequences to Buying Partner

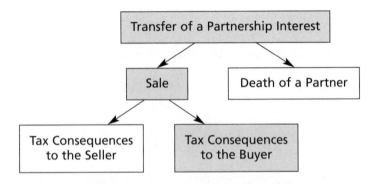

Read:

Code Sections 742; 743(a)-(d); 752(a), (d); 754; 755.
Treas. Reg. §§ 1.743-1(a)-(e), -1(j)(1)-(3)(i); 1.754-1; 1.755-1(a)(1), -1(b)(1)-(3).

A. Background

Under the Revised Uniform Partnership Act, a person may become a partner in the partnership only with the consent of all of the partners.[1] Without the consent of the other partners, all a partner could sell, and an in-coming partner could receive, would be the right to a share of the profits and losses of the partnership and right to receive distributions. All remaining rights and duties would remain with the selling partner.[2]

> **Practice Alert:** A determination must be made as to whether a transfer of an interest without the consent of the remaining partners (*i.e.*, a sale of the profits and losses of the partnership and right to receive distributions) constitutes a sale for federal tax purposes.

---

1. RUPA § 401(i).
2. RUPA §§ 502; 503.

B. Discussion of Rules

1. Partner's Basis in the Partnership—General Rule

In general, for purposes of determining the partner's basis in a partnership interest that he purchases, the Code follows the entity approach. Thus, rather than purchasing an interest in the underlying assets of the partnership, the partner purchases an interest in the partnership itself. His basis in the partnership interest is the amount he paid for the interest, its cost.[3]

Practice Tip: To determine the cost of a partnership interest, the amount paid for the interest includes any partnership liabilities assumed by the buyer-partner. [Code Sec. 752(d)]

---

2. Exception to the General Rule

In general, the basis of partnership property is not adjusted as the result of a sale of a partnership interest.[4] Because the buyer-partner has paid the fair market value for his interest, this rule may lead to unexpected results.

Example: Ray purchased a one-quarter interest in the Fore Partnership from Sam for $40,000. The partnership, which uses the cash method, owned $160,000 of accounts receivable with a zero basis.

When the Fore Partnership later collected the accounts receivable, one-quarter of the income, or $40,000 of ordinary income, was allocated to Ray. This result holds true even though Ray paid $40,000 for the partnership interest and the partnership has not realized any appreciation in its assets from the time Ray purchased his interest.

In addition, note that when Sam sold his one-quarter interest, to the extent of the uncollected accounts receivable he would have been taxed on the $40,000 of gain (characterized as ordinary income under Section 751(a)). It is that same income that is now allocated to Ray.

In order to avoid this result, the partnership may make an election under Section 754 to adjust the buyer-partner's basis in partnership assets, as provided in Section 743(b). In essence, the buyer-partner is given a cost basis in his share of the partnership's assets.

---

3. Code Secs. 742; 1012.
4. Code Sec. 743(a).

Example: Ray purchased a one-quarter interest in the Fore Partnership from Sam for $40,000. The partnership, which uses the cash method, owned $160,000 of accounts receivable with a zero basis.

If the partnership had elected under Section 754 to adjust Ray's basis in the partnership's assets, his basis in the accounts receivable would have been $40,000. When the $160,000 of accounts receivable were collected, $40,000 would have been allocated to each of the partners. The other three partners would have recognized $40,000 of ordinary income. However, because Ray's basis in the accounts receivable was $40,000, he would not have been required to recognize any income.

Substantial built-in loss. If the partnership has a substantial built-in loss immediately after the purchase, the partnership is required to make the election. A substantial built-in loss exists if the partnership's adjusted basis in its assets exceeds the property's fair market value by more than $250,000.[5]

Electing investment partnership. An electing investment partnership[6] is not required to make the election when it has a substantial built-in loss. Congress created the exception because it believed it would be too administratively difficult to make the adjustment upon the sale of a partnership interest. Instead, a loss limitation is imposed on the buyer-partner. With the limitation, the buyer-partner is not allowed to claim losses from the sale or exchange of partnership property to the extent of the loss recognized by the seller-partner. However, the buyer-partner is permitted to claim losses that exceed the loss recognized by the seller-partner.[7]

Election. Once the partnership has made the Section 754 election, it is applicable to all subsequent taxable years. It can be revoked only with the consent of the Internal Revenue Service.[8]

Practice Tip: To make the Section 754 election, the partnership must file a written statement with its timely-filed tax return (including extensions) for the year in which the transfer occurs. [Treas. Reg. § 1.754-1(b)(1)] However, an election will be treated as timely filed if filed within 12 months of the original due date for the return and all partners report their income consistent with the election for the year of the election and all subsequent years. [Rev. Proc. 92-85, 1992-2 C.B. 490, as amended by Rev. Proc. 93-28, 1993-28 C.B. 344]
The statement must include the name and address of the partnership, be signed by a partner, and contain a declaration that the partnership elects under Section 754 to apply the provisions of Section 734(b) and 743(b). [Treas. Reg. § 1.754-1(b)(1)]

---

5. Code Sec. 743(a), (d).
6. An electing investment partnership is defined in Section 743(e)(6).
7. Code Sec. 743(e)(1), (e)(2). A securitization partnership may avoid both the inside basis adjustment and the loss limitation rule. Code Sec. 743(f).
8. Treas. Reg. § 1.754-1(c)(1).

> **Practice Tip:** If the partnership makes an election under Section 754 to adjust the buyer-partner's basis in partnership assets as provided in Section 743(b), the election also applies to a basis adjustment with respect to distributions of property by the partnership as provided in Section 734(b).

3. Calculating the Buyer-Partner's Basis Adjustment

The amount of the overall basis adjustment is the buyer-partner's outside basis, less his share of inside basis:

outside basis
– <u>share of inside basis</u>
overall basis adjustment

The Code and regulations provide a complex formula for determining the buyer-partner's inside basis.[9] The buyer-partner's share of the partnership's inside basis is the buyer-partner's interest in the partnership's previously taxed capital plus the buyer-partner's share of partnership liabilities.

Inside basis = share of previously taxed capital + share of liabilities

The partner's interest in previously taxed capital is determined by considering a hypothetical disposition by the partnership of all its assets. The assets are sold for cash equal to the asset's fair market value in a taxable transaction. The buyer-partner's interest in previously taxed capital is equal to the amount of cash that the partner would receive, plus (the absolute value of) the amount of tax loss, and minus the amount of tax gain that would have been allocated to the buyer-partner from the hypothetical sale.[10]

partner's share of cash
+ share of tax loss
– <u>share of tax gain</u>
share of previously taxed capital

Next, once the amount of the adjustment has been determined, that amount must be allocated among the partnership's assets.[11] Divide the assets into one group that consists of all capital and hotchpot (Section 1231) assets and one group that consists of all other property, generally ordinary assets. Allocate the basis adjustment between the two groups. The amount allocated to the ordinary asset group is the total amount of income, gain or loss that would be allocated to the partner from a sale of the ordinary property. The amount allocated to the capital and hotchpot (Section 1231) group is the amount of the total adjustment, less the amount allocated to the ordinary asset group. If necessary, an increase can be made to one group of property while a decrease is made to the other group. However, a decrease in basis allocated to the capital and hotch-

---

9. Code Secs. 743(b); 755; Treas. Reg. §§ 1.743-1; 1.755-1(b).
10. Treas. Reg. § 1.743-1(d).
11. Treas. Reg. §§ 1.743-1(e); 1.755-1(a)(1), -1(b).

pot group may not exceed the partnership's basis in the property. If a decrease is greater than the basis, the excess must be applied to reduce the basis of the assets in the ordinary asset group.[12]

Finally, allocate within each group among the properties. For assets in the ordinary asset group, in general, each asset is allocated an amount equal to the amount of income, gain, or loss that would be allocated to the partner from a hypothetical sale.[13]

For assets in the capital and hotchpot group, in general, each asset is allocated an amount equal to the amount of income, gain, or loss that would be allocated to the partner from a hypothetical sale.[14] When making an allocation, the basis of any asset may not be reduced below zero. If the amount allocated to the asset would reduce the basis below zero, the excess amount must be applied to reduce the remaining basis, if any, of other capital gain assets pro rata in proportion to the bases of such assets.[15]

The basis adjustment applies only to the buyer-partner. No actual adjustment is made to the basis of the partnership's assets and no adjustment is taken into consideration when determining the amount of the partnership's income, gains, expenses, deductions, or losses. Rather, the partnership computes its income, computes depreciation, and makes allocations without regard to the adjustment. Then, the partnership adjusts the buyer-partner's share of partnership items, taking into consideration the basis adjustment. In addition, with respect to depreciable property, the amount of the adjustment to depreciable property is treated as a separate asset that can be depreciated.

If partnership property is subsequently distributed to the buyer-partner, the partner's basis in the property is the basis as adjusted under Section 743(b).[16] If the partnership property is distributed to a partner other than the buyer-partner, the amount of the basis adjustment for that property is reallocated to partnership property of the same class.[17]

Practice Tip: The basis adjustment allocated to one class of property may be an increase while the allocation to the other class may be a decrease. This result could be true even if the total amount of basis adjustment is zero. Similarly, the portion of the basis adjustment allocated to one item of property within a class may be an increase while the allocation to another is a decrease. This result would be true even though the basis adjustment allocated to the class is zero.

Practice Tip: The basis adjustment under Section 743(b) does not impact the buyer-partner's capital account. [Treas. Reg. § 1.743-1(j)(2)]

---

12. Treas. Reg. § 1.755-1(b)(2).
13. Treas. Reg. § 1.755-1(b)(3)(i).
14. Treas. Reg. § 1.755-1(b)(3)(ii).
15. Treas. Reg. § 1.755-1(b)(3)(iii)(B).
16. Treas. Regs. §§ 1.732-2(b); 1.743-1(g)(1)(i).
17. Treas. Reg. § 1.743-1(g)(2), -1(g)(3).

Formula for Making Section 743(b) Adjustment:

1. Determine the overall basis adjustment:

> outside basis
> – <u>share of inside basis</u>
> overall basis adjustment

A partner's share of inside basis is his share of previously taxed capital plus his share of liabilities.

> Inside basis = share of PTC + share of liabilities

A partner's share of previously taxed capital is the amount of cash the partner would receive on liquidation, plus the amount of tax loss, less the amount of tax gain the partner would receive on liquidation.

> partner's share of cash
> + share of tax loss
> – <u>share of tax gain</u>
> share of PTC

2. Divide assets into capital and hotchpot (Section 1231) in one group and ordinary assets in another group.

3. Allocate the overall basis adjustment between the two groups.

4. Allocate the group's basis adjustment among the assets in the group.

5. Determine the partner's new inside basis, taking into consideration the adjustment for each asset.

---

4. Relationship of Section 743(b) to Section 704(c)

If a partner contributes appreciated property to a partnership, then later sells his interest, the built-in gain is transferred to the buyer-partner.[18] However, if the seller-partner contributed property with a built-in loss, this loss cannot be transferred to the buyer-partner as part of the basis adjustment under Section 743(b).[19]

Practice Tip: Note that, if a partner contributes depreciated property to a partnership, then later sells his interest, the built-in loss is *not* transferred to the buyer-partner.

---

5. Allocation of Purchase Price to Intangible Assets

When structuring the transaction, the selling partner may sell his partnership interest for more than the amount that is reflected in his capital account. Oftentimes,

---

18. Treas. Reg. § 1.704-3(a)(7).
19. Code Sec. 704(c)(1)(C).

this additional amount will represent goodwill, going concern value, or some other intangible generated by the partnership. If the partnership has made an election under Section 754, a portion of the purchase price must be allocated to any intangible assets described in Section 197(d).

Practice Tip: Intangible assets identified in Section 179(d) include:
- Goodwill;
- Going concern value;
- Covenant not to compete; and
- A franchise.

The amount of the allocation is determined under the residual method of valuation.[20] Under the residual method, the value of all assets other than intangible assets identified under Section 197(d) is subtracted from the total purchase price.[21] This residual amount is allocated to the Section 197(d) intangible assets. If there are intangible assets other than going concern value or goodwill, a portion of the remainder amount is allocated to those intangible assets first, up to the asset's fair market value. Then the remaining amount is allocated to goodwill and going concern value.[22] When the adjustment is made under Section 743(b), the partner will receive an inside basis equal to the amount of the purchase price allocated to the intangible asset.

C. Application of Rules

Example 1. Without Section 704(c) property. Annika and Boris formed an equal partnership. Each contributed $1,000 cash, which the partnership used to buy Greenacre, Yellowacre, an inventory of widgets and an inventory of gadgets.

A year later, Annika sold her partnership interest to Christy for $1,000. Immediately after the sale and not reflecting Christy's basis adjustment, the balance sheet appeared as follows:

Asset	Adj. Basis	FMV	Partner	Adj. Basis	Cap. Acct.
Widgets	$500	$250	Christy	$1,000	$1,000
Gadgets	500	500	Boris	1,000	1,000
Greenacre	500	750		$2,000	$2,000
Yellowacre	500	500			
Total:	$2,000	$2,000			

The amount of the adjustment is Christy's outside basis, $1,000, less her share of inside basis. To determine Christy's share of the partnership's inside basis, determine

---

20. Code Sec. 1060(d); Treas. Reg. 1.755-1(a)(2).
21. Treas. Reg. 1.755-1(a)(4).
22. Treas. Reg. 1.755-1(a)(5).

Christy's interest in the partnership's previously taxed capital plus Christy's share of partnership liabilities. Christy's interest in previously taxed capital is determined by considering a hypothetical disposition by the partnership of all its assets. The assets are sold for cash equal to the asset's fair market value in a taxable transaction. The result would be:

Asset	Adj. Basis	FMV	Gain/Loss	Christy's Share
Widgets	$500	$250	<$250>	<$125>
Gadgets	500	500	-0-	-0-
Greenacre	500	750	250	125
Yellowacre	500	500	-0-	-0-
Total	$2,000	$2,000		

In a hypothetical liquidation, Christy would receive:

Share of cash:	$1,000
Share of tax loss:	+ 125
Share of tax gain:	− 125
Share of PTC:	$1,000

Because there are no partnership liabilities, her share of the inside basis would be $1,000 and her overall adjustment would be zero (outside basis of $1,000, less her share of inside basis, $1,000).

Next, once the adjustment has been determined, that amount must be allocated among the partnership's assets. The two parcels of land are allocated to the capital and hotchpot (Section 1231) asset group and the widgets and gadgets are allocated to the ordinary asset group.

The sale of the ordinary assets would result in a net loss of $125.

Asset	Adj. Basis	FMV	Gain/Loss	Christy's Share
Widgets	$500	$250	<$250>	<$125>
Gadgets	500	500	-0-	-0-
Net				<$125>

Thus, a loss of $125 is allocated to the ordinary asset group.

The amount allocated to the capital and hotchpot (Section 1231) group is the amount of the total adjustment (zero), less the amount allocated to the ordinary group (loss of $125), or $125.

Total adjustment:	$-0-
Allocation to ordinary group:	− <125>
Allocation to capital/hotchpot group:	$125

For assets in the ordinary asset group, each asset is allocated an amount equal to the amount of income, gain, or loss that would be allocated to the partner from a hypothetical sale. Thus, with respect to the inventory of widgets, Christy would be allocated a loss of $125 and there would be no allocation to the inventory of gadgets.

For assets in the capital and hotchpot group, each item is allocated an amount equal to the amount of income, gain, or loss that would be allocated to the partner from the hypothetical sale of the item. Thus, for Greenacre, Christy would be allocated a gain of $125 and no amount would be allocated for Yellowacre.

The adjustment is made to Christy's inside basis in the items as follows:

Asset	Current Share of Basis	Adjustment	New Inside Basis
Widgets	$250	<$125>	$125
Gadgets	250	-0-	250
Greenacre	250	125	375
Yellowacre	250	-0-	250
Total	$1,000	$-0-	$1,000

Example 2. With Section 704(c) property. Doris and Eiffel formed an equal partnership. Doris contributed $50,000 and Gainacre, which had a fair market value of $50,000 and an adjusted basis of $25,000. Eiffel contributed $100,000 cash. The partnership used the cash to purchase Blueacre, an inventory of widgets and an inventory of gadgets.

The following year, Doris sold her interest to Grant for $120,000. At the time of the transfer, Doris's outside basis was $75,000. Immediately after the sale, and not reflecting Grant's basis adjustment, the partnership's balance sheet appeared as follows:

Asset	Adj. Basis	FMV	Partner	Adj. Basis	Cap. Acct.
Widgets	$40,000	$45,000	Grant	$120,000	$120,000
Gadgets	10,000	2,500	Eiffel	100,000	120,000
Gainacre	25,000	75,000		$220,000	$240,000
Blueacre	100,000	117,500			
Total:	$175,000	$240,000			

The amount of the adjustment is Grant's outside basis, $120,000, less his share of inside basis. To determine Grant's share of the partnership's inside basis, determine Grant's interest in the partnership's previously taxed capital plus Grant's share of partnership liabilities. Grant's interest in previously taxed capital is determined by considering a hypothetical disposition by the partnership of all its assets. The assets are sold for cash equal to the asset's fair market value in a taxable transaction. The result would be:

Asset	Adj. Basis	FMV	Gain/Loss	Grant's Share
Widgets	$40,000	$45,000	$5,000	$2,500
Gadgets	10,000	2,500	<7,500>	<3,750>
Gainacre	25,000	75,000	50,000	37,500*
Blueacre	100,000	117,500	17,500	8,750
Total		240,000		

* Of the total gain of $50,000, $25,000 represents built-in gain under Section 704(c) that must be allocated to Grant because he succeeds to Doris's interest and she had contributed the land with a built-in gain. The remaining $25,000 of gain would be allocated equally between the partners.

In a hypothetical liquidation, Grant would receive:

Share of cash:	$120,000
Share of tax loss:	+ 3,750
Share of tax gain:	− 48,750
Share of PTC:	$75,000

Because there are no partnership liabilities, his share of inside basis would be $75,000 and his overall adjustment would be $45,000 (outside basis of $120,000, less his share of inside basis, $75,000).

Next, once the adjustment has been determined, that amount must be allocated among the partnership's assets. The two parcels of land are allocated to the capital and hotchpot (Section 1231) asset group and the widgets and gadgets are allocated to the ordinary asset group.

The sale of the ordinary assets would result in a net loss of $1,250.

Asset	Adj. Basis	FMV	Gain/Loss	Grant's share
Widgets	$40,000	$45,000	$5,000	$2,500
Gadgets	10,000	2,500	<7,500>	<3,750>
Net				<$1,250>

Thus, a loss of $1,250 is allocated to the ordinary asset group.

The amount allocated to the capital and hotchpot (Section 1231) group is the amount of the total adjustment, $45,000, less the amount allocated to the ordinary group, loss of $1,250, or $46,250.

Total adjustment:	$45,000
Allocation to ordinary group:	– <1,250>
Allocation to capital/hotchpot group:	$46,250

For assets in the ordinary asset group, each asset is allocated an amount equal to the amount of income, gain, or loss that would be allocated to the partner from a hypothetical sale. Thus, with respect to the inventory of widgets, Grant would be allocated $2,500 of gain, and for the inventory of gadgets Grant would be allocated a loss of $3,750.

For assets in the capital and hotchpot group, each item is allocated an amount equal to the amount of income, gain, or loss that would be allocated to the partner from the hypothetical sale of the item. Thus, for Gainacre, Grant would be allocated $37,500, and for Blueacre Grant would be allocated $8,750.

The adjustment is made to Grant's inside basis in the items as follows:

Asset	Current Share of Basis	Adjustment	New Inside Basis
Widgets	$20,000	$2,500	$22,500
Gadgets	5,000	<3,750>	1,250
Gainacre	-0-	37,500	37,500
Blueacre	50,000	8,750	58,750
Total	$75,000	$45,000	$120,000

D. Problems

1. On January 1, Matt purchased a one-third interest in Consulting Partnership for $51,000. At the time of purchase, the partnership had the following assets:

Asset	Adj. Basis	FMV
Cash	$3,000	$3,000
Acct. Rec.	-0-	30,000
Land	60,000	120,000

(a) The partnership had not made an election under Section 754.

    (1) What are the tax consequences to Matt when Consulting Partnership collects the accounts receivable?

    (2) What are the tax consequences if, before Consulting Partnership collects the accounts receivable, Matt sells his partnership interest to Nye for $51,000?

(b) Alternatively, the partnership had made an election under Section 754.

    (1) What are the tax consequences to Matt at the time he purchased the interest?

    (2) What are the tax consequences to Consulting Partnership when Matt purchased the interest?

    (3) What are the tax consequences to the other partners in Consulting Partnership?

    (4) What are the tax consequences to Matt when Consulting Partnership collects the accounts receivable?

---

2. The Production Partnership is a cash method general partnership. All of the assets were purchased by the partnership. The partnership made a Section 754 election.

On January 1, Russ purchased Quincy's interest for $30,000 cash. Immediately after the purchase, and not reflecting Russ's basis adjustment, the balance sheet appeared as follows:

Asset	Adj. Basis	FMV	Liabilities:		$15,000
Acct. Rec.	$-0-	$15,000	Partner	Adj. Basis	Cap. Acct.
Inventory	-0-	30,000	Ovid	$30,000	$30,000
Building	30,000	45,000	Perry	30,000	30,000
Land	60,000	15,000	Russ	30,000	30,000
Total:	$90,000	$105,000		$90,000	$105,000

Both the land and the building are hotchpot (Section 1231) assets.

What is Russ's inside basis in each of the assets?

---

3. Application:

(a) Could you explain to a buying partner what the tax consequences of a Section 754 election would be?

(b) Who decides whether to make a Section 754 election? How do you know?

(c) When must the election be made? How must the election be made?

(d) Draft a template of a statement the partnership could attach to its return for the year it makes the election.

(e) With respect to the election:

    (1) Would you advise the partnership to make a Section 754 election prior to a new partner purchasing an interest?

(2) Would you advise the partner to condition his purchase of the interest on the partnership making the election?

(3) Could the position of the partnership and the partner be adverse?

(4) Is it important to determine who you represent?

Overview Problem — Putting It All Together

Stacey, Bill, and Olivia have operated the coffee shop for a number of years. While Olivia has really enjoyed being a partner in the partnership, she has decided that it is time for her to do something different. She has always wanted to design women's apparel. With the financial security the partnership has given her, she is ready to leave the partnership and give designing a try. However, she also wants to make sure that Stacey and Bill have someone to take over the responsibilities she has been handling. After some intense discussions with Charles, she decides he could take on her responsibilities and that she would like to sell her partnership interest to him.

Currently, the partnership has the following items:

	Adj. Basis	FMV
Cash	$50,000	$50,000
Acct. Rev.	-0-	40,000
Coffee bean inventory	30,000	30,000
Misc. supplies	25,000	25,000
Espresso machine	2,000	10,000
Building	100,000	100,000

The partners held a partnership meeting to discuss Olivia leaving and Charles joining the partnership. Even though Stacey and Bill will be sad to see her go, they understand her desire to try something new.

The partners need to determine the consequences of Olivia leaving and Charles joining the partnership. You have been invited to the meeting to advise them.

1. With respect to Olivia leaving the partnership:

    (a) How would you determine the sales price for her interest?

    (b) How will Olivia leaving impact the partnership? Will it cause a termination of the partnership?

    (c) What will you tell Olivia regarding the tax consequences of her leaving the partnership? What will you tell the other partners?

2. With respect to Charles joining the partnership:

    (a) What decision will the partners have to make?

    (b) How will you advise the partners? Charles? The partnership?

    (c) Can you represent both the partners and the partnership? Do you represent Charles? Is it important to know? Why?

3. Should the partners have any non-tax concerns? If so, what are they?

4. As the attorney for the partnership, what steps should you take to reflect Olivia's departure and Charles' entry into the partnership?

Practitioner's Checklist

    ☐ Will the partnership make an election under Section 754?

Items to include in the partnership or operating agreement:

    ☐ Language that partnership will make Section 754 election.

    ☐ If the election is not made at the formation of the partnership, explain who will decide if the election subsequently will be made.

VII.

Distributions from the Partnership to a Partner

Overview Problem

Stacey, Bill, and Olivia have operated the coffee shop for a number of years. They each have put a lot of time and effort into the business. Except for a small salary they pay themselves each year, none of the partners has withdrawn anything from the partnership. Instead, they have used the profits to expand the business, and, in profitable years, make several long-term investments. In addition, throughout the years each partner has made additional contributions to the partnership.

Stacey mentioned to Bill and Olivia that she would like to purchase a cabin and spend two-to-three days a week there. However, to be able to afford the purchase, she will have to withdraw some of her investment in the partnership. In addition, if she makes the purchase, Stacey will no longer be available to work full time in the business.

Bill and Olivia support Stacey. But, they want to be sure her decisions do not unnecessarily disrupt the coffee shop business or inadvertently cause any adverse tax consequences.

The partners have set a time for a partnership meeting to discuss Stacey's plans. You have been invited to the meeting to advise them.

Distributions from the Partnership to a Partner

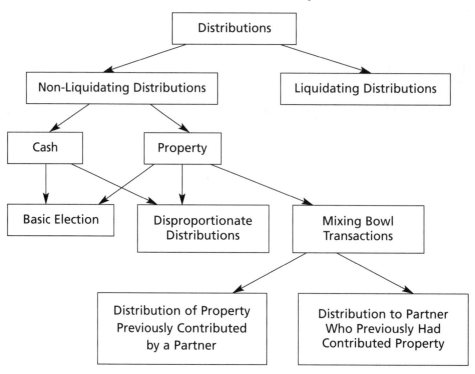

Chapter 23

Non-Liquidating Distributions of Cash and/or Property

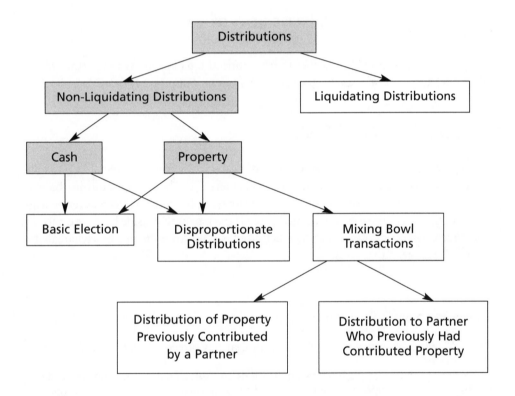

Read:

Code Sections 731(a), (b); 732(a), (c), (d); 733.
Treas. Reg. §§ 1.731-1(a), -1(b); 1.732-1(a), -1(c)(1)-(3), -1(d)(1)-(3); 1.733-1.

A. Background

Congress determined that a transfer of cash or property to a partnership in exchange for a partnership interest generally should not be a taxable event. The partner continues to have an indirect ownership interest in the property. Stated differently, he has a continuity of his investment. Any gain or loss realized in the property is deferred.[1]

If a partner acquires an interest in a partnership through a contribution of property, including money, to the partnership, his basis in his partnership interest is the amount of money and the adjusted basis of the property at the time of the contribution.[2] The basis is increased by gain or income and decreased by loss or deductions allocated to the partner. The partner's basis in his partnership interest is referred to as his "outside basis."

The basis of assets contributed to a partnership is the basis in the hands of the contributing partner.[3] The partnership's transferred basis in the assets is referred to as the "inside basis."

B. Discussion of Rules

Just as Congress provided for the tax-free contribution of property to a partnership, it also provided, in most cases, for the tax-free withdrawal of property from a partnership.

1. Distribution of Cash

Impact on outside basis. A partner's withdrawal of cash from a partnership generally is not a taxable event to the partner or the partnership.[4] The partner's outside basis is reduced by the amount of cash distributed.[5] However, because basis can never be negative, to the extent the cash distributed exceeds the partner's outside basis, the partner must recognize gain.[6] The gain is characterized as gain from the sale or exchange of a partner's partnership interest.

Practice Note: Cash withdrawn from a partnership represents either:
- Previously contributed capital; or
- An allocable share of income or gain that has previously been taxed to the partner.

Prior to withdrawal, both of the above items are reflected in the partner's outside basis. Thus, it is appropriate not to tax the withdrawal and to reduce the partner's outside basis by the amount of the withdrawal. If the partner receives a cash distribution that exceeds his previously contributed capital or share of previously taxed income or gain, it is appropriate to tax him on this accession to wealth.

---

1. Code Sec. 721.
2. Code Sec. 722. The basis is increased by the amount (if any) of gain recognized under Section 721(b).
3. Code Sec. 723. The basis is increased by the amount (if any) of gain recognized under Section 721(b) by the contributing partner at the time of the contribution.
4. Code Sec. 731(a).
5. Code Secs. 705(a)(2); 733(1).
6. Code Sec. 731(a)(1).

The rule applies to actual cash distributions and transactions that are treated as cash distributions. For example, a reduction in the partner's individual liabilities (*e.g.*, through assumption by the partnership) is treated as a cash distribution. Similarly, the forgiveness of a debt owed to the partnership is treated as a distribution of cash to the partner.[7]

Advance or draw. An advance or draw against a partner's distributive share of income is treated as a loan, and not a distribution of cash. On the last day of the partnership's taxable year, the advance or draw is treated as a cash distribution.[8]

Impact on capital account. When a partner withdraws cash from a partnership, he is reducing his economic investment in the partnership. Accordingly, his capital account is reduced by the amount of the distribution.

2. Distribution of Property

Impact on outside basis. The contribution of property to a partnership is not a taxable event. Similarly, a partner's withdrawal of property from a partnership generally is not a taxable event to the partner or the partnership.[9]

> **Practice Note:** A distribution of property to a partner may be taxable if:
> - There is a disproportionate distribution of property; [See Code Sec. 751(b), discussed in Chapter 25.] or
> - The distribution is part of a "mixing bowl" transaction. [Code Secs. 704(c); 737, discussed in Chapter 26 and 27.]

In general, the partner takes the property with the partnership's inside basis, a transferred basis. And, his outside basis is reduced by the basis of the property distributed.[10] Thus, just as the gain or loss inherent in property was preserved in the property upon contribution by a partner to the partnership, it also is preserved upon distribution of the property from the partnership to a partner.

To the extent the basis in the property distributed is larger than the partner's outside basis, the basis in the property is reduced to reflect the partner's outside basis before the asset is distributed.[11] Then, upon distribution of the asset, the partner will have a zero outside basis, and he takes the property with the reduced basis. For purposes of determining the length of time the partner has held the property, he can include (tack) the partnership's holding period onto his own holding period.[12]

---

7. Treas. Reg. § 1.731-1(c)(2).
8. Treas. Reg. § 1.731-1(a)(1)(ii).
9. Code Sec. 731(a), (b).
10. Code Secs. 731(a); 732(a)(1); 733(2). The partnership does not recognize any gain or loss on the distribution. Code Sec. 731(b); Treas. Reg. § 1.731-1(b).
11. Code Sec. 732.
12. Code Secs. 735(b); 1223. For purposes of determining the length of time the partner has held the inventory, the partner may not tack the partnership's holding period onto his own. Code Sec. 735(b).

Rule: Upon a distribution of property to a partner, the partner's outside basis prior to distribution is reflected in the combination of the partner's remaining outside basis and the distributed property's basis.

Basis prior to distribution = basis after distribution + basis in property distributed.

If both cash and property are distributed, the consequences of the cash distribution are considered before the consequences of the property distribution.

Impact on capital account. The partner's capital account is reduced by the fair market value of the property. If the partner takes the property subject to a liability, his capital account is reduced by the net value of the property distributed. If the fair market value of the property is different than its book value, the book gain or loss must be reflected in the capital accounts prior to the distribution. Then, the distributee partner's capital account will be reduced based on the fair market value of the asset.[13]

Example: Elle, Filene, and Gustav are equal partners in a partnership. The partnership balance sheet appears as follows:

Asset	Basis	FMV	Partner	AB	Cap. Acct.
Cash	$48,000	$48,000	Elle	$3,000	$20,000
Gainacre	2,000	12,000	Filene	24,000	20,000
	$50,000	$60,000	Gustav	23,000	20,000
				$50,000	$60,000

The partnership distributes the land to Elle. At the time of the distribution, Gainacre had a fair market value of $15,000. There is no tax gain or loss associated with a distribution, but there is a $3,000 book gain (fair market value $15,000, less book basis of $12,000). The book gain must be allocated equally among the partners, or $1,000 each. Their capital accounts are increased from $20,000 to $21,000. Then, when Gainacre is distributed to Elle, her capital account is reduced by $15,000, from $21,000 to $6,000. After the distribution of Gainacre, the partnership balance sheet would appear as follows:

Asset	Basis	FMV	Partner	AB	Cap. Acct.
Cash	$48,000	$48,000	Elle	$1,000	$6,000
			Filene	24,000	21,000
	$48,000	$48,000	Gustav	23,000	21,000
				$48,000	$48,000

Alternatively, the partnership may elect to reflect its assets at fair market value and restate capital accounts to reflect current fair market values, then distribute the property.[14]

---

13. Treas. Reg. § 1.704-1(b)(2)(iv)(e)(1).
14. Treas. Reg. § 1.704-1(b)(2)(iv)(f)(5)(ii).

Steps For Distribution of Cash and/or Property From a Partnership:
When cash and/or property is distributed to a partner:

Cash:

1st: Reduce the partner's basis by the amount of the cash distribution.

2nd: If the amount of cash distribution exceeds the partner's basis, the partner must recognize gain to the extent of the excess, resulting in a zero basis.

3rd: Reduce the partner's capital account by the amount of the cash distribution.

Property:

4th: Compare the inside basis of property to be distributed to the partner to the partner's outside basis.

5th: If the partner's outside basis is less than the property's inside basis, reduce the basis in the property to equal the partner's outside basis. Distribute the property.

6th: Reduce the partner's outside basis by the property's inside basis.

7th: If necessary, adjust the partners' capital accounts for any book gain or loss. Then, reduce the distributee partner's capital account by the net value of the property.

a. Distribution of More Than One Property

The partnership may distribute several pieces of property to the partner. The partner takes each property with the partnership's inside basis. His outside basis is reduced by the bases of all the property distributed.

If the sum of the inside bases of all the property distributed is greater than the partner's outside basis, the basis of the property must be reduced so that the partner's outside basis is equal to the total of the bases in the assets distributed. The objective of the statute is to preserve the amount of ordinary income in any distributed unrealized receivables or inventory. Thus, the statutory scheme of reducing the basis in the distributed assets, to the extent possible, prevents a reduction in the basis of the unrealized receivables and inventory assets.

To reduce the basis of the assets distributed, first, identify all unrealized receivables and inventory items to be distributed to the partner. Allocate basis to those assets in an amount equal to the partnership's basis.[15]

Definitions:

Unrealized receivables: include, to the extent not previously included in income, any right to payment for services rendered. They also include the right to payment for goods delivered to the extent the proceeds would be treated as amounts received from the sale or exchange of property other than a cap-

---

15. Code Sec. 732(c)(1)(A)(i).

ital asset. They also include any gain that would be characterized as ordinary income under the depreciation recapture provisions.[16]

Inventory: includes those assets held for sale to customers and any items held by the partnership that are not characterized as a capital or hotchpot (Section 1231) item.[17]

If the partner does not have sufficient basis to allocate to unrealized receivables and inventory, the partnership's basis in those assets must be reduced. If any of the properties have unrealized depreciation, reduce the basis by the amount of unrealized depreciation. If necessary, proportion the reduction based on the amount of deprecation in the assets.[18] If an additional reduction is needed, the bases of the assets are reduced in proportion to their respective (new) adjusted bases so as to equal the partner's outside basis.[19] The assets are distributed with the adjusted bases.

Second, if the partner has any remaining outside basis after making the allocation to unrealized receivables and inventory, the remaining portion is allocated to the other distributed property. First, allocate basis to those assets in an amount equal to the partnership's basis.[20]

If the partner does not have sufficient remaining basis to allocate to the other assets, the partnership's basis in the asset must be reduced. If any of the properties have unrealized depreciation, reduce the basis by the amount of unrealized depreciation. If necessary, proportion the reduction based on the amount of deprecation in the assets.[21] If an additional reduction is needed, the bases of the assets are reduced in proportion to their respective (new) adjusted bases so as to equal the partner's remaining outside basis.[22]

The partner takes each property with the partnership's inside basis, adjusted as provided above. His outside basis is reduced to zero.

b. Distributee Partner's Election

In certain circumstances, a different basis rule may apply. If the property is distributed:

- within two years from the time the partner acquired his interest by purchase, exchange, or inheritance;
- the partnership did not have a Section 754 election in effect at the time the partner acquired the interest; and
- the partner makes an election under Section 732(d),

then, the basis of the property will be determined as if the partnership had made the Section 754 election.[23] The basis of the property is adjusted as provided for under Sec-

---

16. Code Sec. 751(c).
17. Code Sec. 751(d).
18. Code Sec. 732(c)(1)(A)(ii), (c)(3)(A).
19. Code Sec. 732(c)(1)(A)(ii), (c)(3)(B).
20. Code Sec. 732(c)(1)(B)(i).
21. Code Sec. 732(c)(1)(B)(ii), (c)(3)(A).
22. Code Sec. 732(c)()1)(B)(ii), (c)(3)(B).
23. See discussion of the Section 754 election in Chapter 22.

Reduction of Partnership's Inside Basis

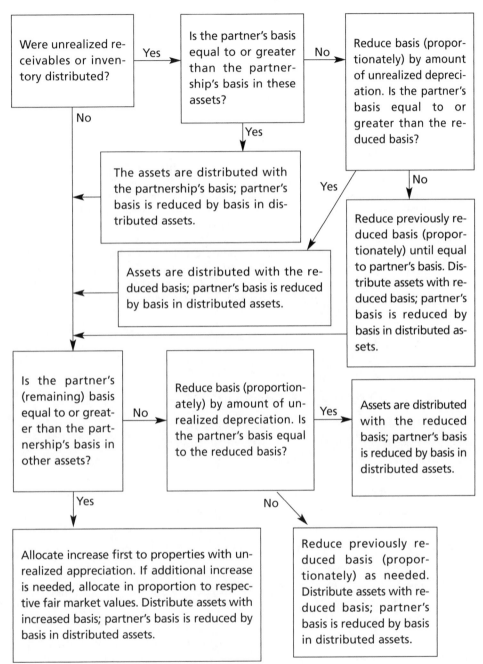

tion 743(b). (The mechanics of this adjustment are discussed in Chapter 22.) This basis is the basis used in determining the reduction in the partner's basis upon distribution of the property and the basis the partner takes in the property. The election only applies to the property distributed; it has no application with respect to property retained by the partnership.[24]

---

24. Treas. Reg. §1.732-1(d)(1)(vi).

If the fair market value of the partnership property, excluding cash, at the time the partner acquired his interest is greater than 110 percent of the partnership's adjusted basis in the assets, the Internal Revenue Service may require the basis to be adjusted. The Service may require the adjustment even if the distribution is not made within two years of the time the partner acquired his interest.[25] Under the regulations, the adjustment will be required only in those situations when the absence of the election would cause a shift in basis from nondepreciable property to depreciable property.[26]

> **Practice Tip:** If the property is depreciable, the partner must make the Section 732(d) election on his tax return for the year in which the distribution occurs. If the property is not depreciable, he must make the election on his tax return for a year that is no later than the first year in which the basis of the property is pertinent in determining his income tax. [Treas. Reg. § 1.732-1(d)(2)]
> When making the election, the partner must attach a schedule to his return. The schedule must include a statement that the partner elects to adjust the basis of property received in a distribution and include the computation of the special basis adjustment for the property distributed and the properties to which the adjustment has been allocated. [Treas. Reg. § 1.732-1(d)(3)]

c. Distribution of Marketable Securities

Marketable securities include financial instruments (*e.g.*, stock and bonds) and foreign currency that are actively traded. They include interests in a common trust fund, a mutual fund, and any financial instrument convertible into money or marketable securities.[27] Because the securities are easy to value and are liquid, when distributed from the partnership they are treated in the same manner as cash distributions. To the extent of the fair market value of the security on the date of distribution, the distribution is treated as a distribution of cash.[28] The basis in the hands of the partner is the basis as determined under the rules for distributions of property to a partner from the partnership.

If the fair market value of the security is greater than the partner's outside basis, the partner must recognize gain to the extent of the excess. When gain is recognized, the partner's basis in the security is its basis as determined under the above rules, increased by the amount of gain recognized.[29]

Exceptions. A distribution of marketable securities is not treated like a distribution of cash if:[30]

---

25. Code Sec. 732(d).
26. Treas. Reg. § 1.732-1(d)(4)(ii).
27. Code Sec. 731(c)(2).
28. Code Sec. 731(c)(1). The amount of the distribution of marketable securities that is treated as a distribution of cash may be reduced in some circumstances. See Code Sec. 731(c)(3)(B).
29. Code Sec. 731(c)(4).
30. Code Sec. 731(c)(3)(A).

- The security was contributed to the partnership by the distributee partner; or
- The partnership is an investment partnership and the partner contributed only money and/or securities.

3. Ordering Rules

The order in which adjustments are made to a partner's outside basis can be important for several reasons, including determining if a loss must be deferred because of insufficient basis or gain must be reported because a cash distribution exceeds the partner's basis. Distributions to a partner are taken into consideration on the day the distribution is made. An advance or "draw" against a distributive share is treated as a distribution made on the last day of the partnership's taxable year. The order in which year-end allocations and distributions are taken into consideration is as follows:[31]

- First, on the last day of the partnership's taxable year, increase the partner's basis by the amount of the distributive share of partnership income.
- Second, decrease the outside basis for year-end distributions of cash, then of property.
- Third, decrease the basis by the amount of the distributive share of partnership deductions and losses.
- Fourth, if sufficient basis, decrease the basis by the amount of any losses carried forward.

Practice Tip: The characterization of a payment to a partner made during the year as a withdrawal, loan, or advance can impact the tax consequences to the partner. Accordingly, the partner and the partnership should clearly establish whether the partner has an obligation to repay any of the amount and under what circumstances.

---

4. Subsequent Disposition of Property Distributed to a Partner

Congress was concerned about partners distributing property from the partnership to a partner and the partner selling it in an individual capacity to achieve a more favorable tax consequence (*i.e.*, converting ordinary income into long-term capital gain). Accordingly, the Code requires retaining the ordinary income treatment upon the distribution and sale of unrealized receivables, inventory, and recapture gain.

Unrealized receivables. If the property distributed to the partner comes within the definition of an unrealized receivable, its character as ordinary continues in the hands

---

31. Code Sec. 706(a).

of the partner, regardless of the use to which the partner may put the property or how long the partner holds the property before selling it.[32]

Inventory items. If the property distributed to the partner comes within the definition of inventory, for five years following distribution its character as ordinary continues in the hands of the partner, regardless of the use to which the partner may put the property. After five years, the character is determined in the hands of the partner.[33] If the property meets the definition of both an unrealized receivable and inventory, the character of the property in the hands of the partner is that of an unrealized receivable.

Recapture gain. If the property had any potential recapture income at the time of distribution, the recapture is preserved in the hands of the partner.[34]

Practice Tip:
Section 724 preserves ordinary income treatment upon contribution of property by a partner to a partnership.
Section 735 preserves ordinary income treatment upon distribution of property from a partnership to a partner.

C. Application of Rules

In the following examples, ignore any implications from the applicability of Section 751(b).

Example 1. Distribution of cash. Anita was a partner in the Green Partnership. Her outside basis was $10,000 and her capital account was $50,000. Anita withdrew $2,000 from the partnership.

Anita's withdrawal of cash is not a taxable event to her or the Green Partnership. Her outside basis is reduced by the amount of cash distributed, or reduced from $10,000 to $8,000.

Anita's withdrawal has reduced her economic investment in the partnership. Accordingly, her capital account is reduced by the amount of the distribution, or reduced from $50,000 to $48,000.

---

32. Code Sec. 735(a). If the partner disposes of the unrealized receivables in a transaction that qualifies for non-recognition, the characterization rule applies to the property received in the exchange in the same manner as it applied to the unrealized receivables. Code Sec. 735(c)(2).

33. Code Sec. 735(a). For purposes of determining the length of time the partner has held the inventory, the partner may not tack the partnership's holding period onto his own. Code Sec. 735(b). If the partner disposes of the inventory in a transaction that qualifies for non-recognition, the characterization rule applies to the property received in the exchange in the same manner as it applied to the inventory. Code Sec. 735(c)(2).

34. Code Secs. 1245(b)(5); 1250(d)(5).

Example 2. Distribution of cash in excess of basis. Betty was a partner in the Blue Partnership. Her outside basis was $10,000 and her capital account was $50,000. Betty withdrew $15,000 from the partnership.

Betty's withdrawal of cash, by itself, is not a taxable event to the partner or the partnership. Her outside basis is reduced by the amount of cash distributed. However, because her basis can never be negative, to the extent the cash distributed exceeds her outside basis, Betty must recognize gain. The cash distribution exceeds her outside basis by $5,000. Her basis in the partnership is reduced to zero and the $5,000 gain is characterized as gain from the sale or exchange of her partnership interest.

Betty's withdrawal has reduced her economic investment in the partnership. Accordingly, her capital account is reduced by the amount of the distribution, or reduced from $50,000 to $35,000.

Example 3. Draws/advances from partnership. Casey was a partner in the Orange Partnership. His outside basis was $10,000 and his capital account was $2,000. During the partnership's taxable year, Casey received $8,000 in draws, or advances.

At the end of the partnership's taxable year, Casey's allocable share of partnership income was $5,000. His basis is increased from $10,000 to $15,000.

The draws/advances are treated as distributions on the last day of the partnership's taxable year. Casey's withdrawal of cash, by itself, is not a taxable event to the partner or the partnership. His outside basis is reduced by the amount of cash distributed, or reduced from $15,000 to $7,000.

Casey's capital account increased from $2,000 to $7,000 on account of the allocable share of partnership income. It is decreased by the amount of the distribution, or reduced from $7,000 to a negative $1,000.

Example 4. Distribution of property. Devon was a partner in the Yellow Partnership. His outside basis was $15,000 and his capital account was $20,000. The partnership distributed Blackacre to Devon. Blackacre's basis was $3,000 and its fair market value was $5,000.

The withdrawal of property by Devon from Yellow Partnership generally is not a taxable event. Devon takes the property with the partnership's inside basis, or $3,000. His outside basis is reduced by the basis of the property distributed, from $15,000 to $12,000. His capital account is reduced by the fair market value of the property, from $20,000 to $15,000.

Example 5. Distribution of property—partnership basis greater than partner's basis. Edith was a partner in the Violet Partnership. Her outside basis was $15,000 and her capital account was $20,000. The partnership distributed Whiteacre to Edith. Whiteacre's basis was $18,000 and its fair market value was $10,000.

The withdrawal of property by Edith from Violet Partnership generally is not a taxable event. Edith takes the property with the partnership's inside basis. However, the partnership's basis in Whiteacre is larger than Edith's outside basis. Accordingly,

Whiteacre's basis is reduced to reflect Edith's outside basis before Whiteacre is distributed, or to $15,000. Upon distribution of Whiteacre, Edith will have a zero outside basis and Whiteacre will have a basis of $15,000.

Edith's capital account is reduced by the fair market value of Whiteacre, or reduced from $20,000 to $10,000.

Example 6. Distribution of cash and property. Fritz was a partner in the Red Partnership. His outside basis was $15,000 and his capital account was $50,000. The partnership distributed $10,000 cash and Greenacre to Fritz. Greenacre's basis was $18,000 and its fair market value was $10,000.

If both cash and property are distributed, the consequences of the cash distribution are considered before the consequences of the property. Fritz's withdrawal of cash is not a taxable event to him or the partnership. His outside basis is reduced by the amount of cash distributed, or reduced from $15,000 to $5,000.

Fritz's withdrawal has reduced his economic investment in the partnership. Accordingly, his capital account is reduced by the amount of the distribution, or reduced from $50,000 to $40,000.

The partnership's basis in Greenacre is larger than Fritz's outside basis (after reduction for the cash distribution). Accordingly, Greenacre's basis is reduced to reflect Fritz's outside basis before Greenacre is distributed, or to $5,000. Upon distribution of Greenacre, Fritz will have a zero outside basis and Greenacre will have a $5,000 basis.

Fritz's capital account is reduced by the fair market value of Greenacre, or reduced from $40,000 to $30,000.

Example 7. Distribution of properties — partnership basis greater than partner's basis. Gerhardt was a partner in the Pink Partnership. His outside basis was $15,000 and his capital account was $50,000. The partnership distributed Countyacre and Cityacre to Gerhardt. Countyacre's basis was $10,000 and its fair market value was $12,000; Cityacre's basis was $10,000 and its fair market value was $5,000.

The withdrawal of property by Gerhardt from the Pink Partnership generally is not a taxable event. Gerhardt takes the property with the partnership's inside basis. However, the partnership's basis in Countyacre and Cityacre combined, $20,000, is larger than Gerhardt's outside basis, $15,000. Accordingly, the basis in the property must be reduced by $5,000. The amount of the reduction, $5,000, must be allocated among the assets distributed so that Gerhardt's outside basis is allocated among the two properties distributed.

There are no unrealized receivables or inventory items. With respect to the other distributed property, the amount by which the basis should be reduced is allocated first to other assets with unrealized depreciation. Cityacre has depreciated by $5,000. Accordingly, the reduction is allocated to its basis, reducing it from $10,000 to $5,000.

Upon distribution of Countyacre and Cityacre, Gerhardt will have a zero outside basis. He will take Countyacre with a basis of $10,000 and Citycacre with a basis of

$5,000. His capital account is reduced by the fair market value of Countyacre and City-acre, or from $50,000 to $33,000.

Example 8. Distribution of properties—partnership basis greater than partner's basis. Hennepin was a partner in the Aqua Partnership. His outside basis was $4,000 and his capital account was $50,000. The partnership distributed the following assets to him:

Asset	Adj. Basis	FMV
Acct. Rec.	$-0-	$1,000
Inventory	7,000	8,000
Whiteacre	3,000	9,000
Total:	$10,000	$18,000

The distribution of property to Hennepin generally is not a taxable event. Hennepin takes the property with the partnership's inside basis. However, the partnership's basis in the accounts receivable, inventory, and Whiteacre combined, $10,000, is larger than his outside basis, $4,000. Accordingly, the basis in the property must be reduced by $6,000. The amount of the reduction, $6,000, is allocated among the assets to be distributed so that Hennepin's outside basis is equal to the total of the bases in the assets distributed.

To reduce the basis of the assets distributed, first, allocate basis to unrealized receivables and inventory in an amount equal to the partnership's basis, or zero and $7,000, respectively. Because Hennepin does not have sufficient basis to allocate to unrealized receivables and inventory, the partnership's basis in those assets must be reduced. If any of the properties have unrealized depreciation, reduce the basis by the amount of unrealized depreciation. Neither asset has unrealized depreciation. Thus, the bases of the assets are reduced to the partner's outside basis. The basis in the inventory is reduced to $4,000. Upon distribution, his outside basis would be decreased from $4,000 to zero. Because he has no remaining basis, Whiteacre's basis is reduced to zero. In sum, he takes the assets with the following basis:

Asset	Adj. Basis
Acct. Rec.	$-0-
Inventory	4,000
Whiteacre	-0-
Total:	$4,000

His capital account is reduced by the value of the property distributed, or from $50,000 to $32,000.

Example 9. Distribution of properties—partnership basis greater than partner's basis. Imex was a partner in the Rose Partnership. His outside basis was $10,000 and his capital account was $50,000. The partnership distributed the following assets to him:

Asset	Adj. Basis	FMV
Acct. Rec.	$6,000	$8,000
Blackacre	3,000	500
Whiteacre	3,000	500
Total:	$12,000	$9,000

The distribution of property to Imex generally is not a taxable event. Imex takes the property with the partnership's inside basis. However, the partnership's basis in the accounts receivable, Blackacre, and Whiteacre combined, $12,000, is larger than his outside basis, $10,000. Accordingly, the basis in the property must be reduced by $2,000. The amount of the reduction, $2,000, is allocated among the assets to be distributed so that Imex's outside basis is equal to the total of the bases in the assets distributed.

To reduce the basis of the assets distributed, first, allocate basis to unrealized receivables in an amount equal to the partnership's basis, or $6,000. The unrealized receivables are distributed with a $6,000 basis, reducing his outside basis to $4,000.

His remaining basis, $4,000, is allocated to the other distributed property. However, the amount is insufficient to allocate to Blackacre and Whiteacre. Accordingly, the partnership's basis in these assets must be reduced. The basis is reduced by the proportionate amount of unrealized depreciation. Because both properties have decreased in value by the same proportionate amount, $2,500, the reduction is made proportionately between the properties, or $1,000 each.

Imex takes the property with the partnership's inside basis, adjusted as follows:

Asset	Adj. Basis
Acct. Rec.	$6,000
Whiteacre	2,000
Blackacre	2,000
Total:	$10,000

His outside basis is reduced to zero. His capital account is reduced by the value of the distributions, from $50,000 to $41,000.

Example 10. Election by partner. Jordan acquired a one-third interest in Teal Partnership, which owned Gainacre. The partnership did not have a Section 754 election in effect at that time. One year later, Teal Partnership distributed Gainacre to Jordan. Gainacre had a basis of $90,000 and fair market value of $120,000. Jordan made an election under Section 732(d).

Jordan's basis in Gainacre is determined as if the partnership had made the Section 754 election. As adjusted under Section 743(b), the basis would be $100,000 ($40,000 basis in his share under Section 743(b) and the remaining $60,000 share allocable to the other two partners).[35]

Example 11. Characterization. Katrina was a partner in the Indigo Partnership. The partnership distributed accounts receivable to her. The accounts receivable had a zero basis and fair market value of $40,000. Seven years later, Katrina sold the accounts receivable for $50,000, recognizing $50,000 of gain.

The accounts receivable are unrealized receivables. Accordingly, the character of the gain is ordinary regardless of the use to which Katrina may put the property or how long she held them before selling.

---

35. The computation of the adjustment is discussed in Chapter 22.

D. Cases and Materials

Rev. Rul. 94-4, 1994-1 C.B. 196

ISSUE: If a deemed distribution of money under 752(b) of the Internal Revenue Code occurs as a result of a decrease in a partner's share of the liabilities of a partnership, is the deemed distribution taken into account at the time of the distribution or at the end of the partnership taxable year?

LAW: Under 752(b), a decrease in a partner's share of partnership liabilities is considered a distribution of money to the partner by the partnership. The partner will recognize gain under 731(a)(1) if the distribution of money exceeds the adjusted basis of the partner's interest immediately before the distribution.

Section 1.731-1(a)(1)(ii) of the Income Tax Regulations provides that for purposes of 731 and 705, advances or drawings of money or property against a partner's distributive share of income are treated as current distributions made on the last day of the partnership taxable year with respect to that partner.

Rev. Rul. 92-97, 1992-2 C.B. 124, treats a deemed distribution of money to a partner resulting from a cancellation of debt as an advance or drawing under 1.731-1(a)(1)(ii) against that partner's distributive share of cancellation of indebtedness income.

HOLDING: A deemed distribution of money under 752(b) resulting from a decrease in a partner's share of the liabilities of a partnership is treated as an advance or drawing of money under 1.731-1(a)(1)(ii) to the extent of the partner's distributive share of income for the partnership taxable year. An amount treated as an advance or drawing of money is taken into account at the end of the partnership taxable year. A deemed distribution of money resulting from a cancellation of debt may qualify for advance or drawing treatment under this revenue ruling and under Rev. Rul. 92-97.

E. Problems

1. Kale has been a partner in the Chemical Partnership for several years. Her outside basis was $10,000 and her capital account was $50,000. What are the tax consequences to Kale under the following alternative distributions:

(a) Kale withdrew $5,000 from the partnership.

(b) Alternatively, Kale withdrew $20,000 from the partnership.

(c) Alternatively, Chemical Partnership distributed Blueacre to Kale. Blueacre had a basis of $7,000 and fair market value of $40,000.

(d) Alternatively, Chemical Partnership distributed Greenacre to Kale. Greenacre had a basis of $12,000 and fair market value of $40,000.

(e) Alternatively, Chemical Partnership distributed $5,000 and Whiteacre to Kale. Whiteacre had a basis of $3,000 and fair market value of $10,000.

(f) Alternatively, Chemical Partnership distributed $5,000 and Blackacre to Kale. Black-acre had a basis of $13,000 and fair market value of $10,000.

(g) Alternatively, Chemical Partnership distributed accounts receivable and Yellowacre to Kale. The accounts receivable had a zero basis and a fair market value of $5,000. Yellowacre had a basis of $3,000 and fair market value of $10,000.

(h) Alternatively, Chemical Partnership distributed an inventory of Whatnots and an inventory of Widgets to Kale. The inventory of Whatnots had a basis of $6,000 and a fair market value of $15,000; the Widgets had a basis of $24,000 and a fair mar-ket value of $30,000.

(i) Alternatively, Chemical Partnership distributed inventory to Kale. The inventory had a zero basis and a fair market value of $5,000. One year later, Kale sold the inven-tory for $6,000. What if Kale had waited six years before she sold the inventory?

---

2. Lily purchased an interest in Development Partnership, a cash basis taxpayer. The following month, it distributed accounts receivable to her. The accounts receivable had a zero basis and fair market value of $5,000. Development Partnership had not made a Section 754 election.

(a) What will the impact be to Lily when she collects the accounts receivable?

(b) What action might Lily want to take? Why?

(c) How would she do that? Does she have to obtain the consent of the Development Partnership?

---

3. Application:

(a) If the partners want to begin making distributions from the partnership, what ad-vice might you give them?

(b) When would you advise a partner to make a Section 732(d) election?

(c) Create a template to use for when a partner wants to make a Section 732(d) election.

F. Advanced Problems—Looking Forward

Without conducting any research, consider the following questions:

1. If a partner receives a cash distribution that exceeds his basis and must, therefore, recognize gain, how is the gain that is recognized at the partner level reflected at the part-nership level? Does it matter? Why or why not?

2. If a partner receives a distribution of property and, because his outside basis is less than the partnership's basis in the asset, he must reduce the asset's basis. Will this cause a distortion in the balance sheet? Is this a concern? Why or why not?

3. Should it matter if the partner is receiving a non-liquidating versus a liquidating distribution?

Chapter 24

Partnership Election

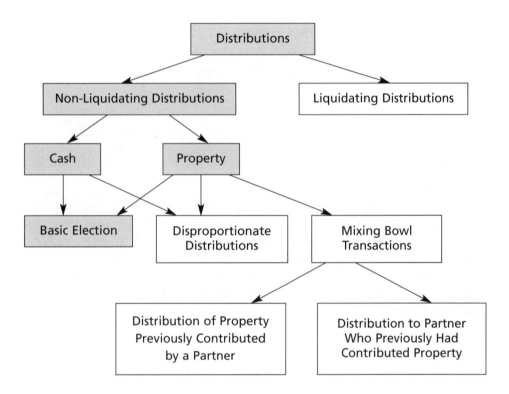

Read:

Code Sections 734; 754; 755.
Treas. Reg. §§ 1.734-1(a), -1(b)(1), -1(c); 1.754-1; 1.755-1(a)(1), -1(c).

A. Background

Recall that, in general, a partner does not recognize gain or loss when he receives a distribution of cash from a partnership.[1] Rather, the partner's outside basis is reduced

---

1. Code Sec. 731(a). The partnership does not recognize any gain or loss on the distribution. Code Sec. 731(b); Treas. Reg. § 1.731-1(b).

by the amount of cash distributed.[2] However, to the extent the cash distributed exceeds the partner's outside basis, the partner must recognize gain.[3]

Similarly, a partner does not recognize gain or loss when he receives a distribution of property from a partnership. Rather, the partner's outside basis is reduced by the basis of the asset distributed.[4] To the extent the basis in the property is larger than the partner's outside basis, the basis in the property is reduced to reflect the partner's outside basis, then the asset is distributed.[5] The partner will then have a zero outside basis.

B. Discussion of Rules

1. Impact of Distribution on Partnership — General Rule

When a partnership distributes cash to a partner in excess of the partner's outside basis, the partner must recognize gain to the extent of the excess.[6] Because the partner recognizes gain, but no adjustments are made to the bases of the partnership property, the partnership's balance sheet may become distorted.

Similarly, when a partnership distributes property to a partner, the bases of the assets retained by the partnership are not affected.[7] This rule applies even in those situations where the partner was required to adjust the basis of the property being distributed (*i.e.*, the partner's outside basis was less than the basis of the asset being distributed).[8] Because the partner adjusted the basis in the distributed property, but no adjustments were made to any remaining partnership property, the partnership's balance sheet may become distorted.

Practice Tip: A distortion in a partnership's balance sheet may occur when:
- The partner recognized gain to the extent a cash distribution exceeded his outside basis; or
- The basis in property distributed to the partner was reduced because the partner had insufficient outside basis.

---

2. Code Sec. 733(1).

3. Code Sec. 731(a)(1).

4. Code Secs. 731(a); 733(2). The partnership does not recognize any gain or loss on the distribution. Code Sec. 731(b); Treas. Reg. §1.731-1(b).

5. Code Sec. 732.

6. Code Sec. 731(a)(1).

7. Code Sec. 734(a).

8. Code Sec. 732(a)(2).

Example: Harry, Ignatius, and Jerry are equal partners in a partnership. The partnership balance sheet appears as follows:

Asset	Basis	FMV	Partner	AB	Cap. Acct.
Cash	$6,000	$6,000	Harry	$3,000	$6,000
Land	3,000	12,000	Ignatius	3,000	6,000
	$9,000	$18,000	Jerry	3,000	6,000
				$9,000	$18,000

The partnership distributes $6,000 of cash (equal to the amount of his capital account) to Harry in liquidation of his entire interest. Because Harry's outside basis is only $3,000, Harry must recognize $3,000 of gain (the excess of the cash distribution over Harry's outside basis). Note that the partnership assets reflect $9,000 of gain in the land, 1/3 of which, $3,000, would have been allocable to Harry if he had remained in the partnership and the asset was sold.

When a partnership distributes cash or property to a partner, the bases of the assets retained by the partnership are not affected. Thus, after the liquidation of Harry's interest, the partnership balance sheet would appear as follows:

Asset	Basis	FMV	Partner	AB	Cap. Acct.
Land	$3,000	$12,000	Ignatius	$3,000	$6,000
	$3,000	$12,000	Jerry	3,000	6,000
				$6,000	$12,000

Even though the gain in the land that was allocable to Harry (and arguably reported by Harry) was $3,000, no adjustment has been made to the basis in the land. This distortion is reflected in the disparity between the inside basis of the partnership assets, $3,000, and the total of the partners' outside basis, $6,000.

If the partnership sells the land for $12,000, it will recognize gain of $9,000. One-half of the gain, $4,500, would be allocated to each of Ignatius and Jerry and their outside basis would each be increased. They each would be recognizing $1,500 more gain than they would have if the property had been sold while Harry was still a partner in the partnership.

After the sale of the land, the partnership's balance sheet would appear as follows:

Asset	Basis	FMV	Partner	AB	Cap. Acct.
Cash	$12,000	$12,000	Ignatius	$7,500	$6,000
	$12,000	$12,000	Jerry	7,500	6,000
				$15,000	$12,000

Again, there is a distortion, reflected in the disparity between the inside basis of the partnership's assets, $12,000, and the total of the partners' outside basis, $15,000. It also is reflected in the disparity between the partner's outside basis and capital accounts. If the partnership were to liquidate, the $12,000 of cash would be distributed equally between Ignatius and Jerry, with each receiving $6,000. They would both recognize a loss of $1,500 (cash distribution of $6,000, less outside basis of $7,500), eventually recognizing a loss to offset the amount of gain that had previously been taxed to Harry upon liquidation of his partnership interest, then again taxed to them upon the sale of the land.

2. Exception to the General Rule

The partnership may make an election under Section 754 to adjust the inside basis of the partnership assets under Section 734(b). The adjustment corrects for an imbalance caused by a partner recognizing gain on the distribution of cash or adjusting the basis of distributed property.

When a partnership distributes cash to a partner in excess of the partner's outside basis, so that the partner must recognize gain in the amount of the excess, the amount of the Section 734(b) adjustment is the amount of gain recognized. The adjustment must be made to capital and hotchpot (Section 1231) assets.[9]

When a partner is required to adjust the basis of the property being distributed because the partner's outside basis is less than the basis of the asset being distributed, the amount of the adjustment is the amount of reduction in the property's basis. The upward adjustment is made to property of the same class of property that gave rise to the adjustment. Thus, the partnership property must be divided into two groups, one group containing capital and hotchpot (Section 1231) assets and the second group containing all remaining (ordinary) assets. Only the group with the same character of assets as that distributed by the partnership to the partner should be given a basis adjustment.[10]

Within the applicable group of assets, allocate the upward adjustment first to properties with unrealized appreciation in proportion to their appreciation (but only to the extent of the unrealized appreciation). Allocate any remaining adjustment in proportion to the fair market value of the property.[11]

If the partnership does not have assets of the character that must be adjusted, the adjustment is carried forward until the partnership acquires such property and an adjustment can be made.[12]

Practice Tip: To make the Section 754 election, the partnership must file a written statement with its timely-filed tax return (including extensions) for the year in which the distribution occurs. [Treas. Reg. § 1.754-1(b)] However, an election will be treated as timely filed if filed within 12 months of the original due date for the return and all partners report their income consistently with the election for the year of the election and all subsequent years. [Rev. Proc. 92-85, 1992-2 C.B. 490, as amended by Rev. Proc. 93-28, 1993-28 C.B. 344]

The statement must include the name and address of the partnership, be signed by a partner, and contain a declaration that the partnership elects under Section 754 to apply the provisions of Section 734(b) and 743(b). [Treas. Reg. § 1.754-1(b)]

Depreciable assets. If the asset is depreciable and the basis has been increased because of the election, to the extent of the increase, the partnership is treated as having ac-

---

9. Treas. Reg. § 1.755-1(c)(1)(ii).
10. Treas. Reg. § 1.755-1(c)(1)(i).
11. Treas. Reg. § 1.755-1(c)(2)(i).
12. Treas. Reg. § 1.755-1(c)(4).

quired a separate asset that was placed in service on the date of the distribution. That portion may be depreciated using an appropriate recovery method. The original portion of the basis continues to be depreciated using the traditional method used by the partnership.[13] If the asset is depreciable and the basis has been decreased, the decrease is taken into consideration over the property's remaining useful life.[14]

Practice Tip: The allocation impacts the partnership and the partners going forward. It is not unique to the partner receiving the distribution.

Practice Tip: If the partnership makes an election under Section 754 to make a basis adjustment with respect to distributions of property by the partnership as provided in Section 734(b), the adjustment to the buyer-partner's basis in partnership assets as provided in Section 743(b) also applies.

Practice Tip: If the partnership makes an adjustment to the bases of partnership property under Section 734(b), it must attach a statement to its partnership return for the year of the distribution setting forth the computation of the adjustment and the partnership properties to which the adjustment has been allocated. [Treas. Reg. § 1.734-1(d)]

Example: Harry, Ignatius, and Jerry are equal partners in a partnership which has made an election under Section 754. The partnership balance sheet appears as follows:

Asset	Basis	FMV	Partner	AB	Cap. Acct.
Cash	$6,000	$6,000	Harry	$3,000	$6,000
Land	3,000	12,000	Ignatius	3,000	6,000
	$9,000	$18,000	Jerry	3,000	6,000
				$9,000	$18,000

The partnership distributes $6,000 of cash (equal to the amount of his capital account) to Harry in liquidation of his entire interest. Because Harry's outside basis is only $3,000, Harry must recognize $3,000 of gain (the excess of the cash distribution over Harry's outside basis).

Because the partnership has made a Section 754 election, it must adjust the inside basis of the partnership assets under Section 734(b). The amount of the adjustment is the amount of the excess (*i.e.*, the amount of gain recognized), or $3,000. The adjustment must be made to capital and hotchpot (Section 1231) assets. Because the land is a capital asset, the partnership increases its basis by $3,000. After the adjustment, the partnership balance sheet would be as follows:

---

13. Treas. Reg. § 1.734-1(e)(1).
14. Treas. Reg. § 1.734-1(e)(2).

Asset	Basis	FMV	Partner	AB	Cap. Acct.
Land	$6,000	$12,000	Ignatius	$3,000	$6,000
	$6,000	$12,000	Jerry	3,000	6,000
				$6,000	$12,000

Basis Adjustment under Section 734(b)

| Partnership distributes cash to a partner in excess of the partner's outside basis. | The partnership had to adjust the basis of the property being distributed because the partner's outside basis was less than the basis of the asset being distributed. |

↓

| The amount of the adjustment is the amount of the excess (i.e., the amount of gain recognized). |

| The amount of the adjustment is the amount of reduction in the property's basis. |

↓

| Divide the partnership property into two groups, one group containing capital and hotchpot (Section 1231) assets and the second group containing all remaining (ordinary) assets. Adjust only the basis of the capital and hotchpot assets. |

| Divide the partnership property into two groups, one group containing capital and hotchpot (Section 1231) assets and the second group containing all remaining (ordinary) assets. Adjust the basis of the group of assets with the same character as that distributed by the partnership. |

↓

| Within the applicable group of assets, allocate the upward adjustment first to properties with unrealized appreciation in proportion to their appreciation. |

↓

| Within the applicable group of assets, allocate any remaining adjustment in proportion to the fair market value of the property. |

C. Application of Rules

Example 1. Distribution of cash. Georgia, Hal, and Inez were equal general partners in a partnership with a balance sheet that appeared as follows:

Asset	Adj. Basis	FMV	Partners	Adj. Basis	Cap. Acct.
Cash	$11,000	$11,000	Georgia	$10,000	$11,000
Land	19,000	22,000	Hal	15,000	11,000
Total:	$30,000	$33,000	Inez	5,000	11,000
				$30,000	$33,000

While an election under Section 754 was in effect, the partnership distributed the $11,000 to Georgia. Because her basis was only $10,000, she recognized $1,000 of gain.

The amount of the Section 734(b) adjustment is the amount of gain Georgia had to recognize, or $1,000. The adjustment must be made to capital and hotchpot (Section 1231) assets. Thus, the basis of the land is increased by $1,000. After the adjustment, the partnership's balance sheet would appear as follows:[15]

Asset	Adj. Basis	FMV	Partners	Adj. Basis	Cap. Acct.
Land	$20,000	$22,000	Hal	$15,000	$11,000
Total:	$20,000	$22,000	Inez	5,000	11,000
				$20,000	$22,000

Example 2. Distribution of property. Jackie, Kandi, and Lanna formed a partnership. Jackie contributed $50,000 and Blackacre, which had a fair market value of $50,000 and adjusted basis of $25,000, in exchange for a one-third general partnership interest. Kandi and Lanna each contributed $100,000 in exchange for a one-third general partnership interest. The partnership used the $250,000 cash to purchase Greenacre for $100,000 and Whiteacre for $50,000. It also purchased an inventory of Widgets for $40,000, an inventory of Gadgets for $50,000, and an inventory of Whatnots for $10,000.

Seven years later, the partnership's balance sheet appeared as follows:

Asset	Adj. Basis	FMV	Partners	Adj. Basis	Cap. Acct.
Widgets	$40,000	$45,000	Jackie	$75,000	$120,000
Gadgets	50,000	60,000	Kandi	100,000	120,000
Whatnots	10,000	2,500	Lanna	100,000	120,000
Blackacre	25,000	75,000		$275,000	$360,000
Greenacre	100,000	117,500			
Whiteacre	50,000	60,000			
Total:	$275,000	$360,000			

While an election under Section 754 was in effect, the partnership distributed the inventory of Gadgets and Whiteacre to Jackie.

---

15. Treas. Reg. § 1.734-1(b)(1) Ex. 1.

Because Jackie's basis was only $75,000 and the total basis of the assets distributed to her was $100,000 (basis of $50,000 in the Gadgets and $50,000 in Whiteacre), she must reduce the basis of the property being distributed to her by $25,000. First, basis is allocated to the inventory in an amount equal to the partnership's basis. Thus, the inventory of Gadgets is allocated a basis of $50,000.

Second, her remaining outside basis, $25,000, is allocated to property to be distributed other than the unrealized receivables and inventory in an amount equal to the partner's basis.[16] Thus, the remaining basis of $25,000 is allocated to Whiteacre, causing a $25,000 reduction in Whiteacre's basis.[17]

When a partner is required to adjust the basis of the property being distributed because the partner's outside basis is less than the basis of the asset being distributed, the amount of the adjustment under Section 734(b) is the amount of reduction in the property's basis, or $25,000. The upward adjustment is made to the same class of property that gave rise to the adjustment. Thus, the partnership property should be divided into two groups, one group containing capital and hotchpot (Section 1231) assets and the second group containing all remaining (ordinary) assets. Blackacre and Greenacre are allocated to the capital and hotchpot group. Because Whiteacre is a capital asset, an adjustment is made only to assets in the capital and hotchpot asset group.

Within the group of capital and hotchpot assets, the upward adjustment is made first to properties with unrealized appreciation in proportion to their appreciation.

Asset	Adj. Basis	FMV	Appreciation
Blackacre	$25,000	$75,000	$50,000
Greenacre	100,000	117,500	17,500
Total:			$67,500

Blackacre: 50,000/67,500 x 25,000 = 18,519

Greenacre: 17,500/67,500 x 25,000 = 6,481

The basis adjustment will be as follows:

Asset	Adj. Basis	Adjustment	New Basis
Blackacre	$25,000	$18,519	$43,519
Greenacre	100,000	6,481	106,481
Total:			$150,000

The partnership's balance sheet would appear as follows:[18]

Asset	Adj. Basis	FMV	Partners	Adj. Basis	Cap. Acct.
Widgets	$40,000	$45,000	Kandi	100,000	120,000
Whatnots	10,000	2,500	Lanna	100,000	120,000
Blackacre	43,519	75,000		$200,000	$240,000
Greenacre	106,481	117,500			
Total:	$200,000	$240,000			

---

16. Code Sec. 732(c)(1)(B)(i).

17. See Code Sec. 732(c)(1).

18. See Treas. Reg. § 1.755-1(c)(5). This problem ignores any implication from the applicability of Section 751(b).

D. Problems

1. Mindy, Nellie, and Orlando are equal partners in a general partnership. The partnership balance sheet was as follows:

Asset	Adj. Basis	FMV	Partners	Adj. Basis	Cap. Acct.
Cash	$90,000	$90,000	Mindy	$20,000	$100,000
Pinkacre	60,000	130,000	Nellie	70,000	100,000
Realacre	10,000	80,000	Orlando	70,000	100,000
Total:	$160,000	$300,000		$160,000	$300,000

The partnership distributed $50,000 to Mindy. After the distribution, Mindy had a one-fifth interest worth $50,000.

(a) What are the consequences to Mindy and the partnership if the partnership has not made a Section 754 election? Reconstruct the balance sheet after the distribution.

(b) What are the consequences to Mindy and the partnership if the partnership has made a Section 754 election? Reconstruct the balance sheet after the distribution.

---

2. Perry, Quidly, and Reynold are equal partners in a general partnership. The partnership balance sheet was as follows:

Asset	Adj. Basis	FMV	Partners	Adj. Basis	Cap. Acct.
Cash	$90,000	$90,000	Perry	$50,000	$100,000
Acct. Rec.	-0-	10,000	Quidly	80,000	100,000
Greenacre	90,000	100,000	Reynold	90,000	100,000
Blueacre	40,000	100,000		$220,000	$300,000
Total:	$220,000	$300,000			

The partnership distributed Greenacre to Perry in liquidation of his interest.

(a) What are the consequences to Perry and the partnership if the partnership has not made a Section 754 election? Reconstruct the balance sheet after the distribution.

(b) What are the consequences to Perry and the partnership if the partnership has made a Section 754 election? Reconstruct the balance sheet after the distribution.

---

3. Application:

(a) How would you explain to the partners the disparity that could be caused at the partnership level when cash or property is distributed?

(b) When would you advise the partnership to make a Section 754 election?

(c) Who decides whether the partnership will make the election? How do you know?

(d) Create a template to use for when a partnership wants to make a Section 754 election.

Chapter 25

Disproportionate Distributions

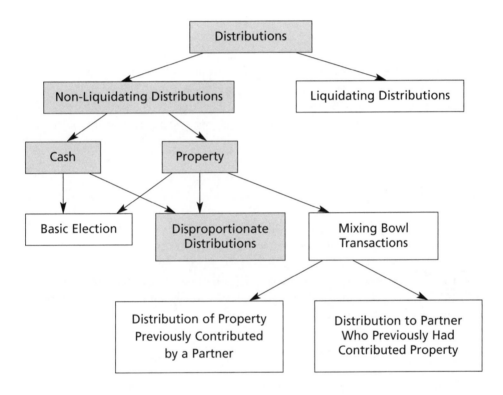

Read:

Code Section 751(b).
Treas. Reg. § 1.751-1(b).

A. Background

Recall that, in general, a partner does not recognize gain or loss when he receives a distribution of cash from a partnership.[1] Rather, the partner's outside basis is reduced

---

1. Code Sec. 731(a). The partnership does not recognize any gain or loss on the distribution. Code Sec. 731(b); Treas. Reg. § 1.731-1(b).

by the amount of cash distributed.[2] However, to the extent the cash distributed exceeds the partner's outside basis, the partner must recognize gain.[3]

Similarly, a partner does not recognize gain or loss when he receives a distribution of property from a partnership. Rather, the partner's outside basis is reduced by the basis of the asset distributed.[4] To the extent the basis in the property is larger than the partner's outside basis, the basis in the property is reduced to reflect the partner's outside basis, then the asset is distributed.[5] The partner will then have a zero outside basis.

B. Discussion of Rules

While the general rule is that there are no tax consequences when property is distributed from a partnership to a partner, there are three exceptions to the rule. The first exception, disproportionate distributions, is discussed in this chapter. The second exception, distributions of property previously contributed by a partner, is discussed in the following chapter. The third exception, distributions to a partner who had previously contributed appreciated property, is discussed in Chapter 27.

1. Rationale

Each partner has an indirect ownership in the underlying partnership property. Each partner is also responsible for an allocable share of the underlying gain or loss in each partnership item. Determining how much of the partnership gain or loss a partner is responsible for is only part of the picture. The other part is the character of the gain or loss. In general, a partner will prefer long-term capital gain over ordinary gain and an ordinary loss over a capital loss, whether long term or short term. However, Congress does not permit the partners to effectively shift the character of the income, gain, or loss among the partners when making a distribution.

Example: Jack and Jill were equal partners in the Hill Partnership. The partnership owned the following assets, all of which were acquired by the partnership:

Asset	Adjusted Basis	Fair Market Value
Cash	$10,000	$10,000
Inventory	20,000	60,000
Blackacre	10,000	50,000

The partnership purchased Blackacre five years ago and holds it for investment purposes. If the partnership sold the inventory and the land, it would

---

2. Code Sec. 733(1).
3. Code Sec. 731(a)(1).
4. Code Secs. 731(a); 733(2). The partnership does not recognize any gain or loss on the distribution. Code Sec. 731(b); Treas. Reg. §1.731-1(b).
5. Code Sec. 732.

have $40,000 of ordinary income and $40,000 of long-term capital gain. The gain would be allocated as follows:

	Jack	Jill
Ordinary income	$20,000	$20,000
Long-term capital gain	20,000	20,000
Total gain:	$40,000	$40,000

In the alternative, if it distributed the inventory to Jack and Blackacre to Jill and they both sold the property, they would each realize the following:

	Jack	Jill
Ordinary income	$40,000	$-0-
Long-term capital gain	-0-	40,000
Total gain:	$40,000	$40,000

While each partner still would be reporting a total of $40,000, Jack would have converted $20,000 of long-term capital gain into ordinary income, and Jill would have converted $20,000 of ordinary income into long-term capital gain. The Code does not allow the partners to shift the character of the income, gain, or loss in this way.

If the partnership does make a distribution to a partner from just one category of property, the Code restructures the transaction and treats the partner as having received a proportionate amount from each category.

Example: If the partnership distributed the inventory to Jack, the distribution would be a disproportionate distribution. He is receiving too much of the ordinary income property and not enough of the capital asset property.

Under Section 751(b), the transaction is restructured and Jack is treated as if he had received one-half of the ordinary income property and one-half of the long-term capital gain property.

While the rationale behind the need for restructuring the transaction is not difficult to understand, the mechanics of the restructuring are a bit daunting.

2. Steps to Restructure the Transaction

First, divide the assets into two categories. The first category contains unrealized receivables and substantially appreciated inventory.

Unrealized receivables. Unrealized receivables include, to the extent not previously included in income, any right to payment for services rendered. They also include the right to payment for goods delivered to the extent the proceeds would be treated as amounts received from the sale or exchange of property other than a capital asset. They also include any gain that would be characterized as ordinary income under the depreciation recapture provisions.[6]

---

6. Code Sec. 751(c).

Example: Collections Partnership holds only accounts receivable. If the partnership is a cash method taxpayer, the accounts receivable are unrealized receivables. In contrast, if the partnership is an accrual method taxpayer, the accounts receivable are not unrealized receivables.

Substantially appreciated inventory. Inventory includes those assets held for sale to customers and any items held by the partnership that are not characterized as a capital or hotchpot (Section 1231) item.[7] The inventory is substantially appreciated if the aggregate fair market value of the inventory exceeds 120 percent of the adjusted inside basis of the inventory.[8] If inventory was acquired for the principal purpose of causing the partnership's inventory to not be substantially appreciated, that inventory will be disregarded.[9]

If an item comes within the definition of both unrealized receivables and inventory items, it is considered in determining if the inventory is substantially appreciated. If the inventory is not substantially appreciated, and the asset meets the definition of unrealized receivables, it will continue to be considered an unrealized receivable.

Example: Developer Partnership is an accrual basis taxpayer with a balance sheet as follows:

Asset	Adj. Basis	FMV	Partners	Adj. Basis	Cap. Acct.
Cash	$3,000	$3,000	Arthur	$17,000	$20,000
Acct. Rec.	14,000	14,000	Brindle	17,000	20,000
Lots for sale	10,000	20,000		$34,000	$40,000
Land	7,000	3,000			
Total:	$34,000	$40,000			

The accounts receivable do not come within the definition of unrealized receivables. The lots held for sale and the accounts receivable both come within the definition of inventory.

The aggregate fair market value of the inventory is $34,000. The aggregate adjusted basis is $24,000. The inventory is substantially appreciated because the aggregate fair market value, $34,000, exceeds 120 percent of the adjusted inside basis of the inventory, $28,800 (120% of $24,000).

The second category contains all remaining assets, generally cash and capital and hotchpot (Section 1231) assets.

Step One: Luke, Mitzi, and Nalli were equal partners in Prop Partnership. The partnership's balance sheet appeared as follows:

---

7. Code Sec. 751(d).
8. Code Sec. 751(b)(3)(A).
9. Code Sec. 751(b)(3)(B).

Asset	Adj. Basis	FMV	Partner	AB	Cap. Acct.
Cash	$30,000	$30,000	Luke	$18,000	$30,000
Inventory	18,000	30,000	Mitzi	18,000	30,000
Stock	6,000	30,000	Nalli	18,000	30,000
Total:	$54,000	$90,000		$54,000	$90,000

The partnership distributes the inventory to Luke in complete liquidation of his interest.

The inventory is substantially appreciated because the fair market value, $30,000, exceeds 120 percent of the adjusted inside basis of the inventory, or $21,600.

The assets are divided into two categories:

Unrealized receivables/inventory	Other
Inventory	Cash
	Stock

Second, determine the recipient partner's interest in each asset, based on his ownership interest in the partnership before the distribution.

Step Two: Luke's interest in the partnership assets is as follows:

Unrealized receivables/inventory	Other
$10,000 Inventory	$10,000 Cash
	$10,000 Stock
Total: $10,000	$20,000

Third, determine the recipient partner's interest in each asset after the distribution based on his ownership interest in the partnership. Include his interest in the distributed property.

Step Three: Luke is no longer a partner in the partnership, so does not have an interest in its assets. But, the assets distributed to him are as follows:

Unrealized receivables/inventory	Other
$30,000 Inventory	$-0-
Total: $30,000	$-0-

Fourth, comparing the partner's interests before and after the distribution, determine the category and amount of which he now owns too little and the category and amount of which he now owns too much.

Step Four: Luke's interest in the partnership assets before distribution:

Unrealized receivables/inventory	Other
$10,000	$20,000

Luke's interest after distribution:

Unrealized receivables/inventory	Other
$30,000	$-0-
Net: $20,000	<$20,000>

He received $20,000 more than his share of the inventory and received $20,000 too little of the other property.

Fifth, take into consideration only the amount of the partnership assets the partner did not receive in a sufficient amount. Distribute those assets (in that amount) from the partnership to the partner. Use the same rules with respect to distributions of cash and property that generally apply to non-liquidating distributions. This step is sometimes referred to as a phantom distribution.

Practice Tip: The partners may provide for a phantom distribution from any of the assets in the class; the distribution does not need to be a proportionate amount of each asset. If the partners do not have an agreement regarding the allocation, the regulations provide a default rule that the phantom distribution will be prorata. [Treas. Reg. § 1.751-1(g)]

Step Five: Luke received $20,000 too little of the other property. Accordingly, the partnership distributes to him a prorata amount of each asset, or $10,000 of cash and $10,000 of stock.

Luke's $18,000 basis is reduced first by the $10,000 cash distribution to $8,000. It is then reduced by the basis in the stock. The distribution to him is 10,000/30,000 of the value of the property. The correlative basis is 1/3 x 6,000, or $2,000. Thus, his basis is reduced from $8,000 to $6,000.

Luke's capital account is reduced for the distributions, or from $30,000 to $10,000.

After the distribution of cash and stock, the balance sheet would appear as follows:

Asset	Adj. Basis	FMV	Partner	AB	Cap. Acct.
Cash	$20,000	$20,000	Luke	$6,000	$10,000
Inventory	18,000	30,000	Mitzi	18,000	30,000
Stock	4,000	20,000	Nalli	18,000	30,000
Total:	$42,000	$70,000		$42,000	$70,000

Sixth, the recipient partner sells the assets that were just distributed to him back to the partnership in exchange for a portion of the asset that was actually distributed to him. The general rules applicable to dispositions of property apply to the partner and the partnership. Thus, both parties recognize any gain or loss realized and take a cost basis in any asset purchased.

Step Six: Under the phantom distribution, the partnership distributed $10,000 of cash and stock with a basis of $2,000 and fair market value of $10,000 to Luke.

Luke sells these assets to the partnership in exchange for inventory. He sells the $10,000 of cash for $10,000 of inventory. He has no gain or loss on the disposition of the cash and his basis in the inventory is $10,000.

He sells the $10,000 of stock for $10,000 of inventory. He recognizes $8,000 of gain on the disposition ($10,000 amount realized, less $2,000 basis). His basis in the inventory is $10,000, giving him a combined basis in the purchased inventory of $20,000.

The partnership has sold $20,000 of inventory. It recognizes $8,000 of gain (amount realized of $20,000, less $12,000 basis). The gain is allocated equally between Mitzi and Nalli, increasing each of their bases by $4,000. The partnership has a cost basis in the stock of $10,000.

The balance sheet now appears as follows:

Asset	Adj. Basis	FMV	Partner	AB	Cap. Acct.
Cash	$30,000	$30,000	Luke	$6,000	$10,000
Inventory	6,000	10,000	Mitzi	22,000	30,000
Stock	14,000	30,000	Nalli	22,000	30,000
Total:	$50,000	$70,000		$50,000	$70,000

Seventh, considering the total amount distributed to the partner and the portion that was purchased by the partner in the previous step, determine the remaining amount that must be distributed to the partner. Use the same rules with respect to non-liquidating distributions of cash and property that generally apply to distributions.

Step Seven: As originally structured, the partnership distributed $30,000 of accounts receivable to Luke. Through the phantom distribution and sale, Luke purchased $20,000 of inventory from the partnership. Thus, he needs a distribution of $10,000 of inventory to end up with a total of $30,000 of inventory.

Luke's basis of $6,000 is reduced by the basis in the inventory, or reduced to zero. His capital account is reduced by $10,000 to zero. His basis in the $30,000 of inventory is $26,000.

The balance sheet would appear as follows:

Asset	Adj. Basis	FMV	Partner	AB	Cap. Acct.
Cash	$30,000	$30,000	Mitzi	$22,000	$30,000
Stock	14,000	30,000	Nalli	22,000	30,000
Total:	$44,000	$60,000		$44,000	$60,000

C. Application of Rules

Example: The balance sheet of Complex Partnership was as follows:

Asset	Adj.	FMV	Partner	Adj. Basis	Cap. Acct.
Cash	$36,000	$36,000	Anika	$18,000	$36,000
Acct. Rec.	-0-	36,000	Brandy	18,000	36,000
Stock	18,000	36,000	Cher	18,000	36,000
Total	$54,000	$108,000		$54,000	$108,000

The partnership distributed $18,000 of cash to Anika. After the distribution, she had a one-fifth interest in the partnership.

First, divide the assets into two categories. The first category contains unrealized receivables and substantially appreciated inventory. The second category contains all remaining assets, generally cash and capital and hotchpot (Section 1231) assets.

Unrealized receivables/inventory	Other
Accounts receivable	Cash
	Stock

Second, Anika's interest in the partnership assets before the distribution was as follows:

Unrealized receivables/inventory	Other
$12,000 Accounts receivable	$12,000 Cash
	$12,000 Stock
Total: $12,000	$24,000

Third, Anika's interest in the partnership assets after the distribution and the distributed property is as follows:

Unrealized receivables/inventory	Other
As a one-fifth partner:	
$7,200 accounts receivable	$3,600 cash
	$7,200 stock
Individually:	
$-0-	$18,000 cash
Total: $7,200	$28,800

Fourth, determine the category and amount in which Anika now owns too little and the category and amount in which she now owns too much.

Anika's interest in the partnership assets before distribution:

Unrealized receivables/inventory	Other
Total: $12,000	$24,000

Anika's interest after distribution:

Unrealized receivables/inventory	Other
Total: $7,200	$28,800
Net: <$4,800>	$4,800

She received $4,800 too little of the inventory and $4,800 too much of the other property.

Fifth, since Anika did not get enough of the accounts receivable to the extent of $4,800, the partnership distributes $4,800 of accounts receivable to her. Because they have a zero basis, they do not reduce her basis. Her capital account is reduced by $4,800, from $36,000 to $31,200. After the distribution, the balance sheet would appear as follows:

Asset	Adj.	FMV	Partner	Adj. Basis	Cap. Acct.
Cash	$36,000	$36,000	Anika	$18,000	$31,200
Acct. Rec.	-0-	31,200	Brandy	18,000	36,000
Stock	18,000	36,000	Cher	18,000	36,000
Total	$54,000	$103,200		$54,000	$103,200

Sixth, Anika sells the accounts receivable to the partnership in exchange for cash (the asset she actually received). She recognizes $4,800 of gain on the disposition (amount realized of $4,800, less adjusted basis of zero).

The partnership does not recognize any gain or loss on the disposition of the cash. It takes a cost basis of $4,800 in the accounts receivable. After the purchase of the accounts receivable, the balance sheet would appear as follows:

Asset	Adj.	FMV	Partner	Adj. Basis	Cap. Acct.
Cash	$31,200	$31,200	Anika	$18,000	$31,200
Acct. Rec.	4,800	36,000	Brandy	18,000	36,000
Stock	18,000	36,000	Cher	18,000	36,000
Total	$54,000	$103,200		$54,000	$103,200

Seventh, distribute Anika's remaining portion of the asset that was distributed to her. The original distribution was $18,000 of cash. She received $4,800 upon the sale of the accounts receivable. The difference, $13,200, is now distributed to her. Her basis is reduced for the cash distribution, from $18,000 to $4,800. Her capital account is reduced by $13,200, or from $31,200 to $18,000.

After the dust settles, Anika has $18,000 in cash and the partnership's balance sheet appears as follows:

Asset	Adj.	FMV	Partner	Adj. Basis	Cap. Acct.
Cash	$18,000	$18,000	Anika	$4,800	$18,000
Acct. Rec.	4,800	36,000	Brandy	18,000	36,000
Stock	18,000	36,000	Cher	18,000	36,000
Total	$40,800	$90,000		$40,800	$90,000

D. Problems

1. The balance sheet of the partnership was as follows:

Asset	Adj.	FMV	Partner	Adj. Basis	Cap. Acct.
Cash	$18,000	$18,000	Billy Jo	$9,000	$18,000
Acct. Rec.	-0-	9,000	Bobby Jo	9,000	18,000
Blueacre	9,000	27,000	Betty Jo	9,000	18,000
Total	$27,000	$54,000		$27,000	$54,000

The partnership distributed the accounts receivable to Billy Jo, reducing her ownership in the partnership from one-third to one-fifth.

(a) What are the consequences to Billy Jo and the partnership?

(b) Who should benefit from the basis increase in Blueacre?

(c) If the partnership owned Blackacre in addition to Blueacre:
   (1) Which property could be used in the phantom distribution?
   (2) Does it matter if Blackacre has depreciated in value? Would it make Blackacre a better asset to use in the phantom distribution?

---

2. Application:

(a) If the partners want to make a distribution from the partnership to a partner, what might you want to recommend?

(b) Will the partners provide for an allocation other than prorata in a phantom distribution? If yes, how would they do so?

(c) How difficult will it be for the accountant to compute the consequences of a disproportionate distribution?

Chapter 26

Mixing Bowl Transaction— Distribution of Previously Contributed Property

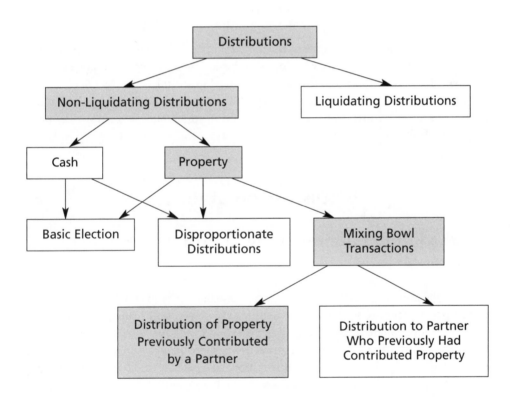

Read:

Code Section 704(c)(1)(B), (c)(2).
Treas. Reg. § 1.704-4(a)(1)-(3), -4(a)(5) Ex. 1, -4(b), -4(d)(4), -4(e)(1), -4(e)(2), -4(f)(1).

A. Background

Recall that a distribution of property from a partnership to a partner generally is not a taxable event to the partner or the partnership.[1] In general, the partner takes the property with the partnership's inside basis, a transferred basis. And, his outside basis is reduced by the basis of the property distributed.[2] Thus, just as the gain or loss inherent in property was preserved in the property upon contribution by a partner to the partnership, it also is preserved upon distribution of the property from the partnership to a partner.

In addition, recall that, prior to contribution of property to a partnership, the partner is the owner of the property. Thus, any gain or loss that arises in the property prior to contribution belongs to the partner individually and must be allocated to, and reported by, the contributing partner. It cannot be shifted to the other partners.[3] The amount of built-in gain or loss is the difference between the fair market value, or book value, and the adjusted tax basis of the property.[4]

After contribution of the property, the partnership is the owner of the property. Any gain or loss that arises after contribution must be allocated among and reported by the partners. The amount of post-contribution gain or loss is measured by the difference between the selling price and the property's fair market, or book, value. Unlike pre-contribution gain or loss, post-contribution gain or loss is allocated among the partners and reflected in the partners' capital accounts.

B. Discussion of Rules

1. Distribution of Previously Contributed Property— General Rule

While the general rule is that there are no tax consequences when property is distributed from a partnership to a partner, there are three exceptions to the rule. The first exception, disproportionate distributions, was discussed in the previous chapter. The second exception, distributions of property previously contributed by a partner, is discussed in this chapter. The third exception, distributions to a partner who had previously contributed appreciated property, is discussed in the following chapter.

Under the second exception, there is a tax consequence when:[5]

- Property is distributed from a partnership to a partner;
- The property was previously contributed by a different partner to the partnership with a built-in gain or loss; and

---

1. Code Sec. 731(a), (b).
2. Code Secs. 731(a); 732(a)(1); 733(2).
3. Code Sec. 704(c)(1)(A); Treas. Reg. § 1.704-3(a)(1).
4. Treas. Reg. § 1.704-3(a)(3)(ii).
5. Code Sec. 704(c)(1)(B).

- The property is distributed within seven years from the time of contribution.

Note that, in the absence of such a rule, a partner could escape the built-in gain or loss in contributed property by having the partnership distribute the property, rather than sell the property. In addition, because of the basis allocation rules of Section 732, the built-in gain or loss would be shifted to the recipient partner.

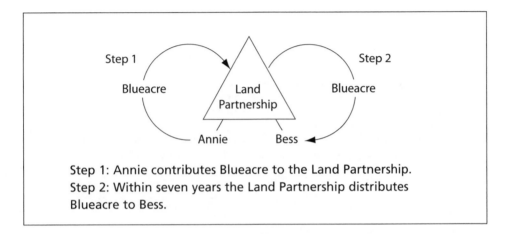

Step 1: Annie contributes Blueacre to the Land Partnership.
Step 2: Within seven years the Land Partnership distributes Blueacre to Bess.

When property previously contributed by a partner with built-in gain or loss is subsequently distributed to another partner, several tax events occur. First, the contributing partner must recognize the built-in gain or loss on the property, determined as if the property had been sold for its fair market value as of the date of distribution. The character of the gain or loss is the same character that the partnership would have recognized upon sale of the property. The contributing partner's basis is adjusted by the amount of gain or loss.[6]

Next, the partnership's inside basis in the property is increased or decreased to reflect the gain or loss recognized by the contributing partner.[7] Then the property is distributed by the partnership to the partner.

The regulations contain an anti-abuse provision that allows the Internal Revenue Service to apply the rules in a manner that is consistent with the intent of the statute. The Service can restructure a transaction so that it is consistent with the applicable tax treatment.[8]

Steps When Previously Contributed Property Is Distributed within Seven Years of Contribution:

Step 1:   Determine the amount of built-in gain or loss that would have been generated if the property had been sold for its fair market value as of the date of distribution. Allocate that gain or loss to the

---

6. Code Secs. 704(c)(1)(B); 705(a)(1)(A), (a)(2)(A); Treas. Reg. § 1.704-4(a)(1)-(3), -4(b)(1), -4(e)(1).

7. Code Sec. 704(c)(1)(B)(iii); Treas. Reg. § 1.704-4(e)(2).

8. Treas. Reg. § 1.704-4(f).

contributing partner. Determine the character of the gain or loss as if the partnership had sold the property.

Step 2: Adjust the contributing partner's basis for the amount of gain or loss.

Step 3: Adjust the partnership's inside basis in the property by the amount of gain or loss recognized by the contributing partner.

Step 4: Distribute the property to the partner using the general rules applicable to distributions of property.

Practice Tip: Section 704(c) may apply and the built-in gain or loss be allocated to a partner who contributed property to a partnership if:
- The partnership sells property that had been contributed to the partnership with a built-in gain or loss; or
- The partnership distributes property that had been contributed by a partner to the partnership to another partner within seven years from the date of contribution.

2. Exception to the General Rule

The requirement that gain or loss be recognized does not apply in three situations. First, if the property is distributed to the same partner who originally contributed the property, no gain or loss is required to be recognized. Since the partner is receiving the property back, there is no opportunity for shifting of the built-in gain or loss. Accordingly, there is no need to recognize the built-in gain or loss upon distribution.[9]

Second, if:

- The partner who contributed the property also receives a distribution of property;
- The distributed property is like-kind; and
- The distribution occurs within 180 days of the distribution to the non-contributing partner or the due date of the contributing partner's tax return for the taxable year of the distribution,

then, the transaction is treated as a like-kind exchange. The contributing partner may reduce the amount of gain or loss that would be recognized upon the deemed sale of the contributed property by the amount of gain or loss in the like-kind property. In sum, to the extent the transaction would have qualified as a like-kind exchange if a third party had been used as an intermediary, the transaction should continue to qualify.[10]

Third, if the partner is a successor to the contributing partner and the property had been contributed with a built-in loss, the successor partner is not entitled to the built-

---

9. Code Sec. 704(c)(1)(B). The same rule applies if the property is distributed to the contributing partner's successor-in-interest.

10. Treas. Reg. § 1.704-4(d)(3).

in loss. Rather, the property is deemed to have been contributed to the partnership with a basis equal to its fair market value.[11]

C. Application of Rules

Example 1. Annie contributed Greenacre to the Land Partnership in exchange for an equal general partnership interest. Greenacre had a basis of $5,000 and fair market value of $15,000. Bess contributed $15,000 of cash in exchange for an equal general partnership interest. Land Partnership held the property for investment purposes.

Two years later, Land Partnership distributed Greenacre to Bess. At the time of distribution its fair market value was still $15,000. Annie's basis was $5,000. Bess's basis was $15,000 and her capital account was $15,000.

Annie must recognize the built-in gain on the property, determined as if the property had been sold for its fair market value as of the date of distribution. If the property was sold at the date of distribution for its fair market value, the partnership would have recognized $10,000 of gain (fair market value of $15,000, less basis of $5,000). Because the partnership held the property for investment purposes, the gain is characterized as long-term capital gain. Annie's basis is increased by $10,000, from $5,000 to $15,000.

The partnership's basis in Greenacre is increased by $10,000, from $5,000 to $15,000. Then the property is distributed by the partnership to Bess. Upon distribution of the property, her basis is reduced by $15,000, from $15,000 to zero, and her basis in Greenacre is $15,000. Bess's capital account is reduced by $15,000, from $15,000 to zero.

Example 2. Connie contributed Whiteacre to the Management Partnership in exchange for an equal general partnership interest. Whiteacre had a basis of $5,000 and fair market value of $15,000. Doug contributed $15,000 of cash in exchange for an equal general partnership interest. Management Partnership used the traditional method for making Section 704(c) allocations. It held the property for investment purposes.

Two years later, Management Partnership distributed Whiteacre to Doug. At the time of distribution, its fair market value was $13,000. Connie's basis was $5,000. Doug's basis was $15,000 and his capital account was $15,000.

Connie must recognize the built-in gain on the property, determined as if the property had been sold for its fair market value as of the date of distribution. If the property was sold at the date of distribution for its fair market value, the partnership would have recognized $8,000 of gain (fair market value of $13,000, less basis of $5,000). All of this gain represents the built-in gain at the time Connie contributed the property to the partnership, as limited by the ceiling rule. Because the partnership held the property for investment purposes, the gain is characterized as long-term capital gain. Connie's basis is increased by $8,000, from $5,000 to $13,000.

---

11. Code Sec. 704(c)(1)(C).

The partnership's basis in Whiteacre is increased by $8,000, from $5,000 to $13,000. Then the property is distributed by the partnership to Doug. Upon distribution of the property, his basis is reduced by $13,000, from $15,000 to $2,000, and his basis in Whiteacre is $13,000. Doug's capital account is reduced by $13,000, from $15,000 to $2,000.

Example 3. Eunice was a partner in Investment Partnership. She had contributed Yellowacre with a basis of $10,000 and fair market value of $20,000 in exchange for an equal general partnership interest.

Two years later, the value of Yellowacre was still $20,000. The partnership distributed Orangeacre to Eunice. At the time of distribution, it had a basis of $10,000 and fair market value of $20,000. In addition, the partnership distributed Yellowacre to Freddy, a partner in the Investment Partnership. At the time of the distributions, Eunice's basis was $10,000 and Freddy's basis was $20,000.

Generally, Eunice must recognize the built-in gain on the property, determined as if the property had been sold for its fair market value as of the date of distribution. If the property was sold at the date of distribution for its fair market value, the partnership would have recognized $10,000 of gain (fair market value of $20,000, less basis of $10,000). However, the gain is reduced by the amount of the built-in gain of Orangeacre in the hands of Eunice. Because there is $10,000 of built-in gain in Orangeacre, she is not required to recognize any gain.

Upon distribution of Orangeacre to Eunice, she reduces her basis by $10,000, from $10,000 to zero, and her basis in Orangeacre is $10,000. Upon distribution of Yellowacre, Freddy reduces his basis by $10,000, from $20,000 to $10,000, and his basis in Yellowacre is $10,000.

D. Problems

1. Jeb contributed Gainacre to Investment Partnership in exchange for a one-third general partnership interest. At the time of contribution, Gainacre had a basis of $5,000 and fair market value of $20,000. Investment Partnership only holds property for investment purposes. For purposes of Section 704(c), the partnership uses the traditional method.

Two years later, Investment Partnership distributed Gainacre to Kayla, a partner in the partnership. At the time of distribution, Jeb's basis was $30,000. Kayla's basis was $20,000 and her capital account was $50,000. What are the tax consequences to the partnership and to Jeb under the following alternatives:

(a) At the time of the distribution, its fair market value was still $20,000.

(b) At the time of the distribution, its fair market value was $22,000.

(c) At the time of the distribution, its fair market value was $15,000.

(d) At the time of the distribution, its fair market value was $3,000.

2. Application:

(a) How would you explain to a partner who has not received any property or cash from the partnership that he has a tax liability because property was distributed to one of his partners?

(b) Do you think it is a good idea to use a partnership to carry out a like-kind exchange? Why or why not? What might be a better option?

Chapter 27

Mixing Bowl Transaction— Distribution of Other Property to Partner Who Contributed Appreciated Property

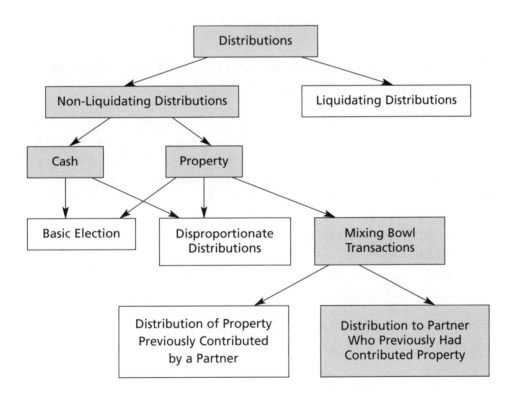

Read:

Code Section 737.
Treas. Reg. §§ 1.737-1(a), -1(b), -1(c)(1), -1(d); 1.737-3(a), -3(b), -3(c)(1); 1.737-4(a).

A. Background

Recall that a distribution of property from a partnership to a partner generally is not a taxable event to the partner or the partnership.[1] In general, the partner takes the property with the partnership's inside basis, a transferred basis. And, his outside basis is reduced by the basis of the property distributed.[2] Thus, just as the gain or loss inherent in property was preserved in the property upon contribution by a partner to the partnership, it also is preserved upon distribution of the property from the partnership to a partner.

If a partner who is not acting in his capacity as a partner transfers property to a partnership, the transaction is treated as a sale. The partner must recognize gain or loss on disposition of the property. The partnership will take a cost basis in the property.

B. Discussion of Rules

1. Distribution of Other Property to Partner Who Had Contributed Property — General Rule

While the general rule is that there are no tax consequences when property is distributed from a partnership to a partner, there are three exceptions to the rule. The first exception, disproportionate distributions, was discussed in the Chapter 25. The second exception, distributions of property previously contributed by a partner, was discussed in the previous chapter. The third exception, distributions to a partner who had previously contributed appreciated property, is discussed in this chapter.

Under the third exception, there is a tax consequence on the distribution of property to a partner when:[3]

- Property was previously contributed by the distributee partner to the partnership with a built-in gain;
- Other property (not including money) is distributed by the partnership to the partner within seven years of the contribution; and
- The partnership retains the property contributed by the partner.

Note that, in the absence of such a rule, a partner could dispose of property with a built-in gain in exchange for other property but not recognize gain on the disposition.

---

1. Code Sec. 731(a), (b).
2. Code Secs. 731(a); 732(a)(1); 733(2).
3. Code Sec. 737.

Practice Tip: Built-in gain will be allocated to a partner who contributed property to a partnership if:
- The partnership distributes other property to the partner within seven years from the date of contribution; or
- The partner is not acting in his capacity as a partner in transferring the property to the partnership.

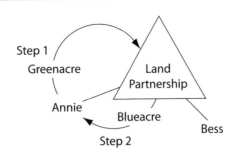

Step 1: Annie contributes Greenacre to the Land Partnership.
Step 2: Within seven years the partnership distributes Blueacre to Annie.

When a partner who previously contributed property with built-in gain to a partnership within seven years receives a distribution of other property, several tax events occur. (The consequences of the distribution are considered after the consequences of any cash distributions.)

First, the contributing partner must recognize gain in an amount that is the lesser of two amounts. The first amount is the fair market value of the distributed property, reduced by the partner's outside basis immediately before the distribution. The second amount is the amount of the net precontribution gain of the partner. Net precontribution gain is the net gain the distributee partner would have recognized under Section 704(c) if all the property contributed by that partner within seven years of the current distribution had been distributed to another partner at the time of the distribution to the contributing partner. The character of the gain is the same character that the partnership would have recognized upon sale of the contributed property.[4]

Next, the partner's basis is increased by the amount of gain.[5]

Finally, the partnership's inside basis in the contributed property is increased to reflect the gain recognized by the partner.[6] The property is distributed by the partnership to the partner.

---

4. Code Sec. 737(a), (b).
5. Code Sec. 737(c)(1).
6. Code Sec. 737(c)(2).

The regulations contain an anti-abuse provision that allows the Internal Revenue Service to apply the rules in a manner that is consistent with the intent of the statute. The Service can restructure a transaction so that it is consistent with the applicable tax treatment.[7]

Practice Tip: Both Section 704(c)(1)(B) and Section 737 may apply to different partners upon the distribution of a single piece of property.

Angie contributed Yellowacre and Bart contributed stock to a partnership. Both the land and the stock had a built-in gain at the time of contribution.

Three years later, the partnership distributed Yellowacre to Bart. Under Section 704(c)(1)(B) Angie must recognize gain and under Section 737 Bart must recognize gain.

Steps When a Partner Who Previously Contributed Property Is Distributed Property Within Seven Years of Contribution:

Step 1: First, temporarily reduce the fair market value of the distributed property (not including cash) by the partner's outside basis. The partner's basis is that basis immediately before the distribution, reduced, but not below zero, by any cash distributed.

Step 2: Second, compute the amount of the net precontribution gain of the partner. Net precontribution gain is the net gain the distributee partner would have recognized under Section 704(c) if all the property contributed by that partner within seven years of the current distribution had been distributed to another partner at the time of the distribution to the contributing partner.

Step 3: Determine which amount is the lesser amount, the amount determined under Step 1 or the amount determined under Step 2. The contributing partner must recognize gain equal to the lesser amount. The character of the gain is the same character that the partnership would have recognized upon sale of the contributed property.

Step 4: The partner's basis is increased by the amount of gain determined in Step 3.

Step 5: The partnership's inside basis in the contributed property is increased to reflect the gain recognized by the partner.

Step 6: Distribute the property to the partner using the general rules applicable to the distribution of property.

---

7. Treas. Reg. § 1.737-4.

2. Exception to the General Rule

In general, if the property distributed was previously contributed by that partner, that property is not taken into consideration in determining the amount of gain the partner must recognize.[8]

3. Pre-Emption by Other Provisions

If the disguised sales rules (of Section 707(a)(2)(B)) or the like-kind exchange treatment (of Section 704(c)(2)) also apply to the transaction, those Sections take precedence.[9] In addition, the provisions of Section 737 do not apply if Section 751(b), applicable to disproportionate distributions, applies.[10]

4. Distribution of Marketable Securities Treated as Distribution of Cash

Marketable securities include financial instruments (*e.g.*, stock and bonds) and foreign currency that are actively traded. They include interests in a common trust fund, a mutual fund, and any financial instrument convertible into money or marketable securities.[11] Because the securities are easy to value and are liquid, to the extent of the fair market value of the security on the date of distribution, the distribution is treated as a distribution of cash.[12]

A distribution of marketable securities is not treated like a distribution of cash if:[13]

- The security was contributed to the partnership by the distributee partner; or
- The partnership is an investment partnership and the partner contributed only money and/or securities.

C. Application of Rules

Example 1. Derris and Rife formed an equal partnership. Derris contributed Greenacre, which had a basis of $10,000 and fair market value of $15,000. Rife contributed $15,000 of cash. Three years later, the partnership used the $15,000 cash to purchase Blueacre.

---

8. Code Sec. 737(d)(1).
9. Treas. Reg. § 1.704-3(a)(5).
10. Code Sec. 737(d)(2).
11. Code Sec. 731(c)(2).
12. Code Sec. 731(c)(1). The amount of the distribution of marketable securities that is treated as a distribution of cash may be reduced in some circumstances. See Code Sec. 731(c)(3)(B).
13. Code Sec. 731(c)(3)(A).

The following year, when the fair market value of Blueacre was still $15,000, the partnership distributed it to Derris. At the time of the distribution Derris's basis was $5,000, and his capital account was $20,000.

Derris had previously contributed property with built-in gain, then received a distribution of other property within seven years. Accordingly, he must recognize gain in an amount that is the lesser of two amounts. The first amount is the fair market value of the distributed property, $15,000, reduced by his basis immediately before the distribution, $5,000, or $10,000. The second amount is the amount of the net precontribution gain. The amount of net precontribution gain in Greenacre is $5,000. The lesser of the two amounts is the second amount, $5,000.

Derris's basis is increased by the amount of the gain. Accordingly, his basis is increased by $5,000, from $5,000 to $10,000. Then, his basis is reduced to reflect the distribution of the property. Derris's basis is reduced from $10,000 to zero and he takes a $10,000 basis in Blueacre. His capital account is reduced by $15,000, or from $20,000 to $5,000.

The partnership's basis in Greenacre is increased to reflect the gain recognized by Derris, or increased by $5,000, from $10,000 to $15,000.

Example 2. Pointjack and Rhiener formed an equal partnership. Pointjack contributed Blackacre, which had a basis of $10,000 and fair market value of $15,000. Rhiener contributed $15,000 of cash. Three years later, the partnership used the $15,000 cash to purchase Whiteacre.

The following year, when the fair market value of Whiteacre was still $15,000, the partnership distributed it to Pointjack. At the time of the distribution Pointjack's basis was $12,000, and his capital account was $20,000.

Pointjack had previously contributed property with built-in gain, then received a distribution of other property within seven years. Accordingly, he must recognize gain in an amount that is the lesser of two amounts. The first amount is the fair market value of the distributed property, $15,000, reduced by his basis immediately before the distribution, $12,000, or $3,000. The second amount is the amount of the net precontribution gain. The amount of net precontribution gain in Blackacre is $5,000. The lesser of the two amounts is the first amount, $3,000.

Pointjack's basis is increased by the amount of the gain. Accordingly, his basis is increased by $3,000, from $12,000 to $15,000. Then, his basis is decreased to reflect distribution of the property. Pointjack's basis is reduced from $15,000 to zero and he takes a $15,000 basis in Whiteacre. His capital account is reduced by $15,000, from $20,000 to $5,000.

The partnership's basis in Blackacre is increased to reflect the gain recognized by Pointjack, or increased by $3,000, from $10,000 to $13,000.

Example 3. Windsor and Hoover formed an equal partnership. Windsor contributed Lossacre, which had a basis of $20,000 and fair market value of $15,000. Hoover contributed $15,000 of cash. Three years later, the partnership used the $15,000 cash to purchase Gainacre.

The following year, when the fair market value of Gainacre was still $15,000, the partnership distributed it to Windsor. At the time of the distribution Windsor's basis was $5,000, and his capital account was $20,000.

Because the property Windsor had previously contributed (Lossacre) did not have a built-in gain, Section 737 does not apply. Windsor's basis is reduced from $5,000 to zero and he takes a $5,000 basis in Gaineacre. His capital account is reduced by $15,000, or from $20,000 to $5,000.

Example 4. Rowdy and Picasso formed an equal partnership. Rowdy contributed Yellowacre, which had a basis of $10,000 and fair market value of $15,000. Picasso contributed Pinkacre, which had a basis of $8,000 and a fair market value of $15,000.

Three years later, when the fair market value of Pinkacre was still $15,000, the partnership distributed it to Rowdy. At the time of the distribution Rowdy's basis was $5,000 and his capital account was $20,000; Picasso's basis was $7,000.

Picasso must recognize the built-in gain on Pinkacre. If the property was sold at the date of distribution for its fair market value, the partnership would have recognized $7,000 of gain (fair market value of $15,000, less basis of $8,000). All of this gain represents the built-in gain at the time Picasso contributed Piinkacre to the partnership. Picasso's basis is increased by $7,000, from $7,000 to $14,000. The partnership's basis in Pinkacre is increased by $7,000, from $8,000 to $15,000.

Rowdy had previously contributed property with built-in gain, then received a distribution of other property within seven years. Accordingly, he must recognize gain in an amount that is the lesser of two amounts. The first amount is the fair market value of the distributed property, $15,000, reduced by his basis immediately before the distribution, $5,000, or $10,000. The second amount is the amount of the net precontribution gain. The amount of net precontribution gain in Yellowacre is $5,000. The lesser of the two amounts is the second amount, $5,000.

Rowdy's basis is increased by the amount of the gain. Accordingly, his basis is increased by $5,000, from $5,000 to $10,000. The partnership's basis in Yellowacre is increased to reflect the gain recognized by Rowdy, or increased by $5,000, from $10,000 to $15,000.

Pinkacre is then distributed by the partnership to Rowdy. Rowdy's basis is reduced to zero and he takes a $10,000 basis in Pinkeacre. His capital account is reduced by $15,000, or from $20,000 to $5,000.

D. Problems

1. Sonny and Cher formed an equal partnership. Sonny contributed Gainacre, which had a basis of $3,000 and fair market value of $20,000. Cher contributed $20,000 of cash. Three years later, the partnership used the $20,000 cash to purchase Lotsacre.

The following year, when the fair market value of Lotsacre was still $20,000, the partnership distributed it to Sonny. At the time of the distribution Sonny's basis was $5,000 and his capital account was $50,000. What are the tax consequences of the distribution to Sonny and the partnership?

2. Oscar and Felix formed an equal partnership. Oscar contributed Backacre, which had a basis of $15,000 and fair market value of $20,000. Felix contributed $20,000 of cash. Three years later, the partnership used the $20,000 cash to purchase Frontacre.

The following year, when the fair market value of Frontacre was still $20,000, the partnership distributed it to Oscar. At the time of the distribution Oscar's basis was $5,000 and his capital account was $50,000. What are the tax consequences of the distribution to Oscar and the partnership?

3. Curley and Moe formed an equal partnership. Curley contributed Sideacre, which had a basis of $25,000 and fair market value of $20,000. Moe contributed $20,000 of cash. Three years later, the partnership used the $20,000 cash to purchase Pastacre.

The following year, when the fair market value of Pastacre was still $20,000, the partnership distributed it to Curley. At the time of the distribution Curley's basis was $25,000 and his capital account was $50,000. What are the tax consequences of the distribution to Curley and the partnership?

4. Mary Ellen and Jim Bob formed an equal partnership. Mary Ellen contributed City-acre, which had a basis of $15,000 and fair market value of $20,000. Jim Bob contributed stock, which had a basis of $10,000 and fair market value of $20,000.

Three years later, when the fair market value of the stock was still $20,000, the partnership distributed it to Mary Ellen. At the time of the distribution Mary Ellen's basis was $5,000 and her capital account was $50,000 and Jim Bob's basis was $20,000. What are the tax consequences of the distribution to Mary Ellen, Jim Bob, and the partnership?

5. Application:

(a) How would you explain to a partner who contributed property to a partnership, anticipating tax-free treatment, that, some years later, he must recognize some or all of the gain realized on the transfer?

(b) What strategies will you employ when determining the tax consequences of a mixing bowl transaction that involves both Section 704(c) and Section 737?

E. Advanced Problems — Looking Forward

Without conducting any research, consider the following question:

Should the analysis change if the distribution happens within one or two years of the contribution of appreciated property?

Chapter 28

Liquidating Distributions

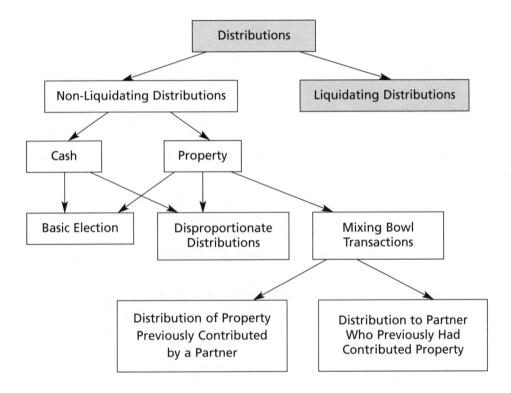

Read:

Code Section 736.
Treas. Reg. § 1.736-1.

A. Background

Under the Uniform Partnership Act, in general, a partner's leaving the partnership may cause the partnership to dissolve and terminate.[1] Under the Revised Uniform Partner-

---

1. UPA § 29-31.

ship Act (RUPA), a partner's leaving the partnership is referred to as dissociation.[2] A partner has the power to dissociate from a partnership at any time. However, the partner does not always have the right to dissociate. In some situations, a partner's dissociation is considered wrongful and he will be liable for damages caused by his departure.[3]

Practice Tip: A partnership may intend to be in existence for:
- A term of years;
- For the length of time necessary to complete a specific undertaking; or
- Until the partners decide to discontinue operating as a partnership (at-will).

Under the RUPA, a partner's dissociation from a partnership may cause the partnership to dissolve and terminate.[4] For example, a partner's voluntarily leaving an at-will partnership will cause a dissolution of the partnership.[5]

Practice Alert: An event that causes dissolution of a partnership under state law may not be considered dissolution of a partnership for federal tax purposes. [See Code Sec. 708(b) and Chapter 32.]

B. Discussion of Rules

A partner can retire from the partnership either by liquidating his interest[6] or retiring by ceasing to be a partner under state law.[7] The tax consequences of the payments the partner receives from the partnership will depend on how they are characterized. All payments to a retiring partner, or a deceased partner's successor in interest, will fall into one of two categories, either a payment for the partner's interest in partnership property (Section 736(b)) or other payments (Section 736(a)).

Definition: Liquidation is the termination of a partner's entire interest in a partnership by means of a distribution, or series of distributions, from the partnership to the partner.[8]

---

2. RUPA § 601.
3. RUPA § 602.
4. RUPA § 801.
5. RUPA § 801(1).
6. Code Sec. 761(d); Treas. Reg. 1.761-1(d).
7. Treas. Reg. 1.736-1(a)(1)(ii).
8. Code Sec. 761(d).

> **Practice Note:** To the extent a retiring partner's interest in the partnership's assets is determined in an arm's-length agreement, the value generally is accepted as correct. [Treas. Reg. 1.736-1(b)(1)]

1. Payments for Partner's Interest in Partnership Property (Section 736(b))

a. General Rule

Payments covered. Subject to certain exclusions, Section 736(b) covers payments made to a partner for his interest in partnership property.

Tax Treatment. To the extent payments are made for a partner's interest in partnership property, the general rules for non-liquidating distributions (discussed in Chapters 23 through 27) are applied.[9] For example:

- A partner does not recognize gain or loss when he receives a distribution of cash from a partnership,[10] except to the extent the cash distributed exceeds the partner's outside basis.[11] His outside basis is reduced by the amount of cash distributed.[12]
- A partner does not recognize gain or loss when he receives a distribution of property from a partnership. The partner's outside basis is reduced by the basis of the asset distributed.[13] To the extent the basis in the property is larger than the partner's outside basis, the basis in the property is reduced to reflect the partner's outside basis, then the asset is distributed.[14] To the extent the basis in the property is less than the partner's outside basis, the basis in the property is increased, then the asset is distributed.[15]
- Ignoring unrealized receivables and unstated goodwill for purposes of defining unrealized receivables, if the distribution constitutes a disproportionate distribution under Section 751(b), the transaction will be restructured.
- If the partnership has made a Section 754 election, the basis in partnership assets will be adjusted as provided under Section 734(b).
- To the extent allowed, a retiring partner may tack the partnership's holding period in distributed assets.[16]

---

9. Code Sec. 736(b).
10. Code Sec. 731(a). The partnership does not recognize any gain or loss on the distribution. Code Sec. 731(b); Treas. Reg. § 1.731-1(b).
11. Code Sec. 731(a)(1).
12. Code Sec. 733(1).
13. Code Sec. 731(a), 733(2). The partnership does not recognize any gain or loss on the distribution. Code Sec. 731(b); Treas. Reg. § 1.731-1(b).
14. Code Sec. 732(b), (c)(1)(A), (c)(1).
15. Code Sec. 732(b), (c)(1)(B), (c)(2).
16. Code Sec. 735(b).

- If unrealized receivables or inventory are distributed, the character as ordinary is preserved (indefinitely for unrealized receivables and five years for inventory).[17]

Timing. Payments are taken into account in the year made by the partnership.[18] Under the rules related to non-liquidating distributions,[19] the partner's basis is reduced by each distribution.[20] The partner recognizes income only when a cash distribution exceeds his basis.[21] A partner who is receiving fixed payments may elect to effectively report a pro rata portion of the gain or loss each time he receives a payment.[22] If there is a loss and the property distributed consists only of cash, unrealized receivables, and inventory items, the partner will recognize the loss in the year the final payment has been made.[23]

b. Exception to General Rule

If the payment is:

- To a general partner;
- For his interest in partnership property;
- The partnership is a service partnership; and
- The payment is for—[24]
  - Unrealized receivables, or
  - Partnership goodwill when the partnership agreement does not expressly provide for such payment (sometimes called unstated goodwill)

then, the payment is not covered by Section 736(b).

Service partnership. A service partnership is one in which capital is not a material income producing factor. In turn, capital is not a material income producing factor if substantially all of the gross income of the business is from fees, commissions, or other compensation for personal services.[25] Accordingly, for this purpose, the extent to which the partnership owns capital is irrelevant. Rather, the source of the income is important.

Example: Five doctors formed Medical Partnership. The partnership acquired a large medical complex from which to run the partnership business. Even though the partnership has a large capital investment, its income is primarily from compensation for the services of its doctors. Accordingly, capital is not a material income producing factor.

Unrealized receivables. For purposes of this provision, unrealized receivables do not include recapture gain.[26]

---

17. Code Sec. 735(a).
18. Treas. Reg. 1.736-1(a)(5).
19. See Code Secs. 731; 732.
20. Code Secs. 731; 732; 733.
21. See Code Sec. 731(a)(1).
22. Treas. Reg. 1.736-1(b)(6).
23. Treas. Reg. 1.731-1(a)(2).
24. Code Sec. 736(a), (b)(2), (b)(3).
25. Treas. Reg. 1.704-1(e)(1)(iv).
26. Code Sec. 751(c).

Definition: Unrealized receivables include, to the extent not previously in-cluded in income, any right to payment for services rendered; they also in-clude the right to payment for goods delivered to the extent the proceeds would be treated as amounts received from the sale or exchange of property other than a capital asset.[27]

Goodwill. The partners can provide for the payment of goodwill in the partnership agreement (stated goodwill). Or, they can include it in any modifications to the agreement, whether written or oral, made in a year prior to the date of filing the income tax return for the year of the liquidation.[28] To be respected, the payments must be reasonable.[29]

2. Other Payments (Section 736(a))

Payments covered. Two types of payments fall under Section 736(a). First, it in-cludes those amounts excepted from coverage under Section 736(b). Thus, if the pay-ment is:

- To a general partner;
- For his interest in partnership property;
- The partnership is a service partnership; and
- The payment is for—[30]
  - Unrealized receivables, or
  - Unstated goodwill,

then, the payment is covered by Section 736(a).

To the extent of the partner's share of the partnership's inside basis in unrealized re-ceivables, the payment is treated as a distribution (*i.e.*, covered by Section 736(b)). Only the amount in excess of the partner's share of inside basis is covered by Section 736(a).[31]

Similarly, if the partnership agreement does not provide a payment for goodwill, to the extent of the partner's share of the partnership's inside basis in goodwill, the pay-ment is treated as a distribution (*i.e.*, covered by Section 736(b)). Only the amount in excess of the partner's share of inside basis is covered by Section 736(a).[32]

Second, a payment that is not for a partner's interest in the partnership's property (sometimes called a premium payment) is covered by Section 736(a).[33]

Tax Treatment. Payments that come within Section 736(a) are treated as either a distributive share of profits or a guaranteed payment.[34] If the amount of the payment depends on the income of the partnership, the payment is treated as a distributive

---

27. Code Sec. 751(c).
28. Code Sec. 761(c); Treas. Reg. 1.761-1(c).
29. Treas. Reg. 1.736-1(b)(1), -1(b)(3).
30. Code Sec. 736(a), (b)(2), (b)(3).
31. Treas. Reg. 1.736-1(b)(2).
32. Code Sec. 736(b)(2)(B), (b)(3); Treas. Reg. 1.736-1(b)(3).
33. Treas. Reg. 1.736-1(a)(3). It is irrelevant whether the partnership is a service partnership.
34. Treas. Reg. 1.736-1(a)(3).

share.[35] If the payment does not depend on the income of the partnership, it is treated as a guaranteed payment.[36] If the partnership uses its own assets to make the payment, it has disposed of property and must recognize any gain or loss realized.

Timing. A partner includes a distributive share in income for his taxable year within which the partnership's taxable year ends.[37] The partner includes a guaranteed payment in income in the year the partnership is entitled to claim a deduction.[38]

Practice Alert: If a general partner is retiring from a service partnership, the parties can plan for whether the payment for goodwill will be treated as a non-liquidating distribution on one hand or a distributive share or guaranteed payment on the other.

If the partnership agreement specifically provides that the partner will be paid for goodwill, it will be treated as a non-liquidating distribution.

If the partnership agreement does not provide for such payment, and makes the payment dependent on the income of the partnership, it will be treated as a distributive share. If the payment does not depend on the income of the partnership, it will be treated as a guaranteed payment.

---

3. Allocation of Installment Payments

If the partner receives payments in installments, each installment must be allocated between the two possible types of payments (*i.e.*, between those covered by Section 736(a) and those covered by Section 736(b)). If the payments are of a fixed amount and paid over a fixed amount of time, the portion treated as a non-liquidating distribution (Section 736(b) payments) is the yearly installment payment, multiplied by the fixed payments related to payments for the partner's interest in the partnership property (Section 736(b) payments), divided by the total of all fixed payments. The remainder of each payment is for items that are treated as a distributive share of income or guaranteed payments under Section 736(a).[39]

Formulas for Fixed Payments:

Portion of payment = Yearly payment x <u>(Section 736(b) payment)</u>
allocable to Section 736(b)   Total payments

Portion of payment allocable to Section 736(a) = yearly payment – portion of payment allocable to Section 736(b).

---

35. Code Sec. 736(a)(1), (a)(2); Treas. Reg. 1.736-1(a)(3)(i).
36. Code Sec. 736(a)(1), (a)(2); Treas. Reg. 1.736-1(a)(3)(ii). Guaranteed payments are discussed in Chapter 30.
37. Treas. Reg. 1.736-1(a)(4), -1(a)(5).
38. Treas. Reg. 1.736-1(a)(4), -1(a)(5).
39. Treas. Reg. 1.736-1(b)(5)(i).

If the payments are contingent (not of a fixed amount), the payment is allocated first to payments for items that come under Section 736(b) (payments for the partner's interest in the partnership assets). Any remaining amount is treated as payments for items that come under Section 736(a).[40]

Alternatively, the parties may agree as to the allocation of the payments. Under such an agreement, the amount allocated to items that come under Section 736(b) cannot exceed the partner's total value in partnership property at the time of retirement.[41]

C. Application of Rules

Example. Designing Partnership was a general partnership that provided architectural consulting services. Geoffrey retired from the partnership. At the time of his retirement, the Designing Partnership balance sheet appeared as follows:

Asset	Adj.	FMV	Partner	Adj. Basis	Cap. Acct.
Cash	$90,000	$90,000	Geoffrey	$45,000	$80,000
Acct. Rec.	-0-	30,000	Handel	45,000	80,000
Stock	20,000	60,000	Izzy	45,000	80,000
Whiteacre	15,000	60,000		$135,000	$240,000
Total:	$125,000	$240,000			

Geoffrey received $90,000 in liquidation of his interest. The partnership agreement did not include any provision for the payment of goodwill.

Because Geoffrey is a general partner and Designing Partnership is a service partnership, the accounts receivable are not treated as non-liquidating distributions (*i.e.*, they are treated as Section 736(a) payments). In addition, the premium payment, $10,000 ($90,000 payment, less $80,000 capital account) is not treated as a non-liquidating distribution (*i.e.*, is treated as a Section 736(a) payment). Geoffrey's share of the following items comes within Section 736(a):

Asset	FMV
Acct. Rec.	10,000
Premium	10,000
Total:	$20,000

Because the payments are made without regard to the partnership income they are treated as guaranteed payments. Geoffrey includes the payments in his income in the year the partnership is entitled to a deduction.

The payment for his share of the cash, stock, and Whiteacre are Section 736(b) payments. His share of the following items comes within Section 736(b):

---

40. Treas. Reg. 1.736-1(b)(5)(ii).
41. Treas. Reg. 1.736-1(b)(5)(iii).

Asset	FMV
Cash	$30,000
Stock	20,000
Whiteacre	20,000
Total:	$70,000

In determining if there has been a disproportionate distribution, unrealized receivables and unstated goodwill are ignored. Thus, because the partnership does not have any substantially appreciated inventory, the distribution is not a disproportionate distribution under Section 751(b).

The payment covered by Section 736(b) is treated in the same manner as a non-liquidating distribution. Upon distribution of $70,000 of cash, Geoffrey's basis is reduced to zero, and he recognizes $25,000 of gain.

D. Cases and Materials

Smith v. Commissioner
313 F.2d 16 (10th Cir. 1962), aff'g 37 T.C. 1033 (1962)

This case is here on the Smiths' Petition To Review a decision of the Tax Court of the United States which was adverse to them.

The facts necessary for our disposition of the case are not in dispute. In January, 1947, V. Zay Smith (petitioner) and three other individuals formed a partnership known as Geophoto Services (Geophoto) for the purpose of engaging in the business of evaluating geological structures based upon aerial photography, which was to be used in the search for petroleum and petroleum reserves. Petitioner, at the time of World War II, was a geologist and, from his experience as a photo intelligence officer in the Navy, conceived the idea of using aerial photography for evaluating geological structures in the search for oil and petroleum.

The original partnership agreement was for a period of five years. Immediately prior to its expiration and on December 31, 1952, the articles of partnership were revised to provide a means of expelling one of the partners.

The partnership prospered during the next four years of the 5 year period of the partnership agreement, with petitioner receiving substantial net income for his share. In January, 1957, the other three partners voted to expel petitioner as a partner in Geophoto. In accordance with paragraph 25 of the revised articles, petitioner received the consideration agreed upon therein. The total amount of $77,000.00 was paid to petitioner in the form of a check for $72,740.71 and an automobile of an agreed upon value of $4,259.29. It was stipulated, however, that the book value of petitioner's interest in the partnership on the date in question was $53,264.61, thereby leaving a payment to him of $2,045.45 as salary and a payment of $21,689.94 as a "premium", for a total payment over and above his partnership interest of $23,735.39.

In their income tax return for the year 1957, petitioners reported the excess over and above his partnership interest in the amount of $23,735.39 as a capital gain—this figure includes the salary payment of $2,045.45. The Commissioner of Internal Revenue determined that the entire excess of $23,735.39 was ordinary income and, accordingly, made a deficiency assessment of $6,992.20 in their income tax for 1957.

Petitioners thereafter filed a petition with the Tax Court alleging that the Commissioner, in determining taxable income for the year 1957, erroneously included the $23,735.39 payment as ordinary income and requested the Tax Court to determine that there was no deficiency due on the 1957 income tax. The Commissioner's position before the Tax Court was that the $23,735.39 payment to petitioner was in liquidation of his interest in the partnership and, accordingly, it was taxable as ordinary income under Section 736(a) of the Internal Revenue Code of 1954, 26 U.S.C. § 736(a). Specifically, the Commissioner contended that the $2,045.45 salary payment should be taxed as a guaranteed payment under paragraph (2) of subsection (a) and the remainder as a distributive share of partnership income under paragraph (1) thereof.

Petitioners argued that the questioned amount was a payment for "good will" and should be treated as a capital gain under section 736(b) of the Act, 26 U.S.C. § 736(b). Specifically, they urged that paragraph (2)(B) of subsection (b) applied. Beyond any question, the $2,045.45 was ordinary income and no further discussion of that item is necessary.

The Tax Court rejected petitioners' contention and, in holding that the questioned amount should be treated as ordinary income, acknowledged this was a case of first impression. The provisions of Section 736 first became embodied in the tax law by the enactment of the 1954 Internal Revenue Code. This was the first time the Congress attempted to specifically cover by statute the tax situation arising when a partnership interest is in fact liquidated by payments from the partnership to the retiring or withdrawing partner. The situation here is not that of a partner selling his interest to another partner or a third party. If that was the situation, the government concedes, and we agree, that Section 741 of the Internal Revenue Code of 1954, 26 U.S.C. 741, would be applicable, as contended by the taxpayer. We agree with the Tax Court that under the facts Section 736 provides the proper tax treatment.

From a careful reading of Section 736 and consideration of the Senate Finance Report made at the time the new legislation was before the Congress, the intended scope of such Section appears clear. Paragraph (2)(B) of subsection (b) exempts from ordinary income treatment payments made for good will only when the partnership agreement so provides specifically and does not permit an intent to compensate for good will to be drawn from the surrounding circumstances as the taxpayer here urges us to do. In fact, the partnership agreement here specifically states "* * * In determining the value or the book value of a deceased or retiring partner's interest, no value shall be assigned to good will, * * *."

The discussion in 6 Mertens, Law of Federal Income Taxation, § 35.81, pp. 232–233, of the questioned statute supports the position of the government:

> "Partnership good will has an ambivalent character under Section 736 of the 1954 Code. Because of the difficulties on the one hand of valuing good will and on the other hand the inequities which might result if good will were required to be disregarded in every case, Section 736(b)(2), in effect, permits an election as to the treatment of partnership good will.

> "If the partnership agreement provides for a specific payment as to good will and such amount is not in excess of the reasonable value of the partner's share

of good will, good will is considered a partnership asset and payments with respect thereto are treated as 'Section 736(b) Payments.' The capitalizing of good will may be desirable from the point of view of the retiring partner or deceased partner's successor. The retiring partner is entitled to capital gain treatment on the amount of the payments allocable to good will. The deceased partner's successor will have a basis equal to the date of death valuation for payments allocable to good will. While this treatment is beneficial to the retiring partner or deceased partner's successor, the continuing partners will not be allowed a deduction or exclusion for such payments.

"On the other hand, if the partnership agreement does not treat good will as partnership property under Section 736(b), the payments relating thereto fall under Section 736(a). Such payments are taxable as ordinary income to the recipient, and may be excluded from the current income of the partnership or deducted therefrom. The treatment of good will under Section 736(a) is favorable to continuing partners since they are permitted to expense the cost of acquiring the withdrawing partner's interest in partnership good will.

"The treatment of good will under the 1954 Code would appear to be one of the principal tax factors to be taken into account in drafting partnership agreements. In most cases it would be desirable for the partners to agree in advance as to whether partnership good will is to be capitalized or not. If the partnership agreement fails to provide for the treatment of good will, the agreement may be so amended at the time of termination of an interest. Section 761(d) of the 1954 Code also permits a partnership agreement to be modified up to the time for filing the partnership return for the taxable year. It is doubtful, however, that the remaining partners could act adversely to the interest of the withdrawing partner after he had left the partnership."

For additional expressions of the same view, see Rabkin and Johnson, Federal Income, Gift and Estate Taxation, §16.11 (5), pp. 1678–1679; Tenen, Tax Problems Of Service Partnerships, 16 N.Y.U. Institute on Federal Taxation 137, 158–160 (1958); Egger, Sales of Partnership Interests and Death or Retirement of Partner, 15 N.Y.U. Institute on Federal Taxation 115, 119–120 (1957).

The case of Commissioner of Internal Revenue v. Lester, 366 U.S. 299, 81 S.Ct. 1343, 6 L.Ed.2d 306, is analogous to this case. It involved a situation where a divorced taxpayer and his former wife entered into a written agreement for periodic payments by him to his former wife. The agreement provided that in the event any of the parties three children should marry, become emancipated or die, the payments should "be reduced in a sum equal to one-sixth of the payments which would thereafter otherwise accrue." The taxpayer deducted the whole of these periodic payments in the taxable years of 1951 and 1952. The government sought to recover tax deficiencies for those years equal to one-half of the periodic payments made contending that the quoted language of the written agreement sufficiently identified 1/2 of the periodic payments as having been "payable for the support" of the taxpayer's minor children under §22(k) of the Internal Revenue Code of 1939 and, therefore, not deductible by him under §23(u) of the Code. The Supreme Court held "that the Congress intended that, to come within the exception portion of 22(k), the agreement providing for the periodic payments must specifically state the amounts or parts thereof allocable to the support of the children" (366 U.S. at page 301, 81 S.Ct. at page 1345) and said that by this statute "the Congress was in effect giving the husband and wife the power to shift a portion of the tax burden from the wife to the husband by the use of a simple provision in the settlement agreement which fixed the specific portion of the periodic payment made to the wife as payable for the support of the children. Here the agreement does not so specifically provide." (366 U.S. at 304, 81 S.Ct. at 1347). The court also noted that "it (the statute) does not say that 'a sufficiently clear purpose' on the part of the parties would satisfy" but "It says that the written instrument must 'fix' that amount, or 'portion of the payment' which is to go to the support of the children." (366 U.S. at page 305, 81 S.Ct. at page 1347).

This reasoning would appear to be particularly applicable here and we think the payment in question should be treated as ordinary income rather than capital gain since the articles of partnership do not specifically provide that the payment is for good will. If intent is to be determined by something other than the plain language of the partnership agreement, uncertainty and confusion will becloud the issue and the efforts of Congress to clarify a complex situation will go for naught. Important, also, is the fact that this result treats fairly both the expelled partner and the remaining partners as the tax consequences are determined in advance by the contract to which they all agreed.

The decision of the Tax Court is Affirmed.

Commissioner v. Jackson Investment Co.
346 F.2d 187 (9th Cir. 1965), rev'g 41 T.C. 575 (1964)

The Commissioner of Internal Revenue has brought this petition to review decisions of the Tax Court (41 T.C. 675 (1964)) involving federal income taxes for the taxable years 1956 through 1958. The amounts in controversy involve distributions made by respondents, Jackson Investment Company and West Shore Company, partners in George W. Carter Company, to a retiring partner, Ethel M. Carter. Petitioner concluded that the distributions were not deductible expenses, and, consequently, assessed deficiencies against Jackson in the aggregate amount of $9,848.18 and against West Shore in the aggregate amount of $15,577.85. The Tax Court, however, rendered a decision adverse to the Commissioner. The Commissioner subsequently petitioned for review, invoking this court's jurisdiction under Section 7482 of the Internal Revenue Code of 1954.

The question presented for our consideration involves the construction of Section 736 of the Internal Revenue Code of 1954. That section, drafted as part of a series of provisions intended to clarify and simplify the tax laws with respect to partnerships, provides as follows:

> § 736. Payments to a retiring partner or a deceased partner's successor in interest.
>
> (a) Payments considered as distributive share or guaranteed payment.—Payments made in liquidation of the interest of a retiring partner or a deceased partner shall, except as provided in subsection (b), be considered—
>
> (1) as a distributive share to the recipient of partnership income if the amount thereof is determined with regard to the income of the partnership, or
>
> (2) as a guaranteed payment described in section 707(c) if the amount thereof is determined without regard to the income of the partnership.

(b) Payments for interest in partnership. —

(1) General rule. — Payments made in liquidation of the interest of a retiring partner to a deceased partner shall, to the extent such payments (other than payments described in paragraph (2)) are determined, under regulations prescribed by the Secretary or his delegate, to be made in exchange for the interest of such partner in partnership property, be considered as a distribution by the partnership and not as a distributive share or guaranteed payment under subsection (a).

(2) Special rules. — For purposes of this subsection, payments in exchange for an interest in Partnership property shall not include amounts paid for —

(A) unrealized receivables of the partnership (as defined in section 751(c)), or

(B) good will of the partnership, except to the extent that the partnership agreement provides for a payment with respect to good will.

The intended purpose of this provision was to permit the participants themselves to determine whether the retiring partner or the remaining partners would bear the tax burdens for payments in liquidation of a retiring partner's interest. Thus, under the general approach of subsection (a), the tax burden is borne by the retiring partner — he recognizes the payments as taxable income, and the remaining partners are allowed a commensurate deduction from partnership income. Under subsection (b), the general rule conceives an approach of nonrecognition of ordinary income to the retiring partner, but places the tax burden on the partnership by denying a deduction from income for the payments. This latter subsection, however, adopts a special rule — (b)(2) (B) — in an express effort to assist the participants to decide inter sese upon the allocation of the tax burden. This special rule lies at the heart of the present controversy. Under this rule, payments for the good will of the partnership are deductible by the partnership (and hence recognizable as ordinary income to the retiring partner) "except to the extent that the partnership agreement provides for a payment with respect to good will." If the partnership agreement provides for a payment with respect to good will, the tax burden is allocated to the partnership — no deduction is allowed and the retiring partner need not recognize the payments as ordinary income. In the present case, petitioner contends that this exception under Section 736(b)(2)(B) applies, and thus the deductions taken by the partnership should be disallowed. We must determine, therefore, whether the parties intended to place the tax burden on the partnership by expressly incorporating into the partnership agreement a provision for payment to the retiring partner with respect to good will.

It is undisputed that the original Partnership Agreement did not contain a provision for partnership good will or a payment therefor upon the withdrawal of a partner. On May 7, 1956, however, the three partners executed an instrument entitled "Amendment of Limited Partnership Agreement of George W. Carter Co." (Tr. 62-75.) This instrument provided for Ethel Carter's retirement, and bound the partnership to compensate Ethel in the amount of $60,000.00 in consideration for her withdrawal. After the necessary adjustment of the figures, it was determined that $19,650.00 of the amount was in return for Ethel's "15% Interest in the fair market value of all the net assets of the partnership." The other $40,350.00, the amount in controversy here, was referred to as "a guaranteed payment, or a payment for good will." (Tr. 66.) The $40,350.00 was paid by the partnership in three annual parts, and deductions were made for good will expense in the partnership net income for each of the years. It is these deductions that petitioner challenges.

The decision of the Tax Court (six judges dissenting), concluded that the document entitled "Amendment of Limited Partnership Agreement of George W. Carter Co." was not a part of the partnership agreement, and therefore, the exception of Section 736(b)(2)(B) was not applicable. As a result, the court held that the amounts in question were legitimate deductions from the partnership income under the terms of Section 736(a)(2). The court founded its conclusion on the fact that the "Amendment" was solely designed to effect a withdrawal of one of the partners; it was not at all concerned with any continued role for Ethel in the partnership affairs.

We cannot agree with the interpretation of the majority of the Tax Court. We find this view unduly interferes with the clear objective of the statute, i.e., to permit and enable the partners to allocate the tax burdens as they choose, and with a minimum of uncertainty and difficulty. If a partnership agreement such as the one involved here, had no provision regarding the withdrawal of a partner, and the partners negotiated to compensate the retiring partner with payments that could be treated by the recipient at capital gain rates, the statutory scheme should not be read to frustrate the parties' efforts. An amendment to the partnership agreement which incorporates the plan of withdrawal and which designates the amount payable as being in consideration for the partnership good will seems clearly to be an attempt to utilize Section 736(b)(2)(B), affording capital gain rates to the retiring partner but precluding an expense deduction for the partnership. Simply because the subject matter of the amendment deals only with the liquidation of one partner's interest, we should not thwart whatever may be the clear intent of the parties by holding the amendment is not part of the partnership agreement. The Internal Revenue Code of 1954 expressly touches upon modifications of partnership agreements, and it gives no support to the thesis that an amendment dealing with the withdrawal of a partner cannot be considered a part of the partnership agreement. Section 761(c) provides:

> "Partnership Agreement.—For purposes of this subchapter, a partnership agreement includes any modifications of the partnership agreement made prior to, or at, the time prescribed by law for the filing of the partnership return for the taxable year (not including extensions) which are agreed to by all the partners, or which are adopted in such other manner as may be provided by the partnership agreement."

We hold, therefore, in harmony with the intent of the parties to the partnership, that the "Amendment of Limited Partnership Agreement of George W. Carter Co." was a modification of the partnership agreement within the meaning of Section 761(c). As such, the requirement of a provision in the partnership agreement as specified in Section 736(b)(2)(B) is satisfied.

There remains, however, an additional requirement to call into operation Section 736(b)(2)(B), viz., that the provision for payment in the partnership agreement be with respect to good will. As noted above, the payment of the $40,350.00 was inartistically described in the Amendment as a "guaranteed payment, or a payment for good will." The "guaranteed payment" terminology seems to expressly incorporate Section 736(a)(2), which would permit an expense deduction to the partnership, while recognizing the payments as ordinary income to the retiring partner. The "good will" language, on the other hand, would appear directed to Section 736(b)(2)(B), which results in the opposite tax consequences. In resolving this conflict, we feel the most helpful guide is to pay deference to what we may determine was the revealed intent of the parties. An examination of the entire amendment leads us to conclude that, notwithstanding the use of the words "guaranteed payment," the parties intended to invoke Section 736(b)(2)(B), not Section 736(a)(2). The Amendment expressly states the following (which we find impossible to harmonize with the majority opinion of the Tax Court or the arguments advanced by respondents in their brief):

> "It is recognized by all the parties hereto that the prior agreements among the partners do not provide for any payment to any partner in respect to good will in the event of the retirement or withdrawal of a partner, but George W. Carter Company will nevertheless make a payment to Ethel M. Carter in respect to good will as herein provided in consideration of her entering into this agreement and her consent to retire from the partnership upon the terms herein expressed." (Tr. 66.) (Emphasis added.)

The meaning of this language as well as the words chosen to express it leads to the conclusion that the $40,350.00 was to be a payment "in respect to good will," with the parties intending to be governed by the tax consequences of Section 736(b)(2)(B). The concluding paragraph of Judge Raum's dissenting opinion in the Tax Court, joined in by five other judges, expresses in our judgment sound reasoning, and we incorporate it here as a summary statement of our viewpoint:

> "To fail to give effect to the plain language thus used by the parties is, I think, to defeat the very purpose of the pertinent partnership provisions of the statute, namely, to permit the partners themselves to fix their tax liabilities inter sese. Although the May 7, 1956, agreement may be inartistically drawn, and indeed may even contain some internal inconsistencies, the plain and obvious import of its provisions in respect of the present problem was to amend the partnership agreement so as to provide specifically for a goodwill payment. This is the kind of thing that section 736(b)(2)(B) dealt with when it allowed the partners to fix the tax consequences of goodwill payments to a withdrawing partner. And this is what the partners clearly attempted to do here, however crude may have been their effort. I would give further effect to that effort, and would not add further complications to an already overcomplicated statute." (41 T.C. at 684.)

The decision of the Tax Court is reversed, and the matter is remanded to that court for further proceedings consistent with this opinion.

E. Problems

1. The Moving-On Partnership is a cash method general partnership that provides consulting services. All of the assets were purchased by the partnership. Ovid would like to end his participation in the partnership. The partnership balance sheet appears as follows:

Asset	Adj. Basis	FMV	Partner	Adj. Basis	Cap. Acct.
Cash	$45,000	$45,000	Ovid	$20,000	$35,000
Building	-0-	15,000	Perry	30,000	35,000
Land	45,000	45,000	Quincy	40,000	35,000
Total:	$90,000	$105,000		$90,000	$105,000

(a) If Ovid sold his interest:

    (1) What is the minimum amount for which Ovid should be able to sell his interest?

    (2) Could he obtain more than that minimum amount? If so, why?

    (3) What would be the tax consequences to Ovid if he sold his interest for $35,000 cash?

(b) Alternatively, if Ovid retired:

    (1) What is the minimum amount the partnership should pay Ovid for his interest?

    (2) Could he obtain more than that minimum amount? If so, why?

    (3) Will Ovid receive any payment for goodwill? How do you know? Who makes the decision?

    (4) Will Section 751(b) (addressing disproportionate distributions) be applicable?

    (5) What would be the tax consequences to Ovid if he retired and received $35,000, plus a $10,000 premium payment?

---

2. Application:

(a) When would you advise your client to sell his interest to the remaining partners (or a third party) versus liquidate his interest? When would you advise your client to liquidate his interest rather than sell to the remaining partners (or a third party)?

(b) Draft language for a partnership agreement addressing payments to a retiring partner for goodwill.

(c) What steps might you take to assure the partners (and you) that the Internal Revenue Service will respect the structure of the transaction?

Overview Problem—Putting It All Together

Stacey, Bill, and Olivia have operated the coffee shop for a number of years. They each have put a lot of time and effort into the business. Except for a small salary they pay themselves each year, none of the partners has withdrawn anything from the partnership. Instead, they have used the profits to expand the business, and, in profitable years, make several long-term investments. In addition, throughout the years each partner has made additional contributions to the partnership.

Stacey mentioned to Bill and Olivia that she would like to purchase a cabin and spend two-to-three days a week there. However, to be able to afford the purchase, she will have to withdraw some of her investment in the partnership. In addition, if she makes the purchase, Stacey will no longer be available to work full time in the business.

Bill and Olivia support Stacey. But, they want to be sure her decisions do not unnecessarily disrupt the coffee shop business or inadvertently cause any adverse tax consequences.

The partners have set a time for a partnership meeting to discuss Stacey's plans. You have been invited to the meeting to advise them.

1. What tax consequences do you anticipate?

2. How many different ways could you structure a transaction to meet Stacey's objectives?

3. To determine which potential consequences you and the partners must plan for, what additional information will you ask for?

4. What specific issues do you anticipate might need the attention of an accountant familiar with partnership tax?

5. What non-tax issues might you be concerned about?

Practitioner's Checklist

☐ Will the partnership allow cash distributions?

☐ Will the partnership allow distributions of property?

☐ How will a departing partner's interest in the partnership be valued (including whether the value will include goodwill or any other intangible asset)?

Items to include in the partnership or operating agreement:

Distributions:

☐ How decisions are made regarding whether the partnership will make cash distributions to partners.

☐ How decisions are made regarding whether the partnership will distribute property to a partner.

☐ Language that partnership will make Section 754 election.

☐ If the Section 754 election is not made at the formation of the partnership, explain who will decide if the election subsequently will be made.

Partner's leaving the partnership:

☐ Method for a partner to provide notice when he intends to leave the partnership.

☐ Any buy-sell provisions.

☐ Method for valuing a partner's interest in the partnership (including whether the value will include goodwill or any other intangible asset).

☐ How a departing partner's interest will be liquidated by the partnership, including whether the buy-out payments can be made on an installment basis.

☐ Whether a partner's leaving the partnership will cause the partnership to dissolve.

Dissolution:

☐ Events that will cause a dissolution of the partnership.

☐ Events that will not cause a dissolution of the partnership.

VIII.

Transactions between a Partner and the Partnership

Overview Problem

Stacey, Bill, and Olivia have just formed a partnership to own and operate the coffee shop and are in the process of working out the details. They plan to operate the business out of the corner shop of a commercial building owned by Bill. Olivia, who contributed a substantial amount of cash, is primarily interested in making sure that the business is successful so that she can receive a good return on her investment. She plans to stay with the business for only a few years, then leave the partnership to open a flower shop. Stacey plans to spend a substantial amount of her time working at the shop, but needs to be certain she earns enough money to pay her mortgage.

The partners are pretty clear about their personal objectives for the partnership. But, they are not sure how to structure their various arrangements to make sure they achieve those goals. Nor do they want their individual objectives to interfere with those of another partner. In addition, they would like to obtain the best overall tax result possible, without taking any controversial positions.

The partners have set a time for a partnership meeting to discuss the arrangements between the partners and between the partners and the partnership. You have been invited to the meeting to advise them.

Transactions between a Partner and the Partnership

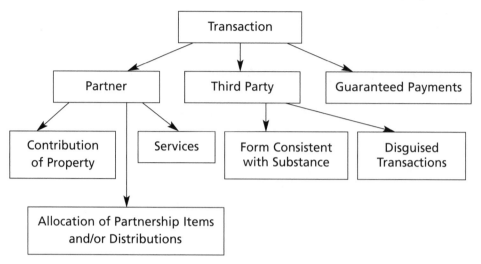

Chapter 29

Transactions in Capacity Other Than as Partner

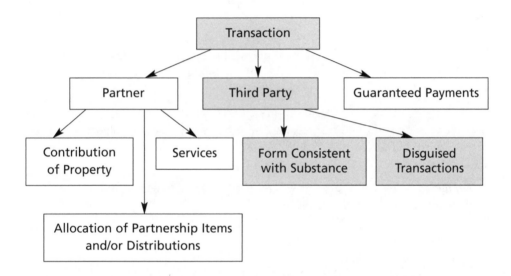

Read:

Code Sections 267(a)(2), (e)(1), (e)(2); 707(a), (b).
Treas. Reg. §§ 1.707-1(a), -1(b); 1.707-3(a)(1), -3(a)(2), -3(b)(1), -3(b)(2), -3(c), -3(d).

A. Background

1. State Law

Property. A partnership can be viewed as an aggregate of the partners or as a separate entity. The Uniform Partnership Act follows the approach that a partnership is an aggregate of the partners. As such, all property contributed to or acquired by the partnership is partnership property.[1] However, each partner is a co-owner of partnership property with the other partners, holding it as tenants-in-partnership.[2]

---

1. UPA §8(1).
2. UPA §25(1).

The Revised Uniform Partnership Act follows the approach that a partnership is a separate entity.[3] Property acquired by the partnership, either through contribution or direct acquisition, is considered property of the partnership and not of the partners individually.[4]

Salary. A partnership is an association of two or more people to carry on as co-owners a business for profit.[5] Under the default rules, each partner is entitled to an equal share of the profits and losses and no partner is entitled to a salary.[6]

2. Federal Law

Gross Income and disposition of property. Gross income includes income from all sources derived. It includes compensation for services, interest, rent, and gain derived from dealings in property.[7]

The gain derived from dealings in property is the excess of the amount realized over the adjusted basis.[8] Unless otherwise provided, the gain realized must be recognized, *i.e.*, reported on the taxpayer's income tax return.[9]

The amount of loss from a disposition of property is the excess of the adjusted basis over the amount realized. The taxpayer can recognize the loss, *i.e.*, report the loss on his tax return, if it was incurred while engaged in a business or in a transaction entered into for profit.[10]

Limitation on losses. If a taxpayer sells property to a related person and realizes a loss, he may not be able to recognize the loss.[11]

Rule: If:
- There was a disposition of property;
- There was a loss on disposition;
- The loss would otherwise be allowed under the Code; and
- The sale was made to a related party,

then, the sellor may not claim the loss from the disposition.

Tax consequences on formation of a partnership. Congress determined that a transfer of cash or property to a partnership in exchange for a partnership interest generally should not be a taxable event. The partner continues to have an indirect ownership interest in the property. Stated differently, he has a continuity of his investment. Any gain or loss in the property is deferred.[12]

---

3. RUPA § 201(a).
4. RUPA § 203.
5. UPA § 6(1); RUPA §§ 101(6); 202.
6. UPA § 18(a), (f); RUPA § 401(b), (h).
7. Code Sec. 61(a).
8. Code Sec. 1001(a).
9. Code Sec. 1001(c).
10. Code Sec. 165(a), (c)(1), (c)(2).
11. Code Sec. 267(a).
12. Code Sec. 721.

If a partner acquires an interest in a partnership through a contribution of property, including money, to the partnership, his basis in his partnership interest is the amount of money and the adjusted basis of the property at the time of the contribution.[13] The basis is increased by gain or income and decreased by loss or deductions allocated to the partner. The basis of assets contributed to a partnership is the basis in the hands of the contributing partner, decreased by allowable depreciation.[14]

B. Discussion of Rules

A partner is not restricted to interacting with the partnership only as a partner. He may act in his capacity as an independent third party. In such cases, the tax consequences are consistent with a transaction between the partnership and a third party.

1. Compensation for Services, Rent, Interest

a. Services

Capacity as a partner. As a partner in a partnership, the partner may be expected to render services through the partnership. In exchange, the partner will receive a share of the partnership profits.[15] He will report any such profits as part of his allocable share of partnership items. His basis will be increased by the amount of gain or income allocated to him.

Not in capacity as a partner. If the partner is not acting in his capacity as a partner, he may render services as an independent contractor to the partnership.[16] In this case, the partner must recognize the payment he receives as compensation for services. He includes the amount in his gross income based on his individual accounting method.

The partnership may be able to claim an expense deduction if the payment qualifies as an ordinary and necessary expense under Section 162 or is deductible under some other provision.

Example: Gary is a partner in Investment Partnership. The partnership hires Gary to prepare the partnership's tax return. Investment Partnership may deduct the amount paid to Gary as an ordinary and necessary expense.

Higgins is a partner in the Acquisition Partnership. As part of the partnership's acquisition of Blackacre, it hires Higgins to verify ownership and validity of

---

13. Code Sec. 722. The basis is increased by the amount (if any) of gain recognized under Section 721(b).

14. Code Sec. 723. The basis is increased by the amount (if any) of gain recognized under Section 721(b) by the contributing partner at the time of the contribution.

15. If the partner provides services in exchange for his partnership interest, he must report the value of the interest received as gross income. See discussion of receipt of a partnership interest in exchange for services in Chapter 5.

16. Code Sec. 707(a)(1).

title to the property. The amount paid to Higgins is not a deductible ordinary and necessary expense. Rather, it must be capitalized as part of the acquisition cost of Blackacre.

Even though a partner generally is expected to contribute services to the partnership in his capacity as a partner (or be hired to provide services as an independent contractor), there is some support for the position that a partner may render services to the partnership as an employee.[17] Any tax benefits that would be available to other employees would be available to the employee-partner.

Disguised services. Some payments, though in form structured as a distribution of partnership income, may be treated as compensation if they are in substance paid for services rendered by the partner not in his capacity as a partner. If:[18]

- A partner performs services for the partnership;
- There is a related direct or indirect allocation and distribution from the partnership; and
- When considered together, the transaction is properly characterized as a transaction between the partnership and a partner not acting in his capacity as a partner,

then the transaction will be treated as one between the partnership and a third party.

Practice Tip: When a partner provides services to a partnership it might be characterized as any of the following, depending on the facts and circumstances:
- Services provided in exchange for a partnership interest;
- Services rendered as a partner in the partnership;
- Services rendered in exchange for a guaranteed payment;
- Services rendered not in the partner's capacity as a partner (*i.e.*, as an independent contractor or employee); or
- Services in form an allocation of partnership income, but in substance performance of services rendered not in partner's capacity as a partner (*i.e.*, rendered as an independent contractor).

---

b. Rental of Property

Not in capacity as a partner. If the partner is not acting in his capacity as a partner and enters into an arrangement through which the partnership may use the partner's property, the transaction is treated as a rental or lease arrangement. The partner must recognize income upon receipt of the rental or lease payments. He includes the amounts in his gross income consistent with his individual accounting method.[19]

---

17. Armstrong v. Phinney, 394 F.2d 661 (5th Cir. 1968).
18. Code Sec. 707(a)(2)(A).
19. Code Sec. 707(a)(1).

The partnership may be able to claim an expense deduction if it qualifies as an ordinary and necessary expense under Section 162 or is deductible under some other provision.

Example: ImaJean is a partner in Rental Partnership. In the ordinary course of its business, the partnership rents ImaJean's property and pays her monthly rent. Rental Partnership may deduct the rent paid to ImaJean as an ordinary and necessary expense under Section 162.

Jim is a partner in the Purchases Partnership. The partnership, in form, leases Whiteacre from Jim, paying him monthly "rent." However, in substance, the transaction is a purchase of Whiteacre by Purchases Partnership from Jim. The amount paid to Jim is not an ordinary and necessary expense. Rather, it is part of the purchase price of Whiteacre. The partnership is not entitled to a deduction for the payments.

Similarly, if the partnership enters into an agreement allowing the partner to use partnership property, the transaction is treated as a rental or lease arrangement. The partnership must recognize the rental or lease payments as income, consistent with its accounting method.[20]

The partner may be able to claim an expense deduction if the payment qualifies as an ordinary and necessary expense under Section 162 or qualifies as a deduction under some other provision.[21]

Practice Tip: When a partner allows a partnership to use his individual property, the transaction might be characterized as any of the following, depending on the facts and circumstances:
- Use of partner's individual property in exchange for a guaranteed payment; or
- Rental of individual property where partner is not acting in his partner capacity (*i.e.*, is acting as a third party).

---

c. Use of Money

Capacity as a partner. A partner may contribute money to a partnership. The contribution is reflected in his outside basis and in his capital account.

Not in capacity as a partner. The partner, not acting in his capacity as a partner, may loan the partnership money. The partner must include interest in his gross income and the partnership will be entitled to claim a deduction for the interest paid.

---

20. Id.
21. Id.

Similarly, the partnership may loan money to a partner not acting in his capacity as a partner. The partnership must include interest in its gross income and the partner will be entitled to claim a deduction for the interest paid.[22]

Practice Tip: When a partner allows a partnership to use his money, the transaction might be characterized as any of the following, depending on the facts and circumstances:
- Contribution of money to the partnership in exchange for a partnership interest;
- Use of the partner's money in exchange for a guaranteed payment; or
- Loan of the partner's money where the partner is not acting in his partner capacity (*i.e.*, is acting as a third party).

---

d. Limitation

The deduction may be deferred in certain circumstances. For the deferral to be applicable, the following elements must be present as of the close of the payor-taxpayer's taxable year. First, the payor must be on the accrual method of accounting, allowing the amount to be deducted, depreciated, or amortized regardless of whether it is paid.[23]

Second, the recipient must be on the cash basis method of accounting or otherwise not be required to include the amount in gross income until it is paid.[24]

Third, the payor and recipient must have one of the following relationships:[25]

- A partnership and a partner;[26]
- The partnership and person if they are, directly or indirectly, partners in another partnership;[27] or
- If the transaction is related either to the operations of the partnership or to an interest in the partnership, any person related to one of the above partners.[28]

In determining who is a partner in a partnership, constructive ownership rules apply.[29]

If the three elements are present, the payor is not allowed to take a deduction until the amount is actually paid.[30] In essence, an accrual basis taxpayer is placed on the cash basis with respect to a related payee so that the inclusion in income and deduction occur in the same year.

---

22. Code Sec. 707(a)(1).
23. Code Sec. 267(a)(2)(B).
24. Code Sec. 267(a)(2)(A).
25. Code Sec. 267(a)(2)(B), (e).
26. Code Sec. 267(e)(1)(B)(i).
27. Code Sec. 267(e)(1)(C).
28. Code Sec. 267(e)(1)(D).
29. Code Sec. 267(e)(3). A partner is not considered as constructively owing a partnership interest owned by his partner. Code Sec. 267(e)(3)(A).
30. Code Sec. 267(a)(2), (e). The deferral provision is not applicable if the partnership owns low-income housing and pays qualifying expenses or interest to a qualified five-percent or less partner or any person related to a qualified five-percent or less partner. Code Sec. 267(e)(5).

Practice Alert: The requirement that a deduction be deferred does not apply if the payment is a guaranteed payment. [Code Sec. 267(e)(4). See discussion of guaranteed payments in Chapter 30.]

Example: Related Partnership, an accrual basis taxpayer, is owned equally by Dolly and Polly, both cash basis taxpayers. Related Partnership enters into a contract with Dolly for Dolly to provide services to the partnership in exchange for $100. Dolly completes the services in year 1, but Related Partnership does not pay Dolly until year 2. The payment by the partnership to Dolly would be deductible.

Related Partnership is an accrual basis taxpayer. Dolly, as a cash basis taxpayer, is not required to include any amount in income in year 1. Because Dolly is a partner in Related Partnership, they have one of the identified relationships. Thus, the deduction deferral applies and Related Partnership is not entitled to claim a deduction for the $100 in year 1. The partnership can take a deduction in year 2 when Dolly is actually paid and will include the amount in her gross income.

Practice Tip: If:
- The payor is required to make a payment to the payee;
- The payor is on the accrual method of accounting and the payment is otherwise deductible, depreciable, or amortizable;
- The payee is on the cash basis method of accounting or otherwise not required to include the amount in income until actually received;
- No actual payment has been made; and
- The payor and payee have a relationship defined in Section 267(e)(1);

then, the payor is effectively placed on the cash basis method of accounting and may claim a deduction only when the payment is actually made.

---

2. Transfer of Property

a. Disposition of Property

Capacity as a partner. A partner may contribute property to a partnership. The contribution is reflected in both his outside basis and in his capital account.

Not in capacity as a partner. If a partner who is not acting in his capacity as a partner transfers property to a partnership, the transaction is treated as a sale. The partner must recognize gain or loss on disposition of the property. The partnership will take a cost basis in the property.

Similarly, if the partnership transfers property to a partner not acting in his capacity as a partner, the transaction is treated as a sale. The partnership must recognize gain or loss on disposition of the property. The partner will take a cost basis in the property.[31]

Disguised sales. Some transactions, though in form structured as a distribution of partnership income, may be treated as a sale if the allocation is in substance a payment to purchase the partner's property. If:[32]

- A partner transfers property to a partnership;
- There is a related direct or indirect allocation and distribution from the partnership; and
- When considered together, the transaction is properly characterized as a transaction between the partnership and a partner not acting in his capacity as a partner,

then, the transaction will be treated as one between the partnership and a third party.

Similarly, if the transaction is structured as a distribution of partnership property, it may be treated as a sale if the distribution is in substance a payment to purchase the partner's property. If:[33]

- A partner directly or indirectly transfers money or property to a partnership;
- There is a related direct or indirect transfer of money or other property by the partnership to the partner; and
- When considered together, the transaction is properly characterized as a sale of property,

then the transaction will be treated as a sale between the partner and the partnership or between partners acting not as partners.

If, within a two-year time frame, a partner transfers property to a partnership and the partnership transfers money or other consideration to the partner, the transfer is presumed to be a sale of the property by the partner to the partnership. The presumption can be rebutted, based on the facts and circumstances.[34] In contrast, if a partner transfers property to a partnership and the partnership transfers money or other consideration to the partner, and the transfers occur more than two years apart, the transfer is presumed not to be a sale. The presumption can be rebutted, based on the facts and circumstances.[35]

---

31. Id.
32. Code Sec. 707(a)(2)(A).
33. Code Sec. 707(a)(2)(B).
34. Treas. Reg § 1.707-3(c)(1). The order of the transactions is not relevant.
35. Treas. Reg § 1.707-3(d). The order of the transactions is not relevant.

Practice Note: If:
- Within a two-year time period, a partner transfers property to a partnership and the partnership transfers money or other consideration to the partner; and
- The partner does not treat the transaction as a sale,

Then, he must attach a Form 8275, Disclosure Statement, to his return disclosing his treatment of the transaction.

The disclosure must include: [Treas. Reg § 1.707-8(b)]
- A caption identifying the statement as a disclosure under Section 707;
- The item for which the disclosure is being made;
- The amount of each item; and
- The facts affecting the potential tax treatment of the items under Section 707.

Practice Tip: When a partner provides property to a partnership it might be characterized as any of the following, depending on the facts and circumstances:
- Property contributed to a partnership in exchange for a partnership interest;
- Sale of a partner's individual property to a partnership where the partner is not acting in his partner capacity (*i.e.*, is acting as a third party);
- An allocation of partnership income or gain to the partner that is in substance a sale of the partner's property to the partnership;
- A distribution of partnership property to the partner that is in substance a sale of the partner's property to the partnership; or
- A contribution of the partner's property to a partnership that is treated as a sale of the property to the partnership because it was followed by a related distribution within seven years to the partner of other partnership property. [See discussion in Chapter 27.]

---

b. Limitation

No deduction for a loss is allowed on sales between a partner and the partnership if the partner owns more than 50 percent of the capital interest or profits interest in the partnership.[36] In determining a partner's ownership in a partnership, constructive ownership rules apply.[37]

---

36. Code Sec. 707(b)(1)(A); Treas. Reg § 1.707-1(b)(1)(i).

37. Code Sec. 707(b)(3). A partner is not considered as constructively owing a partnership interest owned by his partner. Code Sec. 707(b)(3).

> **Practice Tip:** The loss realized by a partner or the partnership must be otherwise allowable before the disallowance rule applicable to losses from the sale of property to a related party has any application. For example, Jill, a partner in the Rental Partnership, sold a boat she had used for personal purposes to the partnership. She realized a loss on the disposition. Jill may not recognize the loss because it is a personal loss. The fact that she sold the boat to a partnership in which she was a partner does not impact the tax consequences of the transaction.

Similarly, no deduction for a loss is allowed when a partnership sells property to another partnership where partners own more than 50 percent of the capital interest or profits interest in both partnerships.[38]

> **Rule:** A loss realized on the sale of property may not be recognized if:
> - There was a disposition of property;
> - The taxpayer realized a loss;
> - The loss would otherwise be allowed under the Code; and
> - The sale was between a more than 50-percent partner and a partnership or between two partnerships where the same parties own more than 50 percent of each partnership.

If a loss was disallowed because it was between a partner and a partnership or between two partnerships and there is a subsequent sale or exchange of the property, gain from disposition is recognized only to the extent it exceeds the loss that was disallowed.[39] The loss can be utilized to offset the gain only in situations where there is a gain on disposition of the property. Similarly, the loss can be utilized only to the extent of gain on disposition of the property. It cannot be used as a means of generating a loss.

> **Practice Alert:** If gain from the sale of partnership property is not recognized because it was offset by a previously disallowed loss [as provided for under Section 707(b)(1) and Section 267(d)], the basis of each partner's interest in the partnership is increased by the partner's share of the gain that is not recognized. [Rev. Rul. 96-10, 1996-1 C.B. 138.]

c. Characterization Issues

If the sale occurs between certain related parties, the Code may dictate the character of the gain on disposition. If the sale occurs between:

---

38. Code Sec. 707(b)(1)(B); Treas. Reg § 1.707-1(b)(1)(i).
39. Code Secs. 707(b)(1); 267(d); Treas. Reg § 1.707-1(b)(1)(ii).

- A partnership and a person owning, directly or indirectly, more than 50 percent of the capital interest or profits interest; or
- Two partnerships in which the same persons own, directly or indirectly, more than 50 percent of the capital interests or profits interests,

and, in the hands of the buyer, the asset would not be characterized as a capital asset, then the gain is characterized as ordinary. The rule applies regardless of whether it is a direct or indirect sale.[40]

3. Need for Making Determination

In some circumstances, the net tax results are the same, regardless of whether the partner is acting in his capacity as a partner or is acting as a third party. However, in some circumstances, determining the relationship of the partner to the partnership may be important.

First, if the partner can be classified as an employee, certain Code provisions may provide beneficial treatment. For example, in some circumstances, an employee may be able to exclude amounts that are paid for meals and lodging.[41] Or, an employee may be able to obtain employer-provided group life insurance and exclude the benefit from gross income.[42] Finally, other fringe benefits may be excludable from an employee's gross income.[43]

Second, if the payment is a distributive share, the character of the income will be determined at the partnership level.

Third, whether the partner is acting as a third party or in his capacity as a partner may impact the timing of including the income or claiming the deduction. If the amount is part of the partner's distributive share, it must be reported on the partner's individual return for the year during which the partnership year ends. If the partner is not acting in his capacity as a partner, the year he includes the amount in income or claims a deduction is determined by his accounting method. Similarly, the year the partnership includes the amount in income or claims a deduction is determined by the partnership's accounting method. However, the partnership's deduction may be limited by Section 267(a)(2) and (e).

Practice Tip: It may be important to determine whether the person is acting in his capacity as a partner or as an unrelated third party as it may impact:
- Whether an amount may be excluded from gross income;
- The character of the income; and
- The timing of the inclusion or deduction.

Fourth, the classification of a payment may impact the overall tax consequences of the transaction to the partner and the partnership. For example, the partnership may

---

40. Code Sec. 707(b)(2).
41. See Code Sec. 119.
42. Code Sec. 79(a).
43. See, *i.e.*, Code Sec. 132.

attempt to obtain an advantage by disguising a payment that is in actuality to a partner acting in his capacity as a third party as an allocation of a partnership item.

Example: Euclid, Pythagoras, and Galileo were equal partners in the Algebra Partnership. During the year, Euclid performed services for the partnership; the value of the services was $30,000. Because the services were paid in conjunction with the acquisition of a large triangular tract of land, the payment must be capitalized as part of the total cost and is not currently deductible. In addition, during the year, the partnership had $60,000 of gross income.

The transaction could be treated with Euclid acting in his capacity as a third party. As an unrelated third party, Euclid must include the $30,000 paid as compensation for services in his gross income. The partnership is not permitted to deduct any portion of the $30,000 it paid for Euclid's services. Accordingly, it has $60,000 of net income that is allocated equally between the partners, or $20,000 each. The partners report the following amounts of income:

Euclid:	$50,000 ($30,000 plus $20,000)
Pythagoras:	20,000
Galileo:	20,000
Total:	$90,000

Alternatively, the transaction could be treated with Euclid acting in his capacity as a partner. The partners could agree to make a special allocation to Euclid, allocating $30,000 to him, with the remainder divided equally between the partners. Thus, $30,000 would be allocated to Euclid, and the remaining $30,000 would be allocated equally among the partners, or $10,000 each. The partners would report the following amounts of income:

Euclid:	$40,000 ($30,000 plus $10,000)
Pythagoras:	10,000
Galileo:	10,000
Total:	$60,000

By treating Euclid as acting in his capacity as a partner, the partners reduced the total amount of income reported by all the partners by $30,000. Or, seen from a different perspective, the form of the transaction allowed the partnership to effectively deduct the $30,000 paid to Euclid. To the extent Euclid is properly treated as not acting in his capacity as a partner, Section 707(a)(2)(A) prevents the partnership and partners from achieving this result.

Practice Tip:
- Section 707(a)(1) applies when a partner is, in form and substance, acting as a third party.
- Section 707(a)(2)(A) applies when the form of the transaction is an allocation of partnership income to a partner, but the substance of the transaction is a payment by the partnership to the partner, acting not in his capacity as a partner, for services or rent.
- Section 707(a)(2)(B) applies when the payment is in form a distribution of property to a partner, but the substance of the transaction is a sale of property by the partner to the partnership.

4. Determining in Which Capacity a Partner Is Acting

In general. There is no bright line for determining whether a partner is acting in his capacity as a partner or acting as an independent third party. In general, a partner is not acting as a partner when the services are of a limited technical nature or in connection with a specific transaction;[44] a partner who performs services that are on-going and integral to the business of the partnership is acting in his capacity as a partner.[45] Ultimately, the determination must be made based on the substance of the transaction, and not its form.[46]

Legislative history. To assist in determining the character of a transaction, the legislative history of Section 707(a)(2)(A) sets forth factors to consider in determining if the payment is a disguised payment of compensation or disguised sale of property.

First: is there an appreciable risk that the payment will not be made or that it will not be made in full? In general, a partner assumes the risk that a partnership will not have profits. An independent third party does not assume any risk; he expects to be paid, regardless of the profitability of the partnership. The first factor is considered the most important factor.

Second: how long will the partner remain a partner in the partnership? This factor is only relevant if the partner could be described as transitory. Under such circumstances, the concern is that he may have joined the partnership for the sole purpose of structuring the transaction, in form, as an allocation to a partner when, in actuality, the payment is a fee or payment for property. However, if the partner continues in the partnership, the transaction could still be properly characterized as a transaction with an independent third party.

Third: how close in time is the allocation to the partner to the performance of services or use of property? The closer in time, the greater the indication the allocation is actually a disguised payment.

Fourth: based on all the facts and circumstances, does it appear that the partner joined the partnership solely to obtain favorable tax consequences for himself or the partnership that could not have been obtained acting in his individual capacity? Any non-tax motives in becoming a partner are not taken into consideration.

Fifth: is the partner's interest in the partnership small in relation to the allocation? If the interest is small, it may be an indication that the payment is to the partner not in his capacity as a partner. However, if the partner's interest is substantial, it is not an indication the payment was part of his allocable share of partnership income.

The sixth factor is relevant only when dealing with the use of property (and not to the provision of services). Does the requirement that capital accounts be maintained

---

44. Treas. Reg. § 1.707-1(a).
45. Pratt v. Commissioner, 64 T.C. 203 (1975), *aff'd in part, rev'd in part* 550 F.2d 1023 (5th Cir. 1977).
46. Treas. Reg. § 1.707-1(a).

as provided in the regulations make the income allocations[47] associated with the property unfeasible and, therefore, unlikely to be made?

C. Application of Rules

Example 1. Distributive share. Rome, Paris, and London are equal partners in the International Partnership. The partners and the partnership are all accrual basis taxpayers.

In the first year, Rome provided services to the partnership that were integral to the partnership's business in exchange for a special allocation of $10,000 of partnership income. The partners agree to allocate the remaining income equally.

In the first year, International Partnership has $40,000 of net ordinary income. It allocates $10,000 to Rome and allocates the remainder, $30,000, equally among the partners, or $10,000 each. Thus, Rome reports a total of $20,000 and Paris and London each report $10,000 of income.

Example 2. Nonpartner capacity. Oslo, Prague, and Warsaw are equal partners in the Eastern Partnership. The partners and the partnership are all accrual basis taxpayers. The partners agree to allocate net income equally.

In the first year, Oslo provided services to the partnership as an independent contractor in exchange for a payment of $10,000. Before considering the payment to Oslo, Eastern Partnership had $40,000 of ordinary income. It paid Oslo $10,000 and is entitled to claim a $10,000 expense deduction under Section 162. The net income, $30,000 ($40,000 less $10,000 expense deduction) is allocated equally among the partners, or $10,000 each. Thus, Oslo reports a total of $20,000, $10,000 in his non-partner capacity and $10,000 as his distributive share, and Prague and Warsaw each report $10,000 of income.

Note that the net result is the same in Example 1 and Example 2. It does not make a difference whether the partner is acting in his capacity as a partner.

Example 3. Distributive share. Dover, Montpellier, and Syracuse are equal partners in the Northeastern Partnership. The partners and the partnership are all accrual basis taxpayers.

In the first year, Dover provides services to the partnership that were integral to the partnership's business in exchange for a special allocation of $10,000 of partnership income. The partners agree to allocate the remaining income equally. In the first year, Northeastern Partnership has $16,000 or ordinary income and $24,000 of long-term capital gain. It allocates $4,000 of ordinary income and $6,000 of the long-term capital gain, totaling $10,000, to Dover for use of the land. The remaining ordinary income, $12,000, is allocated equally among the partners, or $4,000 each. The remaining long-term capital gain, $18,000, is allocated equally among the partners, or $6,000 each. The partners report the following amounts.

---

47. For an allocation to have economic effect, the partners must agree to maintain the capital accounts in accordance with the regulations. See discussion of allocations in Chapters 15 and 16.

Partner	Nonpartner Ordinary Income	Nonpartner LTCG	Partner Ordinary Income	Partner LTCG
Dover	$4,000	$6,000	$4,000	$6,000
Montpellier	-0-	-0-	4,000	6,000
Syracuse	-0-	-0-	4,000	6,000

Example 4. Nonpartner capacity. Salem, Helena, and Olympia are equal partners in the Northwestern Partnership. The partners and the partnership are all accrual basis taxpayers. The partners agree to allocate net income equally.

In the first year, Salem leases his land (in a non-partner capacity) to the partnership in exchange for a payment of $10,000. Before considering the payment to Salem, Northwestern Partnership has $16,000 of ordinary income and $24,000 of long-term capital gain. It pays Salem $10,000 and is entitled to claim a $10,000 expense deduction under Section 162. The net income, $6,000 ($16,000 of ordinary income less $10,000 expense deduction) is allocated equally among the partners, or $2,000 each. The long-term capital gain is allocated equally among the partners, or $8,000 each. The partners report the following amounts.

Partner	Nonpartner Ordinary Income	Nonpartner LTCG	Partner Ordinary Income	Partner LTCG
Salem	$10,000	-0-	$2,000	$8,000
Helena	-0-	-0-	2,000	8,000
Olympia	-0-	-0-	2,000	8,000

Note that the net result is not the same in Example 3 and Example 4. It does make a difference whether the partner is acting in his capacity as a partner.

Example 5. Timing disparity — nonpartner capacity. Jackson, Atlanta, and Mobil are equal partners in the Southeast Partnership. The partners are cash basis taxpayers and the partnership is an accrual basis taxpayer.

In the first year, Jackson leases his land (in a non-partner capacity) to the partnership in exchange for a payment of $10,000. The partnerships does not pay Jackson at the end of year one. Because Jackson is a cash basis taxpayer, he does not have to include the $10,000 in his income. In addition, the partnership is not permitted to take a deduction until the payment has been made.

Example 6. Related party transaction. Carol owns 60 percent and David owns 40 percent of Alpha Partnership. Carol owns 70 percent and Emma owns 30 percent of Beta Partnership. Carol, David, and Emma are not related to each other. Alpha Partnership sold stock to Beta Partnership for $150. Alpha Partnership's basis in the stock was $200. Alpha Partnership realized a loss of $50 (amount realized of $150 less basis of $200).

No deduction for a loss is allowed when a partnership sells property to another partnership where partners own more than 50 percent of the capital interest or profits interest in both partnerships. Carol owns more than 50 percent of both partnerships. Thus, the loss from the sale of the stock is disallowed. Of that disallowed loss, 60 percent, $30, is allocable to Carol and 40 percent, $20, is allocable to David. Carol must reduce her basis in Alpha Partnership by $30 and David must reduce his basis in Alpha Partnership by $20.

D. Cases and Materials

Pratt v. Commissioner
64 TC 203 (1975), aff'd 550 F.2d 1023 (5th Cir. 1977)

[Author's note: The taxpayer was a partner in two limited partnerships that each operated a shopping center. The taxpayer was a cash basis method taxpayer and the partnerships were accrual method taxpayers. Under the partnership agreement, the taxpayer was due management fees based on a percentage of gross rentals. The management fees were not paid by the partnership to the partners, but the partnerships claimed a deduction for the amounts. The issue before the court was whether the taxpayer was acting as a third party. If he was not, the fees were for services performed as a partner and became part of the partner's distributive share of income.]

* * *

Section 1.707-1(a) of the Income Tax Regulations with respect to a "partner not acting in capacity as partner" states that "In all cases, the substance of the transaction will govern rather than its form." Here, the record indicates that in managing the partnership petitioners were acting in their capacity as partners. They were performing basic duties of the partnership business pursuant to the partnership agreement. Although we have been unable to find cases arising under the 1954 Code concerning when a partner is acting within his capacity as such, a few cases arising under the provisions of the 1939 Code dealt with whether a payment to a partner should be considered as paid to him in a capacity other than as a partner. See *Leif J. Sverdrup*, 14 T.C. 859, 866 (1950); *Wegener v. Commissioner*, 119 F. 2d 49 (5th Cir. 1941), affg. 41 B.T.A. 857 (1940), cert. denied 314 U.S. 643 (1941). In *Wegener*, a joint venture was treated as a partnership for limited purposes, and the taxpayer-partner was found to be acting outside the scope of his partnership duties and in an individual capacity as an oil well drilling contractor, so that payments he received from the "partnership" for carrying out this separate and distinct activity were income to him individually as if he were an outsider. In the *Sverdrup* case, we recognized a payment to a taxpayer by a joint venture between a partnership of which the taxpayer was a member and a third party as compensation for work done on contracts being performed by the joint venture since "This sum was not a part of the income of the partnership of which he was a member, but was paid to him as an individual for services rendered to the joint venture."

Petitioners in this case were to receive the management fees for performing services within the normal scope of their duties as general partners and pursuant to the partnership agreement. There is no indication that any one of the petitioners was engaged in a transaction with the partnership other than in his capacity as a partner. We therefore hold that the management fees were not deductible business expenses of the partnership under section 707(a). Instead, in our view the net partnership income is not reduced by these amounts and each petitioner's respective share of partnership profit is increased or loss is reduced by his credited portion of the management fees in each year here in issue. *Frederick S. Klein, supra.*

Armstrong v. Phinney
394 F.2d 661 (5th Cir. 1968)

Appealing from an adverse judgment in the court below, taxpayer, Tobin Armstrong, presents a novel question for our determination: Under the Internal Revenue Code of 1954 is it legally possible for a partner to be an employee of his partnership for purposes of section 119 of the Code? In granting the government's motion for summary judgment, the District Court answered this question in the negative. We disagree and reverse.

Taxpayer is the manager of the 50,000 acre Armstrong ranch located in Armstrong, Texas. Beef cattle are raised and some of the land contains certain mineral deposits. The ranch is owned by a partnership in which taxpayer has a five percent interest. In addition to his share of the partnership profits and a fixed salary for his services as manager of the ranch, the partnership provides taxpayer certain other emoluments which are the subject of this controversy. The partnership provides a home at the ranch for taxpayer and his family, most of the groceries, utilities and insurance for the house, maid service and provides for the entertainment of business guests at the ranch. Taxpayer did not include the value of these emoluments in his gross income for the years 1960, 1961 or 1962. The Internal Revenue Service determined that these items should have been included and therefore increased his taxable income by approximately $6,000 for each year involved. Taxpayer paid the assessed deficiencies, filed a refund claim, and no action having been taken thereon within the requisite period taxpayer brought this suit seeking to recover the paid deficiencies on the ground that he is an employee of the ranch and that, as such, he comes within the provisions of section 119 of the Internal Revenue Code of 1954 and is therefore entitled to exclude the value of the items in question from his gross income. Taxpayer filed an affidavit in support of his allegations and his deposition was taken. Each side moved for a summary judgment. The court granted the government's motion without an opinion and this appeal ensued.

The case law interpreting the 1939 Internal Revenue Code held that a partner could not be an employee of his partnership under any circumstances, and that therefore no partner could take advantage of the "living expense" exclusion promulgated in the regulations and rulings under the 1939 Code. Commissioner of Internal Revenue v. Robinson, 3 Cir. 1959, 273 F.2d 503, 84 A.L.R. 2d 1211; United States v. Briggs, 10 Cir. 1956, 238 F.2d 53; Commissioner of Internal Revenue v. Moran, 8 Cir. 1956, 236 F.2d 595; Commissioner of Internal Revenue v. Doak, 4 Cir. 1956, 234 F.2d 704. The earlier cases, *Doak* and *Moran*, followed with little discussion by the later cases, were grounded on the theory, present throughout the 1939 Code, that a partnership and its partners are one inseparable legal unit. However, in 1954 Congress rejected this "aggregate theory" in favor of the "entity theory" in cases where "a partner sells property to, or performs services for the partnership." H.R. Rep. No. 1337, 83d Cong., 2d Sess. 67 (1954), U.S. Code Cong. & Admin. News 1954, pp. 4025, 4093. Under the entity approach "the transaction is to be treated in the same manner as though the partner were an outsider dealing with the partnership." Id. This solution to the problem of the characterization of a partner's dealings with his partnership was codified as section 707(a) of the 1954 Code, 26 U.S.C.A. §707(a).

Considering the legislative history and the language of the statute itself, it was manifestly the intention of Congress to provide that in any situation not covered by section 707(b)-(c), where a partner sells to or purchases from the partnership or renders services to the partnership and is not acting in his capacity as a partner, he is considered to be "an outsider" or "one who is not a partner." The terms "outsider" and "one who is not a partner" are not defined by Congress; neither is the relationship between section 707 and other sections of the Code explained. However, we have found nothing to indicate that Congress intended that this section is not to relate to section 119. Consequently, it is now possible for a partner to stand in any one of a number of relationships with his partnership, including those of creditor-debtor, vendor-vendee, *and* employee-employer. Therefore, in this case the government is not entitled to a judgment as a matter of law.

Our reversal of the District Court is not dispositive of the issues upon which rest taxpayers ultimate right of recovery. On the record before us we cannot resolve these issues, nor do we express any opinion on the final outcome of the case. Among the questions which must be answered are whether taxpayer is, in fact, an employee of the partnership; whether meals and lodging are provided for the convenience of the employer; whether living at the ranch is a condition of taxpayer's employment; whether taxpayer's wife and children are also employees and, if not, how much of the $6,000 must be allocated to their meals and lodging. These questions are not meant to be exhaustive, but are merely intended to give an indication of the nature of the inquiry into the merits which must be held on remand.

E. Problems

1. Axel and Bruce were partners in the Management Partnership. The partnership owned and operated a commercial building. Due to faulty wiring in the building, a small fire broke out causing damage to a tenant's property. When the tenant sued to recover damages from the fire, the partnership hired Axel to represent the partnership and paid him $30,000 in legal fees. With respect to Axel and Management Partnership, how is the payment of the fees treated?

---

2. Carrie, Derrick, and Ethel, all cash basis taxpayers, were partners in the Beauty-For-All Partnership. It is an accrual method partnership that owned and operated a hair salon. During the year, the partnership earned $40,000 of ordinary income.

(a) What are the consequences if Carrie leased to the partnership the building in which the business was operated. The partnership paid Carrie $10,000 each year.

(b) Alternatively, Carrie leased to the partnership the building in which the business was operated. What are the consequences if, while the partnership owed Carrie $10,000, it failed to pay her until the following year.

(c) Alternatively, what are the consequences if Carrie permitted the partnership to use the building in which the business was operated. The partnership agreed to make a special allocation of $10,000 each year to Carrie. The partnership distributed $10,000 to Carrie each year.

(d) Alternatively, what are the consequences if Carrie performed services to verify title for the building the partnership purchased to operate its business. The partnership paid Carrie $10,000 for her services.

(e) Alternatively, what are the consequences if Carrie transferred a building she owned, worth $30,000, to the partnership to use in its business. One year later, the partnership distributed stock worth $30,000 to Carrie.

(f) Alternatively, Carrie sold the building to the partnership for $100,000. What are the consequences if she had previously purchased the building for $120,000?

(g) Alternatively, Carrie sold land to the partnership for $100,000. The partnership is in the business of developing subdivisions and offering lots for sale. What are the consequences if she had previously purchased the land for $70,000?

---

3. An architect, a general contractor, and a doctor formed a partnership to build a commercial office building. Once built and leased out, the partners expect the building to earn $100,000 in lease payments each year. The architect designed the building and the general contractor oversaw its construction. The partnership agreement provided that the architect and the contractor each would receive a special allocation of $20,000 for the first two years after the building was leased out. Otherwise, income and losses would be shared equally.

How should the arrangement be treated for tax purposes? What else might you want to know to assist you in determining how the arrangement should be treated for tax purposes?

---

4. What if the partner contributes appreciated property to the partnership. Then, more than two years later, receives a distribution of property from the partnership. Should the transaction be treated as, in substance, a sale?

---

5. Application:

(a) How will you decide which structure will be best for a partner? For the partnership?

(b) What information might you need before you can offer advice?

(c) Can you advise both a partner and the partnership?

Chapter 30

Guaranteed Payments

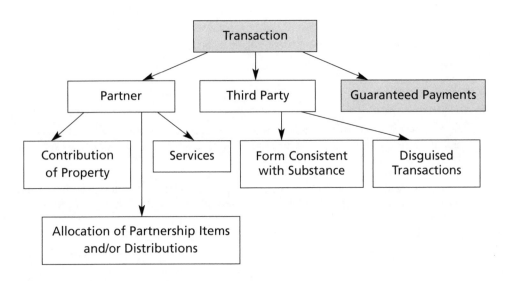

Read:

Code Sections 707(c).
Treas. Reg. § 1.707-1(c).

A. Background

Under the Code, the partnership is treated as an aggregate of the partners for purposes of reporting and paying tax on the partnership's income, gains, deductions, and losses. In general, partnership items are allocated among the partners based on the partnership agreement.[1] If the partnership agreement does not provide an allocation or there is no partnership agreement, the items will be allocated based on the partner's interest in the partnership.[2] The partners report their allocable share on their individual tax return.

---

1. Code Sec. 704(a); Treas. Reg. § 1.704-1(a).
2. Treas. Reg. § 1.704-1(b)(1)(i).

A partner is not restricted to interacting with the partnership only as a partner. He may act in his capacity as an independent third party. In such cases, the tax consequences are consistent with a transaction between the partnership and a third party.

B. Discussion of Rules

1. Identifying Guaranteed Payments

A guaranteed payment is a fixed payment made by a partnership to a partner for services or use of capital that is not dependent on whether the partnership has income or profits. It is considered as having been made regardless of whether there is partnership income.[3]

Practice Note: A guaranteed payment is a hybrid, part distributive share of partnership items and part payment to partner not acting in his capacity as a partner. To be a guaranteed payment:
- The payment must be due to be paid to a partner;
- The payment must be for services or the use of property or money; and
- The amount of the payment must not depend on whether the partnership has profits.

Example: Letti is a partner in the Hybrid Partnership. The partnership agrees to pay her $10,000 each year for services she provides to the partnership. Her services are an integral part of the partnership's activities.

Because the payment is made to her in her capacity as a partner, the payment is for her services, and she is required to be paid irrespective of whether the partnership has any income or profits, the payment is a guaranteed payment.

---

2. Tax Implications of a Guaranteed Payment

The tax consequences to the partner and partnership reflect the hybrid nature of the payments.

Partner. If the parties agree to a guaranteed payment, the partner treats the payment as his distributive share of partnership profits. He must include the amount of the guar-

---

3. Code Sec. 707(c).

anteed payment in his gross income during the year that the partnership year ends in which the partnership deducted the amount or treated the amount as paid or accrued. Whether the partner has actually received the payment is irrelevant.[4]

The income is always characterized as ordinary income; its character does not depend on the character of income received or earned by the partnership for the year in which the payment is considered made.[5]

Partnership. If the partnership agrees to a guaranteed payment, it is allowed an expense deduction for the payment if otherwise allowed in the year deemed paid or accrued. If the payment is a capital expenditure, the partnership is allowed deprecation if the item is depreciable.[6]

Tax Consequences Based on Relationship of Partner to Partnership:

	Partner	**Partnership**
As a Partner	• Receives allocation of partnership items. • Items are included on the taxpayer's individual return for the year in which the partnership's year ends. • Items are characterized at the partnership level.	• No deduction allowed for allocations made to partners.
Guaranteed Payment	• Payment is characterized as ordinary income. • Must be included in income in year deducted by the partnership, regardless of whether amount is actually paid.	• Permitted an expense or depreciation deduction to the extent allowed by the Code based on the partnership's accounting method.
As a Third Party	• Reports items as ordinary income (from compensation, rent, interest, etc.). • Include as required by the partner's method of accounting.	• Permitted an expense deduction or depreciation to the extent allowed by the Code, based on the partnership's accounting method. • Deduction may be deferred if partnership is on accrual method and partner is on cash method.

---

4. Code Sec. 707(c); Treas. Reg. 1.707-1(c).

5. Code Sec. 707(c); Treas. Reg. 1.707-1(c).

6. Code Sec. 707(c); Treas. Reg. 1.707-1(c). Because the payment must be included in the year the deduction is claimed, there is no need for deferral of the deduction under Section 267(a)(2).

C. Application of Rules

Example 1. Patsy had a one-tenth ownership interest in Consulting Services Partnership. The partnership agreement provided it would pay Patsy $10,000 each year for her consulting services, regardless of the income of the partnership.

During the year, the partnership earned $60,000. It paid Patsy $10,000. Because the payment is a fixed payment made by Consulting Services Partnership to Patsy for her services and is not dependent on whether the partnership has income or profits, the payment is a guaranteed payment. She was required to include the payment in her gross income, regardless of whether it was paid.

Consulting Services Partnership deducted the payment. The net income, $50,000, was allocated among the partners based on their ownership interests, with $5,000 being allocated to Patsy. Patsy must include $15,000 in her income, composed of the $10,000 guaranteed payment and $5,000 distributive share of income.

Example 2. Querry was a limited partner in Dentistry Partnership. The partnership agreement provided that all limited partners would receive a 5-percent return on the amount in their capital account. Because the payment is a fixed payment made by Dentistry Partnership for the use of capital and is not dependent on whether the partnership has income or profits, the payment is a guaranteed payment. Querry must include the amount of the payment in his gross income, regardless of whether it was paid. Dentistry Partnership may deduct the payment.

Example 3. Rusty had a one-third ownership interest in Architecture Partnership. The partnership agreement provided that it would pay Rusty $10,000 each year for his services, which were an integral part of the partnership business. The amount was due regardless of the income of the partnership. During the year, the partnership earned $4,000 of income and $9,000 of capital gain.

Because the payment is a fixed payment made by Architecture Partnership to Rusty for his services and is not dependent on whether the partnership has income or profits, the payment is a guaranteed payment. Rusty was required to include the amount in his income regardless of whether it was paid.

After deducting the payment from its income, Architecture Partnership has a net loss of $6,000 ($4,000 of income, less $10,000 guaranteed payment). The net loss is allocated among the partners based on their ownership interests, with $2,000 being allocated to Rusty. In addition, he is allocated one-third of the capital gain, or $3,000.

Rusty must report net income of $8,000, composed of the $10,000 guaranteed payment and $2,000 distributive share of loss. In addition, he must report $3,000 of capital gain.

Example 4. For services rendered in furtherance of the partnership business, Sam was entitled to receive 30 percent of partnership income, but not less than $10,000.

During the year, the partnership had $100,000 of income and Sam's allocable share was $30,000. None of the payment is a guaranteed payment. Rather, it is his distributive share of income.

Example 5. For services rendered in furtherance of the partnership business, Twix was entitled to receive 30 percent of partnership income, but not less than $50,000. During the year, the partnership had $100,000 of income. Because Twix's allocable share of the partnership income would be only $30,000, he must receive a guaranteed payment. Twix will receive a $28,572 guaranteed payment and 30 percent of $71,428 ($100,000 less the $28,572 guaranteed payment), or $21,428 for a total payment of $50,000 ($28,572 guaranteed payment plus $21,428 allocable share).

D. Cases and Materials

Gaines v. Commissioner

T.C. Memo. 1982-731

* * *

These consolidated cases generally involve transactions between the various petitioners and certain real estate partnerships. The issues for our decision are as follows:

* * *

2. Whether Gaines Properties, the general partner of several limited partnerships, should have reported as income certain guaranteed payments, which were accrued on the books of the limited partnerships and claimed as deductions on their partnership returns, but never paid to Gaines Properties;

* * *

Issue No. 2: Guaranteed Payments

FINDINGS OF FACT

On their partnership returns for the year 1973, Lincoln Manor, Brookwood, Gaines Realty, and Riverbend each claimed as deductions certain guaranteed payments to partners. Gaines Properties was a general partner in each of these partnerships. The amounts claimed by the limited partnerships as deductions for guaranteed payments to partners and Gaines Properties' share of those guaranteed payments were as follows:

Partnership	Amount Claimed	Gaines Properties' Share
Lincoln Manor	$74,131.26	$23,750.00
Brookwood	109,666.00	88,666.00
Gaines Realty	125,881.00	91,006.00
Riverbend	216,087.00	104,168.50

Each of the four limited partnerships accrued and claimed deductions for these guaranteed payments. Lincoln Manor, Brookwood, Gaines Realty, and Riverbend all used the accrual method of accounting on their 1973 partnership returns. Gaines Properties reported its income using the cash receipts and disbursements method of accounting.

Gaines Properties never received any of the guaranteed payments and did not report them in its income.

Respondent determined that Gaines Properties should have reported as income the guaranteed payments accrued and deducted by the four limited partnerships. Respondent, however, disallowed portions of the deductions that the four limited partnerships claimed for these guaranteed payments, on the ground that some portions were capital expenditures and not currently deductible.

Issue No. 2: Guaranteed Payments

OPINION

Lincoln Manor, Brookwood, Riverbend, and Gaines Realty accrued and claimed deductions on their partnership returns for certain "guaranteed payments," including guaranteed payments to Gaines Properties, a general partner of each limited partnership. Gaines Properties never received these guaranteed payments. Respondent disallowed to the limited partnerships portions of the claimed deductions for guaranteed payments, including some of the deductions attributable to the guaranteed payments to Gaines Properties. Notwithstanding this partial disallowance of deductions at the partnership level, respondent determined that the *entire amount* of the guaranteed payments to Gaines Properties, including the portion disallowed as deductions at the partnership level, should be included in Gaines Properties' income. Petitioners argue that the guaranteed payments that Gaines Properties did not receive, or at least such payments to the extent that the deductions therefor were disallowed at the partnership level, were not includable in Gaines Properties' income. Respondent argues that Gaines Properties' share of these guaranteed payments was includable in its income regardless of the fact that the deduction was partially disallowed at the partnership level and regardless of the fact that Gaines Properties, which used the cash method of accounting, never received the payments. We agree with respondent.

Section 707(c), as in effect in 1973, provided:

> To the extent determined without regard to the income of the partnership, payments to a partner for services or the use of capital shall be considered as made to one who is not a member of the partnership, but only for the purposes of section 61(a) (relating to gross income) and section 162(a) (relating to trade or business expenses).

This case does in fact involve "guaranteed payments" to a partner within the meaning of section 707(c) of the Code. The fact that no actual payments were made does not affect the status of these transactions as section 707(c) guaranteed payments. "[D]espite the use of the word 'payments' in both § 707(c) and the Regulations thereunder, it is clear that no actual payment need be made; if the partnership deducts the amount under its method of accounting, the 'recipient' partner must include the amount in income in the appropriate year." W. McKee, W. Nelson and R. Whitmire, Federal Taxation of Partnerships and Partners (hereinafter McKee, Nelson and Whitmire), par. 13.03[2], pp. 13–16. See also *Pratt v. Commissioner*, 64 T.C. 203, 213 (1975), affd. on this point and revd. on other grounds 550 F. 2d 1023 (5th Cir. 1977); sec. 1.707-1(c), Income Tax Regs. The parties stipulated that each of the four limited partnerships deducted "guaranteed payments." The partnership agreements of Brookwood and Gaines Realty expressly stated that certain payments to partners "shall constitute guaranteed payments within the meaning of section 707(c) of the Code." While the descriptions of such payments in the partnership agreements are not binding upon us (*Doyle v. Mitchell Bros. Co.*, 247 U.S. 179, 187 (1918)), the payments referred to in those two partnership agreements are clearly fixed sums determined without regard to partnership income. See Sec. 707(c); Sec. 1.707-1(c), Income Tax Regs. Furthermore, it is equally clear that the payments to the partners were for services in their capacities as partners. Respondent in his notices of deficiency determined that these payments were in fact guaranteed payments under section 707(c), and petitioners did not dispute this determination. Accordingly, we hold that the payments here were guaranteed payments within the meaning of section 707(c).

The statutory language of section 707(c) addresses only the character of the guaranteed payments and not the timing. Respondent's regulation under section 707(c), section 1.707-1(c), Income Tax Regs., addresses the timing question, as follows:

> Payments made by a partnership to a partner for services or for the use of capital are considered as made to a person who is not a partner, to the extent such payments are determined without regard to the income of the partnership. However, a partner must include such payments as ordinary income for his taxable year within or with which ends the partnership taxable year in which the partnership deducted such payments as paid or accrued under its method of accounting. See section 706(a) and paragraph (a) of § 1.706-1.

As the regulation makes clear, the statutory authority for the timing of the inclusion of these guaranteed payments is section 706(a), which provides:

> In computing the taxable income of a partner for a taxable year, *the inclusions required by section 702 and section 707(c)* with respect to a partnership *shall be based on the income, gain, loss, deduction, or credit* of the partnership for any taxable year of the partnership ending within or with the taxable year of the partner. (Emphasis supplied.)

The separate reference of section 707(c) guaranteed payments in the timing provisions of section 706(a) was explained by the Senate Report as simply—

> to make clear that payments made to a partner for services or for the use of capital are includible in his income at the same time as his distributive share of partnership income for the partnership year when the payments are made or accrued.... (S. Rept. No. 1622, to accompany H.R. 8300 (Pub. L. No. 591), 83d Cong., 2d Sess. 385 (1954)).

In *Cagle v. Commissioner*, 63 T.C. 86 (1974), affd. 539 F. 2d 409 (5th Cir. 1976), we held that includability and deductibility of guaranteed payments are two separate questions, and specifically that guaranteed payments are not automatically deductible simply by reason of their being included in the recipient's income. In *Cagle*, we stated 63 T.C. at 95:

> We think that all Congress meant was that guaranteed payments should be included in the recipient partner's income in the partnership taxable year ending with or within which the partner's taxable year ends and in which the tax accounting treatment of the transaction is determined at the partnership level. S. Rept. No. 1622, *supra* at pp. 94, 385, 387.

We believe our statement in *Cagle* is an accurate description of the Congressional intent. We have found nothing in the statutory language, regulations, or legislative history to indicate that includability in the recipient partner's income was intended to be dependent upon deductibility at the partnership level.

Petitioners seem to argue that there is a patent unfairness in taxing them on nonexistent income, namely income that they have neither received nor benefitted from (e.g. through a tax deduction at the partnership level). Their argument has a superficial appeal to it, but on closer analysis must fail. Except for certain very limited purposes, guaranteed payments are treated as part of the partner's distributive share of partnership income and loss. Sec. 1.707-1c), Income Tax Regs. For timing purposes guaranteed payments are treated the same as distributive income and loss. Sec. 706(a); sec. 1.706-1(a) and sec. 1.707-1(c), Income Tax Regs. A partner's distributive share of partnership income is includable in his taxable income for any partnership year ending within or with the partner's taxable year. Sec. 706(a). As is the case with a partner's ordinary distributive share of partnership income and loss, any unfairness in taxing a partner on guaranteed payments that he neither receives nor benefits from results from the conduit theory of partnerships, and is a consequence of the taxpayer's choice to do the business in the partnership form. We find no justification in the statute, regulations, or legislative history to permit these petitioners to recognize their income pro rata as deductions are allowed to the partnership. See also *Pratt v. Commissioner,* 64 T.C. 203, 213 (1975), affd. on this ground 550 F. 2d 1023 (5th Cir. 1977). We hold for respondent on the guaranteed payments issue.

* * *

Rev. Rul. 69-180, 1969-1 C.B. 183

Advice has been requested as to the proper method for computing the partners' distributive shares of the partnership's ordinary income and capital gains under the circumstances described below.

F and G are partners in FG, a two-man partnership. The partnership agreement provides that F is to receive 30 percent of the partnership income as determined before taking into account any guaranteed amount, but not less than 100x dollars. The agreement also provides that any guaranteed amount will be treated as an expense item of the partnership in any year in which F's percentage of profits is less than the guaranteed amount. The partnership agreement makes no provision for sharing capital gains.

For the taxable year in question the partnership income before taking into account any guaranteed amount, is 200x dollars, and consists of 120x dollars of ordinary income and 80x dollars of capital gains.

Section 707(c) of the Internal Revenue Code of 1954 provides that, to the extent determined without regard to the income of the partnership, payments to a partner for services or the use of capital shall be considered as made to one who is not a member of the partnership, but only for the purpose of section 61(a) (relating to gross income) and section 162(a) of the Code (relating to trade or business expenses). Section 1.707-1(c) of the Income Tax Regulations provides that for purposes of section 61(a) of the Code guaranteed payments are regarded as a partner's distributive share of ordinary income. Thus, a guaranteed payment is includible in gross income of the recipient as ordinary income, and is deductible by the partnership from its ordinary income as a business expense.

For Federal income tax purposes, F's guaranteed payment, as defined under section 707(c) of the Code is 40x dollars, 100x dollars (minimum guarantee) less 60x dollars distributive share (30 percent of partnership income of 200x dollars). See Example 2 of section 1.707-1(c) of the regulations and Revenue Ruling 66-95, C.B. 1966-1, 169.

After the guaranteed payment is taken into account, the partnership's ordinary income is 80x dollars (120x dollars of ordinary income less the 40x dollars guaranteed payment which is deductible by the partnership as a business expense under section 162 of the Code).

For Federal income tax purposes, the taxable income of the partnership amounts to 160x dollars (80x dollars of ordinary income and 80x dollars of capital gains).

Section 704(b) of the Code and section 1.704-1(b) (1) of the regulations provide that if the partnership agreement does not specifically provide for the manner of sharing a particular item or class of items of income, gain, loss, deduction, or credit of the partnership, a partner's distributive share of any such item shall be determined in accordance with the manner provided in the partnership agreement for the division of the general profits or losses (that is, the taxable income or loss of the partnership as described in section 702(a) (9) of the Code). In applying this rule, the manner in which the net profit or loss (computed after excluding any item subject to a recognized special allocation) is actually credited on the partnership books to the accounts of the partners will generally determine each partner's share of taxable income or loss as described in section 702(a) (9) of the Code. Thus, F and G share the capital gains in the same ratio in which they share the general profits from business operations.

The partnership income for the taxable year, after deduction of the guaranteed payment, is 160x dollars. Of this amount, F's distributive share, as determined above under the partnership agreement is 60x dollars. Therefore, G's distributive share is 100x dollars. Hence, the effective profit sharing ratio for the year in question is 6/16 for F and 10/16 for G. Thus, as provided by section 704 (b) of the Code, the partnership capital gains as well as the partnership ordinary income are to be shared in the ratio of 6/16 for F and 10/16 for G.

Accordingly, the amounts of ordinary income and capital gains to be reported by the partners in this case are as follows:

	F	G	Total
Ordinary income	30x dollars	50x dollars	80x dollars
Guaranteed payment	40x dollars		40x dollars
Total ordinary income	70x dollars	50x dollars	120x dollars
Capital gains	30x dollars	50x dollars	80x dollars
Total	100x dollars	100x dollars	200x dollars

Rev. Rul. 2007-40, 2007-1 C.B. 1426

ISSUE: Is a transfer of partnership property to a partner in satisfaction of a guaranteed payment under section 707(c) a sale or exchange under section 1001, or a distribution under section 731?

FACTS: Partnership purchased Blackacre for $500x. A, a partner in Partnership, is entitled to a guaranteed payment under section 707(c) of $800x. Subsequently, when the fair market value of Blackacre is $800x and Partnership's adjusted basis in Blackacre is $500x, Partnership transfers Blackacre to A in satisfaction of the guaranteed payment to A.

LAW AND ANALYSIS: Section 731(b) provides that no gain or loss shall be recognized to a partnership on a distribution to a partner of property, including money.

Section 707(c) provides that, to the extent determined without regard to the income of the partnership, payments to a partner for services or for the use of capital are considered as made to one who is not a member of the partnership, but only for the purposes of § 61(a) (relating to gross income) and, subject to § 263, for purposes of § 162(a) (relating to trade or business expenses).

Section 61(a)(3) provides the general rule that gross income includes gains derived from dealings in property. In addition, section 1001(a) provides that the gain from the sale or other disposition of property shall be the excess of the amount realized over the adjusted basis provided in section 1011 for determining gain, and the loss shall be the excess of the adjusted basis over the amount realized.

Section 1001(b) further provides, in part, that the amount realized from the sale or other disposition of property shall be the sum of any money received plus the fair market value of the property (other than money) received.

A taxpayer that conveys appreciated or depreciated property in satisfaction of an obligation, or in exchange for the performance of services, recognizes gain or loss equal to the difference between the basis in the distributed property and the property's fair market value. See, e.g., International Freighting Corp., Inc. v. Commissioner, 135 F.2d 310 (2d Cir. 1943), United States v. General Shoe Corp., 282 F.2d 9 (6th Cir. 1960).

A transfer of partnership property in satisfaction of a partnership's obligation to make a guaranteed payment under section 707(c) is a sale or exchange under section 1001. Because the transfer is a sale or exchange under section 1001, it is not a distribution within the meaning of section 731. Accordingly, the nonrecognition rule in section 731(b) does not apply to the transfer.

Partnership realizes a $300x gain when Partnership transfers Blackacre in satisfaction of its section 707(c) guaranteed payment to A, the difference between the adjusted basis of the property ($500x) to the partnership and the property's fair market value ($800x).

HOLDING: A transfer of partnership property to a partner in satisfaction of a guaranteed payment under section 707(c) is a sale or exchange under section 1001, and not a distribution under section 731.

E. Problems

1. Selim had a one-fourth ownership interest in Consulting Partnership. The partnership agreement provided that it would pay Selim $50,000 each year for his services, re-

gardless of the income of the partnership. During the year, the partnership earned $40,000 of income and had a $12,000 short-term capital gain. What are the consequences to Selim and the partnership?

2. Tritt had a one-third ownership interest in Investment Partnership. The partnership agreement provided that it would pay Tritt a 10-percent return on the amount in his capital account each year. For the year, his capital account value was $100,000.

During the year, the partnership earned $40,000 of income and had a $3,000 capital loss. What are the consequences to Tritt and the partnership?

3. Utt had a one-fourth ownership interest in the Interior Design Partnership. The partnership agreement provided that, as compensation for his services, it would pay Utt one-fourth of the partnership income. However, in no event would it pay him less than $50,000. During the year, the partnership earned $100,000 of income. What are the consequences to Utt and the partnership?

4. Application:

(a) When would you advise a partner to insist upon receiving a guaranteed payment?

(b) How would you explain to a partner who, under the partnership agreement is entitled to a guaranteed payment, but is not paid, that he must include the amount in his gross income?

(c) When would you advise the partnership to agree to make a guaranteed payment?

(d) Can you advise both the partner and the partnership? Do you anticipate a possible conflict of interest?

(e) Draft language for a partnership agreement providing a partner a guaranteed payment.

Overview Problem — Putting It All Together

Stacey, Bill, and Olivia have just formed a partnership to own and operate the coffee shop and are in the process of working out the details. They plan to operate the business out of the corner shop of a commercial building owned by Bill. Olivia, who contributed a substantial amount of cash, is primarily interested in making sure that the business is successful so that she can receive a good return on her investment. She plans to stay with the business for only a few years, then leave the partnership to open a flower shop. Stacey plans to spend a substantial amount of her time working at the shop, but needs to be certain she earns enough money to pay her mortgage.

The partners are pretty clear about their personal objectives for the partnership. But, they are not sure how to structure their various arrangements to make sure they achieve those goals. Nor do they want their individual objectives to interfere with those of another partner. In addition, they would like to obtain the best overall tax result possible, without taking any controversial positions.

The partners have set a time for a partnership meeting to discuss the arrangements between the partners and between the partners and the partnership. You have been invited to the meeting to advise them.

1. How many different options are available when addressing the relationship of the partner to the partnership?

2. With respect to Bill:

    (a) How many of those options might apply to meeting Bill's objectives?

    (b) Which option would you recommend to him? Why?

    (c) If Bill agrees with your recommendation, what steps should you take?

3. With respect to Olivia:

    (a) How many of those options might apply to meeting Olivia's objectives?

    (b) Which option would you recommend to her? Why?

    (c) If Olivia agrees with your recommendation, what steps should you take?

4. With respect to Stacey:

    (a) How many of those options might apply to meeting Stacey's objectives?

    (b) Which option would you recommend to her? Why?

    (c) If Stacey agrees with your recommendation, what steps should you take?

5. Do you anticipate a conflict of interest if you offer advice to each of the three partners?

Practitioner's Checklist

☐ Clarify transactions between each partner and the partnership. (Contribution of property? Rental of property? Loan?)

☐ Determine if any partner will receive a guarantee payment.

Item to include in the partnership or operating agreement:

☐ If there is a guaranteed payment, language describing the guaranteed payment.

IX.

Termination of a Partnership

Overview Problem

Stacey, Bill, and Olivia have operated the coffee shop for a number of years. While the shop has been very successful, they all have decided that they would like to explore other opportunities. They are not sure they want to leave the coffee shop business, but are open to suggestions as to how to expand, whether it be franchising the business, merging into a larger coffee chain, or expanding the coffee business into other areas. Olivia has always been interested in opening a fudge factory and Bill has been interested in opening a small book store.

The partners have set a time to meet and discuss their various options. You have been invited to the meeting to advise them.

End of a Partnership

```
              ┌─────────────────────────┐
              │    End of a Partnership  │
              └─────────────────────────┘
               ↙                      ↘
   ┌──────────────────┐      ┌──────────────────┐
   │  Reorganization  │      │   Termination    │
   └──────────────────┘      └──────────────────┘
                             ↙                  ↘
                 ┌──────────────────┐   ┌──────────────────┐
                 │  Discontinuance  │   │ Sale or Exchange │
                 │   of Business    │   │                  │
                 └──────────────────┘   └──────────────────┘
```

Chapter 31

Reorganization

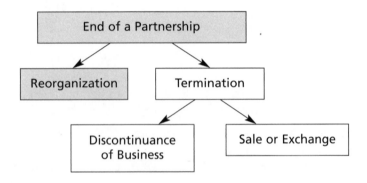

Read:

Code Sections 708(a), (b)(2).
Treas. Reg. § 1.708-1(c)(1)-(4), -1(d)(1)-(4).

A. Background

Under the Revised Uniform Partnership Act, a general partnership may convert into a limited partnership if approved by all the partners or by a number or percentage specified for conversion in the partnership agreement.[1] A limited partnership may be converted into a general partnership if agreed to by all the partners.[2] Under either scenario, the partnership after the conversion is treated as the same entity as that before the conversion, with all the assets and liabilities vesting in the new partnership.[3]

Under a plan of merger, a partnership may merge with one or more other partnerships. The plan must be approved by all the partners or a number or percentage specified for merger in the partnership agreement. If the partnership is a limited partnership, the merger generally must be approved by all the partners.[4] When a merger takes effect, the partnerships, other than the surviving partnership, no longer have a separate

---

1. RUPA § 902.
2. RUPA § 903.
3. RUPA § 904.
4. RUPA § 905.

existence. The assets and liabilities of each of the partnerships vests in the surviving partnership.[5]

B. Discussion of Rules

A partnership, rather than terminating outright, may transform itself by incorporating, merging with another partnership, dividing into separate partnerships, or converting from a general partnership to a limited partnership or vice versa.

1. Incorporation

A partnership may end its partnership status by incorporating. It may structure the incorporation in several different ways, including:[6]

- The partnership contributes all its assets and liabilities to a newly-formed corporation in exchange for stock;
- The partnership terminates and distributes its assets to its partners. The partners then contribute the assets and liabilities to a newly-formed corporation in exchange for stock.
- The partners contribute their partnership interests to a newly-formed corporation in exchange for stock.

The different methods of incorporation may lead to different tax results. For example, to the extent the transfer complies with the requirements of Section 351, it will be tax free. Thus, the parties may select one form over others in order to achieve certain tax results. The Internal Revenue Service has ruled that it will respect the form chosen by the parties.[7] In addition, if the parties elect to convert a partnership into a corporation under state law, and the state law does not require the actual transfer of assets or interests, the transaction will be treated as a contribution of the partnership's assets and liabilities to a newly-formed corporation in exchange for stock. In effect, the partnership is treated as if it had elected to be classified as a corporation for federal tax purposes.[8]

2. Mergers

A partnership may merge with another partnership. The merger may be structured in several different ways, including:

- The partnership transfers its assets and liabilities to a different partnership in exchange for partnership interests. Those interests are then distributed to its partners in a liquidating distribution (often referred to as assets-over form).

---

5. RUPA § 906.
6. See Rev. Rul. 84-111, 1984-2 C.B. 88.
7. Rev. Rul. 84-111, 1984-2 C.B. 88.
8. Rev. Rul. 2004-59, 2004-1 C.B. 1050.

- The partnership may liquidate and distribute its assets to its partners. The partners then contribute the assets and liabilities to a different partnership in exchange for partnership interests (often referred to as assets-up form).
- The partners contribute their (old) partnership interests to a different (new) partnership in exchange for partnership interests. The new partnership liquidates the old partnership (often referred to as interest-over form).

If partners from one of the merged partnerships own more than 50 percent of capital and profits interest in the surviving partnership, the surviving partnership will be considered a continuation of that merged partnership.[9] All other merged partnerships are considered terminated.

If partners from more than one of the merged partnerships own more than 50 percent of capital and profits interest in the surviving partnership, the surviving partnership will be considered a continuation of the partnership that contributed the greatest net value to the surviving partnership. All other merged partnerships are considered terminated.[10]

If partners from any of the merged partnerships do not own more than 50 percent of capital and profits interest in the surviving partnership, then the surviving partnership is considered a new partnership; all other merged partnerships are considered terminated.[11]

Practice Tip: If a partnership is treated as a continuation of the merged partnership, the partnership must file its return for the full taxable year of the continuing partnership. The return must: [Treas. Reg. § 1.708-1(c)(2)]
- State that the partnership is a continuation of a merging or consolidating partnership;
- Identify all of the partnerships that were terminated in the merger or consolidation; and
- Set forth the distributive shares of the partners for the periods before and after the date of the merger.

If the partnership is treated as terminating, it's tax years closes on the date of the merger. It must file a tax return for a tax year ending on that date. [Code Sec. 706(c)(1); Treas. Reg. § 1.708-1(c)(1), -1(c)(2).]

The different methods of merging the partnership with or into another partnership may lead to different tax results. Thus, the parties may select one form over another in order to achieve certain tax results. If the parties select either the assets-over or the assets-up form for the merger, the Service will respect the form.[12] If the parties select the interest-over form or are unclear about the form, the Service will treat the transaction as an assets-over merger.[13]

---

9. Code Sec. 708(b)(2)(A).
10. Treas. Reg. § 1.708-1(c)(1).
11. Id.
12. Treas. Reg. § 1.708-1(c)(3).
13. Treas. Reg. § 1.708-1(c)(3)(i).

Change in liabilities. In determining the liability of a partner for purpose of computing his basis,[14] any increases and decreases associated with the merged partnership and the surviving partnership are netted.[15]

Partner not continuing in surviving partnership. A partner may not want to become a partner in the surviving partnership. Accordingly, his interest may be bought out. If the transaction is structured as an assets-over merger and the merged partnership does not want the buy-out to be treated as a sale under the disguised sale provisions,[16] the form as a buy-out of the partner's interest will be respected if the merger agreement specifies that the surviving partnership is purchasing an interest from a particular partner in the merged partnership and specifies the consideration that is transferred for the interest.[17]

3. Divisions

A partnership may divide into two or more partnerships. It may divide by:

- The partnership transferring its assets and liabilities to at least two new partnerships in exchange for partnership interests. Those interests are then distributed to its partners in a liquidating distribution (often referred to as assets-over form).
- The partnership liquidating and distributing its assets to its partners. The partners then contribute the assets and liabilities to two or more newly-formed partnerships in exchange for partnership interests (often referred to as assets-up form).

If partners in the resulting partnerships owned more than 50 percent of the prior partnership, the resulting partnerships are a continuation of the prior partnership.[18] Any other partnership is considered a new partnership. If none of the resulting partnerships have partners who owned more than 50 percent of the prior partnership, the prior partnership is considered terminated.[19]

The different methods by which a partnership may divide a partnership into two or more partnership may result in different tax consequences. Thus, the parties may select one form over another in order to achieve certain tax results. Accordingly, if the parties select either the assets-over or the assets-up form for the division, the Service will respect the form.[20] If the parties are unclear about the form, the Service will treat the transaction as an assets-over merger.[21]

4. Conversions

A partner can convert a general partnership interest into a limited partnership interest in the same partnership, or vice versa, tax free. The transaction is treated as if

---

14. See Code Sec. 752, discussed in Chapters 6. 7, 19 and 20.
15. Treas. Reg. § 1.752-1(f).
16. See Code Sec. 707(a)(2)(B).
17. Treas. Reg. § 1.708-1(c)(4).
18. Code Sec. 708(b)(2)(B).
19. Treas. Reg. § 1.708-1(d)(1).
20. Treas. Reg. § 1.708-1(d)(3).
21. Treas. Reg. § 1.708-1(d)(3)(i).

the partner had contributed his old partnership interest to the partnership in exchange for the new interest.[22] Similarly, a partnership may convert into a limited liability company, or vice versa, tax free if the new entity continues the business of the old entity.[23]

C. Application of Rules

Example 1. Kelo, LaShawn, and Melinda were equal partners in the Square Partnership. Nemo and Osiris were equal partners in the Circle Partnership. Square Partnership and Circle Partnership merged to form Triangle Partnership, with each partner receiving a one-fifth interest.

Kelo, LaShawn, and Melinda own more than 50 percent of Triangle Partnership. Accordingly, Triangle Partnership is considered a continuation of Square Partnership. Circle Partnership is treated as having terminated.

Example 2. Parish and Quinlen each owned 40 percent and Royce and Sarah each owned 10 percent of Divisive Partnership. The partnership owned Greenacre, Whiteacre, and Blackacre with fair market values of $4,000, $4,000, and $2,000, respectively.

Divisive Partnership contributed Whiteacre to First Partnership and distributed 100 percent of the partnership interests to Parish and Quinlen as equal partners. It contributed Blackacre to Second Partnership and distributed 100 percent of the partnership interests to Royce and Sarah as equal partners. Royce and Sarah are no longer partners in Divisive Partnership. Finally, Divisive Partnership, now referred to as Third Partnership, continued to own Greenacre. Only Parish and Quinlen continued as partners in Third Partnership.

The division was accomplished with an assets-over form; Divisive Partnership is deemed to contribute Whiteacre to First Partnership and Blackacre to Second Partnership. Because Parish and Quinlen, as partners in First Partnership and Third Partnership, owned more than 50 percent of Divisive Partnership, First Partnership and Third Partnership are a continuation of Divisive Partnership. Second Partnership is a new partnership.

---

22. Rev. Rul. 84-52, 1984-1 C.B. 157.
23. Rev. Rul. 95-37, 1995-1 C.B. 130.

Chapter 32

Termination of a Partnership

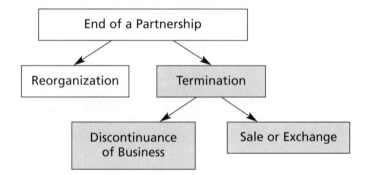

Read:

Code Sections 708(a), (b)(1).
Treas. Reg. § 1.708-1(a), (b).

A. Background

1. Relevant State Law Provisions

Under the Uniform Partnership Act (UPA), in general, a partner's leaving the partnership may cause the partnership to dissolve and terminate.[1] Under the Revised Uniform Partnership Act (RUPA), a partner's leaving the partnership is referred to as dissociation.[2] A partner has the power to dissociate from a partnership at any time.

Under the RUPA, a partner's dissociation from a partnership may cause the partnership to dissolve and terminate.[3] For example, a partner's voluntarily leaving an at-will partnership will cause a dissolution of the partnership.[4]

---

1. UPA § 29-31.
2. RUPA § 601.
3. RUPA § 801.
4. RUPA § 801(1).

Practice Tip: A partnership may intend to be in existence for:
- A term of years;
- For the length of time necessary to complete a specific undertaking; or
- Until the partners decide to discontinue operating as a partnership (at-will).

In general, a partnership continues after dissolution only for the purpose of winding up its business.[5] In winding up the business, the assets of the partnership are applied to discharge its obligations to creditors, including partners who are creditors. Any remaining amount is distributed to the partners in accordance with their rights to distributions.[6] When the winding up of the business is complete, the partnership is terminated.[7]

Practice Alert: An event that causes dissolution of a partnership under state law may not be considered termination of a partnership for federal tax purposes and vice versa.

---

2. Liquidating Distributions

Recall that, in general, a partner does not recognize gain or loss when he receives a distribution of cash from a partnership.[8] Rather, the partner's outside basis is reduced by the amount of cash distributed.[9] However, to the extent the cash distributed exceeds the partner's outside basis, the partner must recognize gain.[10]

Similarly, generally, a partner does not recognize gain or loss when he receives a distribution of property from a partnership. Rather, the partner's outside basis is reduced by the basis of the asset distributed.[11] To the extent the basis in the property is larger than the partner's outside basis, the basis in the property is reduced to reflect the partner's outside basis, then the asset is distributed.[12] The partner will then have a zero outside basis.

---

5. RUPA §802(a).

6. RUPA §807.

7. RUPA §802(a).

8. Code Sec. 731(a). The partnership does not recognize any gain or loss on the distribution. Code Sec. 731(b); Treas. Reg. §1.731-1(b).

9. Code Sec. 733(1).

10. Code Sec. 731(a)(1).

11. Code Secs. 731(a); 733(2). The partnership does not recognize any gain or loss on the distribution. Code Sec. 731(b); Treas. Reg. §1.731-1(b).

12. Code Sec. 732.

B. Discussion of Rules

1. Termination of a Partnership

A partnership is treated as continuing until it terminates.[13] It is terminated under two situations. First, the partnership terminates if no part of the partnership's business continues to be conducted in partnership form. The partners may liquidate the partnership assets, pay off creditors, distribute any remaining amounts to the partners, and terminate the partnership.

Practice Tip: If one partner in a two-partner partnership dies, the partnership is not considered as terminated if the estate or other successor in interest of the deceased partner continues to share in the profits or losses of the partnership. [Treas. Reg. § 1.708-1(b)(1)(i)]

Second, the partnership terminates if there is a sale or exchange of 50 percent or more of the total interests in partnership capital and profits within a 12-month time period.[14] In determining if there has been a sale or exchange of more than 50 percent of partnership interests, all sales during a 12-month time frame are aggregated.[15] Sales between partners are considered.[16]

Some transfers are not considered. If one interest is sold more than once (re-sales), the sale is considered only once. A transfer of an interest by gift, bequest, or inheritance is not considered a sale or exchange. The liquidation of a partner's interest is not considered a sale or exchange.[17]

Practice Tip: The 12-month period is any 12 consecutive months. It is not dependent on the calendar year or the partnership's year for tax purposes.

---

13. Code Sec. 708(a).
14. Code Sec. 708(b)(1); Treas. Reg. § 1.708-1(b)(2). This termination provision does not apply to electing large partnerships. Code Sec. 774(c).
15. Code Sec. 708(b)(1)(B).
16. Treas. Reg. § 1.708-1(b)(2).
17. Id.

2. Effect of Termination of a Partnership

a. *Winding Up and Termination*

When a partnership's business is no longer conducted in partnership form, the partnership affairs are wound up and the partnership is liquidated. The rules that apply to non-liquidating distributions[18] from a partnership apply to distributions from a partnership that is terminating. In general, a partner does not recognize gain or loss when he receives a distribution of cash from a partnership.[19] Rather, the partner's outside basis is reduced by the amount of cash distributed.[20] However, to the extent the cash distributed exceeds the partner's outside basis, the partner must recognize gain.[21]

Similarly, in general, a partner does not recognize gain or loss when he receives a distribution of property from a partnership. Rather, the partner's outside basis is reduced by the basis of the asset distributed.[22] To the extent the basis in the property is larger than the partner's outside basis, the basis in the property is reduced to reflect the partner's outside basis, then the asset is distributed.[23] The partner will then have a zero outside basis.

If the amount of unrealized receivables and substantially appreciated inventory on one hand and capital and hotchpot (Section 1231) assets on the other hand is not proportionate, the rules of Section 751(b) will come into play and recharacterize the transaction so that the partner receives a proportionate amount of each type of asset.[24]

A partnership taxable year closes on the date on which the partnership terminates. If no part of the partnership's business continues to be conducted in partnership form, the partnership terminates on the date on which the winding up of the partnership affairs is completed.

b. *Technical Termination*

If a partnership is deemed terminated because of a sale or exchange of 50 percent or more of the total interests in partnership capital and profits within a 12-month time period, the partnership is deemed to have contributed all of its assets and liabilities to a new partnership in exchange for an interest in the new partnership.[25] The terminated partnership distributes the interests in the new partnership to the purchasing partner

---

18. See, *e.g.*, Code Secs. 731; 732(a); 733; 735. Note that Section 736 generally is not applicable to a complete liquidation of the partnership.

19. Code Sec. 731(a). The partnership does not recognize any gain or loss on the distribution. Code Sec. 731(b); Treas. Reg. § 1.731-1(b).

20. Code Sec. 733(1).

21. Code Sec. 731(a)(1).

22. Code Secs. 731(a); 733(2). The partnership does not recognize any gain or loss on the distribution. Code Sec. 731(b); Treas. Reg. § 1.731-1(b).

23. Code Sec. 732.

24. Rev. Rul. 77-412, 1977-2 C.B. 223. See discussion of Section 751(b) in Chapter 25.

25. Treas. Reg. § 1.708-1(b)(3).

and the remaining partners based on their ownership interests in the terminated partnership. The terminated partnership is liquidated.[26]

The new partnership's basis in the assets is the same as the terminated partnership's basis.[27] No Section 704(c) built-in gain or loss is created, but any built-in gain or loss from the terminated partnership is preserved in the new partnership. No gain is triggered under either the provision addressing distribution of property previously contributed by a partner (Section 704(c)(1)(B)) or other mixing bowl provisions (Section 737). Nor does the termination begin a new seven year period for purposes of those provisions. Rather, a distribution of Section 704(c) property by the new partnership to a partner is subject to Section 704(c) and Section 737 to the same extent it would have been if distributed by the terminated partnership.

The partners' capital accounts in the new partnership are the same as they were in the terminated partnership.[28]

The buyer-partner will have the benefit of basis adjustment in the property of the new partnership if the terminated partnership has made a section 754 election. The election may be made on the final return of the terminated partnership.[29] The basis adjustment is made before the deemed contribution to the new partnership. If the new partnership makes the election, all of the partners are entitled to a basis adjustment with respect to the assets deemed contributed.[30]

Practice Tip: The new partnership may use the terminated partnership's taxpayer identification number. [Treas. Reg. §§ 1.708-1(b)(4); 301.6109-1(d)(2)(iii)]

C. Application of Rules

Example 1. On January 10, 2006, Micah sells his 40 percent partnership interest in Square Partnership to Casey. On May 15, 2006, Darrus sells his 40 percent partnership interest in Square Partnership to Windsor. There has been a sale or exchange of 50 percent or more of the total interests in partnership capital and profits (*i.e.*, there has been

---

26. Treas. Reg. § 1.708-1(b)(4). The partnership terminates on the date of the sale or exchange of the partnership interest which, either alone or in conjunction with other sales and exchanges, results in the transfer of an interest of 50 percent or more of partnership capital and profits. Treas. Reg. § 1.708-1(b)(3).

27. Treas. Reg. § 1.708-1(b)(4).

28. Treas. Reg. §§ 1.708-1(b)(4); 1.704-1(b)(2)(iv)(l).

29. Treas. Reg. § 1.708-1(b)(5).

30. Treas. Reg. § 1.761-1(e).

a sale of 80 percent of partnership interests) within a 12-month time period. The partnership terminates for tax purposes on May 15, 2006.

Example 2. On January 10, 2006, Pointjack sells his 40 percent partnership interest in Oval Partnership to Rhiener. On May 15, 2006, Rhiener sells his 40 percent partnership interest in Square Partnership to Rife. The sale of the 40 percent partnership interest is counted only once. Thus, there has not been a sale or exchange of 50 percent or more of the total interests in partnership capital and profits within a 12-month time period. The partnership does not terminate.[31]

Example 3. Glory and Ossie are equal partners in the Equine Partnership. The partnership's balance sheet appears as follows:

Asset	Adj. Basis	FMV	Partner	Adj. Basis	Cap. Acct.
Cash	$30,000	$30,000	Glory	$25,000	$40,000
Acct. Rec.	-0-	10,000	Ossie	25,000	40,000
Land	20,000	40,000		$50,000	$80,000
Total:	$50,000	$80,000			

None of the assets were contributed to the partnership by a partner. The partnership has not made a Section 754 election.

On March 1, 2006, Glory sells his interest to Saline for $40,000. There has been a sale or exchange of 50 percent of the total interests in partnership capital and profits within a 12-month time period. Equine Partnership terminates.

Equine Partnership is deemed to transfer its assets to a new partnership in exchange for an interest in the new partnership. The new partnership's basis in the assets will be the same as Equine Partnership's basis in the assets,[32] and Equine Partnership will take a basis in the partnership interest equal to the basis of the assets it contributed, or $50,000.[33]

Equine will then distribute one-half of the interest in the new partnership to Ossie and one-half to Saline. Ossie will take the new partnership interest with a basis of $25,000. Saline will take the new partnership interest with a basis of $40,000.[34] Saline will succeed to Glory's capital account. Equine Partnership then liquidates.

After the above transactions, the balance sheet of the new partnership will appear as follows:

Asset	Adj. Basis	FMV	Partner	Adj. Basis	Cap. Acct.
Cash	$30,000	$30,000	Saline	$40,000	$40,000
Acct. Rec.	-0-	10,000	Ossie	25,000	40,000
Land	20,000	40,000		$65,000	$80,000
Total:	$50,000	$80,000			

---

31. Treas. Reg. § 1.708-1(b)(2).
32. Code Sec. 722.
33. Code Sec. 723.
34. Code Sec. 732(b).

D. Cases and Materials

Sirrine Building No. 1 v. Commissioner
T.C. Memo. 1995-185, aff'd 117 F.3d 1417 (5th Cir. 1997)

This matter is before the Court on petitioner's motion to dismiss for lack of jurisdiction filed December 22, 1993, pursuant to Rule 40.

In her notice of final partnership administrative adjustments (hereinafter FPAA) dated January 25, 1993, respondent determined that Sirrine Building No. 1 (Partnership) failed to report long-term capital gain for tax year 1985, in the amount of $3,514,339.

The tax matters partner, M. Allen Winter (petitioner), does not deny that Partnership failed to report capital gain. He alleges instead that the gain should have been reported in 1982; that Partnership incorrectly reported the transaction as an installment sale in 1982, 1983, and 1984; that Partnership was terminated and dissolved prior to December 31, 1984, and thus had no obligation to file (and did not file) a return for 1985; and that Partnership is thus not subject to the audit and deficiency procedures of the Tax Equity and Fiscal Responsibility Act of 1982, Pub. L. 97-248, 96 Stat. 324 (TEFRA) for 1985 because it was no longer in existence. Therefore, petitioner contends, the Court lacks subject matter jurisdiction.

FINDINGS OF FACT

* * *

The following facts are not in dispute. Partnership was formed in 1979 for the purpose of acquiring land, constructing a building thereon, and then leasing or selling the building and land. It financed the construction through an insurance company with a $7 million note secured by a first lien on the property. In 1981, Partnership sold the building for $11,247,464: A $2,265,000 cash downpayment and an $8,982,464 wraparound mortgage. The buyer purchased the building subject to, but not assuming, the $7 million note. The gain on the sale was properly reported under the installment method of accounting.

In 1982, the buyer paid off $2 million of the wraparound mortgage and assumed the remaining balance of the $7 million note, thereby, in effect, paying off the entire purchase price. The wraparound deed of trust was released by Partnership in accordance with the terms of the wraparound note.

The parties agree that Partnership should have recognized gain on the unrecognized installments in 1982, because that was the year in which Partnership was relieved of indebtedness on the building, thereby "collapsing" the installment transaction.

Partnership did not, however, report the gain on the unrecognized installments in 1982. Instead, it continued to report the transaction as an installment sale for the taxable years 1982, 1983, and 1984. Partnership attached to the returns balance sheets and schedules of partnership accounts that reflected the $8,982,464 note, minus applicable payments, as a note receivable.

Partnership did not file a return for 1985 (when the period of limitations for 1982 had apparently expired).

The December 31, 1984, balance sheets filed with the 1984 partnership return reflect the following: [chart omitted]

Respondent contends that the 1982 events did not cause the termination of Partnership and that the financial statements attached to its 1984 return demonstrate that Partnership had not completed, or even embarked upon, the winding-up process.

* * *

Petitioner contends that Partnership was terminated before 1985, and it did not file a partnership return in 1985; thus, he argues that it is not subject to the unified partnership audit and litigation procedures and that the FPAA issued by respondent is invalid.

Respondent counters as follows: Partnership reported an installment sale in 1981 and continued to consistently report the installment sale as an ongoing transaction in 1982, 1983, and 1984. On its face Partnership's 1984 return was not a final return. The returns thus reflect continuing partnership activity. Therefore, Partnership was required to file a return in 1985. We agree with respondent that we have jurisdiction over this proceeding.

The test for determining whether an entity is a partnership is whether

considering all the facts — the agreement, the conduct of the parties in execution of its provisions, their statements, the testimony of disinterested persons, the relationships of the parties, their respective abilities and capital contributions, the actual control of income and the purposes for which it is used, and any other facts throwing light on their true intent — the parties in good faith and acting with a business purpose intended to join together in the present conduct of the enterprise. *Commissioner v. Culbertson*, 337 U.S. 733, 742 (1949).

Here there is no question that at one time a partnership existed. The issue concerns whether it terminated before 1985. The intent of the partners is a question of fact. *Id.* at 741.

Section 708(a) provides that an existing partnership shall be considered as continuing if it is not terminated. Section 708(b), in pertinent part, provides that a partnership shall be considered terminated only if no part of any business, financial operation, or venture of the partnership continues to be carried on by any of its partners in a partnership. Sec. 708(b)(1)(A).

While State law generally determines when the partnership dissolves, the question of termination of a partnership for Federal tax purposes is determined by Federal law. A termination of a partnership is thus distinct from a mere dissolution of a partnership. *Fuchs v. Commissioner*, 80 T.C. 506, 509 (1983). A partnership's taxable year closes on the date on which the partnership terminates. Sec. 1.708-1(b)(1)(iii), Income Tax Regs. The date of termination is, for purposes of section 708(b)(1)(A), the date on which the winding up of the partnership affairs is completed. Sec. 1.708-1(b)(1)(iii)(a), Income Tax Regs.

The Partnership agreement provided:

> Upon dissolution a proper accounting shall be made of the Joint Venture's assets, liabilities and operations from the date of the last previous accounting to the

date of dissolution. The profits or losses realized subsequent to the date of dissolution shall be allocated in accordance with Article VI and proper adjustments made to the Capital Accounts of each Venturer.

Although petitioner contends that the partnership was terminated "prior to January 1, 1985", he does not tell us what the termination date was. In his affidavit attached to the motion to dismiss, petitioner opines that "The 1982 events constituted, as a matter of law and pursuant to Article X of the Joint Venture Agreement, the complete dissolution, winding up, and termination of the partnership." However, in his "response to respondent's response" petitioner states:

If, in fact, the Partnership return for 1983 reflects the activities asserted by Respondent, Respondent may be correct that the Partnership did not terminate in 1982 but continued for tax law purposes into 1983 * * * * However, the continued existence of the Partnership until 1983 is not evidence of its continuing existence in 1985. * * * *

Clearly, by the end of 1983, all of the affairs of the Partnership had been wound up, and only the preparation and filing of tax returns, reflecting the error of S. E. Sirrine Company [a partner] and its accountants in continuing to report the sale on the installment method, continued. There was no continuing business or financial activity or joint venture being conducted by the partners and all affairs of the Partnership had been wound up, including distribution of all of its assets and satisfaction of all of its indebtedness. Whether the Partnership technically terminated in 1982 or 1983 is irrelevant for purposes of determining whether or not it continued in 1985.

Petitioner is mistaken in his view that the specific termination date is irrelevant, because "an existing partnership *shall* be considered as continuing if it is not terminated." Sec. 708(a) (emphasis added). Moreover, the 1983 and 1984 partnership returns do, in fact, show continuing financial activity.

The partnership return for 1983 reports a continuing business enterprise and continued financial operations. It shows accounts payable reduced from $1,400 to zero. It shows trade accounts of $2,969. Partnership was reimbursed by the general contractor for liabilities to subcontractors which had been accrued and capitalized. This required the recomputation of the gross profit ratio to determine the proper amount of the reported installment to be included in income. Partnership wrote off a bad debt in the amount of $1,624. It incurred deductible expenses for professional fees of $525. It continued to deduct interest on the wraparound note. As respondent says:

The fact that the partnership was hiring professionals and paying them for services rendered, writing off uncollectible debts, deducting interest, receiving reimbursement for liabilities that had been capitalized and adjusting the tax books for recomputation of the proper gross profit ratio indicates that the partnership continued its business and financial operations during the taxable year 1983.

The return for 1984 continues to reflect financial activity, though at a reduced level. It reflects a continuing enterprise. In addition to continuing the installment treatment of the sale, Partnership reported $697,539 of interest income and $707,056 in losses. The return reflects unfinished business, in that the partnership had not settled accounts between partners with respect to their capital contributions and in accordance with the partnership agreement. According to the return, for tax accounting purposes the partners' capital accounts totaled $3,454,598 on January 1, 1984, and $3,442,337 on December 31, 1984. The financial statements attached to the return report partners' capital accounts individually and as a total. An entire schedule is devoted to reporting changes in the partners' capital accounts as a result of transactions of the partnership during the year.

Information contained in a tax return is an admission by the taxpayer and indicative of the partners' intention to continue the partnership. In *Fuchs v. Commissioner*, 80 T.C. 506 (1983), we concluded that a partnership was not terminated until at least 1975, even though the partnership dissolved in 1969 when the taxpayer withdrew and ceased to be associated with the carrying on of partnership business. Our conclusion was supported by the fact that the partnership continued to file tax returns after its dissolution, and the taxpayer continued to report receipts from the partnership. Here, Partnership filed returns through 1984, and petitioner reported partnership income (losses) on his individual Federal income tax returns through at least 1984.

The Partnership's return for 1984 reflects that as of the end of that year, no "proper accounting had been made of the assets, liabilities, and operations from the date of the last previous accounting to the date of dissolution", and the individual partners' capital accounts had not been brought to zero, as required by the partnership agreement upon dissolution. In short, the winding up was not completed by December 31, 1984. There was no termination for Federal tax purposes. Sec. 1.708-1(b)(1)(i), Income Tax Regs.

Based on this record, we find that the partnership was not terminated before January 1, 1985, and was thus required to file a partnership return for 1985. The FPAA is therefore valid, and we have jurisdiction to decide this case.

* * *

E. Problems

1. Andy, Barbie, and Carl are equal partners in Circle Partnership. Does Circle Partnership terminate under the following facts:

(a) On January 1, 2007, Andy sells his one-third interest to Danny. On June 30, 2007, Barbie sells her one-third interest to Eugene.

(b) Alternatively, on January 1, 2007, Andy sells his one-third interest to Danny. On June 30, 2007, Danny sells his recently acquired one-third interest to Eugene.

---

2. Application: How can the partners plan to avoid an inadvertent termination of the partnership caused by a sale or exchange of partnership interests? Under state law? Under federal law?

Overview Problem—Putting It All Together

Stacey, Bill, and Olivia have operated the coffee shop for a number of years. While the shop has been very successful, they all have decided that they would like to explore other opportunities. They are not sure they want to leave the coffee shop business, but are open to suggestions as to how to expand, whether it be franchising the business, merging into a larger coffee chain, or expanding the business into other areas. Olivia has always been interested in opening a fudge factory and Bill has been interested in opening a small book store.

The partners have set a time to meet and discuss their various options. You have been invited to the meeting to advise them.

1. Can you utilize any of the various reorganization provisions to assist the partners in exploring their options?

2. If one of the partners wants to leave the business:

   (a) How many ways could you structure the transaction?

   (b) Will a partner's leaving necessarily cause a termination of the partnership? Under federal law? Under state law? Under their partnership agreement?

3. What additional facts might you want to know to assist you in advising the partners?

4. Can you advise all the partners? Or, is there a conflict of interest?

Practitioner's Checklist

☐ Length of existence of the partnership (specific undertaking, a term of years, at will): _____

Item to include in the partnership or operating agreement:

☐ If the partnership is to terminate at a specific time or upon a specific event, including language in the partnership agreement providing for such termination.

X.

Partnership Status

Overview Problem

Stacey, Bill, and Olivia want to own and operate a coffee shop. They are not sure what legal steps they need to take to do so. But, they have heard about partnerships and are thinking that it might be the entity that would work best for them. However, they would like to know more about what the consequences would be if they did decide to operate the coffee shop through a partnership.

The partners have scheduled a meeting to discuss their options. You have been invited to the meeting to advise them.

Chapter 33

Check the Box Regulations

Read:

Code Sections 761(a); 7701(a)(2).
Treas. Reg. §§ 1.761-1(a); 301.7701-1, -2(a), -2(b)(1)-(7), -3(a), -3(b)(1),
-3(c)(1)(i)-(iv), -3(c)(2).

A. Background

1. State Law

State law establishes which entities can be created in the state. State law also sets forth the rights, obligations, and responsibilities of the entity owners to each other, to the entity, between the entity and a third party, and between the owners and a third party. In general, states provide, at a minimum, for partnerships, limited liability companies, and corporations.

Under the Revised Uniform Partnership Act a partnership exists when two or more people carry on as co-owners a business for profit.[1] The partners share the profits of the business and, in addition to the partnership, are individually liable for its debts.[2] While a partnership can arise by operation of law, regardless of whether a certificate has been obtained, all states provide for creation of a partnership by filing with the state.

2. Prior Federal Law

For federal tax purposes, the government is not bound by the state law characterization of an entity. Rather, characterization of an entity for tax purposes is based on federal rules and definitions.[3]

Prior to 1997, federal law classified entities based on their characteristics. In general, it focused on six characteristics:[4]

---

1. RUPA §§ 101(b); 202.
2. RUPA §§ 401(b); 306.
3. Treas. Reg. § 301.7701-1(a).
4. See *United States v. Kintner*, 216 F.2d 418 (9th Cir. 1954), *aff'g* 107 F. Supp. 976 (D. Mont. 1952).

- Association;
- An objective to carry on business and share its profits;
- Continuity of life;
- Centralized management;
- Limited liability; and
- Free transferability of interests.

However, because both a partnership and a corporation are an association and are formed to carry on a business for profit, those two characteristics were not helpful in determining if an entity was a partnership or a corporation. By focusing on the remaining characteristics, continuity of life, centralized management, limited liability and free transferability of interests, the Internal Revenue Service could determine whether the entity had more partnership characteristics or more corporate characteristics.

The result of focusing on the four characteristics was in reality an emphasis on drafting partnership agreements or corporate by-laws with the factors in mind. Regardless of the intent of the parties, parties who failed to incorporate the necessary provisions into their agreements might later have found that their entity was reclassified. For example, even though the parties formed a corporation under state law, for federal tax purposes the Internal Revenue Service might have classified the entity as a partnership. And, partners who formed a partnership under state law might have found the partnership classified as a corporation for federal tax purposes.

With the advent of the limited liability company, the distinction between a corporation and a partnership became blurred. As a result, the characteristics could no longer be relied upon to properly classify an entity as either a corporation or a partnership for federal tax purposes.

B. Discussion of Rules

In 1997, the old characteristic-based system was replaced with the much simpler, and more predictable, check-the-box regulations. The regulations set forth a progression of choices and default rules that can be followed to determine the classification of the entity. The check-the-box regulations only apply to business entities.[5] They do not apply to trusts.[6]

Definition of partnership. The parties need not have formed a partnership under state law to be treated as a separate entity under federal law. For federal tax purposes, a partnership is a joint venture or other contractual arrangement where the participants carry on a business, financial operation, or venture and share the profits.[7] Similarly, if the

---

5. Treas. Reg. § 301.7701-2.
6. Treas. Reg. § 301.7701-2(a).
7. Code Sec. 761(a); Treas. Reg. § 1.761-1(a). See also Commissioner v. Culbertson, 337 U.S. 733 (1949); Luna v. Commissioner, 42 T.C. 1067 (1964).

parties have formed a partnership under state law, but do not meet the definition of a partnership under federal law, the entity may be disregarded for federal tax purpose. For example, if the parties have formed a partnership under state law, but only share expenses, it is not a partnership for federal tax purposes.[8]

Default provisions. Under the default provisions, if the entity is classified as a corporation under state law, it is a corporation for federal tax purposes.[9] Publicly traded partnerships are also classified as corporations for federal tax purpose.[10] If the entity is not a corporation and there are two or more members, the entity is classified as a partnership.[11] If the entity is not a corporation and there is only one owner, the entity is disregarded as an entity separate from its owner (*i.e.*, if owned by an individual, treated as a sole proprietorship; if owned by a corporation, treated as a branch or division).[12]

Election out of default provisions. If the entity is not a corporation and there are two or more members (*i.e.*, under the default rules would be treated as a partnership), the owners can elect to be treated as a corporation.[13] If the entity is not a corporation and there is only one owner (*i.e.*, under the default rules would be disregarded as an entity separate from its owner), the owner can elect to be classified as a corporation.[14]

Election. An election is only required when the owners want a different result than what the default rules provide.[15] The election must be signed by either each member of the entity, including any prior members who would be impacted by the election, or an officer, manager, or member authorized to make the election.[16]

Practice Note: The taxpayer makes an election under the check-the-box regulations by filing a Form 8832, Entity Classification Election.

Once an entity makes an election, it cannot make a subsequent election for 60 months. However, if more than 50 percent of the ownership interests are owned by those who did not have an ownership interest when the first election was made, the Internal Revenue Service may permit the entity to make a subsequent election during the 60-month period.[17]

---

8. Treas. Reg. § 301.7701-1(a)(2).
9. Treas. Reg. § 301-7701-2(b)(1)-(8).
10. Code Sec. 7704; Treas. Reg. § 301-7701-2(b)(7).
11. Treas. Reg. § 301-7701-2(c)(1); -3(b)(1)(i).
12. Treas. Reg. § 301-7701-2(c)(2); -3(b)(1)(ii).
13. Treas. Reg. § 301-7701-3(a).
14. Id.
15. Treas. Reg. § 301-7701-3(a), -3(c)(1).
16. Treas. Reg. § 301.7701-3(c)(2).
17. Treas. Reg. § 301.7701-3(c)(1)(iv).

Practice Note: For federal tax purposes, an entity will be classified as one of the following:
- Disregarded entity;
- Partnership; or
- Corporation.

Entity Classification—Check the Box Regulations

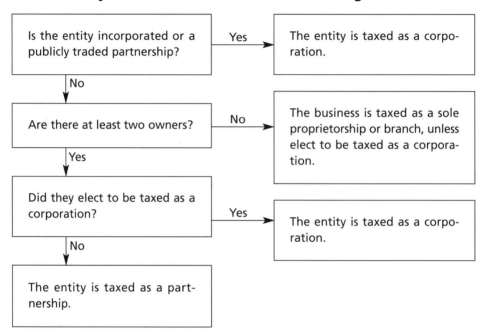

C. Application of Rules

Example 1. Jaggy and Kraal owned adjacent parcels of land. To improve access to both properties they decided to construct a driveway along the common edge. They shared the costs associated with the construction.

Because Jaggy and Kraal are not carrying on a business or financial operation and dividing profits therefrom, they have not created a separate entity for federal tax purposes.[18]

Example 2. Lagusi owns and operates a restaurant as a sole proprietorship. Because the restaurant is not a separate business entity, the check-the-box regulations are inapplicable.

Example 3. Missy and Nellie formed a limited liability company. Because the entity is not a corporation and there are two or more members, under the default rules the en-

---

18. Treas. Reg. § 301.7701-1(a)(2).

tity is classified as a partnership for federal tax purposes. However, they may file a Form 8832, Entity Classification Election, and elect to be classified as a corporation.

D. Problems

1. Which of the following would be considered a separate entity for federal tax purposes:

(a) Lisle and Fredrick own Alpineacres as tenants-in-common. They hold the land for investment.

(b) Gretl and Marta own Vermontacres as tenants-in-common. They developed the land, creating several subdivisions, and offered the lots for sale.

(c) Maria and Gaylord share a recording studio. They each record, produce, and market their own music independently. Except for the studio rent, which they share equally, their financial arrangements are independent.

2. Your clients, Kurt and Brigitta, have formed a partnership to own and operate a music store. Under the check-the-box default rules they are classified as a partnership. Under what circumstances would you advise them to elect to be classified for federal tax purposes as a corporation?

3. Application:

(a) Does the state in which you practice provide standardized forms for the formation of a partnership? If so, do the forms ask for information on whether the owners have joined together to operate the business with an intent to make a profit?

(b) Does your state have a presumption for when parties are considered to be a partnership? If so, when does the presumption apply?

(c) If your clients wanted to make an election under the check-the-box regulations, where would you find Form 8832?

Chapter 34

Family Partnerships

Read:

Code Section 704(e).
Treas. Reg. § 1.704-1(e)(1), -1(e)(3)(a), -1(e)(3)(b).

A. Background

Case law is replete with examples of families attempting to lower their cumulative tax burden by shifting items of income, gain, deduction, or loss among themselves. The Supreme Court case of *Horst v. Helvering*[1] is an example of an attempt by taxpayers to shift income between family members. The taxpayer clipped interest coupons from a bond and gave them to his son. The issue before the court was who was the correct taxpayer to include the coupon interest in income, the dad or the son. The Supreme Court turned to the fruit and tree analysis it had first utilized in *Lucas v. Earl*[2] and stated that the fruit could not be attributed to a different tree from that upon which it grew. Using this axiom, it held that, because the father held the tree (the bond), he should be taxed on the fruit (the interest coupons).[3] In other words, the person who controls the capital that generated the income is the person who should pay tax on the income. To allow otherwise would be to allow taxpayers to shift income between themselves and to the taxpayer with the lowest marginal rate, potentially avoiding or improperly reducing the family's overall tax liability.

The Tax Court case of *Salvatore v. Commissioner*[4] is an example of an attempt by taxpayers to shift gain from the disposition of property between family members. Mrs. Salvatore entered into an agreement to sell an oil and gas station to Texaco. However, after she entered into the sale agreement, she transferred one-half of the property to her five children. The sale was then completed by Mrs. Salvatore and her five children as the sellers. Mrs. Salvatore reported one-half of the gain and her five children reported one-half of the gain.

---

1. 311 U.S. 112 (1940).
2. 281 U.S. 111 (1930).
3. The holding in Horst is sometimes interpreted as requiring the taxpayer who controls the income (rather than the property that generated the income) to report the income.
4. T.C. Memo. 1970-30, *aff'd*, 434 F2d 600 (3d Cir. 1970).

The Internal Revenue Service argued that, even though the form of the transaction was a sale from Mrs. Salvatore and her children to Texaco, the substance of the transaction was a sale of the entire property by Mrs. Salvatore. The transfers to her children should be disregarded and Mrs. Salvatore should report all of the gain. The Tax Court agreed with the Internal Revenue Service.

B. Discussion of Rules

When family members form a partnership, there may be issues regarding whether all members are participating in the partnership or whether the entity is being used as a means to shift income.[5] Accordingly, the entity must meet the general definition of a partnership[6] and not run afoul of assignment of income principles. In addition, special rules apply.

Family. The family of an individual includes his spouse, ancestors, and lineal descendants, and any trust for the primary benefit of such persons.[7]

1. Recognition as a Partner

If capital is a material income-producing factor, a family member will be recognized as a partner only if he owns a capital interest in the partnership. It is not relevant how the family member obtained his partnership interest.[8] Capital is not a material income producing factor if the income of the business consists principally of fees, commissions, or other compensation for personal services performed by members or employees of the partnership. Capital is ordinarily a material income-producing factor if the operation of the business requires substantial inventories or a substantial investment in plant, machine, or other equipment.[9]

2. Allocation of Income

If a partner received his interest from a family member, the donor partner must be adequately compensated. Thus, in general, the donee partner must include his distributive share of partnership items in his gross income. However, income will be re-allocated from the donee to the donor if the donee's share of income is determined without allocating a reasonable amount of compensation for services rendered to the partnership by the donor partner. Similarly, income will be reallocated from the donee

---

5. Family limited partnerships have become popular for use in estate planning. As any issues involving the use of family limited partnerships to lower estate and gift tax do not involve income tax issues, they are not addressed in these materials.

6. See Code Sec. 761(a) and Commissioner v. Culberston, 337 U.S. 733 (1949).

7. Code Sec. 704(e)(3).

8. Code Sec. 704(e)(1).

9. Treas. Reg. § 1.704-1(e)(1)(iv).

to the donor if the donee's share of income is disproportionately greater than the interest in partnership capital he received.[10] The same rules apply if the interest was purchased from a family member.[11]

C. Cases and Materials

Commissioner v. Culbertson
337 U.S. 733 (1949)

* * *

The *Tower* case thus provides no support for [the position of the Tax Court]. We there said that the question whether the family partnership is real for income-tax purposes depends upon

> "Whether the partners really and truly intended to join together for the purpose of carrying on business and sharing in the profits or losses or both. And their intention in this respect is a question of fact, to be determined from testimony disclosed by the 'agreement, considered as a whole, and by their conduct in execution of its provisions.' Drennen v. London Assurance Corp., 113 U.S. 51, 56, 5 S.Ct. 341, 344; Cox v. Hickman 8 H.L.Cas. 268. We see no reason why this general rule should not apply in tax cases where the Government challenges the existence of a partnership for tax purposes." 327 U.S. at page 287, 66 S.Ct. at page 536.

The question is not whether the services or capital contributed by a partner are of sufficient importance to meet some objective standard supposedly established by the *Tower* case, but whether, considering all the facts—the agreement, the conduct of the parties in execution of its provisions, their statements, the testimony of disinterested persons, the relationship of the parties, their respective abilities and capital contributions, the actual control of income and the purposes for which it is used, and any other acts throwing light on their true intent—the parties in good faith and acting with a business purpose intended to join together in the present conduct of the enterprise.

D. Problems

1. Andy is an accountant. He gives his son, Opie, a 10 percent interest in his accounting practice. Did Andy and Opie form a partnership?

---

2. June owns a commercial building subject to a 20-year lease. She transfers the building, subject to the lease, to a partnership with her sons Wally and Beaver. Did June, Wally, and Beaver form a partnership?

---

10. Code Sec. 704(e)(2); Treas. Reg. § 1.704-1(e)(3)(i).
11. Code Sec. 704(e)(3).

3. Angela owns an apartment building that generates $100,000 in rental income each year. She transfers the building to a partnership with her son, Jonathon. Each year, Angela actively manages the apartment building. The value of her services is approximately $20,000 each year. Pursuant to the partnership agreement, partnership income is to be allocated equally between the partners. Will the allocation in the partnership agreement be respected?

Chapter 35

Election Out of Subchapter K

Read:

Code Section 761(a).
Treas. Reg. § 1.761-1(a); -2.

A. Background

State law. Under the Revised Uniform Partnership Act a partnership exists when two or more people carry on as co-owners a business for profit.[1] The partners share the profits of the business and, in addition to the partnership, are individually liable for its debts.[2] While a partnership can arise by operation of law, regardless of whether a certificate has been obtained, all states provide for creation of a partnership by filing with the state.

Federal law. The parties need not have formed a partnership under state law to be treated as a partnership under federal law. For federal tax purposes, a partnership is a joint venture or other contractual arrangement where the participants carry on a business, financial operation, or venture and share the profits.[3] Similarly, if the parties have formed a partnership under state law, but do not meet the definition of a partnership under federal law, the entity may be disregarded for federal tax purpose. For example, if the parties have formed a partnership under state law, but only share expenses, it is not a partnership for federal tax purposes.[4]

---

1. RUPA §§ 101(b); 202.
2. RUPA §§ 401(b); 306.
3. Code Sec. 761(a); Treas. Reg. § 1.761-1(a). See also Commissioner v. Culbertson, 337 U.S. 733 (1949); Luna v. Commissioner, 42 T.C. 1067 (1964).
4. Treas. Reg. § 301.7701-1(a)(2).

B. Discussions of Rules

1. Election Out of Subchapter K

An entity that is a partnership for federal tax purposes generally is governed by the partnership provisions found in subchapter K of the Internal Revenue Code.

Practice Note: The partnership provisions of subchapter K are included in Sections 701 through 761. [Subchapter K also includes the rules for electing large partnerships. See Code Sec. 771 through 777.]

However, under certain circumstances, the owners can elect to have the partnership provisions not apply.

First, if the organization is used for investment purposes only, and not for the active conduct of a business, the owners may elect out of application of the partnership provisions.[5] To be able to elect out, the owners must:[6]

- Own the investment property as co-owners;
- Reserve the right separately to take or dispose of their shares of any property acquired or retained; and
- Not actively conduct business or irrevocably authorize some person acting in a representative capacity to purchase, sell, or exchange the investment property.

Second, if an organization is used for the joint production, extraction, or use of property, but not for the purpose of selling services or property produced or extracted, the owners may elect out of application of the partnership provisions. The owners must:[7]

- Own the property as co-owners;[8]
- Reserve the right separately to take in kind or dispose of their shares of any property produced, extracted, or used; and
- Not jointly sell services or the property produced or extracted.[9]

Third, if an organization is used by dealers in securities for a short period for the purpose of underwriting, selling, or distributing a particular issue of securities, the owners can elect out of application of the partnership provisions.[10]

---

5. Code Sec. 761(a).

6. Treas. Reg. § 1.761-2(a)(2).

7. Treas. Reg. § 1.761-2(a)(3).

8. The owners may own the property in fee, under lease, or under another form of contract granting exclusive operating rights. Treas. Reg. § 1.761-2(a)(3).

9. Each separate participant may delegate authority to sell for periods of not longer than one year. Treas. Reg. § 1.761-2(a)(3).

10. Code Sec. 761(a).

The election to opt out of the partnership provisions does not change the nature of the partnership. Rather, the parties are treated as co-owners of the property and each partner reports on his return his income and deductions with respect to the property. However, with respect to provisions outside subchapter K, and which are not interdependent with subchapter K, the entity is still treated as a partnership. For example, the entity still will come within the definition of partnership in Section 7701 and the check-the-box provisions continue to apply.

Practice Note: If an organization elects out of the partnership provisions (subchapter K), each partner can:
- Compute income or loss from their individual ownership interest;
- Individually elect the method for computing depreciation;
- Qualify for a like-kind exchange treatment; and
- Elect out of the installment method of reporting.

Election. The election must be agreed to by all the owners.[11] Once made, a valid election is irrevocable without the consent of the Internal Revenue Service, as long as the organization continues to qualify.[12]

Practice Note: To make a formal election to elect out of the partnership provisions of subchapter K, the organization files a partnership return with the name and address of the organization. No other information (*e.g.*, income or deductions) should be included on the return. The organization should attach a statement to the return that includes the following: [Treas. Reg. § 1.761-2(b)(2)(i); Rev. Rul. 56-500, 1956-2 C.B. 464. The statement does not need to be signed by every member.]
- Names, addresses, and identification numbers of all the members of the organization;
- Statement that the organization qualifies for the election, and the basis for the qualification;
- Statement that all of the members of the organization elect the exclusion; and
- Information regarding where a copy of the operating agreement may be obtained.

The election should be filed in the first taxable year that the organization receives income or makes or incurs any expenditures treated as a deduction. [Treas. Reg. § 301.6031-1(a)(2)]

An informal election will be deemed to have been made if all of the surrounding facts and circumstances show that it was the intention of the owners at the time of for-

---

11. Id.
12. Treas. Reg. § 1.761-2(b)(3).

mation to be excluded from the partnership provisions.[13] An agreement among the owners to be excluded from the partnership provisions will be considered evidence of such intention. Similarly, the owners of substantially all of the capital interests in the organization reporting their respective share of the income, deductions, and credits of the organization on their individual tax returns will be considered evidence of the owners' intention to make the election.[14]

2. Qualified Joint Ventures

If a husband and wife conduct a qualified joint venture, the venture is not treated as a partnership. Rather, all items of income, gain, loss, deduction, and credit from the venture are allocated between the spouses based on their respective ownership interests. Each spouse treats the items as if they were generated from a sole proprietorship.[15] A "qualified joint venture" is a joint venture that conducts a business, is owned solely by the spouses, both spouses materially participate, and the spouses elect to have Section 761(f) apply.[16]

C. Application of Rules

Example. Mary and Jane formed Investment Partnership to acquire and hold land solely for investment purposes. Pursuant to the partnership agreement, they each have free transferability of their partnership interest and the land may not be subdivided or in any manner developed for sale. Investment Partnership may elect out of application of the partnership provisions.

D. Problem

What questions would you ask your client to help you decide if you should advise him to elect out of the partnership provisions?

---

13. Treas. Reg. § 1.761-2(b)(2)(ii).
14. Id.
15. Code Sec. 761(f)(1). The spouses must file a joint return and each spouse files a Schedule C.
16. Code Sec. 761(f)(2).

Chapter 36

Anti-Abuse Regulations

Read:

Treas. Reg. § 1.701-2(a)-(c), -2(e), -2(h).

A. Background

1. Regulations

If a statute in the Code does not specifically direct the Secretary to issue regulations, the Secretary still has the authority to issue interpretative regulations. Section 7805(a) gives the Secretary the general authority to issue "all needful rules and regulations for the enforcement" of the Code. Regulations issued under this authority are called interpretative (or interpretive) regulations.

The court will follow an interpretative regulation as long as it implements the Congressional mandate in some way. If Congress has directly spoken to the question at issue, and the intent of Congress is clear, the regulation must give effect to the Congressional intent. If Congress has not spoken directly to the question at issue, the court will not determine which potential interpretation is the best, the taxpayer's or the Internal Revenue Service's; rather it will limit itself to determining only whether the Service's interpretation is reasonable. A regulation is considered reasonable if it is consistent with the statutory language and the statute's origin and purpose. A statute's legislative history is often considered in determining its purpose.[1]

2. Non-Statutory Legal Principles

When the Internal Revenue Service and the courts disagree with the taxpayer's characterization of a transaction, they often have turned to legal principles not found in the Code to restructure the transaction. At various times both have looked to the following legal arguments:

- Substance over form;
- Step transaction doctrine;

---

1. NationsBank of N.C., N.A. v. Variable Annuity Life Ins. Co., 513 U.S. 251, 257 (1995).

- A lack of business purpose; and
- The sham transaction doctrine.

Through these provisions, the Service and the courts have restructured transactions, resulting in different tax consequences from those planned by the taxpayer.

B. Discussion of Rules

Given the flexibility partnerships provide, they often are used to carry out tax planning. However, sometimes the taxpayer's use of a partnership and partnership tax provisions appears to be inconsistent with the intent of the partnership provisions.

To help combat the inappropriate use of partnerships in tax avoidance or deferral schemes, the Internal Revenue Service issued regulations incorporating the common law legal principles of substance over form, the step transaction doctrine, business purpose, and sham transactions. These regulations often are referred to as the anti-abuse regulations. The regulations are intended to supplement current common law principles, not supplant them.[2]

1. Abusive Use of a Partnership

Under the first group of regulations, for tax purposes the Service can restructure a transaction into a transaction that is consistent with the intent of the partnership provisions.[3] The intent of the partnership provisions is to allow taxpayers to conduct joint business or investment activities through a flexible economic arrangement without incurring an entity-level tax.[4] To come within this intent, the partnership must meet the following requirements:[5]

- The partnership must be bona fide; each partnership transaction or series of related transactions must be entered into for a substantial business purpose.
- The form of each partnership transaction must satisfy the doctrine of substance over form.
- The tax consequences of the partnership provisions to each partner of partnership operations and transactions between the partner and the partnership must accurately reflect the partners' economic arrangement and clearly reflect the partner's income.

If the transaction meets the business purpose and substance over form doctrines, reflected in the first two requirements, the last requirement does not have to be met if a partnership provision allows the partners to not clearly reflect the income.

---

2. Treas. Reg. § 1.701-2(h).
3. Treas. Reg. § 1.701-2(a)-(c).
4. Treas. Reg. § 1.701-2(a).
5. Treas. Reg. § 1.701-2(a)(1)-(3).

If the partnership was formed for the principal purpose of substantially reducing the present value of the partners' aggregate tax liability and the reduction was achieved in a manner that is inconsistent with the intent of the partnership provisions, the Commissioner can restructure the transaction into one that is consistent with the intent of the partnership provisions.[6] The Commissioner can:[7]

- Disregard the partnership and treat the partners as owning the assets directly;
- Disregard one or more partners;
- Change the partnership's accounting method to one that clearly reflects the partnership's or a partner's income; or
- Reallocate partnership items.

Facts and circumstances. To assist in determining whether the partnership was formed for the principal purpose of substantially reducing the present value of the partners' aggregate tax liability in a manner that is inconsistent with the intent of the partnership provisions, the regulations set forth facts and circumstances to consider.[8] The factors are indicative only; they do not necessarily establish that the partnership was used inconsistent with the intent of the provisions. The presence or absence of any factor does not create a presumption about use of the partnership. The weight to be given to any of the factors depends on the facts and circumstances.[9]

The list of factors, while not exclusive, includes:[10]

- The present value of the partners' federal income tax liability is substantially less than if the partners had owned the partnership assets directly.
- The present value of the partners' federal income tax liability is substantially less than it would have been if purported separate transactions are integrated and treated as steps in a single transaction.
- There are partners who are necessary to achieve the claimed tax results but who have a nominal interest or are substantially protected from any risk of loss.
- Substantially all the partners are related.
- There are special allocations of partnership items that are inconsistent with the purpose of Section 704(b).
- The ownership of property nominally contributed to the partnership is effectively retained by the contributing partner.
- The benefits and burdens of ownership of partnership property are effectively shifted to a distributee partner other than at the time of actual distribution.

2. Abuse Treatment of Partnership as an Entity

Under the second group of regulations, to the extent necessary to carry out the intent of the Code and regulations, the Service can disregard the partnership and treat the

---

6. Treas. Reg. § 1.701-2(b).
7. Id.
8. Treas. Reg. § 1.701-2(c).
9. Id.
10. Treas. Reg. § 1.701-2(c)(1)-(7).

partners as an aggregate of its partners.[11] However, if a Code provision or regulation prescribes the treatment of a partnership as an entity in whole or in part and that treatment and the ultimate tax results, taking into account all relevant facts and circumstance, are clearly contemplated by that provision, the anti-abuse provision will not apply.[12]

C. Application of Rules

Example 1. General Corporation and Darcy decided to form a limited partnership to operate a movie theatre. General Corporation was the general partner with a one percent general partnership interest. Darcy was the limited partner with a 99 percent limited partnership interest. They chose the limited partnership form to provide limited liability to Darcy but not incur an entity-level tax.

The partnership provisions are intended to permit taxpayers to conduct a joint business activity through a flexible economic arrangement without incurring an entity-level tax. Even though Darcy has retained, indirectly, substantially all of the benefits and burdens of ownership of the assets contributed to the partnership, the decision to operate the business through a partnership is consistent with the intent of the partnership provisions. Thus, the Commissioner cannot recast the transaction under the anti-abuse provisions.[13]

Example 2. Elaine and Fern formed a general partnership to manage a commercial building. Elaine and Fern each contributed $10,000. The partnership purchased a building for $100,000, using the $20,000 cash and obtaining a $80,000 non-recourse debt. Elaine and Fern strongly believe that the value of the building will increase significantly in the next ten years.

The partnership agreement provided that capital accounts would be maintained in accordance with the regulations, that partners had an obligation to restore negative capital account balances, and that liquidating distributions would be made in accordance with capital account balances. It also contained a minimum gain chargeback provision. Pursuant to the partnership agreement, all income and expenses would be allocated equally between the partners, except for all depreciation, which would be allocated 80 percent to Elaine and 20 percent to Fern.

The partnership provisions are intended to permit taxpayers to conduct a joint business activity through a flexible economic arrangement without incurring an entity-level tax. The decision to manage the commercial building through a partnership is consistent with this intent.

Section 704(b) allows partnership items to be allocated in a manner that differs from the partners' respective ownership interests, provided that the statutory and regulatory criteria have been met and the allocation has substantial economic effect. Based on the

---

11. Treas. Reg. § 1.701-2(e)(1).
12. Treas. Reg. § 1.701-2(e)(2).
13. Treas. Reg. § 1.701-2(d) Ex. 1.

provisions in the partnership agreement, the allocation of both recourse and non-recourse deductions has substantial economic effect. In addition, the regulations provide that the value of property is presumed to decrease consistent with allowable depreciation. The tax results that will be obtained by Elaine and Fern through the special allocation of depreciation, taking into account all the facts and circumstances, were contemplated by the Section 704(b) provisions.

Thus, even though the partners' overall tax liability may be substantially less than if the partners had owned the property directly, the transaction is not inconsistent with the intent of the partnership provisions. The Commissioner cannot recast the transaction under the anti-abuse provisions.[14]

D. Problems

1. Read Section 701. Are the anti-abuse regulations interpretative or legislative regulations?

---

2. Cathy and Dennis formed an equal general partnership to sell state-of-the art cookware throughout the world. The partnership agreement provided that capital accounts will be maintained in accordance with the regulations, that liquidating distributions will be made in accordance with capital account balances, and both partners have an obligation to restore negative capital account balances. In addition, it provided that all income from sales in the United States will be allocated to Dennis and all income from sales outside the United States will be allocated to Cathy.

Cathy is a resident of the United States and is responsible for marketing outside the United States. Dennis is a nonresident alien who is not subject to income tax from sales generated in the United States; he is responsible for marketing in the United States. At the time they enter into the agreement, they are relatively certain that sales outside the United States will equal sales in the United States.

(a) Will the allocation have substantial economic effect?

(b) What provisions would you provide in support of your position? Will you need to rely on the anti-abuse regulations?

---

3. Can you think of a situation where the government would need to rely on the anti-abuse regulations because no statutory provision, regulatory provision, or case law supports its position?

---

14. Treas. Reg. § 1.701-2(d) Ex. 6.

Chapter 37

TEFRA

Read:

Code Section 761.

A. Background

1. Statutory Notice of Deficiency

If the Internal Revenue Service proposes changes to the taxpayer's income tax return and the taxpayer does not agree to the changes and the disagreement cannot be resolved through Appeals, he will be issued a statutory notice of deficiency. If the taxpayer wants to continue his challenge to the Service's proposed adjustments, he has the option of bringing suit in the United States Tax Court. To do so, the taxpayer must file a petition, generally within 90 days from the date the statutory notice of deficiency was mailed to him.[1]

2. Partnerships

A partnership can be viewed as an aggregate of the partners or as a separate entity. Recall that the Uniform Partnership Act follows the approach that a partnership is an aggregate of the partners. The Revised Uniform Partnership Act (RUPA) follows the approach that a partnership is a separate entity.[2] Under the Code, the partnership is treated as an aggregate of the partners for purposes of reporting and paying tax on the partnership's income, gains, deductions, and losses. In general, partnership items are allocated among the partner based on the partnership agreement.[3] If the partnership agreement does not provide an allocation or there is no partnership agreement, the items will be allocated based on the partners' interest in the partnership.[4] The partners report their allocable share on their individual tax return.

Before the enactment of the partnership-level audit provisions, proposed adjustments to partnership items had to be made where they were reported and the taxes

---

1. I.R.C. §§6212, 6213.
2. RUPA §201(a).
3. Code Sec. 704(a); Treas. Reg. §1.704-1(a).
4. Treas. Reg. §1.704-1(b)(1)(i).

paid—at the partner level. As partnerships became more complex and partners more geographically diverse, making adjustments to each partner's return became unworkable and often was inconsistent as between partners.

B. Discussion of Rules

Sections 6221 through 6234 are often referred to as the TEFRA provisions or unified audit procedures. They were enacted as part of the Tax Equity and Fiscal Responsibility Act of 1982. In general, the provisions provide that examination, administrative, and judicial actions for certain partnerships are conducted at the partnership level. If the TEFRA provisions apply, the Internal Revenue Service can make adjustments to partnership items only by using the TEFRA provisions.[5] However, once the partnership-level audit is complete, each partner is liable for the tax results.[6]

Partnerships covered by TEFRA provisions. In general, a partnership that has 11 or more partners at any time during the taxable year is covered by the provisions. When determining the number of partners, a husband and wife are counted as one partner.[7] However, a partnership that does not come within the TEFRA provisions can elect to be treated as a TEFRA partnership.[8]

Partnership items. For those partnerships covered by the TEFRA provisions, partnership items are determined at the partnership level. Partnership items include:[9]

- Items that appear on the partnership tax return; and
- Other issues that are more appropriately determined through an examination of the partnership's books and records.

Items that appear on the partnership tax return include items such as the partners' distributive share, determination of liabilities, partnership items used for computation purposes only, and the character of an asset.

A non-partnership item is an item that is not a partnership item or is treated as other than a partnership item.[10] An affected item is a type of non-partnership item that is affected by a partnership item.[11]

Tax matters partner. In administrative proceedings, the Internal Revenue Service will deal primarily with the tax matters partner. It is the tax matter partner's responsibility to keep the other partners informed of any administrative or judicial proceedings.[12] However, any partner has the right to participate in partnership administrative proceedings.[13]

---

5. Code Sec. 6221.
6. Code Sec. 6225.
7. Code Sec. 6231(a)(1)(B).
8. Code Sec. 6231(a)(1)(B)(ii).
9. Code Sec. 6231(a)(3).
10. Code Sec. 6231(a)(4).
11. Code Sec. 6231(a)(5).
12. Code Sec. 6223(g).
13. Code Sec. 6224.

The partnership designates a tax matters partner.[14] If the partnership does not make a designation, the general partner having the largest profits interest is the tax matters partner. If more than one partner has an identical interest, the tax matters partner will be the partner whose name appears first alphabetically.[15] If it is not practical for the Internal Revenue Services to apply the largest profits rule, the Commissioner will select as the tax matters partner any person who was a general partner at any time during the taxable year and owned a profits interest. If a general partner cannot be selected, the Commissioner will select any partner who was a partner in the partnership at the close of the taxable year under examination.[16]

The tax matters partner generally receives notice on behalf of the partnership and for non-notice partners of the commencement of partnership proceedings, of interim events, and of the notice of final partnership administrative adjustment. The final partnership administrative adjustment is, for the partnership, the equivalent of a notice of deficiency for an individual.

The tax matters partner has the authority to settle issues for non-notice partners.[17] He may extend the period during which the Service may issue a notice of final partnership administrative adjustment. If the partnership intends to challenge adjustments in the notice, the tax matters partner can choose the forum for pursuing litigation.[18]

Statute of limitations. Generally, the Service may assess a deficiency attributable to partnership items for at least three years after the partnership return is filed.[19] If a petition was filed in response to the notice of final partnership administrative adjustment, the statute is tolled for one year after the decision of the court becomes final.

---

14. Code Sec. 6231(a)(7)(A).
15. Code Sec. 6231(a)(7)(B).
16. Code Sec. 6231(a)(7).
17. Code Sec. 6224(c)(3).
18. Code Sec. 6226.
19. Code Sec. 6229.

Overview Problem — Putting It All Together

Stacey, Bill, and Olivia want to own and operate a coffee shop. They are not sure what legal steps they need to take to do so. But, they have heard about partnerships and are thinking that it might be the entity that would work best for them. However, they would like to know more about what the consequences would be if they did decide to operate the coffee shop through a partnership.

The partners have scheduled a meeting to discuss their options. You have been invited to the meeting to advise them.

1. How would you explain, generally, to the potential partners the tax consequences of electing to be a partnership?

2. If they go forward with operating the coffee shop but do not file for a certificate to be a partnership in their state, will they still be a partnership for state law purposes? For federal tax purposes?

3. With respect to entity classification for federal tax purposes:

    (a) Under the default rules, how will they be characterized? Does it matter if they file for a certificate to be a partnership in their state?

    (b) Will you advise them to elect to be treated as a corporation?

    (c) What additional information, if any, would you need to be able to advise them?

    (d) Who makes the decision? How do you know?

4. With respect to electing out of the partnership tax provisions of subchapter K:

    (a) Will you advise them to elect out of the partnership provisions?

    (b) What additional information, if any, would you need to be able to advise them?

5. Will the TEFRA provisions apply to the partnership?

Practitioner's Checklist

TEFRA

☐ Is there a reason why the partnership would not want to be treated for tax purposes as a partnership?

☐ Is the partnership is family partnership?

  ☐ Do the partners want to elect out of Subchapter K?

☐ Is the partnership covered by TEFRA?

  ☐ If so, has the partnership named a tax matters partner?

  ☐ If not, will it elect to be covered by TEFRA?

Items to include in the partnership or operating agreement:

  ☐ If the partnership will be covered by TEFRA, how a tax matters partner will determined.

  ☐ If the partnership is not covered by TEFRA, when/why it will elect to be covered by TEFRA and how the tax matters partner will be determined.

Index